PAGODA TOEFL

80+ Writing

3rd Edition

파고다교육그룹 언어교육연구소, 안병남(Bobby Ahn) I 저

PAGODA Books

3rd Edition PAGODA TOEFL

80+ Writing

초 판	1쇄 발행	2013년 8월 28일
개정 2판	1쇄 발행	2019년 10월 7일
개정 3판	1쇄 인쇄	2024년 2월 29일
개정 3판	1쇄 발행	2024년 3월 8일

지 은 이 | 파고다교육그룹 언어교육연구소, 안병남(Bobby Ahn)
펴 낸 이 | 박경실
펴 낸 곳 | **PAGODA Books** 파고다북스
출판등록 | 2005년 5월 27일 제 300-2005-90호
주 소 | 06614 서울특별시 서초구 강남대로 419, 19층(서초동, 파고다타워)
전 화 | (02) 6940-4070
팩 스 | (02) 536-0660
홈페이지 | www.pagodabook.com

저작권자 | ⓒ 2019, 2024 파고다아카데미, 파고다에스씨에스, 안병남(Bobby Ahn)

ISBN 978-89-6281-914-4 (13740)

파고다북스	www.pagodabook.com
파고다 어학원	www.pagoda21.com
파고다 인강	www.pagodastar.com
테스트 클리닉	www.testclinic.com

▌ 낙장 및 파본은 구매처에서 교환해 드립니다.

2023년 7월
New iBT TOEFL®의 시작!

TOEFL 주관사인 미국 ETS(Educational Testing Service)는 iBT TOEFL® 시험에서 채점되지 않는 더미 문제가 삭제되면서 시간이 개정 전 3시간에서 개정 후 2시간 이하로 단축됐으며, 새로운 라이팅 유형이 추가되었다고 발표했다. 새로 바뀐 iBT TOEFL® 시험은 2023년 7월 26일 정기 시험부터 시행된다.

- 총 시험 시간 기존 약 3시간 ···› 약 2시간으로 단축
- 시험 점수는 각 영역당 30점씩 총 120점 만점으로 기존과 변함없음

영역	2023년 7월 26일 이전	2023년 7월 26일 이후
Reading	지문 3~4개 각 지문 당 10문제 시험 시간 54~72분	지문 2개 각 지문 당 10개 시험 시간 36분
Listening	대화 2~3개, 각 5문제 강의 3~5개, 각 6문제 시험 시간 41~57분	28문제 대화 2개, 각 5문제 강의 3개, 각 6문제 시험 시간 36분
Speaking	*변함없음 4문제 독립형 과제 1개 통합형 과제 3개 시험 시간 17분	
Writing	2문제 통합형 과제 1개 독립형 과제 1개 시험 시간 50분	2문제 통합형 과제 1개 수업 토론형 과제 1개 시험 시간 30분

목차

이 책의 구성과 특징   6

6주 완성 학습 플랜   8

iBT TOEFL® 개요   9

iBT TOEFL® Writing 개요   16

>> Diagnostic Test   18

>> Integrated Task   26

Part 1.   기초 다지기   30

Lesson 01   노트테이킹   32

     1. 읽고 노트테이킹   34

     2. 듣고 노트테이킹   40

Lesson 02   요약하기   46

     1. 읽고 요약하기   48

     2. 듣고 요약하기   54

Part 2.   실전 굳히기   60

Lesson 01   정리하기   62

     1. 읽고 정리하기   64

     2. 듣고 정리하기   76

Lesson 02   노트&답변 연결하기   84

Test   108

>> Academic Discussion Task ·· 112

Part 1.	기초 다지기	116
Lesson 01	스트레스 관련 표현	122
Lesson 02	분위기 관련 표현	126
Lesson 03	사람들과의 관계 관련 표현	130
Lesson 04	관점의 확장 관련 표현	134
Lesson 05	조언 관련 표현	138
Lesson 06	편리함 관련 표현	142
Lesson 07	시간 활용 관련 표현	146

Part 2.	실전 굳히기	150
Lesson 01	스트레스 관련 주제 문단 구성	154
Lesson 02	분위기 관련 주제 문단 구성	158
Lesson 03	사람들과의 관계 관련 주제 문단 구성	162
Lesson 04	관점의 확장 관련 주제 문단 구성	166
Lesson 05	조언 관련 주제 문단 구성	170
Lesson 06	편리함 관련 주제 문단 구성	174
Lesson 07	시간 활용 관련 주제 문단 구성	178

Test		182

>> Actual Test ·· 186

Actual Test 1	188
Actual Test 2	192

이 책의 구성과 특징

›› New TOEFL 변경사항 및 최신 출제 유형 완벽 반영!

2023년 7월부터 변경된 새로운 토플 시험을 반영, iBT TOEFL® 80점 이상을 목표로 하는 학습자를 위해 최근 iBT TOEFL®의 출제 경향을 완벽하게 반영한 문제와 주제를 골고루 다루고 있습니다.

›› 유형별 표현 정리 제공!

유형별로 자주 쓰이는 유용한 표현들을 예문과 함께 수록해, 실제 시험에 그대로 적용해서 사용할 수 있도록 있도록 구성하였습니다.

›› 단계별로 점진적인 학습 가능!

혼자 공부하는 사람도 충분히 따라올 수 있도록, 효율적인 노트 정리부터 답변 작성하기까지 차근차근 단계별로 학습을 구성하였습니다. 함께 제공되는 예시 노트 및 답변을 통해 학습자가 자신의 답변을 직접 비교해 보고 보완할 수 있습니다.

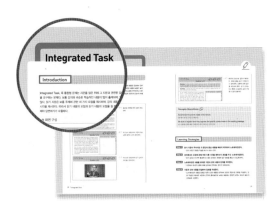

Introduction & Learning Strategies

각각의 문제 유형을 살펴보고, iBT TOEFL® 전문 연구원이 제안하는 효과적인 문제풀이 전략과 예시 문제 학습을 통해 정답을 찾는 능력을 배양합니다.

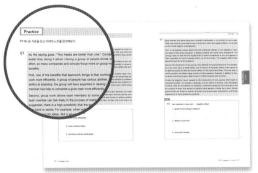

Practice

앞에서 배운 학습 전략을 적용하여, 연습문제를 풀어보며 해당 문제 유형을 집중 공략합니다.

Test

실전과 유사한 유형과 난이도로 구성된 연습문제를 풀며 iBT TOEFL® 실전 감각을 익힙니다.

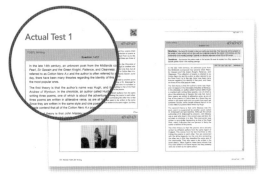

Actual Test

실제 시험과 동일하게 구성된 2회분의 Actual Test를 통해 실전에 대비합니다.

6주 완성 학습 플랜

DAY 1	DAY 2	DAY 3	DAY 4	DAY 5
Diagnostic Test		Integrated Task		
Diagnostic Test	Diagnostic Test Review • 문제 다시 보기 • 노트테이킹 연습하기	Part 1 Lesson 01 • 1. 읽고 노트테이킹 • Practice	Part 1 Lesson 01 • 2. 듣고 노트테이킹 • Practice	Part 1 Lesson 02 • 1. 읽고 요약하기 • Practice

DAY 6	DAY 7	DAY 8	DAY 9	DAY 10
Integrated Task				
Part 1 Lesson 02 • 2. 듣고 요약하기 • Practice	Part 1 Review	Part 2 Lesson 01 • 1. 읽고 정리하기 • Practice	Part 2 Lesson 01 • 2. 듣고 정리하기 • Practice	Part 2 Lesson 02 • Practice

DAY 11	DAY 12	DAY 13	DAY 14	DAY 15
Integrated Task			Academic Discussion Task	
Part 2 Review	Test	Test Review • 문제 다시 보기 • 노트테이킹 연습하기	Part 1 Lesson 01 • Practice	Part 1 Lesson 02 • Practice

DAY 16	DAY 17	DAY 18	DAY 19	DAY 20
Academic Discussion Task				
Part 1 Lesson 03 • Practice	Part 1 Lesson 04 • Practice	Part 1 Lesson 05 • Practice	Part 1 Lesson 06 • Practice	Part 1 Lesson 07 • Practice

DAY 21	DAY 22	DAY 23	DAY 24	DAY 25
Academic Discussion Task				
Part 2 Lesson 01 • Practice	Part 2 Lesson 02 • Practice	Part 2 Lesson 03 • Practice	Part 2 Lesson 04 • Practice	Part 2 Lesson 05 • Practice

DAY 26	DAY 27	DAY 28	DAY 29	DAY 30
Academic Discussion Task			Actual Test	
Part 2 Lesson 06 • Practice	Part 2 Lesson 07 • Practice	Test	Actual Test 1	Actual Test 2

iBT TOEFL® 개요

1. iBT TOEFL® 이란?

TOEFL은 영어 사용 국가로 유학을 가고자 하는 외국인들의 영어 능력을 평가하기 위해 개발된 시험이다. TOEFL 시험 출제 기관인 ETS는 이러한 TOEFL 본연의 목적에 맞게 문제의 변별력을 더욱 높이고자 PBT(Paper-Based Test), CBT(Computer-Based Test)에 이어 차세대 시험인 인터넷 기반의 iBT(Internet-Based Test)를 2005년 9월부터 시행하고 있다. ETS에서 연간 30~40회 정도로 지정한 날짜에 등록함으로써 치르게 되는 이 시험은 Reading, Listening, Speaking, Writing 총 4개 영역으로 구성되며 총 시험 시간은 약 2시간이다. 각 영역별 점수는 30점으로 총점 120점을 만점으로 하며 성적은 시험 시행 약 4~8일 후에 온라인에서 확인할 수 있다.

2. iBT TOEFL®의 특징

1) 영어 사용 국가로 유학 시 필요한 언어 능력을 평가한다.

각 시험 영역은 실제 학업이나 캠퍼스 생활에 반드시 필요한 언어 능력을 측정한다. 평가되는 언어 능력에는 자신의 의견 및 선호도 전달하기, 강의 요약하기, 에세이 작성하기, 학술적인 주제의 글을 읽고 내용 이해하기 등이 포함되며, 각 영역에 걸쳐 고르게 평가된다.

2) Reading, Listening, Speaking, Writing 전 영역의 통합적인 영어 능력(Integrated Skill)을 평가한다.

시험이 4개 영역으로 분류되어 있기는 하지만 Speaking과 Writing 영역에서는 [Listening + Speaking], [Reading + Listening + Speaking], [Reading + Listening + Writing]과 같은 형태로 학습자가 둘 또는 세 개의 언어 영역을 통합해서 사용할 수 있는지를 평가한다.

3) Reading 지문 및 Listening 스크립트가 길다.

Reading 지문은 700단어 내외로 A4용지 약 1.5장 분량이며, Listening은 3~4분 가량의 대화와 6~8분 가량의 강의로 구성된다.

4) 전 영역에서 노트 필기(Note-taking)를 할 수 있다.

긴 지문을 읽거나 강의를 들으면서 핵심 사항을 간략하게 적어두었다가 문제를 풀 때 참고할 수 있다. 노트 필기한 종이는 시험 후 수거 및 폐기된다.

5) 선형적(Linear) 방식으로 평가된다.

응시자가 시험을 보는 과정에서 실력에 따라 문제의 난이도가 조정되어 출제되는 CAT(Computer Adaptive Test) 방식이 아니라, 정해진 문제가 모든 응시자에게 동일하게 제시되는 선형적인 방식으로 평가된다.

6) 시험 응시일이 제한된다.

시험은 주로 토요일과 일요일에만 시행되며, 시험에 재응시할 경우, 시험 응시일 3일 후부터 재응시 가능하다.

7) Performance Feedback이 주어진다.

온라인 및 우편으로 발송된 성적표에는 수치화된 점수뿐 아니라 각 영역별로 수험자의 과제 수행 정도를 나타내는 표도 제공된다.

3. iBT TOEFL®의 구성

시험 영역	Reading, Listening, Speaking, Writing
시험 시간	약 2시간
시험 횟수	연 30~40회(날짜는 ETS에서 지정)
총점	0~120점
영역별 점수	각 영역별 30점
성적 확인	응시일로부터 4~8일 후 온라인에서 성적 확인 가능

시험 영역	문제 구성	시간
Reading	● 독해 지문 2개, 총 20문제가 출제된다. ● 각 지문 길이 700단어 내외, 지문당 10개 문제	36분
Listening	● 대화(Conversation) 2개(각 5문제씩)와 강의(Lecture) 3개(각 6문제씩)가 출제된다.	36분
Break		10분
Speaking	● 독립형 과제(Independent Task) 1개, 통합형 과제(Integrated Task) 3개 총 4개 문제가 출제된다.	17분
Writing	● 통합형 과제(Integrated Task) 1개(20분) ● 수업 토론형 과제 (Writing for Academic Discussion) 1개(9분)	30분

4. iBT TOEFL®의 점수

1) 영역별 점수

Reading	0~30	Listening	0~30
Speaking	0~30	Writing	0~30

2) iBT, CBT, PBT 간 점수 비교

기존에 있던 CBT, PBT 시험은 폐지되었으며, 마지막으로 시행된 CBT, PBT 시험 이후 2년 이상이 경과되어 과거 응시자의 시험 성적 또한 유효하지 않다.

5. 시험 등록 및 응시 절차

1) 시험 등록

온라인과 전화로 시험 응시일과 각 지역의 시험장을 확인하여 신청할 수 있으며, 일반 접수는 시험 희망 응시일 7일 전까지 가능하다.

❶ 온라인 등록

ETS 토플 등록 사이트(https://www.ets.org/mytoefl)에 들어가 화면 지시에 따라 등록한다. 비용은 신용카드로 지불하게 되므로 American Express, Master Card, VISA 등 국제적으로 통용되는 신용카드를 미리 준비해 둔다. 시험을 등록하기 위해서는 회원 가입이 선행되어야 한다.

❷ 전화 등록

한국 프로메트릭 콜센터(00-7981-4203-0248)에 09:00~17:00 사이에 전화를 걸어 등록한다.

2) 추가 등록

시험 희망 응시일 3일(공휴일을 제외한 업무일 기준) 전까지 US $60의 추가 비용으로 등록 가능하다.

3) 등록 비용

2023년 현재 US $220(가격 변동이 있을 수 있음)

4) 시험 취소와 변경

ETS 토플 등록 사이트나 한국 프로메트릭(00-7981-4203-0248)으로 전화해서 시험을 취소하거나 응시 날짜를 변경할 수 있다. 등록 취소와 날짜 변경은 시험 날짜 4일 전까지 해야 한다. 날짜를 변경하려면 등록 번호와 등록 시 사용했던 성명이 필요하며 비용은 US $60이다.

5) 시험 당일 소지품

❶ 사진이 포함된 신분증(주민등록증, 운전면허증, 여권 중 하나)

❷ 시험 등록 번호(Registration Number)

6) 시험 절차

❶ 사무실에서 신분증과 등록 번호를 통해 등록을 확인한다.

❷ 기밀 서약서(Confidentiality Statement)를 작성한 후 서명한다.

❸ 소지품 검사, 사진 촬영, 음성 녹음 및 최종 신분 확인을 하고 연필과 연습장(Scratch Paper)을 제공받는다.

❹ 감독관의 지시에 따라 시험실에 입실하여 지정된 개인 부스로 이동하여 시험을 시작한다.

❺ Reading과 Listening 영역이 끝난 후 10분간의 휴식이 주어진다.

❻ 시험 진행에 문제가 있을 경우 손을 들어 감독관의 지시에 따르도록 한다.

❼ Writing 영역 답안 작성까지 모두 마치면 화면 종료 메시지를 확인한 후에 신분증을 챙겨 퇴실한다.

7) 성적 확인

응시일로부터 약 4~8일 후부터 온라인으로 점수 확인이 가능하며, 시험 전에 종이 사본 수령을 신청했을 경우 약 11-15일 후 우편으로 성적표를 받을 수 있다.

6. 실제 시험 화면 구성

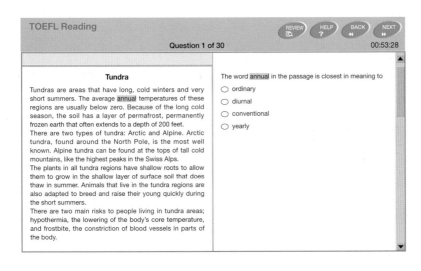

전체 Direction

시험 전체에 대한 구성 설명

Reading 영역 화면

지문은 왼쪽에, 문제는
오른쪽에 제시

Listening 영역 화면

수험자가 대화나 강의를 듣는
동안 사진이 제시됨

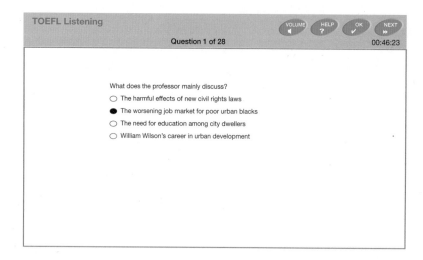

Listening 영역 화면

듣기가 끝난 후 문제 화면이 등장

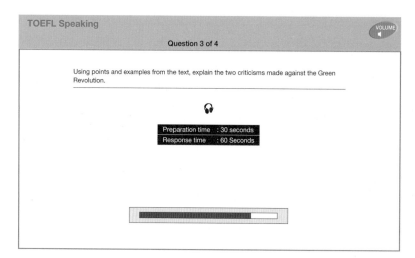

Speaking 영역 화면

문제가 주어진 후, 답변을 준비하는 시간과 말하는 시간을 알려줌

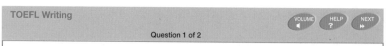

Writing 영역 화면

왼쪽에 문제가 주어지고 오른쪽에 답을 직접 타이핑할 수 있는 공간이 주어짐

복사(Copy), 자르기(Cut), 붙여넣기(Paste) 버튼이 위쪽에 위치함

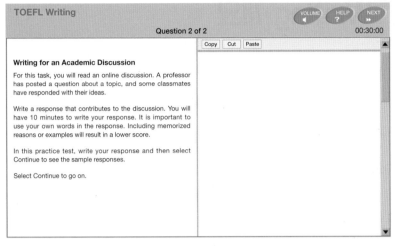

Copy | Cut | Paste

Writing for an Academic Discussion

For this task, you will read an online discussion. A professor has posted a question about a topic, and some classmates have responded with their ideas.

Write a response that contributes to the discussion. You will have 10 minutes to write your response. It is important to use your own words in the response. Including memorized reasons or examples will result in a lower score.

In this practice test, write your response and then select Continue to see the sample responses.

Select Continue to go on.

Writing 영역 화면

왼쪽에 문제가 주어지고 오른쪽에 답을 직접 타이핑할 수 있는 공간이 주어짐

복사(Copy), 자르기(Cut), 붙여넣기(Paste) 버튼이 위쪽에 위치함

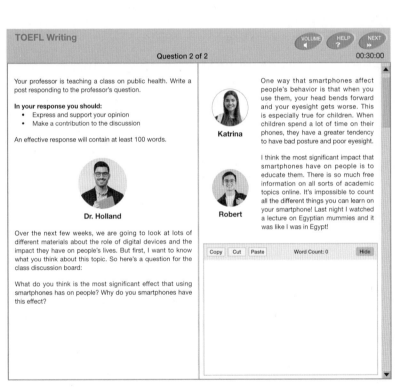

Your professor is teaching a class on public health. Write a post responding to the professor's question.

In your response you should:
- Express and support your opinion
- Make a contribution to the discussion

An effective response will contain at least 100 words.

Dr. Holland

Over the next few weeks, we are going to look at lots of different materials about the role of digital devices and the impact they have on people's lives. But first, I want to know what you think about this topic. So here's a question for the class discussion board:

What do you think is the most significant effect that using smartphones has on people? Why do you smartphones have this effect?

Katrina

One way that smartphones affect people's behavior is that when you use them, your head bends forward and your eyesight gets worse. This is especially true for children. When children spend a lot of time on their phones, they have a greater tendency to have bad posture and poor eyesight.

Robert

I think the most significant impact that smartphones have on people is to educate them. There is so much free information on all sorts of academic topics online. It's impossible to count all the different things you can learn on your smartphone! Last night I watched a lecture on Egyptian mummies and it was like I was in Egypt!

Copy | Cut | Paste   Word Count: 0   Hide

Writing 영역 화면

왼쪽에 문제가 주어지고 오른쪽에 답을 직접 타이핑할 수 있는 공간이 주어짐

복사(Copy), 자르기(Cut), 붙여넣기(Paste) 버튼이 타이핑하는 곳 위쪽에 위치함

iBT TOEFL® Writing 개요

1. Writing 영역의 특징

Writing 영역의 특징으로는 먼저 2개의 문제가 출제된다는 점을 들 수 있고, 단순히 주어진 주제에 대해 글을 쓰는 아주 기본적인 글쓰기에서 끝나는 것이 아니라, 실제 학업 상황에서 빈번하게 경험하게 되는 읽기, 듣기, 그리고 쓰기가 접목된 통합형 과제(Integrated Task)가 등장한다는 점을 그 특징으로 들 수 있다.

Writing 영역의 주요한 특징은 다음의 4가지로 정리할 수 있다.

1) Writing 영역은 2개의 문제로 구성된다.

첫 번째인 통합형(Integrated Task)은 주어진 지문(Reading Passage)을 3분간 읽고, 약 2~3분 가량의 강의자(Lecturer; Speaker)의 강의(Lecture)를 듣고 난 후, 강의자가 지문에 대해 어떤 주장을 하는지 150~225자의 단어(Words)로 20분 동안 요약(Summary)하여 글쓰기를 하는 문제다.

두 번째 문제는 2023년 7월부터 TOEFL 시험이 개정되면서 추가된 새로운 수업 토론형 과제(Writing for an Academic Discussion Task)다. 기존 독립형 과제(Independent Task)를 대체한 이 새로운 유형의 과제에서 온라인 교실 토론이 등장하는데, 다른 두 학생의 의견을 제시한 후 응시자 자신의 의견을 요구한다. 10분 동안 100자 이상의 단어로 온라인 포럼에서 댓글을 작성하듯이 자신의 의견을 표현하는 문제다.

2) 노트 필기(Note-taking)가 가능하다.

읽고, 듣고, 쓰는 문제에서 노트 필기는 매우 핵심적인 기술이다. 따라서 미리 노트 필기의 기술을 배우고 반복 연습해 두어야 한다.

3) Typing만 가능하다.

수험자가 답안을 작성할 때 컴퓨터를 통한 Typing만 가능하도록 제한되어 있다. (Handwriting 불가) 미리 충분한 속도의 영타가 가능하도록 연습해야 한다. 단, Brainstorming이나 Outline은 종이에 작성할 수 있다.

4) 각 문제에 대한 평가 기준이 다르다.

Writing 영역의 핵심적인 특징 중 하나는 두 문제가 각각 다른 평가 기준(Scoring Rubric)을 가지고 있다는 점인데 고득점을 위해서는 이 평가 기준을 반드시 유념해서 답안을 작성해야 한다.

간단히 말해서 통합형 과제의 평가 기준은 내용적인 측면에 더 많은 강조를 두지만, 수업 토론형 과제의 경우 내용적인 측면과 함께 토론에 대한 연관성과 기여도에 신경을 써야 한다는 것이다.

2. Writing 영역의 문제 유형

ETS가 제시하고 있는 Writing 영역의 문제 유형은 구체적으로 다음과 같다.

1) 통합형 과제(Integrated Task)

읽기와 듣기를 기반으로 요약의 글을 완성하는 유형의 문제로서 작문 능력뿐 아니라 독해력과 청취력도 요구된다.

2) 수업 토론형 과제(Writing for an Academic Discussion Task)

주어진 토론 주제에 대해 두 명의 다른 학생의 의견을 읽은 후, 논리적으로 자신의 의견과 이유, 그리고 구체적인 근거를 들어 토론에 기여하는 답안을 작성하는 문제 유형이다. 따라서, 단순히 자신의 생각을 작성하는 능력뿐 아니라 다른 학생들의 의견을 파악하고 토론 주제와 관련성 있는 답변을 구사하는 능력이 요구된다.

Diagnostic Test

실제 TOEFL Writing 시험 구성과 유사한 진단 테스트를 풀어보면서 내 현재 실력이 얼마나 되는지, 취약한 문제 유형은 무엇인지 점검해 보자.

Diagnostic Test

문제 듣기

Writing Section Directions

Make sure your headset is on.

This section measures your ability to use writing to communicate in an academic environment. There will be two writing tasks.

For the first writing task, you will read a passage and listen to a lecture and then answer a question based on what you have read and heard. For the second writing task, you will answer a question based on your own knowledge and experience.

TOEFL Writing

Writing Based on Reading and Listening Directions

For this task, you will read a passage about an academic topic, and you will listen to a lecture about the same topic. You may take notes while you read and listen. Then, you will write a response to a question that asks you about the relationship between the reading passage and the lecture you heard. You may use your notes to help you answer the question.

Typically, an effective response will be 150 to 225 words. Your response will be judged on the quality of your writing and on the completeness and accuracy of the content.

You should allow 3 minutes to read the passage. Then listen to the lecture. Then allow 20 minutes to plan and write your essay.

Many scientists advocate substituting species to support ecosystems where an important contributor to the ecology has disappeared or gone extinct. They argue that the balance must be maintained or the entire ecosystem could collapse. However, there are many flaws with this line of thinking.

Firstly, the loss of a species from an ecosystem is not necessarily a disaster. In many cases, other species have altered their feeding habits to exploit that vacancy and thereby become stronger. This is referred to as species succession, and it occurs naturally, so if we intervene, we are preventing nature from taking its course. We should study the ecosystem to see if any species are filling in the gap. If none are, then maybe we should start to consider substituting another species, but we must do so carefully.

The most serious outcome of introducing a new species is that it may become invasive. Many species that have been introduced to new ecosystems have wreaked havoc upon their new homes. Some of these species introductions were accidental like the zebra mussel, which outcompetes similar shellfish and causes industrial problems. Others were intentional like the cane toad, which was introduced to Australia to control insect populations. Cane toads have no natural predators there, so their population has exploded as they devour many species other than the intended insects.

Species substitution could also disrupt the entire ecosystem. Some experts believe the problems of invasive species can be solved by introducing animals from different populations of the same species. This sounds ideal, but since they are from a different population, they may behave differently and could have a negative effect on the ecosystem as well. For instance, in their native habitat, they may have more competition than in the new area. With less competition, they may overburden the local food chain and cause irreversible damage.

 DT

Diagnostic Test

Directions : You have 20 minutes to plan and write your response. Your response will be judged on the quality of your writing and on how well your response presents the points in the lecture and the relationship to the reading passage. Typically, an effective response will be 150 to 225 words.

Questions : Summarize the points made in the lecture. Be sure to explain how they oppose the specific points made in the reading passage.

Copy | Cut | Paste | Undo | Redo | Hide Word Count | 0

Many scientists advocate substituting species to support ecosystems where an important contributor to the ecology has disappeared or gone extinct. They argue that the balance must be maintained or the entire ecosystem could collapse. However, there are many flaws with this line of thinking.

Firstly, the loss of a species from an ecosystem is not necessarily a disaster. In many cases, other species have altered their feeding habits to exploit that vacancy and thereby become stronger. This is referred to as species succession, and it occurs naturally, so if we intervene, we are preventing nature from taking its course. We should study the ecosystem to see if any species are filling in the gap. If none are, then maybe we should start to consider substituting another species, but we must do so carefully.

The most serious outcome of introducing a new species is that it may become invasive. Many species that have been introduced to new ecosystems have wreaked havoc upon their new homes. Some of these species introductions were accidental like the zebra mussel, which out-competes similar shellfish and causes industrial problems. Others were intentional like the cane toad, which was introduced to Australia to control insect populations. Cane toads have no natural predators there, so their population has exploded as they devour many species other than the intended insects.

Species substitution could also disrupt the entire ecosystem. Some experts believe the problems of invasive species can be solved by introducing animals from different populations of the same species. This sounds ideal, but since they are from a different population, they may behave differently and could have a negative effect on the ecosystem as well. For instance, in their native habitat, they may have more competition than in the new area. With less competition, they may overburden the local food chain and cause irreversible damage.

Writing for an Academic Discussion

Directions: In this assignment, you'll review an online discussion where a professor has posed a question, and fellow students have shared their perspectives. Your task is to provide a response that adds value to the ongoing discussion. During the actual test, you'll have a 10-minute window to craft your response. It is essential to articulate your ideas using appropriate language. Your writing should be centered on the topic introduced by the professor. A logically structured rationale and a well-presented example will contribute to achieving a higher score.

Your professor is teaching a class. Write a post responding to the professor's question.

In your response, you should:
- express and support your opinion
- make a contribution to the discussion

An effective response will contain at least 100 words.
You will have 10 minutes to write it.

Dr. Harlow

Hello, everyone. Today, let's discuss the notion that teaching kids nowadays is trickier due to their extensive engagement with video games, phone chats, and social media updates. We need to consider how these advanced technologies influence children's learning and how we can strike a balance in utilizing technology for education without causing issues.

The question is: Do you believe these new technologies make it more challenging for kids to learn? Let's delve into this and examine how modern gadgets impact their education.

Alex

Thanks, Professor. I totally think that dealing with advanced technology is a big challenge in educating kids today. Video games and constant phone use can distract them from studying. We need to figure out how these distractions affect their learning and development.

Sara

While I agree with Alex about the challenges, I also see some good sides. Instead of just thinking about the problems, we should see how using technology in education can make learning fun for kids. Plus, the skills they learn from using gadgets can be helpful in the future.

Copy Cut Paste   Word Count: 0   Hide

I
Integrated Task

Introduction & Learning Strategies

Part 1. 기초 다지기

❱ Lesson 01   노트테이킹

❱ Lesson 02   요약하기

Part 2. 실전 굳히기

❱ Lesson 01   정리하기

❱ Lesson 02   노트 & 답변 연결하기

Test

Integrated Task

Introduction

Integrated Task, 즉 통합형 문제는 지문을 읽은 뒤에 그 지문과 관련된 강의를 듣고 둘의 내용을 통합하는 답변을 요구하는 문제다. 보통 강의와 비슷한 학술적인 내용이 많이 출제되며, 일상생활과 관련된 내용의 비중은 높지 않다. 읽기 지문은 보통 주제에 관한 세 가지 요점을 제시하며, 강의 내용은 앞선 세 가지 요점에 반박하거나 다른 시각을 제시한다. 따라서 읽기 내용의 요점과 듣기 내용의 요점을 잘 파악하고 서로 어떻게 연결되어 있는지 이해해야 답변하기가 수월하다.

▶ 화면 구성

TOEFL   CONTINUE

Writing based on Reading and Listening Directions

For this task, you will first have three minutes to read a passage about an academic topic. You may take notes on the passage if you wish. The passage will then be removed and you will listen to a lecture about the same topic. While you listen, you may also take notes.

Then you will have 20 minutes to write a response to a question that asks you about the relationship between the lecture you heard and the reading passage. Try to answer the question as completely as possible using information from the reading passage and the lecture. The question does not ask you to express your personal opinion. You will be able to see the reading passage again when it is time for you to write. You may use your notes to help you answer the question.

Typically, an effective response will be 150 to 225 words long. Your response will be judged on the quality of your writing and on the completeness and accuracy of the content. If you finish your response before time is up, you may click on Next to go on to the second writing task.

Now you will see the reading passage for three minutes. Remember it will be available to you again when it is time for you to write. The lecture will begin, so keep your headset on until the lecture is over.

• 안내: 통합형 문제에 관한 설명이 제시된다.

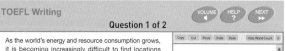

TOEFL Writing   VOLUME   HELP   NEXT

Question 1 of 2

Copy   Cut   Paste   Undo   Redo   Hide Word Count   0

As the world's energy and resource consumption grows, it is becoming increasingly difficult to find locations that can provide resources. One of the locations is the deep sea where there are a lot of thermal vents. A vent is a deep crack on the ocean's floor. This so-called vent mining has recently received attention. There are a number of reasons why vent mining is good.

First, the deep sea has rich metals and minerals. Materials such as gold and iron can be found in enormous supply along these thermal vents. These areas are readily available to humans for harvesting and may even provide larger supplies of metal than land based mines.

• 읽기: 약 250~300단어의 지문이 제시되며 3분의 시간이 주어진다.

TOEFL Writing   VOLUME   HELP   NEXT

Question 1 of 2

• 듣기: 약 250~300단어의 듣기 강의가 약 2분간 주어진다.

TOEFL Writing VOLUME ◀ HELP ? NEXT ▶▶ **Question 1 of 2** **Directions :** You have 20 minutes to plan and write your response. Your response will be judged on the basis of the quality of your writing and on how well your response presents the points in the lecture and their relationship to the reading passage. Typically, an effective response will be 150 to 225 words. **Questions :** Summarize the points made in the lecture you just heard, explaining how they cast doubt on the points made in the reading. As the world's energy and resource consumption grows, it is becoming increasingly difficult to find locations that can provide resources. One of the locations is the deep sea where there are a lot of thermal vents. A vent is a deep crack on the ocean's floor. This so-called vent mining has recently received attention. There are a number of reasons why vent Copy Cut Paste Undo Redo Hide Word Count 0	• 쓰기: 화면과 음성으로 질문이 제시된다. 왼쪽 창에는 읽기 지문을 다시 보여주며, 오른쪽 창에 답안을 작성해야 한다. 듣기 강의는 다시 들을 수 없으며, 글쓰기 제한 시간은 20분이다.

Sample Questions

Summarize the points made in the lecture. Be sure to explain how they oppose the specific points made in the reading passage.

강의에서 제시한 요점을 요약하시오. 읽기 지문의 요점에 대해 강의에서 어떻게 반박하는지 설명하시오.

Learning Strategies

Step 1 읽기 지문이 주어지면 각 문단의 중심 내용을 빠르게 파악하여 노트테이킹한다.

⋯ 읽기 지문은 답변을 작성할 때 다시 볼 수 있다.

Step 2 강의에서는 요점에 관해 어떤 다른 시각을 취하는지 초점을 두고 노트테이킹한다.

⋯ 듣기 강의는 한 번만 들려준다는 점에 유의하고 최대한 많은 정보를 들을 수 있도록 한다.

Step 3 노트테이킹한 내용을 토대로 지문과 강의 내용의 관계를 파악한다.

⋯ 지문에서 제시한 요점에 대해 강의에서 반박하는 경우가 대부분이다.

Step 4 지문과 강의 내용을 연결하여 답변을 작성한다.

⋯ 노트테이킹한 내용을 토대로 지문과 강의 내용을 요약하여 완전한 문장으로 답변을 작성한다. 답변 작성을 완료하면 처음부터 끝까지 훑어보면서 누락된 내용이나 문법적 오류나 오타가 없는지 살펴보며 수정한다.

Part 1

기초 다지기

▶ Lesson 01 **노트테이킹**

❶ 읽고 노트테이킹

❷ 듣고 노트테이킹

▶ Lesson 02 **요약하기**

❶ 읽고 요약하기

❷ 듣고 요약하기

01 노트테이킹

문제 듣기

통합형 문제에서 제한된 시간 내에 빠르게 답안을 작성하기 위해서는 읽기 지문과 강의의 관계를 명확히 이해하고 작성한 답안을 여러 번 읽을 수 있는 시간을 벌어야 한다. 그러기 위해서는 차별화된 노트테이킹 기술이 필요하다. 노트테이킹할 때 유념해야 할 전략은 다음과 같다.

1. 간단히 필기한다.

지문이나 강의에서 나오는 내용을 전부 적기도 어려울뿐더러 그럴 필요도 없다. 요점을 파악하고 그 요점을 간단히 빠르게 적는 것이 중요하다. 답변을 작성할 때 노트를 보면서 '이게 이런 내용이었지'하고 이해할 수 있을 정도로만 적으면 된다. 나만 알아볼 수 있으면 된다는 점을 명심하고 최대한 간단히 적자. 필요 없는 수식어는 모두 빼도 내용 이해에 전혀 지장을 주지 않는다. 참고로, 읽기 지문은 답안을 작성하는 20분동안 계속 읽으며 참고할 수 있다.

2. 핵심만 적는다.

답변에 별 도움이 되지 않는 곁가지 내용을 쓰다가 정작 핵심 내용을 놓치는 상황이 발생할 수도 있다. 무엇이 중요한지 파악하여 그 내용을 적는다. 문단의 내용을 요약할 수 있으면 더 좋다. 강의자가 말한 단어를 받아 적는 것이 아니라 강의를 정확히 이해하는 것이 통합형 문제의 핵심이다.

3. 약자와 기호를 사용한다.

익숙한 단어나 표현은 약자로 짧게 줄여 쓰거나 보기 쉽게 기호를 활용하는 것이 시간 절약에 큰 도움이 된다. 앞서 언급한 것처럼 나만 알아보면 되는 노트이므로, 나만의 약자와 기호를 써도 무방하다. 나중에 글을 쓸 때 참고하기 쉽게 한눈에 이해되고 보기 편하게 쓰는 것이 가장 좋다. 영어로 쓰기 편할 때는 영어로, 한글로 쓰기 편할 때는 한글로 쓰면서 노트테이킹하는 것도 빨리 필기할 수 있는 방법이다.

> Ex 가격이 오르자 고객이 줄었다.
> price ↑ → customer ↓

● 약자와 기호

약자	단어	약자	단어
bgt	budget	w/ & w/o	with & without
AD	advertisement	esp.	especially
HR	human resources	yr	year
HQ	headquarters	intro	introduction
hr	hour	info	information
min	minute	prof	professor
pls	please	stud	student
ex 또는 e.g.	for example	ppl	people
i.e.	in other words, that is	vs.	in contrast to
etc.	et cetera, and so on	cf.	compare
24/ 7	24 hours a day, seven days a week	est.	established
ASAP	as soon as possible	no.	number
asst.	assistant	Ave.	avenue
bldg.	building	dist.	district
corp.	corporation	ft.	foot, feet
dept.	department	gov.	government, governor
mgmt	management	Inst.	institution
approx.	approximately	pop.	population
appt.	appointment	univ.	university

기호	단어	기호	단어
%	percent	≠	not, different
↑	increase	→	cause, produce, lead to
↓	decrease	←	because of, come from
&	and	〈	smaller, less
−	or	〉	larger, bigger, more
@	at	~	approximately, about
+	moreover, in addition	↔	opposite to
=	is, equal to, refer to	#	number

읽기 지문은 스스로 읽는 속도를 조절할 수 있고 답변을 작성하는 공간이 지문 바로 옆에 제공되기 때문에 굳이 노트테이킹이 필요하지는 않다. 답변 작성에 필요한 중요 부분만 몇 단어씩 짧게 적어두면 충분하다. 읽기 지문에서 보통 주제에 관한 세 가지 요점을 제시하므로, 순서대로 번호와 함께 적어두면 보기 편하다.

| Example

> The deep sea vents are a rich source of metals and minerals that are increasingly difficult to find on land. And materials such as gold and iron can be found in enormous supply along these thermal vents. These areas are readily available to humans for harvesting and may even provide larger supplies of metal than land based mines. In addition, extraction of the minerals from the sea floor sediment would also be much easier than removing them from ore.

노트

주제　deep sea vents = source of metals & minerals → extract

1. ↑ supply than land based mines
2. mineral extraction = easier

위 문단의 주제는 'deep sea vents 근처에서 광물을 추출해야 한다'이다. 따라서 이 문장을 가장 상위 분류로 정리한 뒤에 다음에 따라오는 세부 내용을 차례로 정리한다.

1) 육지에 있는 광맥보다 더 많은 광물을 공급한다는 것
2) 광물 추출이 더 쉽다는 것

이 사실들을 차례로 정리해두면 정보를 한눈에 파악하기 쉽다.

해석 심해 분출구는 육지에서는 점점 더 찾기 힘들어지는 금속과 광물의 풍부한 원천이다. 그리고 금과 철 같은 물질의 엄청난 양이 이 열수 분출구를 따라 발견될 수 있다. 이런 지역은 인간이 채광하기 쉬우며, 육지에 있는 광맥보다 더 많은 금속을 공급할 수도 있다. 또한, 해저 퇴적물에서 광물을 추출하는 것은 광석에서 광물을 분리하는 것보다 훨씬 쉬울 것이다.

Practice

정답 및 해석 | P. 5

>> 다음 지문을 읽고 노트를 완성하시오.

Q1

Many large companies have cafeterias where their employees can eat their lunches. This has many benefits. Employees do not have to use their break to travel to and from restaurants. Thus, they have more time to relax and enjoy their meals. Additionally, they can talk to their coworkers about non-work topics and form closer relationships.

> **노트**
>
> 주제   company cafeteria's benefits
>
>   1. X waste time finding restaurants → _____
>
>   2. talk to coworkers → _____

Q2

The governments of many countries invest millions of dollars in space exploration every year. However, many editorials have been published that say this is a complete waste of money. Most people do not see any profit gained from space exploration, but they pay for it with their taxes. Not only that, but searching the galaxy for planets that are Earth-like but unreachable is a pointless exercise.

> **노트**
>
> 주제   invest $ on space exp. = waste of $
>
>   1. no profit gained → _____
>
>   2. Earth-like planets → _____

Q3

Many people choose to take package tours when they go on vacation, but that is not recommended. People on package tours spend most of their time crammed into tour buses, so they cannot enjoy the scenery. Moreover, when they arrive at a tourist attraction, they are hurried through the experience so they cannot really enjoy any aspect of their trip.

> **노트**
>
> 주제 package tour → X recommend
>
> 1. _____ → can't enjoy scenery
> 2. _____ → have to hurry

Q4

Cities that host professional sports teams can receive two major benefits. First, the team's stadium creates hundreds of new jobs, and the ticket sales, refreshments, and team merchandise all bring in revenue to the city. Second, the team brings attention to the city, which can make it more prominent on the national level and attract sports fans and other tourists to the city.

> **노트**
>
> 주제 cities hosting pro. sports teams → profit
>
> 1. stadium → _____ → _____
> 2. attention to city → _____

Q5

Many cultures practice arranged marriage in the past, but that tradition has faded from much of the world. However, some studies indicate that they were more successful than love marriages. For example, the rate of divorce has only increased as arranged marriage has been abandoned. This is because the family is less involved. Moreover, love marriages are often based on passion instead of compatibility, which means that they are destined to fail while arranged marriages are more likely to last.

> **노트**
>
> 주제　arranged marriage = better than love m.?
>
> 　　　1. _____
>
> 　　　2. love m. = passion / arr. m. = compatibility

Part 1
Integrated Task

Q6

Although fast food restaurants serve convenient, inexpensive, and tasty meals and snacks, people should not visit these establishments. Fast food poses many health risks. The menu items can cause many health problems due to their high salt and sugar content. Not only that, but they can make people overweight if they eat them too often. They contain a lot of fat and empty calories, which quickly become fat deposits in the body.

> **노트**
>
> 주제　don't buy fast food = many health risks
>
> 　　　1. ↑ salt & sugar content
>
> 　　　2. _____

Q7

Although watching movies that are produced within your own culture may be easier because of shared language and ideas, watching movies from other cultures can be very rewarding. Watching a movie that is in another language requires a level of concentration that people often don't apply to movie watching. So they get more involved in the story. In addition, you may be exposed to new ideas and values that do not exist in your own culture that can enrich your understanding of the world.

노트

주제   watching movie from other cultures = rewarding

      1. another lang. = requires concentration → more involved in the story

      2. _____

Q8

Most drivers on the roads today rely on GPS navigation systems to find their way. These devices are useful, but people should not become completely dependent upon them for several reasons. First, people do not learn the routes that they are taking as they would if they studied a map before leaving. Second, the devices constantly need to be updated, so people can easily become lost or have accidents if they do not question their instructions.

노트

주제   X depend on GPS navi.

      1. ppl do not learn the routes → rely too much on GPS

      2. _____

Q9

Many lesser crimes are punished by making the person complete community service. This is an effective method because it forces the person to become involved in society instead of hiding them from it like a prison. They must work to help other people while they contemplate their own wrongdoing. Furthermore, it is much more effective than imposing a fine, since some people are happy to pay a fine and continue to break the law.

노트

주제　lesser crime → punishment: comm. service = effective

1. ppl get involved in society, not hiding → think about their crime

2. _____

Q10

Parents often require their children to do chores around the house. Although some people question the wisdom of this practice, it actually has many benefits for the children. First of all, having children take part in chores prepares them for later in their lives when they will have to do such work alone. Also, it teaches them how to share responsibility, which will help them to interact better with roommates and coworkers when they are older.

노트

주제　children doing house chores = beneficial

1. _____

2. _____

강의는 읽기 지문과 달리 딱 한 번만 들을 수 있기 때문에 노트테이킹이 필수이고 중요성 역시 더 크다. 읽기 지문에서 제시된 요점의 개수만큼(보통 3개) 강의에서도 같은 개수의 요점이 나온다. 정확히 말하면, 읽기 지문에서 제시된 요점들에 관해 강의에서 차례로 반박하거나 다른 의견을 제시한다. 따라서 읽기 지문에서 했던 노트테이킹과 같은 번호를 매칭하며 강의 요점을 적어 두면 나중에 답변을 정리하기가 더 쉽다. 다만 적는 데 집중하다가 뒤에 나오는 내용을 놓치지 않도록 주의해야 한다. 빠르고 간단한 노트테이킹이 가장 중요하다.

Example

🎧 P1_00

> Now, first of all, about there being a lot of metal resources near these thermal vents, yes, this is true. But, we don't have any technology that could mine these metals. I mean, first, you need a way to sort the metals from the ocean sediment. This is not possible at the moment; the technology still needs to be developed. And, even if you could sort the metals from the sediment, you would need a way to transport the metals to the surface of the ocean. These technologies just don't exist right now.

노트

주제	It is true that there are lots of metals near thermal vents, but tech X.
	1. sort metals from ocean sediment = possible X
	2. can't transport metals to ocean surface

위 문단의 주제는 'thermal vents 근처에 metal resources가 많은 것은 사실이나 우리는 이런 금속을 채굴할 수 있는 기술을 갖고 있지 않다'이다. 따라서 이 문장을 가장 상위 분류로 정리한 뒤에 이어서 나오는 세부 내용을 차례로 정리한다.

1) 바다 침전물에서 금속을 분류하는 것은 현재 불가능하다는 것
2) 해수 표면으로 금속을 운반할 기술은 존재하지 않는다는 것

이 사실들을 차례로 정리해두면 정보를 한눈에 파악하기 쉽다.

해석 자, 우선, 이런 열수 분출구 근처에 많은 금속 자원이 있다는 점, 네, 이건 사실입니다. 하지만 우리는 이런 금속을 채굴할 수 있는 기술을 갖고 있지 않아요. 내 말은, 우선 바다 퇴적물에서 금속을 분류할 방법이 필요합니다. 이것은 지금으로서는 불가능해요. 기술을 개발해야 합니다. 그리고 퇴적물에서 금속을 분류할 수 있다 해도, 해수면으로 그 금속을 운반할 방법이 필요할 겁니다. 이런 기술은 현재는 존재하지 않습니다.

Practice

정답 및 해석 | P. 9

>> 다음 강의를 듣고 노트를 완성하시오.

Q1

Listen to the lecture. 🎧 P1_01

노트

주제	hiking = beneficial

1. low-impact exercise & fresh air

2. _____

Q2

Listen to the lecture. 🎧 P1_02

노트

주제	universal min. wage = bad idea

1. _____

2. take $ from other import. gov't programs

Listen to the lecture. 🎧 P1_03

노트

주제 | essay @ home = final exam → bad idea
1. do all research on one day – X study
2. _____

Q4

Listen to the lecture. 🎧 P1_04

노트

주제 | doctor resi. program → restructure
1. long shift → _____
2. _____ → _____

Q5

Listen to the lecture. 🎧 P1_05

노트

주제   world = overpopulated? No

1. _____

2. _____

Q6

Listen to the lecture. 🎧 P1_06

노트

주제   ride sharing service = not good

1. backgr. check X sufficient = _____

2. _____

Q7

노트

주제   tutoring program = positive

1. _____

2. _____

Q8

노트

주제   T/F q. = X evaluate student knowledge

1. _____

2. _____

Q9

Listen to the lecture. 🎧 P1_09

노트

주제 keep voting age at 18

    1. _____

    2. _____

Q10

Listen to the lecture. 🎧 P1_10

노트

주제 antibacterial use → negative result

    1. _____

    2. _____

Lesson

02 요약하기

문제 듣기

통합형 문제에서는 읽기 지문의 내용과 강의의 내용을 요약해야 하므로 요약하는 연습이 필수적이다. 앞서 학습한 노트테이킹을 토대로 살을 붙여서 요약문을 작성하는데, 이때 기억해야 할 점은 다음과 같다.

◎ 1. 중심 내용 파악하기

앞에서 정리했던 노트테이킹을 보며 지문과 강의의 핵심 내용, 즉 주장하는 내용이 무엇인지를 파악한다. 지문에서는 주제가 제시된 뒤에 그 주제를 뒷받침하는 세부 요점 3개가 나오고, 강의에서는 교수가 '지문의 내용에 동의하지 않는다/내 생각은 다르다'라고 하면서 지문에서 나온 세부 요점 3개에 반박하거나 다른 관점을 제시한다.

> **Ex** 지문의 주장: A는 B이다.
> 1. A가 B인 첫 번째 이유는 다음과 같다.
> 2. A가 B인 두 번째 이유는 다음과 같다.
> 3. A가 B인 세 번째 이유는 다음과 같다.
>
> 강의의 주장: A는 B가 아니다./A가 B라는 주장에는 오류가 있다.
> 1. A가 B가 아닌 첫 번째 이유는 다음과 같다.
> 2. A가 B가 아닌 두 번째 이유는 다음과 같다.
> 3. A가 B가 아닌 세 번째 이유는 다음과 같다.

◎ 2. 노트테이킹한 내용을 완전한 문장으로 만들기

앞서 적어두었던 노트 필기 내용을 바탕으로 이제 완전한 문장을 만들어본다. 원래 내용과 똑같이 쓰려고 하지 않아도 되고, 내가 아는 단어와 표현을 활용해 풀어서 쓰면 된다. 이를 paraphrasing(다른 말로 바꾸어 표현하기)이라고 하며, 이는 토플의 모든 영역에서 아주 중요한 요소이다. paraphrasing을 할 때는 특정 단어를 같은 뜻을 가진 다른 단어로 바꾸어 쓰거나 주어와 목적어의 자리를 바꾸는 등 다양한 방법으로 새로운 문장을 구성해볼 수 있다.

◎ paraphrasing에 유용한 단어와 표현을 정리해보자.

부정적인, 해로운		긍정적인, 유익한	
worse	～보다 더 나쁜, 안 좋은	better	～보다 더 좋은, 나은
negative	부정적인	positive	긍정적인
harmful	해로운, 유해한	beneficial	유익한, 이로운
detrimental	해로운	effective	효과적인, 실질적인

찬성하다, 동의하다		반대하다, 맞서다	
accept	받아들이다, 수락하다	oppose	반대하다, 겨루다
agree	동의하다	defy	저항하다, 반항하다
comply	동의하다, 응하다	disagree	동의하지 않다, 반대하다
support	지지하다	dispute	반박하다, 이의를 제기하다
approve	찬성하다, 승인하다	disapprove	반대하다, 불만을 나타내다
설명하다		믿다, ~라고 여기다	
explain	설명하다	think	생각하다, 믿다
describe	서술하다, 묘사하다	assume	추정하다, 상정하다
define	정의하다	consider	고려하다, 여기다
illustrate	설명하다, 예증하다	feel	(생각, 느낌이) 들다
clarify	명확히 하다, 분명히 말하다	believe	믿다
주장하다		~하게 하다, 허락하다	
argue	주장하다, 논증하다	let	~하게 하다, 허락하다
assert	주장하다, 확고히 하다	allow	~하게 하다, 허락하다
claim	주장하다, 요구하다	enable	~가 가능하게 하다
contend	주장하다, 겨루다	make it possible to V	~하는 것을 가능하게 하다
야기하다, 기여하다		필요로 하다, 요구하다	
cause	초래하다, 야기하다	need	필요로 하다
contribute	기여하다, ~의 원인이 되다	demand	요구하다
responsible for	~의 원인이 되다	ask	요구하다, 요청하다
generate	발생시키다, 만들어내다	require	필요로 하다, 요구하다
produce	만들어내다, 초래하다	feel necessity for	필요를 느끼다

◎ 알아두면 좋은 명사

장점	advantage, benefit, merit, strength	연결	link, connection, association, tie
단점	disadvantage, drawback, weakness, shortcoming	상황	circumstances, surroundings, environment, situation
문제	problem, issue, difficulty, trouble	책무	responsibility, duty, obligation, liability
대안	substitute, alternative, replacement, another option	실수	mistake, error, fault, blunder
이유/근거	reason, grounds, rationale, cause	비용	expense, cost, expenditure, spending

1. 읽고 요약하기

지문을 요약하기 위해서는 핵심 내용을 파악하는 연습을 해야 한다. 긴 문장이나 한 문단을 읽고 핵심이 무엇인지 간단히 정리해보는 연습은 큰 도움이 된다. 이는 질문에 맞는 답변을 하는 데 도움을 주기도 한다. 앞서 학습한 노트테이킹 연습에서 정리했던 주제로 요약하는 연습을 해보자. paraphrasing 기술을 활용하는 것이 좋다.

Example

> The deep sea vents are a rich source of metals and minerals that are increasingly difficult to find on land. Materials such as gold and iron can be found in enormous supply along these thermal vents. These areas are readily available to humans for harvesting and may even provide larger supplies of metal than land based mines. Extraction of the minerals from the sea floor sediment would also be much easier than removing them from ore.

노트

주제	deep sea vents = source of metals & minerals → extract

1. ↑ supply than land based mines
2. mineral extraction = easier

Q. According to the passage, what are the advantages of deep sea vent mining?

지문에 의하면, 심해 분출구 채광의 이점은 무엇인가?

위에 적어둔 노트를 보고 완전한 문장으로 바꿔보자.

주제 Deep sea vents are a good source of metals and minerals. Therefore, extracting the minerals from the area would be very beneficial for the following reasons.

1. They can also provide larger supplies than land based mines do.
2. In addition, mineral extraction can be much easier.

해석 심해 분출구는 육지에서는 점점 더 찾기 힘들어지는 금속과 광물의 풍부한 원천이다. 금과 철 같은 물질의 엄청난 양이 이 열수 분출구를 따라 발견될 수 있다. 이런 지역은 인간이 채광하기 쉬우며, 육지에 있는 광맥보다 더 많은 금속을 공급할 수도 있다. 또한, 해저 퇴적물에서 광물을 추출하는 것은 광석에서 광물을 제거하는 것보다 훨씬 쉬울 것이다.

Practice

정답 및 해석 | P. 12

>> 제시된 주제를 참고로 노트를 완성하고, 주어진 질문에 대한 답변을 완성하시오.

Q1

Many people like to drink soft drinks with their meals instead of water. Unfortunately, this is bad for your health in a number of ways. For example, soft drinks contain a lot of sugar and they are very acidic, which means that they can damage your teeth. On top of that, they offer nothing good to your body. They contain very few nutrients so the calories they provide are basically empty. Unneeded calories often lead to weight gain.

노트

주제   soft drinks → bad for health

1. _____

2. _____

Q. According to the passage, why is drinking soft drinks not recommended?

Q2

Avocados are unique fruit that provides many health benefits. One, it is very nutritious and contains important vitamins like B, C, E, and potassium. In addition, avocados are also a rich source of monounsaturated fat, which is very good for the heart and arterial health.

노트

주제   avocado – benefits

1. _____

2. _____

Q. According to the passage, how are avocados beneficial?

Q3

It is a widely held belief that children who begin studying foreign languages early in their life generally reach and maintain a higher level of fluency. Research has proven this idea to be correct for a few reasons. Children appear to have a preexisting mental ability to understand and use grammar easily. Second, they constantly mimic the speech of others, which allows them to adopt new words freely.

> **노트**
>
> 주제 study foreign language early – high level
>
> 1. _____
>
> 2. _____

Q. According to the passage, why does starting to learn languages early in life allow people to become more fluent?

Q4

Sleep is very beneficial for people's health. First of all, it provides the body with down time to relax and repair itself. That is why sleep is an important part of recovering from an illness. On top of that, it also gives the brain time to process new information and create new mental pathways. This is what happens during dreaming.

> **노트**
>
> 주제 benefits of sleeping
>
> 1. _____
>
> 2. _____

Q. According to the passage, what are the benefits of sleeping?

Q5

Most school districts rely upon standardized tests to determine what level of academic achievement students have reached. Unfortunately, these tests are flawed for a number of reasons. One is that such tests only measure a small part of cognitive abilities. Another is that some people cannot perform well when tested in this way. Therefore, standardized tests are not a viable way to assess achievement.

노트

주제 standardized test = flawed

1. _____

2. _____

Q. According to the passage, why are standardized tests flawed?

Q6

Although many students and parents question whether playing team sports at school is necessary, it actually has many benefits for children. Obviously, playing sports provides students with regular exercise, which is important for their health. Team sports also require them to work together toward a common goal. This is a skill that will be very valuable to them throughout their lives.

노트

주제 team sports = beneficial

1. _____

2. _____

Q. According to the passage, why should students be required to play team sports at school?

Q7

One of the methods suggested for controlling global warming is to plant entire forests of trees. This has many advantages for people and the planet. As most people know, trees take in carbon dioxide and release oxygen. This reduces CO_2 levels in the atmosphere, and CO_2 is an important greenhouse gas. What people may not realize is that they also pull water out of the ground and release it through their leaves as water vapor. This can form into low level clouds that block the Sun's rays.

노트

주제   control global w. → plant trees

1. _____

2. _____

Q. According to the passage, how does planting trees help fight global warming?

Q8

In many countries, students do not have to pay tuition to attend university. This system has many advantages for both students and society. On the one hand, charging tuition makes it impossible for many qualified students to attend university. Placing a financial barrier in front of students promotes inequality in society. On the other hand, having a well educated population makes society function better as a whole. Therefore, making university free apart from fees would make society better.

노트

주제   no tuition for univ. → beneficial

1. _____

2. _____

Q. According to the passage, why should universities not charge tuition?

Q9

In general, teachers in the United States are not paid well, and this needs to change for many reasons. For one thing, paying teachers a low salary reduces their motivation to teach, which means that their students are not getting the best education possible. For another thing, a low salary forces teachers with families to take on additional work to pay their bills. This causes a lot of stress that can damage both their physical and mental health.

> 노트
>
> 주제　teachers not paid well → change
>　　　1. _____
>　　　2. _____

Q. According to the passage, why should teachers in the Unites States receive more pay?

Integrated Task

Part 1

Q10

Many people say that people should become vegetarians because it is better for the environment and people's health. However, there are many disadvantages to such a diet. First, some vegetarian alternative foods like almond milk require huge amounts of water, which can harm the environment. Second, many nutrients that are easily gotten from animal products are difficult to get from plants, so people are forced to take supplements to stay healthy.

> 노트
>
> 주제　vegetarian diet → beneficial?
>　　　1. _____
>　　　2. _____

Q. According to the passage, what are the disadvantages of a vegetarian diet?

2. 듣고 요약하기

읽기 지문과 마찬가지로 강의 내용을 정리한 노트를 보며 완전한 문장으로 만드는 연습을 한다. 읽기 지문에 반박하거나 다른 의견을 제시하는 요점을 잘 파악하여 요약하는 것이 핵심이다. 여기에서도 paraphrasing이 유용하게 쓰인다.

| Example

🎧 P1_00

Now, first of all, about there being a lot of metal resources near these thermal vents, yes, this is true. But, we don't have any technology that could mine these metals. I mean, first, you need a way to sort the metals from the ocean sediment. This is not possible at the moment; the technology still needs to be developed. And, even if you could sort the metals from the sediment, you would need a way to transport the metals to the surface of the ocean. These technologies just don't exist right now.

노트

주제 | It is true that there are lots of metals near thermal vents, but X tech.
1. sort metals from ocean sediment = X possible
2. can't transport metals to ocean surface

Q. Why does the lecture say deep sea vent mining is not a good idea?
강의는 왜 심해 분출구 채굴이 좋은 생각이 아니라고 하는가?

위에 적어둔 노트를 보고 완전한 문장으로 바꿔보자.

주제 | It is true that there are lots of metals near thermal vents, but we <u>simply don't have any technology for this kind of mining.</u>
1. Right now, it is <u>impossible to sort the metals from the ocean sediment.</u>
2. In addition, we <u>don't have any technology for transporting these metals to ocean surface.</u>

해석 자, 우선, 이런 열수 분출구 근처에 많은 금속 자원이 있다는 점, 네, 이건 사실입니다. 하지만 우리는 이런 금속을 채굴할 수 있는 기술을 갖고 있지 않아요. 내 말은, 우선 바다 퇴적물에서 금속을 분류할 방법이 필요합니다. 이것은 지금으로서는 불가능해요. 기술을 개발해야 합니다. 그리고 퇴적물에서 금속을 분류할 수 있다 해도, 해수면으로 그 금속을 운반할 방법이 필요할 겁니다. 이런 기술은 현재는 존재하지 않습니다.

Practice

>> 제시된 주제를 참고로 노트를 완성하고, 주어진 질문에 대한 답변을 완성하시오.

Q1

Listen to the lecture. 🎧 P1_11

노트

주제	pet ownership = bad for pets
	1. _____
	2. _____

Q. According to the passage, why is pet ownership bad for the pets themselves?

Q2

Listen to the lecture. 🎧 P1_12

노트

주제	cold weather & catching cold
	1. _____
	2. _____

Q. According to the passage, how does cold weather indirectly make people sick?

Q3

> **노트**
>
> 주제 Internet's benefits
>
> 1. _____
>
> 2. _____

Q. According to the passage, what are the benefits of the Internet?

Q4

> **노트**
>
> 주제 single-sex schools – drawbacks
>
> 1. _____
>
> 2. _____

Q. According to the passage, what are the drawbacks of single-sex schools?

Q5

노트

주제 lottery – not good

1. _____

2. _____

Q. According to the passage, what are the negative aspects of winning a lottery?

Q6

노트

주제 uniform @ work = X good idea

1. _____

2. _____

Q. According to the passage, why is wearing a uniform at work a bad idea?

Q7

노트

주제   eye doctor – X get corrective surgery

      1. _____

      2. _____

Q. According to the passage, why do eye doctors not get corrective surgeries?

Q8

노트

주제   computers in classroom → side effect

      1. _____

      2. _____

Q. According to the passage, what are the side effects of using computers in a classroom?

Q9

Listen to the lecture. 🎧 P1_19

노트

주제   bear = hibernation? No

1. _____

2. _____

Q. According to the passage, why is bear not a hibernating animal?

Q10

Listen to the lecture. 🎧 P1_20

노트

주제   video game = beneficial to children

1. _____

2. _____

Q. According to the passage, how is playing video games beneficial for children?

Part 2

실전 굳히기

◎ Lesson 01   정리하기
    ❶ 읽고 정리하기
    ❷ 듣고 정리하기

◎ Lesson 02   노트 & 답변 연결하기

01 정리하기

문제 듣기

답변을 작성할 때는 지문과 강의의 요점이 각각 어떻게 연결되어있는지 생각하며 해야 한다.

읽기(지문)		듣기(강의)
주제	⬌	주제 반박
요점 1	⬌	요점 1 반박
요점 2	⬌	요점 2 반박
요점 3	⬌	요점 3 반박

위의 표에 제시된 것처럼 읽기(지문)와 듣기(강의)는 내용이 서로 밀접하게 연결되어있다는 점을 기억하자. 하나의 주제에 대해 읽기에서 먼저 어떤 의견을 제시하면 듣기에서 그 의견에 반박한다. 따라서 지문을 읽으면서 뒤에 나올 강의가 대강 어떤 내용일지 유추가 가능하다. 강의는 결국 지문 내용과 반대이기 때문이다. 다음의 예시를 살펴보자.

공룡이 살던 시대의 거대한 새인 아르젠타비스 마그니피센스는 날지 못했을 것이다.

지문의 도입부에서 위와 같이 주장한다면, 강의의 도입부 주장은 무엇이 될까? 당연히 '이 새가 날 수 있었다/날았을 가능성이 있다'고 주장할 것이다.

이제 다음 문단으로 넘어가 요점 1이 등장한다.

거대한 새인 아르젠타비스 마그니피센스는 날개가 그 몸집에 비례해 엄청나게 길었지만 다리는 생각보다 매우 짧아 날개를 퍼덕이며 날아오르려 하면 땅에 날개가 부딪쳐 날지 못했다. 또한 다리는 짧을 뿐만 아니라 약하고 가늘어서 공중에 뛰어올라 날개를 움직이는 것도 어려웠다.

그렇다면 강의의 요점 1은 무엇일까? 이 내용에 반박하는 내용, 즉 '날개는 그만큼 길지 않았다/다리가 그만큼 짧고 약하지 않았다'는 내용일 수도 있고, 이 새가 이런 약점을 극복하기 위해 취했던 다른 방법이 있었을 거라고 제시할 수도 있다. 그 방법에는 경사진 땅에서 도움닫기를 하거나 날개를 펼친 뒤에 절벽에서 뛰어내리는 방법 등이 있을 수 있다.

요점 1이 마무리되고 다음 문단에서 요점 2가 제시된다.

> 새가 날기 위해 필요한 가슴 근육을 아르젠타비스 마그니피센스에게서는 잘 찾아볼 수 없다. 이 새의 가슴 근육은 너무 약해 보여서 무게를 지탱하기 어려워 보인다.

그렇다면 강의의 요점 2는 무엇일까? 가슴 근육이 약하지 않았다는 증거를 제시하거나, 약한 가슴 근육을 극복하고 날 만한 다른 방법이 있었을 거라고 설명할 것이다. 이 방법 중 하나는 상승하는 난기류를 타고 날개를 많이 움직일 필요 없이 몇 시간 동안 나는 것이다.

마지막으로 요점 3이 나온다.

> 아르젠타비스 마그니피센스는 너무 커서 포식자가 몇 없었으므로 날아서 도망칠 필요가 별로 없었고, 그러다가 나는 능력을 잃었을 것이다.

그렇다면 강의의 요점 3은 무엇일까? 이 새를 위협하는 포식자가 분명히 존재했다고 증거를 제시하거나, 새가 날아야 했던 다른 이유를 댈 수도 있다. 즉, 이 새가 사실 죽은 동물을 먹는 새였으며, 죽은 동물을 찾기 위해서는 공중에서 날며 넓은 지역을 둘러봐야 했으므로 비행의 필요성이 분명히 존재했다고 반박할 수 있다.

위의 예시처럼 지문과 강의의 긴밀한 관계를 염두에 두면 내용을 더 쉽게 이해할 수 있을 뿐 아니라 강의에서 어떤 내용이 제시될지도 유추할 수 있고, 더욱 정확한 답변을 할 수 있다.

Example - Reading

As the world's energy and resource consumption grows, it is becoming increasingly difficult to find locations that can provide resources. One source that holds great reserves of minerals is deep sea thermal vents. A vent is a deep crack on the ocean's floor where sea water is heated and filled with minerals. The concept of vent mining has recently received attention, but these are fragile ecosystems with many unique species. Still, there are a number of reasons why vent mining should be carried out.

First, the deep sea vents are a rich source of metals and minerals that are increasingly difficult to find on land. Materials such as gold and iron can be found in enormous supply along these thermal vents. These areas are readily available to humans for harvesting and may even provide larger supplies of metal than land based mines. Extraction of the minerals from the sea floor sediment would also be much easier than removing them from ore.

Secondly, although thermal vents are home to a number of very unique animals that cannot exist elsewhere, we would not have to put those organisms in danger. Much of the minerals from thermal vents can be found as much as two kilometers away from the vent itself. Mining at this distance would not damage these fragile habitats while still yielding the desired resources.

Finally, mineral extraction in the deep sea can be regulated by international law. Many critics say that miners would recklessly mine since it would be very difficult to oversee their operations. But there are many laws and agencies that can regulate mining near the vents. One of these agencies is the International Seabed Authority which was established by the Law of the Sea Convention. This agency ensures that companies follow the strict regulations for ocean mining and do not destroy the environment with their activities.

세계의 에너지와 자원 소비가 증가함에 따라 자원을 제공할 수 있는 장소를 찾는 것이 점점 더 어려워지고 있다. 엄청난 광물 매장량을 보유한 한 원천이 심해의 열수 분출구이다. 분출구는 해저에 있는 깊은 틈으로, 이곳에서는 해수가 데워지고 광물로 가득 차있다. 분출구 채광이라는 개념은 최근에 주목을 받아왔지만, 이곳은 많은 독특한 종들이 서식하는 연약한 생태계이다. 그럼에도 분출구 채광을 해야 하는 많은 이유가 있다.

첫째, 심해 분출구는 육지에서는 점점 더 찾기 힘들어지는 금속과 광물의 풍부한 원천이다. 금과 철 같은 물질의 엄청난 양이 이 열수 분출구를 따라 발견될 수 있다. 이런 지역은 인간이 채광하기 쉬우며, 육지에 있는 광맥보다 더 많은 금속을 공급할 수도 있다. 해저 퇴적물에서 광물을 추출하는 것은 역시 광석에서 광물을 제거하는 것보다 훨씬 쉬울 것이다.

둘째로, 열수 분출구가 다른 곳에서는 존재할 수 없는 아주 독특한 많은 동물들의 서식지라 해도, 이 생물들을 위험에 처하게 할 필요는 없다. 열수 분출구에서 나오는 많은 광물이 분출구에서 2km까지 떨어진 곳에서 발견될 수 있다. 이런 거리에서 채굴하면 이 연약한 서식지에 손상을 입히지 않으면서 원하는 자원을 여전히 산출할 수 있을 것이다.

마지막으로, 심해에서 광물을 채굴하는 것은 국제법으로 규제할 수 있다. 비판하는 사람들 다수는 광부들의 활동을 감독하기가 아주 어렵기 때문에 이들이 무분별하게 채광할지 모른다고 말한다. 그러나 분출구 근처의 채광을 규제할 수 있는 많은 법과 단체가 있다. 이런 단체 중 하나가 국제 해양법 협약에 따라 설립한 국제 해저 기구이다. 이 단체는 기업들이 바다에서 채광할 때 반드시 엄격한 규정을 따르고 채광 활동으로 환경을 파괴하지 않도록 한다.

주제　deep sea vents mining = advantageous 심해 분출구 채광 = 이점

1. rich source of metals & minerals 금속 & 광물의 풍부한 원천
   - gold & iron available 금 & 철을 구할 수 있음
   - larger supply than land based mines 육지 기반 광산보다 더 많은 공급량
   - extraction much easier 추출이 훨씬 쉬움

2. X danger for animals 동물들에게 위험 X
   - mine far from vents 분출구에서 멀리 떨어져 채굴

3. regulate by int'l law 국제법으로 규제
   - oversee companies, strict regulations 회사들 감독, 엄격한 규제

읽기 지문을 요약할 때는 주제를 맨 위에 쓴 뒤에 주제를 뒷받침하는 내용들을 1, 2, 3의 소제목으로 나열한다. 이 소제목들 아래에 더 작은 세부 사항들을 정리해두면 보기 편하다.

>> 제시된 지문을 읽고 아래의 노트를 완성해보자.

Q1   As the saying goes, "Two heads are better than one." Completing a project as a team is better than doing it alone. Having a group of people divide work can help save time and effort, so many companies and schools focus more on group work. Teamwork brings several benefits.

First, one of the benefits that teamwork brings is that working as a team helps to carry out work more efficiently. A group of people has various abilities. If a team member in a group is skillful at statistics, the group will have expertise in dealing with data. The abilities that each member has help to complete a given task more efficiently.

Second, group work allows team members to come up with various creative ideas. Each team member can talk freely in the process of making a group decision. As various ideas are suggested, there is a high possibility that the group will have creative solutions to problems they have to tackle. For example, when writing an essay, an individual can face limitations in brainstorming for ideas. But a group of people can think of more various and creative ideas than a single individual.

Another benefit of having a group of people tackle a problem is that teamwork can make team members actively participate in the work. This is because team members will feel more responsible for what they do in the group, and they will work harder to achieve positive results. They know that the others are depending on them, so they have more reason to perform.

노트

주제   project: team > alone

    1. work more efficiently

     -

    2. more creative ideas

     -

    3. members actively participate

     -

Q2 Many animals and plants have been imported intentionally or by accident to new areas. These new species transported to new environments often have negative effects. Let us take a look at these negative consequences.

First, a new species always upsets the local ecological balance. A new species is never just added to the native ecosystem. It always competes with some native ecosystems. The damage does not end with the displacement of native competitors as the new species is often unsuitable as food for species further up the food chain. The negative effects thus spread through the whole ecosystem.

Second, the introduction of new species often destroys the local environment. For example, the cane toad, native to South Africa, was introduced to Australia, where it has spread at an alarming speed and has had harmful effects on the local environment. The cane toad, a natural predator, has killed a large number of native species in Australia. In addition to this, its poison sometimes poses a direct threat to children and pets when touched.

Finally, the negative impact caused by the introduction of new species often leads to economic burdens. For example, mesquites, a shrub native to America, were introduced to Africa. After the introduction of mesquites, commonly planted for land restoration and as a source of wood, they started to displace native species in Africa. As a result, African governments are forced to commit economic and bureaucratic resources to control the replacement of native species by mesquites.

노트

주제   new species in new envi. → negative effect

    1. upset local ecology's balance

     -

     -

    2. destroy local envi.

     -

     -

    3. economic burden

     -

Part 2 Integrated Task

Q3

In England before the Industrial Revolution of the late 18th century, manufactured goods such as cloth and thread were produced manually at homes and small workshops. This so-called "putting-out system" developed into the factory system. There are several reasons why the development of the factory system was first made possible in England.

First, the advent of new technologies resulted in the accelerated development of the factory system. The development of steam engines played an especially pivotal role in the spread of the factory system. The introduction of steam engines to factories made it possible to generate a considerable amount of energy that individual workers at home could not create.

Second, the development of the factory system in England was the result of the introduction of property rights. Stable and strict rules of law that protected private property encouraged property holders to develop their property and efficiently allocate resources based on the operation of the market. This, in turn, caused property owners to invest more in new factories.

Finally, this system helped factory owners reduce production costs, especially transportation costs. Before the advancement of the system, raw materials and equipment had been supplied for workers who worked at home. This would have cost business owners considerable amounts of money for transportation. In this case, naturally, they preferred the factory system in which they could reduce the cost of transporting raw materials and goods.

노트

주제   development of factory system in England

1. new technologies

-

2. intro. of property rights

-

-

3. owners: reduce production costs, esp. trans. costs

-

Q4

It is well known that fossil fuels will not power the world for much longer. In fact, hydrogen fuel will most likely replace fossil fuels as the main source of global energy in a very short period of time. There are many reasons why hydrogen fuel will replace fossil fuels.

First of all, hydrogen is not only more abundant than fossil fuels, but also renewable. One day, the world will use up fossil fuel reserves and be forced to use alternative energy sources. Hydrogen is one of the most abundant elements in the universe and is therefore much more readily available than fossil fuels. This means hydrogen can be used as a potential source of energy and the world will never run out of hydrogen.

Another point is the problem of pollution. When we burn fossil fuels to generate energy, carbon dioxide, a greenhouse gas, builds up in the atmosphere. As the amount of carbon dioxide in the air increases, global temperatures rise. However, the only byproduct of hydrogen fuel engines is water. This in no way harms the environment and seems to be the most logical choice for the world's next energy supply.

Finally, as the cost of acquiring and maintaining hydrogen fuel cell engines decreases, consumers will have no reason not to use them. Already, hydrogen fuel cell engines cost less to maintain than combustion engines since hydrogen fuel engines malfunction much less often. As the engines operated by hydrogen become cheaper to buy, they will turn out to be the best replacement for combustion engines.

노트

주제   hydrogen fuel will replace fossil f.

　　1. hydrogen = abundant & renewable

　　　-

　　2. pollution X

　　　-

　　　-

　　3. costs less

　　　-

Q5

Many people think that increasing energy prices is the most effective way to save limited sources of energy. They believe that if gasoline prices increase because of raising gas taxes, gasoline can be conserved. However, the policy of increasing gas taxes cannot be a solution to saving energy, especially gasoline. There are several reasons why this policy is inefficient and problematic.

Firstly, one reason why this policy is inefficient is that people will not stop consuming gasoline even if gasoline prices increase. For example, even though the government raised the price of cigarettes from $2 to $4, a 100% increase, smokers who could not find a substitute for cigarettes did not reduce their consumption of cigarettes by 100%. Likewise, no matter how much gasoline prices increase, people will not give up using it.

Secondly, increasing gas taxes can put a financial burden on people. In particular, this increase may burden poor families that live on the outskirts of the city because of high housing prices. The families have to commute to work by car, so they would have to spend too much money on buying gasoline if prices of gasoline increased.

Thirdly, there are much better ways of conserving gasoline like making cars more fuel efficient. Governments should make car manufacturers develop cars that use less gasoline, such as hybrid gas-electric vehicles that can be operated partially by electricity. Without raising the prices of gasoline, governments can easily achieve their goal of conserving gasoline.

노트

주제   ↑ energy price = saving source of energy? No

1.
- ppl will not give up b/c there's no substitute

2.
- esp. poor families living on the outskirts
- commuting by car = too much $

3.
- making fuel-efficient cars(hybrid ones)

Q6 Due to the lack of written history documenting England during the Dark Ages, debate has arisen as to the true origins of the English people who now inhabit the country. Some contend that they are descended from the tribes who lived there long before the Roman occupation, known as the Celts. Others claim that most people are descended from the people who invaded soon after, referred to as Anglo-Saxons. However, the majority of the evidence suggests that the latter is true.

Firstly, the arrival of Anglo-Saxons into the British Isles was not the result of exploration or trade. It was actually a mass migration from what is now North Central Europe. Constant pressure and invasions from the East forced the majority of the Angles and the Saxons to flee their homeland. When they arrived in England, they quickly displaced the Celtic population, forcing them into the farthest corners of the land. The Anglo-Saxons rapidly became the dominant population.

Secondly, the language of England is directly derived from the Anglo-Saxons. Modern English can be clearly traced back to their Germanic languages and not those of the Celts. Indeed, apart from a few terms that were adopted by the invaders, there is no evidence of Celtic languages in England. Rather, Celtic tongues survive in Wales, Ireland, and Scotland, clearly supporting the theory that the people of modern day England are Anglo-Saxons.

Thirdly, a recent genetic study of the DNA of people living in the eastern portion of England has provided compelling proof. The mapping of the human genetic code has made determining people's background easier and much more accurate. The DNA profiles of the people sampled were virtually identical to the profiles of people living in modern day Germany and Denmark, which is the area from which the Anglo-Saxons came.

노트

주제 origins of English ppl = Anglo-Saxons?

1.
- invasion → Angles & Saxons ran away from homeland
- arrived in England → displaced Celtic

2.
- directly from Anglo-Saxons
- no evidence of Celtic lang. in England

3.
- almost identical to Germany / Denmark ppl
  = where Anglo-Saxons came from

The Everglades is a large area of wetlands in southern Florida that contain abundant plant and animal life. However, recent environmental issues have threatened the unique ecology of the region. If these issues are not addressed, the Everglades may disappear.

One serious issue for the Everglades is invasive species, which are plants and animals that have been introduced from other parts of the world. One such species is the paperbark tree from Australia. The tree's native habitat is very similar to the Everglades, which allows it to spread rapidly. Paperbark trees take over the sawgrass marshes that comprise most of the Everglades, turning them into swamp.

An even more serious problem for the region is water pollution. The two main pollutants are chemical fertilizers used in farming and mercury released from power plants burning fossil fuels. The fertilizers change the chemical composition of the soil, killing marsh grasses and encouraging other plants like cotton tails to grow. Mercury builds up in animals' bodies as they feed on each other. This eventually kills many animals and makes fish unsafe to eat.

The most serious threat to the Everglades is its decreased water supply. Wetlands need a large supply of slow moving water to exist. Dams and canals were built to prevent flooding and divert water for farming and residential areas. This led to insufficient water flow to the area. So, large sections of the Everglades are simply drying up, removing the habitat from the plants and animals that depend upon it.

노트

주제   issues threatening the Everglades → they may disappear

  1. invasive plants & animals

    -

  2. water pollution

    -

  3. ↓ water supply

    -

    -

Q8

Sometimes, the introduction of new species can result in several negative consequences, so the government is considering a law to restrict importing, buying, and selling of non-native species of animals. However, this law should not be implemented for the following reasons.

First of all, the law might be used to force pet owners to give up ownership of their pets. This law could have an immediate effect on pet owners who currently have non-native species animals since they have to worry about their pets being taken away. Most of these animals are kept inside the owner's homes, so they rarely come into contact with native species. Since they are not much of a threat, their owners should be allowed to keep them.

Second, implementing the law is expensive because conducting studies to find out whether non-native species cause damage when they are released to the wild requires a lot of money. A variety of new animals, ranging from a marine species, such as the zebra mussel, to pets, have been introduced or transported to the US intentionally or accidentally, and it costs a lot to investigate the consequences of their release to the wild.

Another reason to oppose this law is that the law is not reasonable because it applies a single standard to the entire country. For example, South American rabbits cannot survive long in northern parts of the US simply because the regions are too cold for them to survive. Therefore, it is unreasonable to apply the law to the entire US.

노트

주제	gov't law = restrict importing/buying/selling non-native species → shouldn't be implemented

1. pet owners will give up their pets

   -

2. cost

   -

3. not reasonable

   -

Scattered across the Atlantic coast of the United States there are shallow, round depressions in the land. They are called Carolina bays, and the bay part of their name comes from a type of tree that is commonly found in them and not the fact that they often hold water. The origin of the bays remains undetermined, but many scientists think that they may have been created by large meteors that exploded above the ground for the following reasons.

First, the depressions that form the bays are shaped in a way that is consistent with impact craters created by fragments of meteors that exploded above the ground. When that happens, most of the fragments strike the ground at an angle, which makes an oval crater with one side deeper than the other. The deeper side will have fine, crushed material piled high on its edge. The bays are ovals that lie in a northwest to southeast direction, their southeastern rim is higher, and it is usually made of white sand. This suggests that they were likely formed in this way.

Second, the sand contained in the bays is different from the sand found in the Atlantic coastal region. The normal sand has a coating of iron compounds, but the sand in the bays lacks this coating. The absence of iron can be explained by the intense heat that would result from a meteor impact. This heat would have melted the iron, causing it to vaporize and be blown away. So, as the meteor fragments created the bays, they could have left behind sand that does not have the usual iron coating.

Third, scientists have found buckyballs in some of the bays, which may point to an object from space striking the Earth. Buckyballs are unique carbon structures that are composed of 60 tightly interconnected carbon atoms. They are made when carbon is exposed to intense heat and pressure. These conditions can be created during a meteor strike. So the meteor fragments that made the bays could have also created the buckyballs that were found in them.

노트

주제 | Carolina bays – their origin = large meteors?

1.
- similar to impact craters created by meteors
- oval shape

2.
- not found in Atlantic coast
- absence of iron = meteor impact's intense heat

3.
- carbon structures that can be made from meteor strike
- found in some of the bays

Q10

In the densely populated Northeastern Unites States, many cities have been linked by express trains for decades, and high-speed rail service has been operating since 2000 linking Boston, NYC, Philadelphia, and Washington DC. This type of transportation system has many advantages, and for those reasons, the next area to receive this kind of service should be California, between San Francisco and Los Angeles.

Firstly, railroad tracks are cheaper and easier to maintain than roads. Asphalt roads must frequently be repaired due to damage from the vehicles that use them and the weather, so they are a constant drain on the economy. This is extremely expensive and uses up a large portion of the government's budget for infrastructure. By comparison, railways are much easier to maintain and need to be repaired far less often. Since the tracks are made from steel and they are attached to concrete, they are much more durable than asphalt.

Secondly, creating a high-speed rail system will help to relieve traffic congestion. The streets and highways in the Los Angeles area have some of the worst traffic congestion in the whole country, and it is only getting worse. If they were provided with an alternative way to travel, many people would prefer to use that. A high-speed rail system would provide them with such an alternative. So, if people can ride trains, there will be fewer cars on the road, which would mean less congestion on the road.

Thirdly, a high-speed rail system is an environmentally friendly form of transportation. High-speed trains use far less energy to transport people than cars. Since cars travel much more slowly than high-speed trains, they must use a lot more energy to cover the same distance. This means that they also produce more emissions than the high-speed trains do. So, high-speed trains are more energy-efficient, and they produce far less pollution than a highway full of cars.

노트

주제   high-speed trains = advantages → California

1.
- asphalt repair too frequent → $$$
- railways repair = less often, more durable

2.
- provide alternative way to travel
- ppl use more → less traffic

3.
- use less energy than cars

Example - Listening

P2_00

We all know there is a definite need to meet the world's demand for mineral resources, and vent mining seems to be one of the best options for collecting these resources. However, I don't think that the reading accurately discusses vent mining. Let's look at the points in the reading, because honestly, they just don't make sense to me.

Now, first of all, about there being a lot of metal resources near these thermal vents, yes, this is true. But, we don't have any technology that could mine these metals. I mean, first, you need a way to sort the metals from the ocean sediment. This is not possible at the moment; the technology still needs to be developed. And, even if you could sort the metals from the sediment, you would need a way to transport the metals to the surface of the ocean. These technologies just don't exist right now.

The second point the author made that mining can be performed two kilometers away from the thermal vents, well, this certainly is not far away enough to guarantee the safety of the ecosystem there. I mean, sure, two kilometers may seem like a large distance, but mining uses some very toxic chemicals that would be very difficult to contain underwater. If the chemicals from the mining actually spread to the ecosystem, the effects might be simply disastrous to the organisms that make their homes at the vents.

Finally, the standards mentioned in the reading only apply to vents that are located within international waters. But, companies would most likely want to mine at vents closer to coastlines. Vents located near these coastlines are not within the jurisdiction of international law. That is, companies would mine in the territorial waters of the country to which the coast belongs. Many of these places have absolutely no form of regulation on vent mining activities, so regulating their activities would be impossible.

광물 자원에 대한 세계의 수요를 맞출 필요가 분명히 있다는 점은 우리 모두 알고 있고, 분출구 채광은 이런 자원을 모으는 데 가장 좋은 선택지 중 하나처럼 보입니다. 하지만 나는 지문이 열수 분출구 채광을 정확하게 논의하고 있다고 생각하지 않아요. 지문의 요점들을 살펴보도록 하죠. 솔직히 저는 이해가 되지 않으니까요.

자, 우선, 이런 열수 분출구 근처에 많은 금속 자원이 있다는 점, 네, 이건 사실입니다. 하지만 우리는 이런 금속을 채굴할 수 있는 기술을 갖고 있지 않아요. 내 말은, 우선 바다 퇴적물에서 금속을 분류할 방법이 필요합니다. 이것은 지금으로서는 불가능해요. 기술을 개발해야 합니다. 그리고 퇴적물에서 금속을 분류할 수 있다 해도, 해수면으로 그 금속을 운반할 방법이 필요할 겁니다. 이런 기술은 현재는 존재하지 않습니다.

채광이 열수 분출구에서 2km 떨어진 곳에서 이루어질 수 있다는 필자의 두 번째 요점은 글쎄요, 이건 분명 그곳 생태계의 안전을 보장하기에 충분히 먼 거리가 아닙니다. 내 말은, 2km가 먼 거리처럼 보일지 모르지만, 채광할 때 매우 유독한 화학 물질을 몇 가지 사용하는데, 이는 물속에서 통제하기가 아주 어려울 겁니다. 만약 채광에 쓰이는 화학 물질이 실제로 생태계에 퍼지면 그 영향은 분출구를 서식지로 삼는 생물들에게 그저 재앙일 수도 있습니다.

마지막으로, 지문에서 언급된 기준은 공해 내에 있는 열수 분출구에만 적용됩니다. 그러나 기업들은 해안선과 더 가까이 있는 분출구에서 채광하고 싶을 겁니다. 이런 해안선 근처에 위치한 분출구들은 국제법의 관할 구역 내에 있지 않아요. 즉, 기업들은 그 해안이 속한 나라의 영해 내에서 채광할 겁니다. 이런 장소들 중 다수는 열수 분출구 채광 행위에 관한 어떤 형태의 규정도 전혀 가지고 있지 않기에 그들의 활동을 규제하는 것은 불가능할 겁니다.

주제   deep sea vents mining = X advantageous 심해 분출구 채광 = 이점 없음

1. no technology 기술 없음
   - sorting metals 금속 분류
   - transporting them to ocean surface 그것들을 해수면으로 운송

2. X danger for animals? 동물들에게 위험하지 않다?
   - mine far from vents → not enough 분출구에서 먼 곳에서 채광 → 충분하지 않음
   - toxic chemicals can still harm marine species
     유독성 화학 물질이 여전히 해양 종들에게 해를 입힐 수 있음

3. regulate by int'l law? 국제법으로 규제?
   - only apply to int'l waters 공해에만 적용
   - companies mine near coastlines = X jurisdiction
     기업들이 해안선 근처에서 채광 = 관할 구역 없음

Part 2
Integrated Task

읽기 노트와 마찬가지로 강의를 요약할 때 역시 주제를 맨 위에 쓴 뒤에 주제를 뒷받침하는 내용들을 1, 2, 3의 소제목으로 나열한다. 이 소제목들 아래에 더 작은 세부 사항들을 정리해두면 보기 편하다.

>> 강의를 듣고 아래의 노트를 완성해보자.

Q1
Listen to the lecture. 🎧 P2_01

노트

| 주제 | working as a team = not good |

1. not efficient

   - _____

   - _____

2. creative ideas? no

   - _____

   - _____

3. ppl don't work harder in a group

   - _____

Q2
Listen to the lecture. 🎧 P2_02

노트

| 주제 | new species in a new envi. cause problems? No |

1. disturb ecology? Not really

   - _____

2. destroy the natives?

   - _____

   - _____

3. economic burden?

   - _____

Q3

Listen to the lecture. 🎧 P2_03

노트

주제 | 3 reasons for the rise of factory system in England → problems

1. many breakthroughs? no
   - _____
   - _____

2. property rights X contribute
   - _____

3. cost ↓ X
   - _____

Q4

Listen to the lecture. 🎧 P2_04

노트

주제 | hydrogen fuel can replace fossil f. soon? No

1. _____
   - the kind of H. used for H. fuel engines is artificial & complicated to make

2. _____
   - byproduct = water, true
   - but the process of making that H. requires fossil f. too → pollution

3. _____
   - H. fuel engine = platinum = rare & expensive

Listen to the lecture. 🎧 P2_05

노트

주제   ↑ energy price = saving source of energy? Yes

1. _____

   - use gas economically(e.g. X drive a short distance)

2. _____

   - we have public transp.(bus, subway, train…)
   - ppl can carpool too

3. _____

   - encourage making more fuel-efficient cars
   - ppl will demand these cars

Listen to the lecture. 🎧 P2_06

노트

주제   origins of English ppl = Anglo-Saxons? Not clear

1. _____

   - displaced Celtic? No, Celtics # too large
   - can't displace that many ppl

2. _____

   - conquered ppl often use their ruler's language too
   - Celts adopting Anglo-Saxon language? Not really…

3. _____

   - DNA samples came from a small area where Anglo-Saxons would
     have arrived

Listen to the lecture. 🎧 P2_07

노트

주제   issues threatening the Everglades → there is hope

1. invasive plants & animals

- _____

2. water pollution

- _____

3. ↓ water supply

- _____

- _____

Q8

Listen to the lecture. 🎧 P2_08

노트

주제   gov't law = restrict importing / buying / selling non-native species
→ good idea

1. pet owners will give up their pets

- _____

2. cost

- _____

- _____

3. not reasonable?

- _____

노트

주제   Carolina bays – their origin = large meteors?

1. depressions' shape

\- _____

2. sand is different

\- _____

\- _____

3. buckyballs

\- _____

\- _____

Listen to the lecture. 🎧 P2_10

노트

주제　high-speed trains = advantages → California X

　　1. cheaper & easier to maintain than roads

　　- _____

　　2. relieve traffic congestion

　　- _____

　　- _____

　　3. environ. friendly

　　- _____

문제 듣기

지문(읽기)과 강의(듣기)를 노트테이킹한 내용을 토대로 답변을 작성하는 과정을 살펴보자.

<u>노트</u>

지문(읽기)		강의(듣기)
주제	⬌	주제 반박
요점 1	⬌	요점 1 반박
요점 2	⬌	요점 2 반박
요점 3	⬌	요점 3 반박

답변

읽기 주제 + 듣기 주제 반박
읽기 요점 1 + 듣기 요점 1
읽기 요점 2 + 듣기 요점 2
읽기 요점 3 + 듣기 요점 3

As the world's energy and resource consumption grows, it is becoming increasingly difficult to find locations that can provide resources. One source that holds great reserves of minerals is deep sea thermal vents. A vent is a deep crack on the ocean's floor where sea water is heated and filled with minerals. The concept of vent mining has recently received attention, but these are fragile ecosystems with many unique species. Still there are a number of reasons why vent mining should be carried out.

First, the deep sea vents are a rich source of metals and minerals that are increasingly difficult to find on land. Materials such as gold and iron can be found in enormous supply along these thermal vents. These areas are readily available to humans for harvesting and may even provide larger supplies of metal than land based mines. Extraction of the minerals from the sea floor sediment would also be much easier than removing them from ore.

Secondly, although thermal vents are home to a number of very unique animals that cannot exist elsewhere, we would not have to put those organisms in danger. Much of the minerals from thermal vents can be found as much as two kilometers away from the vent itself. Mining at this distance would not damage these fragile habitats while still yielding the desired resources.

Finally, mineral extraction in the deep sea can be regulated by international law. Many critics say that miners would recklessly mine since it would be very difficult to oversee their operations. But there are many laws and agencies that can regulate mining near the vents. One of these agencies is the International Seabed Authority which was established by the Law of the Sea Convention. This agency ensures that companies follow the strict regulations for ocean mining and do not destroy the environment with their activities.

노트

주제   deep sea vents mining = advantageous 심해 분출구 채광 = 이점

1. rich source of metals & minerals 금속 & 광물의 풍부한 원천
   - gold & iron available 금 & 철을 구할 수 있음
   - larger supply than land based mines 육지 기반 광산보다 더 많은 공급량
   - extraction much easier 추출이 훨씬 쉬움

2. X danger for animals 동물들에게 위험 X
   - mine far from vents 분출구에서 멀리 떨어져 채굴

3. regulate by int'l law 국제법으로 규제
   - oversee companies, strict regulations 회사들 감독, 엄격한 규제

세계의 에너지와 자원 소비가 증가함에 따라 자원을 제공할 수 있는 장소를 찾는 것이 점점 더 어려워지고 있다. 엄청난 광물 매장량을 보유한 한 원천이 심해의 열수 분출구이다. 분출구는 해저에 있는 깊은 틈으로, 이곳에서는 해수가 데워지고 광물로 가득 차있다. 분출구 채광이라는 개념은 최근에 주목을 받아왔지만, 이곳은 많은 독특한 종들이 서식하는 연약한 생태계이다. 그럼에도 분출구 채광을 해야 하는 많은 이유가 있다.

첫째, 심해 분출구는 육지에서는 점점 더 찾기 힘들어지는 금속과 광물의 풍부한 원천이다. 금과 철 같은 물질의 엄청난 양이 이 열수 분출구를 따라 발견될 수 있다. 이런 지역은 인간이 채광하기 쉬우며, 육지에 있는 광맥보다 더 많은 금속을 공급할 수도 있다. 해저 퇴적물에서 광물을 추출하는 것은 역시 광석에서 광물을 제거하는 것보다 훨씬 쉬울 것이다.

둘째로, 열수 분출구가 다른 곳에서는 존재할 수 없는 아주 독특한 많은 동물들의 서식지라 해도, 이 생물들을 위험에 처하게 할 필요는 없다. 열수 분출구에서 나오는 많은 광물이 분출구에서 2km까지 떨어진 곳에서 발견될 수 있다. 이런 거리에서 채굴하면 이 연약한 서식지에 손상을 입히지 않으면서 원하는 자원을 여전히 산출할 수 있을 것이다.

마지막으로, 심해에서 광물을 채굴하는 것은 국제법으로 규제할 수 있다. 비판하는 사람들 다수는 광부들의 활동을 감독하기가 아주 어렵기 때문에 이들이 무분별하게 채광할지 모른다고 말한다. 그러나 분출구 근처의 채광을 규제할 수 있는 많은 법과 단체가 있다. 이런 단체 중 하나가 국제 해양법 협약에 따라 설립한 국제 해저 기구이다. 이 단체는 기업들이 바다에서 채광할 때 반드시 엄격한 규정을 따르고 채광 활동으로 환경을 파괴하지 않도록 한다.

We all know there is a definite need to meet the world's demand for mineral resources, and vent mining seems to be one of the best options for collecting these resources. However, I don't think that the reading accurately discusses vent mining. Let's look at the points in the reading, because honestly, they just don't make sense to me.

Now, first of all, about there being a lot of metal resources near these thermal vents, yes, this is true. But, we don't have any technology that could mine these metals. I mean, first, you need a way to sort the metals from the ocean sediment. This is not possible at the moment; the technology still needs to be developed. And, even if you could sort the metals from the sediment, you would need a way to transport the metals to the surface of the ocean. These technologies just don't exist right now.

The second point the author made that mining can be performed two kilometers away from the thermal vents, well, this certainly is not far away enough to guarantee the safety of the ecosystem there. I mean, sure, two kilometers may seem like a large distance, but mining uses some very toxic chemicals that would be very difficult to contain underwater. If the chemicals from the mining actually spread to the ecosystem, the effects might be simply disastrous to the organisms that make their homes at the vents.

Finally, the standards mentioned in the reading only apply to vents that are located within international waters. But, companies would most likely want to mine at vents closer to coastlines. Vents located near these coastlines are not within the jurisdiction of international law. That is, companies would mine in the territorial waters of the country to which the coast belongs. Many of these places have absolutely no form of regulation on vent mining activities, so regulating their activities would be impossible.

노트

주제   deep sea vents mining = X advantageous 심해 분출구 채광 = 이점 없음

1. no technology 기술 없음
   - sorting metals 금속 분류
   - transporting them to ocean surface 그것들을 해수면으로 운송

2. X danger for animals? 동물들에게 위험하지 않다?
   - mine far from vents → not enough 분출구에서 먼 곳에서 채광 → 충분하지 않음
   - toxic chemicals can still harm marine species
     유독성 화학 물질이 여전히 해양 종들에게 해를 입힐 수 있음

3. regulate by int'l law? 국제법으로 규제?
   - only apply to int'l waters 공해에만 적용
   - companies mine near coastlines = X jurisdiction
     기업들이 해안선 근처에서 채광 = 관할 구역 없음

광물 자원에 대한 세계의 수요를 맞출 필요가 분명히 있다는 점은 우리 모두 알고 있고, 분출구 채광은 이런 자원을 모으는 데 가장 좋은 선택지 중 하나처럼 보입니다. 하지만 나는 지문이 열수 분출구 채광을 정확하게 논의하고 있다고 생각하지 않아요. 지문의 요점들을 살펴보도록 하죠. 솔직히 저는 이해가 되지 않으니까요.

자, 우선, 이런 열수 분출구 근처에 많은 금속 자원이 있다는 점, 네, 이건 사실입니다. 하지만 우리는 이런 금속을 채굴할 수 있는 기술을 갖고 있지 않아요. 내 말은, 우선 바다 퇴적물에서 금속을 분류할 방법이 필요합니다. 이것은 지금으로서는 불가능해요. 기술을 개발해야 합니다. 그리고 퇴적물에서 금속을 분류할 수 있다 해도, 해수면으로 그 금속을 운반할 방법이 필요할 겁니다. 이런 기술은 현재는 존재하지 않습니다.

채광이 열수 분출구에서 2km 떨어진 곳에서 이루어질 수 있다는 필자의 두 번째 요점은 글쎄요, 이건 분명 그곳 생태계의 안전을 보장하기에 충분히 먼 거리가 아닙니다. 내 말은, 2km가 먼 거리처럼 보일지 모르지만, 채광할 때 매우 유독한 화학 물질을 몇 가지 사용하는데, 이는 물속에서 통제하기가 아주 어려울 겁니다. 만약 채광에 쓰이는 화학 물질이 실제로 생태계에 퍼지면 그 영향은 분출구를 서식지로 삼는 생물들에게 그저 재앙일 수도 있습니다.

마지막으로, 지문에서 언급된 기준은 공해 내에 있는 열수 분출구에만 적용됩니다. 그러나 기업들은 해안선과 더 가까이 있는 분출구에서 채광하고 싶을 겁니다. 이런 해안선 근처에 위치한 분출구들은 국제법의 관할 구역 내에 있지 않아요. 즉, 기업들은 그 해안이 속한 나라의 영해 내에서 채광할 겁니다. 이런 장소들 중 다수는 열수 분출구 채광 행위에 관한 어떤 형태의 규정도 전혀 가지고 있지 않기에 그들의 활동을 규제하는 것은 불가능할 겁니다.

답변 연결

Reading	Listening
주제 deep sea vents mining = advantageous	deep sea vents mining = X advantageous
1. rich source of metals & minerals - gold & iron available - larger supply than land based mines - extraction much easier	1. no technology - sorting metals - transporting them to ocean surface
2. X danger for animals - mine far from vents	2. X danger for animals? - mine far from vents → not enough - toxic chemicals can still harm marine species
3. regulate by int'l law - oversee companies, strict regulations	3. regulate by int'l law? - only apply to int'l waters - companies mine near coastlines = X jurisdiction

읽기&듣기 연결 → 실제 답변 써보기

도입: Reading과 Listening의 주제

The reading and the lecture both talk about the potential of vent mining. The reading says that there are three reasons why vent mining should be carried out. However, the lecturer argues that the reasons given in the reading are unconvincing.

지문과 강의 둘 다 열수 분출구 채광의 잠재력에 관해 말하고 있다. 지문은 열수 분출구 채광이 시행되어야 하는 세 가지 이유가 있다고 한다. 하지만 강의자는 지문에서 주어진 이유들은 설득력이 없다고 주장한다.

문단 1: Reading의 주장 1과 Listening의 반박

Firstly, the reading states that vent mining is a good idea because there are a lot of precious metals and minerals near thermal vents. Although the lecturer admits that there are a lot of metals at thermal vents, he argues that it is too difficult to get them. This is because we do not have the technology necessary to sort the metals from the sediment at the bottom of the ocean, nor to transport them to the surface of the ocean.

첫째로, 지문은 열수 분출구 근처에 귀금속과 광물이 많이 있기 때문에 열수 분출구 채광이 좋은 생각이라고 말한다. 강의자는 열수 분출구에 많은 금속이 있다는 점은 인정하지만, 그러한 금속을 얻는 것이 너무 어렵다고 주장한다. 왜냐하면 해저 침전물에서 그 금속들을 분리하거나 그것들을 해수면으로 운송하는 데 필요한 기술을 가지고 있지 않기 때문이다.

문단 2: Reading의 주장 2와 Listening의 반박

Secondly, the reading states that vent mining can be done in ways that will not harm marine life near the vents. Much of the minerals are found up to two kilometers away from the vents and their fragile ecosystems. According to the lecture, however, toxic chemicals used in mining are difficult to contain, and they can spread regardless of how far away mining is performed.

둘째로, 지문은 열수 분출구 채광이 분출구 근처의 해양 생물들을 해치지 않는 방법으로 진행될 수 있다고 한다. 많은 광물이 분출구와 그 섬세한 생태계에서 2km까지 떨어진 곳에서 발견된다. 그러나 강의에 따르면, 채굴에 사용되는 유독성 화학 물질은 통제하기 어려우며, 얼마나 멀리서 채굴을 하든 관계없이 확산할 수 있다고 한다.

문단 3: Reading의 주장 3과 Listening의 반박

Thirdly, the reading goes on to say that vent mining in the deep sea can be regulated by international law. However, the lecturer casts doubt on this claim, stating that companies can mine in territorial waters where international law does not apply. This means that international law cannot prevent companies from recklessly extracting metals in the deep sea.

셋째로, 지문은 계속해서 심해의 분출구 채굴이 국제법으로 규제될 수 있다고 말한다. 하지만 강의자는 기업들이 국제법이 적용되지 않는 영해에서 채광할 수 있다고 하며 이러한 주장에 의문을 제기한다. 이는 기업들이 심해에서 금속을 무분별하게 채굴하는 것을 국제법이 막을 수 없다는 의미다.

어휘 potential n 잠재력, 가능성 | unconvincing adj 설득력이 없는 | precious metal 귀금속 | sediment n 침전물 | the bottom of the ocean 해저 | marine life 해양 생물 | regardless of ~에 관계없이, 상관없이 | regulate v 규제하다, 단속하다 | cast doubt on 의문을 제기하다 | recklessly adj 무분별하게 | extract v 뽑아내다, 채굴하다, 추출하다

Part 2 Integrated Task

>> 제시된 지문을 읽고 아래의 노트를 완성해보자.

Q1

The top priority for any company is to increase its profits. In order to do so, companies must regularly assess their performance in the market and find new strategies suitable for rapidly changing their economic circumstances. Such strategies often involve releasing new products onto the market, and this can be done in three ways.

One strategy for increasing a company's sales is to develop an entirely new product by using the company's image. For example, if a renowned car company develops a motorcycle, the company can use its popularity to sell the product. Consumers who intend to buy a motorcycle will probably choose this particular motorcycle because of the company's image. Consumers will naturally think that the motorcycles will be just as good as the cars the company produces, so they will buy its motorcycles without any doubt.

The second strategy for raising a company's sales is to make a new version of an existing product. For example, if a soft drink company that is famous for its cola creates a version with an added fruit flavor, the company can easily increase sales. Consumers who love the original cola drink will be inclined to try this variation of the original product. The new cola benefits from both the familiarity that customers have with the old version and their curiosity about the newer one.

The final strategy is to make a partnership with another company. For example, if a company that makes chocolate forms a partnership with an ice cream company, the two companies can easily produce chocolate ice cream products together. In this case, both companies can increase their sales in a short period of time because they both receive a percentage of the new sales of the new chocolate ice cream. The brand images of both companies contribute to those sales.

Listen to the lecture. 🎧 P2_11

Reading 노트

주제   ↑ profit by releasing new products, 3 ways

    1.
       - consumers buy b/c the comp's image

    2.
       - consumers' familiarity & curiosity

    3.
       - 2 comps → new product
       - brand images of both comps

Listening 노트

주제   ↑ profit by releasing new products, 3 ways?

1.
  -

2.
  -
  -

3.
  -
  -

노트 & 답변 연결

주제	읽기 The reading and the lecture both talk about strategies companies can use to raise profits by producing new products. 듣기
요점 1	읽기 Firstly, the reading states that 듣기 On the contrary, the lecturer claims that
요점 2	읽기 Secondly, in the reading, the author argues that 듣기 However, the lecturer says that
요점 3	읽기 Thirdly, the reading goes on to say that 듣기 However, the lecturer contradicts this opinion, arguing that

Intentionally setting a forest fire, called prescribed fire or controlled burning, is widely used in national parks across America. Prescribed fire is widely used because of the benefits that it brings to all of the organisms that live in the forest. However, there are disadvantages far outweigh the benefits of burning forests.

First, in the process of burning forests on a regular basis, many animals are killed. Some argue that animals can escape from the fire. However, what about the young animals that cannot get away from these fires? For example, young birds are not able to fly and therefore will be trapped and die. And even adult animals can become trapped as forest fires spread very rapidly.

Second, like all fires, prescribed fire releases harmful greenhouse gases into the air. The carbon dioxide that is emitted when trees burn is one of the gases that contributes to global warming. As we all know, global warming has a detrimental impact on the planet. For example, global warming makes many areas arid and this harms the forests.

Third, prescribed fire is a waste of time and resources. That is because naturally occurring fire happens in areas where prescribed fire has already been carried out. This happens because of occasional lightning strikes, camping accidents, or just senseless acts of arson. Either way, firefighters and residents must work to put out these fires again, which means that prescribed fire is a waste of time and resources.

Listen to the lecture. 🎧 P2_12

Reading 노트

주제   prescribed fire – disadvantages > benefits

     1. animals are killed

       -

     2.

       - CO_2 → global warming

     3.

       - natural fire occurs in the same area anyway → have to put out

주제   prescribed fire – disadvantages > benefits?

    1.

      -

    2.

      -

    3.

      -

주제	읽기 The reading and the lecture both talk about prescribed fire. The article says that such artificial fire leads to several negative consequences. 듣기 However, the lecturer argues that prescribed fire is not as harmful or inefficient as the reading argues.
요점 1	읽기 Firstly, the reading states that 듣기 However, according to the lecturer,
요점 2	읽기 Secondly, in the reading, the author argues that 듣기 In contrast, the lecturer claims that
요점 3	읽기 Thirdly, the reading goes on to say that 듣기 However, the lecturer contradicts this opinion by stating that

Q3

Recycling is useful in that it reuses materials in the creation of new products without the need to gather as many new raw materials. Single-stream recycling is a process that allows recyclable materials to be thrown away in one bag without any sorting. Sorting is done at a single-stream recycling center by a machine that automatically separates the collected materials. However, this method has been shown to have many disadvantages.

First, single-stream recycling is dangerous. The sorting machine at a single-stream recycling center is responsible for separating paper, glass, and plastic. Though the sorting machine at the recycling plant sorts materials automatically, it frequently breaks glass bottles. Employees at the plant have to manually remove these broken pieces of glass and are at risk of causing serious injury to their hands.

Second, this method also leads to a waste of valuable resources. This method of sorting various materials in one bag is far from perfect. Sometimes, broken glass will get mixed in with collected paper. This may contaminate paper so that it cannot be used for its intended purpose. In this case, high-quality paper has to be used for making cheap boxes instead. This clearly shows precious materials can be wasted.

A third problem is that single-stream recycling is too expensive. The cost of building a single-stream recycling center is up to three times higher than the cost of building a traditional recycling plant. Many cities have very limited budgets to use for such facilities. For cities that already have a working recycling system, it is unreasonable to switch to a single-stream recycling solution.

Listen to the lecture. 🎧 P2_13

Reading 노트

주제   single-stream recycling(recycle together w/o sorting)
       → sort by a machine = many disadvantages

   1.

      - sorting machine → sort paper, glass, plastic… → can hurt employees

   2.

      - sorting = X perfect(glass get mixed w. paper, etc.)
       → paper X used for intended purpose

   3.

      - 3 X more $$$ than building a traditional recycling plant
      - cities have limited budgets

Listening 노트

주제 single-stream recycling(recycle together w/o sorting)
→ sort by a machine = many disadvantages?

1.

-

2.

-

-

3.

-

노트 & 답변 연결

주제	**읽기** The reading and the lecture both talk about single-stream recycling. The article says that this method results in many disadvantages.
	듣기 However,
요점 1	**읽기** Firstly, the reading says that
	듣기 On the contrary, the lecturer disagrees with this argument. She claims that
요점 2	**읽기** Secondly, in the reading, the author argues that
	듣기 The lecturer's point is that
요점 3	**읽기** Thirdly, the reading goes on to say that
	듣기 Although the lecturer admits that the cost of building a single-stream recycling plant is higher than the cost of building an ordinary plant, she claims that

Q4

Hydroelectric dams change the power of falling water into electricity, and they are the most realistic means of generating power. A hydroelectric dam extracts energy from a reusable source of energy, water, which is stored in a large reservoir behind a dam. Compared to other methods of power generation, hydroelectric dams are the most efficient.

The cost of operating a hydroelectric dam is very low compared to the cost of operating traditional power plants that burn fossil fuels. The reason for this is that the dams do not require much money to generate power. If there are enough rainfall and water flow, the amount of energy produced by hydroelectric dams can be tremendous. Because of these relatively low dam operation costs, hydroelectric energy is seen as a low-cost renewable energy source.

Another advantage of hydroelectric dams is environmental friendliness. Hydroelectric dams do not harm the environment. Since hydroelectric dams do not burn fossil fuels, the dams do not emit carbon dioxide, which means that the dams do not release greenhouse gases that directly devastate the environment.

Finally, hydroelectric dams do not harm wildlife either, especially river wildlife. Hydroelectric dams use fish ladders, which are structures designed to allow fish to pass dams. So for example, salmon can reach their spawning grounds by swimming across dams safely through these fish ladders.

Listen to the lecture. 🎧 P2_14

| Reading 노트 |

주제   hydroelectric dams = the most efficient power generator

1.

  -

  -

2.

  - don't burn fossil fuel → No CO_2

3.

  - use fish ladder → fish can pass dams

Listening 노트

주제   hydroelectric dams = not that perfect

     1.

       -

     2.

       -

     3.

       -

노트 & 답변 연결

주제	**읽기** The reading and the lecture both talk about hydroelectric dams. The article says that these dams bring several benefits. **듣기** However,
요점 1	**읽기** Firstly, the reading argues that **듣기** Although the lecturer admits that
요점 2	**읽기** Secondly, the reading claims that **듣기** However, the lecturer's point is that
요점 3	**읽기** Thirdly, the reading goes on to explain that **듣기** Even though the lecturer agrees that some fish like salmon can use these ladders, he states that

The Internet seems to benefit society as a whole. Further, through the Internet, users share information on a global scale. It is becoming increasingly clear that the Internet offers us waves of opportunities. There is no doubt that the Internet brings several benefits.

First, the information that the Internet provides is useful and valuable. If you enter any topic on a search engine, a huge amount of useful information related to it would instantly come up. This is much faster and easier than going to a library, where it could take hours to find the information that you need. Thanks to the Internet, you do not need to look up the information in the library any more.

Second, the Internet allows ordinary people to access a lot of information that they could not in the past. Before the Internet, a few groups monopolized information. If someone wanted to obtain specific information, he or she had to pay for it. However, today, even poor people who cannot afford to attend college can get specific information or knowledge easily on the Internet.

Finally, the Internet increases the rate at which information or ideas are shared. Many Internet users are willing to share what they know. For example, if someone knows how to travel around Europe in economical ways, they will post the information on their website so that many people can obtain the information.

Listen to the lecture. 🎧 P2_15

Reading 노트

주제　Internet brings benefits to society.

1. info. = useful & valuable
   -
   -

2.
   -

3.
   -

Listening 노트

주제   Internet brings benefits to society? → sometimes causes problems

       1.

         -

         -

       2.

         -

       3.

         -

         -

노트 & 답변 연결

주제	읽기
	듣기
요점 1	읽기 Firstly, the reading says that
	듣기 On the contrary, the lecturer claims that
요점 2	읽기
	듣기 In contrast, the lecturer says that
요점 3	읽기 Thirdly, the reading goes on to explain that
	듣기

Part 2 / Integrated Task

Q6

Menhaden are small but important fish that have been disappearing from the Chesapeake Bay in Virginia. The government has recommended that the fishing industry drastically limit the amount of menhaden that is harvested from the bay in order to protect the fishing industry and the species. There are some reasons why this is not the best solution.

First, it is better to remove a predator to prevent the decrease in a fish population because they are not careful about which fish they catch. Fishermen do not take very young fish so that the population can continue to grow. Some scientists say that the striped bass plays a major role in reducing the number of menhaden. This means a main cause of the extinction of these fish is the bass, so removing the bass would be more effective.

Second, the government's proposal would have a negative effect on agriculture. Menhaden are used as an important source of protein for animal feed that is given to livestock and poultry. If the government limits the amount of menhaden caught, the agriculture industry will suffer greatly. Their animals will not consume enough protein, which will slow down their growth.

Third, reducing the amount of menhaden caught would cause many people to lose their jobs in the fishing industry. The government's proposal would affect the fishing industry directly, but it would also affect the whole economy in the end. For example, if many people became unemployed because of the government's proposal, consumer spending in the local area would drop significantly. This would make the local economy become sluggish.

Listen to the lecture. 🎧 P2_16

Reading 노트

주제

1.

 -

2.

 -

 -

3.

 -

주제

   1.

     -

   2.

     -

     -

   3.

     -

     -

노트 & 답변 연결

주제	읽기	
	듣기	However, the lecturer argues that
요점 1	읽기	Firstly,
	듣기	
요점 2	읽기	Secondly,
	듣기	
요점 3	읽기	Thirdly,
	듣기	

Q7 Since the first pterosaur fossils were discovered, there has been much debate as to whether or not these creatures were capable of powered flight like birds and bats are today. As flying reptiles, their body shape does bear similarities to modern bird species, and their wing structure is similar to that of bats. However, there are many factors that indicate that they couldn't actually have flown under their own power, but may have glided instead.

Firstly, pterosaurs would have had too low of a metabolism for flight. They were an order of reptiles, and as such they would have been cold-blooded. Reptiles depend upon their environment for warmth, so they are only capable of short bursts of energy. Considerable energy is required for taking off from the ground and flapping wings to maintain altitude and increase speed. However, this energy expenditure would have been impossible for organisms with such a slow metabolism.

Secondly, the body structure of pterosaurs would have made them far too heavy for flight. When compared to modern bats and birds, they had uniformly heavier bone structure. In addition, some species of pterosaurs were truly massive, with estimated wingspans of over 10 meters. Such huge bodies would have made them extremely heavy. So heavy that their wings could not have generated enough downward thrust to take off.

Thirdly, the feeble hind legs of pterosaurs would not have been capable of launching their bodies into the air. For an animal to begin flying under its own power, it must be able to leap off of the ground high enough to flap its wings. However, pterosaurs had short legs that were not muscular enough to propel them into the air. Their wings would have collided with the ground, thwarting any attempt at powered flight.

Listen to the lecture. 🎧 P2_17

Reading 노트

주제

1.
-
-

2.
-
-

3.
-
-

Listening 노트

주제

    1.
-
-

    2.
-
-

    3.
-
-

노트 & 답변 연결

주제	읽기
	듣기
요점 1	읽기
	듣기
요점 2	읽기
	듣기
요점 3	읽기
	듣기

White nose syndrome is an infection caused by a fungus that grows on the snouts and wings of bats. The infection causes the bats to wake up frequently when they are hibernating during the winter. This increases their metabolism when they cannot feed to replenish their fat stores, slowly starving them to death. Since it is a serious threat to the bat population of North America, scientists have proposed several possible ways to combat the fungus.

Some scientists have suggested that the fungus is being spread by humans, so people should be prevented from entering caves with large bat populations. First detected in a cave in New York, the fungus spread to 25 states and 5 Canadian provinces in just 8 years. Since the fungus can survive on clothing, human visitors would appear to explain its rapid spread. Therefore, people, and tourists in particular, should be barred from entering infected caves.

Another way to help the afflicted bats is to study European bat populations that seem to be resistant to the fungus. It is believed that the fungus was most likely introduced to North America from Europe. According to the scientists, while the fungus is already widespread in Europe, most of the infected European bats are healthy. If the reason behind their resistance can be determined, perhaps it could be utilized to save their North American cousins.

Yet another way of addressing the issue lies in a limitation of the fungus. The organism is psychrophilic, which means that it prefers cooler conditions to grow in. In fact, if it is exposed to temperatures over 20 degrees centigrade, it cannot survive. So, if the air temperature in infected caves could be raised slightly, that would cause it to die off. This solution would not be simple to implement, but it could have a dramatic effect on the spread of the syndrome.

Listen to the lecture. 🎧 P2_18

Reading 노트

주제

1.

    -

2.

    -

3.

    -

    -

Listening 노트

주제

   1.
-
-

   2.
-
-

   3.
-

노트 & 답변 연결

주제	읽기
	듣기
요점 1	읽기 First of all,
	듣기
요점 2	읽기 Next, the author claims that
	듣기
요점 3	읽기 Finally, the reading passage suggests that
	듣기

According to various ancient records, there once existed a fabulously wealthy kingdom called Ophir that traded with the Eastern Mediterranean. They supplied huge amounts of luxury goods including sandalwood, gems, gold, and ivory. However, the documents provide little information regarding its location. For the following reasons, many scholars think that the Kingdom of Ophir was located somewhere in South Asia.

Firstly, South Asia seems to have been a likely location for Ophir when looking at the goods that were imported to the Eastern Mediterranean. Gold and gems could be imported from anywhere, but sandalwood trees are native to India and Pakistan in South Asia, and they were the only suppliers of the trees until fairly recently. In addition, Asian elephants have been a source of ivory for thousands of years. Therefore, Ophir is likely to have been located in South Asia because most of its goods originated from South Asia.

Secondly, the Kingdom of Ophir was located quite far from its trading partners in the Eastern Mediterranean. The records say that merchant ships of the Eastern Mediterranean returned from Ophir every three years full of trade goods. Some scientists suggest that Ophir was located in the Middle East or Africa, but those areas are far too close. It must have been much farther away for the voyage to take three years to return to the Eastern Mediterranean.

Thirdly, according to the records, the terms that were used for the trade goods from Ophir are the same as or very similar to the names they had in South Asia. Some of the imported goods were quite exotic, so no local terms existed for them in the Eastern Mediterranean. It is still common practice today to borrow words for new things from the culture that introduced them. A prime example of this is the many words that English has adopted from other languages for new things or ideas.

Listen to the lecture. 🎧 P2_19

Reading 노트

주제

    1.

       -

       -

    2.

       -

    3.

       -

Listening 노트

주제

    1.

        -

        -

    2.

        -

        -

    3.

        -

        -

노트 & 답변 연결

주제	읽기 듣기 However, the lecturer argues that
요점 1	읽기 듣기 While the lecturer admits that
요점 2	읽기 듣기 However, the lecturer contradicts this idea by mentioning
요점 3	읽기 듣기 However, the lecturer suggests that

The Glen Canyon Dam was constructed on the Colorado River in northern Arizona to regulate water flow. By building it, a manmade reservoir called Lake Powell was created. Although the dam has performed its task quite well, many people have demanded that it be removed, which would drain Lake Powell. However, there are many important reasons to continue using the dam.

First, Lake Powell is a major vacation spot that attracts an average of 2 million people per year. These people come to enjoy the lake and its rugged surroundings, which are made more beautiful by the plants that grow along its shores. This lake makes tourism the main industry of the region, generating the majority of the area's revenue. Therefore, the entire local economy would be crippled if the dam were removed.

Second, it would be extremely difficult to satisfy the demand for water if the dam were removed. This is because regulating the flow of water from the upper to the lower Colorado River Basin was the original purpose of constructing the dam. The dam provides a reliable source of water to the surrounding area and the communities downriver, which would be parched desert without it. This is the most efficient way to provide water to the people and agriculture that depend upon the Colorado River.

Third, draining the lake and removing the dam would have a negative effect on the surrounding ecosystem. The Colorado River descends from the Rocky Mountains full of sediment, and the dam prevents some of that sediment from continuing downstream. This makes the water cleaner and keeps the river channel deeper. Therefore, the dam creates a pleasant environment for wildlife downstream by removing that sediment, which is beneficial for the ecosystem.

Listen to the lecture. 🎧 P2_20

Reading 노트

주제

    1.

      -

      -

    2.

      -

    3.

      -

Listening 노트

주제

   1.
     -
     -
   2.
     -
     -
   3.
     -
     -

노트 & 답변 연결

주제	읽기
	듣기 On the other hand,
요점 1	읽기 Firstly, the author states that
	듣기 However, the lecturer suggests that
요점 2	읽기
	듣기 Yet again, the lecturer points out that
요점 3	읽기
	듣기

Test

Q1

It is a well established fact that many plants either fold up their leaves or close up their flowers after night falls. This behavior is called nyctinasty, and while scientists fully understand the physical process responsible for this ability, the reasons behind this behavior remain a mystery. Many hypotheses have been proposed to explain this behavior, and these are three of the most popular ones.

The first is that the plants are trying to protect themselves from the cold. Even in tropical climates, temperatures are typically lower at night than they are during the day. When the leaves are unfolded, their surface area is increased, which is ideal for gathering sunlight to perform photosynthesis. However, at night, increased surface area means that more heat will be lost into the cool air. The internal parts of flowers are also delicate, so closing can protect them from the effects of the cold.

The second is that the leaves and flowers close so that they will collect less dew. When they are open, they will collect more moisture, which can be used by fungi and other parasites to grow on them. For flowers, moisture is even more of a problem. If they are filled with water, insects will not visit them, and moisture will affect how their pollen works. They need their pollen to stick to insects temporarily so they will transport it, but water will cement it to the insects, keeping them from depositing it on another flower.

The third is that plants can limit their exposure to light by closing at night. Like animals, plants have daily and yearly cycles that determine their activity levels called circadian rhythms. This cycle is particularly important for reproduction, so they have to use the length of the day to track the seasons. So, by closing their leaves at night, they can avoid unusually bright nighttime conditions that could throw off their circadian rhythms.

 T1

Directions : You have 20 minutes to plan and write your response. Your response will be judged on the basis of the quality of your writing and on how well your response presents the points in the lecture and their relationship to the reading passage. Typically, an effective response will be 150 to 225 words.

Questions : Summarize the points made in the lecture. Be sure to explain how they oppose the specific points made in the reading passage.

It is a well established fact that many plants either fold up their leaves or close up their flowers after night falls. This behavior is called nyctinasty, and while scientists fully understand the physical process responsible for this ability, the reasons behind this behavior remain a mystery. Many hypotheses have been proposed to explain this behavior, and these are three of the most popular ones.

The first is that the plants are trying to protect themselves from the cold. Even in tropical climates, temperatures are typically lower at night than they are during the day. When the leaves are unfolded, their surface area is increased, which is ideal for gathering sunlight to perform photosynthesis. However, at night, increased surface area means that more heat will be lost into the cool air. The internal parts of flowers are also delicate, so closing can protect them from the effects of the cold.

The second is that the leaves and flowers close so that they will collect less dew. When they are open, they will collect more moisture, which can be used by fungi and other parasites to grow on them. For flowers, moisture is even more of a problem. If they are filled with water, insects will not visit them, and moisture will affect how their pollen works. They need their pollen to stick to insects temporarily so they will transport it, but water will cement it to the insects, keeping them from depositing it on another flower.

The third is that plants can limit their exposure to light by closing at night. Like animals, plants have daily and yearly cycles that determine their activity levels called circadian rhythms. This cycle is particularly important for reproduction, so they have to use the length of the day to track the seasons. So, by closing their leaves at night, they can avoid unusually bright nighttime conditions that could throw off their circadian rhythms.

Q2

There are approximately 5,880 species of mammals currently living on our planet. Nearly all of these animals are contained within two categories: marsupial and placental mammals. Marsupial mammals give birth after only a few weeks, and their young finish developing in an outer pouch of skin. In contrast, placental mammals are pregnant for much longer, and their offspring are much better adapted for survival when born. This means that marsupial mammals are inherently inferior to placental mammals.

Firstly, when a marsupial is born, it is at a very early stage of development compared to placental mammals. It must climb inside its mother's pouch unaided, or it will die. Once inside the pouch, a marsupial has access to its mother's nipples, but if she cannot find enough food, she will not be able to produce milk for the baby. So, even in the pouch, the infant is still vulnerable to environmental influences. Conversely, many placental mammals are much more developed when born and can move around independently just a few hours after birth.

Secondly, the internal body temperature of marsupials varies widely, which shows that they are more primitive than placental mammals. An infant marsupial cannot control its body temperature, so it must stay in its mother's pouch. However, even as an adult, a marsupial's body temperature is heavily influenced by its environment, which makes them more like cold-blooded animals. Such variation makes them vulnerable to extreme temperatures, unlike placental mammals that maintain a high internal temperature regardless of environmental conditions.

Thirdly, some evidence shows that marsupials are unable to compete with placental mammals. Most marsupials flourish in Australia, whereas placental mammals live everywhere. However, since marsupials exist in the fossil record on all continents, this means that marsupials used to live in places other than Australia, but most of them died out due to placental mammals. This is further proven by the fact that placental mammals have recently been introduced to Australia, and now marsupials are being outcompeted even there.

🎧 T2

Directions : You have 20 minutes to plan and write your response. Your response will be judged on the basis of the quality of your writing and on how well your response presents the points in the lecture and their relationship to the reading passage. Typically, an effective response will be 150 to 225 words.

Questions : Summarize the points made in the lecture. Be sure to explain how they oppose the specific points made in the reading passage.

Copy Cut Paste Undo Redo   Hide Word Count 0

There are approximately 5,880 species of mammals currently living on our planet. Nearly all of these animals are contained within two categories: marsupial and placental mammals. Marsupial mammals give birth after only a few weeks, and their young finish developing in an outer pouch of skin. In contrast, placental mammals are pregnant for much longer, and their offspring are much better adapted for survival when born. This means that marsupial mammals are inherently inferior to placental mammals.

Firstly, when a marsupial is born, it is at a very early stage of development compared to placental mammals. It must climb inside its mother's pouch unaided, or it will die. Once inside the pouch, a marsupial has access to its mother's nipples, but if she cannot find enough food, she will not be able to produce milk for the baby. So, even in the pouch, the infant is still vulnerable to environmental influences. Conversely, many placental mammals are much more developed when born and can move around independently just a few hours after birth.

Secondly, the internal body temperature of marsupials varies widely, which shows that they are more primitive than placental mammals. An infant marsupial cannot control its body temperature, so it must stay in its mother's pouch. However, even as an adult, a marsupial's body temperature is heavily influenced by its environment, which makes them more like cold-blooded animals. Such variation makes them vulnerable to extreme temperatures, unlike placental mammals that maintain a high internal temperature regardless of environmental conditions.

Thirdly, some evidence shows that marsupials are unable to compete with placental mammals. Most marsupials flourish in Australia, whereas placental mammals live everywhere. However, since marsupials exist in the fossil record on all continents, this means that marsupials used to live in places other than Australia, but most of them died out due to placental mammals. This is further proven by the fact that placental mammals have recently been introduced to Australia, and now marsupials are being outcompeted even there.

Test
Integrated Task

II
Academic
Discussion Task

Introduction & Learning Strategies

Part 1.   기초 다지기

유형 1. 찬성/반대 | 유형 2. 아이디어 말하기

- Lesson 01   스트레스 관련 표현
- Lesson 02   분위기 관련 표현
- Lesson 03   사람들과의 관계 관련 표현
- Lesson 04   관점의 확장 관련 표현
- Lesson 05   조언 관련 표현
- Lesson 06   편리함 관련 표현
- Lesson 07   시간 활용 관련 표현

Part 2.   실전 굳히기

- Lesson 01   스트레스 관련 주제 문단 구성
- Lesson 02   분위기 관련 주제 문단 구성
- Lesson 03   사람들과의 관계 관련 주제 문단 구성
- Lesson 04   관점의 확장 관련 주제 문단 구성
- Lesson 05   조언 관련 주제 문단 구성
- Lesson 06   편리함 관련 주제 문단 구성
- Lesson 07   시간 활용 관련 주제 문단 구성

Test

Academic Discussion Task

Introduction

Academic Discussion Task는 교수의 논제 제시와 논제에 대한 두 학생들의 답변으로 이루어진다. 교수가 논의할 주제를 제시할 때에는, 1) 제시한 주제에 대한 찬성/반대 유형과 2) 자신의 아이디어를 말해야 하는 두 가지 유형으로 나눌 수 있다. 따라서, 주제의 유형에 따라서 답변의 첫 문장, 즉 인트로부터 달라져야 하고, 수험자는 이에 대해 오류 없는 완벽한 문장으로 그에 대한 대비를 철저히 할 필요가 있다.

◉ 화면 구성

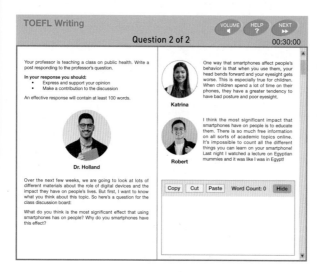

* 교수가 제시한 논제에 대한 토론 참여
* 두 명의 학생이 각자 의견을 제시
* 주어진 논제에 대한 자신의 의견을 간단히 기술 (100단어 / 10분)

Sample Questions 💬

Your professor is teaching a class. Write a post responding to the professor's question.

In your response, you should:
* express and support your opinion
* make a contribution to the discussion

An effective response will contain at least 100 words. You will have 10 minutes to write it.

당신의 교수님께서 강의 중입니다. 교수님의 질문에 답하는 글을 쓰세요.
  * 당신의 의견을 표현하고 뒷받침하세요
  * 토론에 기여하세요
효과적인 답변은 최소한 100단어를 포함할 것입니다. 당신은 10분 동안 글을 작성할 수 있습니다.

Dr. Springer: Today, we will delve into a thought-provoking topic that centers around government spending. Our focus will be on the question of whether it is important for the government to allocate funds towards things that are beautiful, rather than solely practical endeavors. In your opinion, should the government spend money on things that are beautiful, not just on those that are practical?

오늘은 정부 지출을 중심으로 한 생각할 여지가 있는 주제에 대해 탐구할 것입니다. 우리의 초점은 정부가 실용적인 노력뿐만 아니라 아름다운 것에 자금을 할당하는 것이 중요한지에 관한 문제입니다. 여러분이 생각하기에, 정부는 실용적인 노력뿐만 아니라 아름다운 것에도 돈을 써야 될까요?

Jeorge: I completely agree with the statement. Investing in aesthetically pleasing projects and initiatives not only enhances the visual appeal of our surroundings but also contributes to the overall well-being and happiness of the population. Beautiful infrastructure, public spaces, and cultural landmarks can attract tourists, boost local economies, and foster a sense of pride among citizens.

이 주장에 완전히 동의합니다. 아름다운 프로젝트와 계획에 투자함으로써 우리 주변의 시각적 매력이 향상되는 것뿐만 아니라 전체적인 웰빙과 시민들의 행복에 기여할 수 있습니다. 아름다운 인프라, 공공 공간 및 문화적 명소는 관광객을 유치하고 지역 경제를 촉진하며 시민들 사이에 자부심을 유발할 수 있습니다.

April: While I appreciate the value of beauty, I believe that practicality should be the primary focus of government spending. Limited resources should be allocated towards addressing pressing issues such as healthcare, education, and infrastructure. Practical investments can directly improve the quality of life and provide essential services to the population, ensuring long-term sustainability and progress.

아름다움의 가치를 고려하긴 하지만, 나는 정부 지출에 있어서 실용성이 주요 관심사여야 한다고 생각합니다. 제한된 자원은 의료, 교육 및 인프라와 같은 긴요한 문제에 할당되어야 합니다. 실용적인 투자는 직접적으로 삶의 질을 높이고 주민들에게 필수적인 서비스를 제공하여 장기적인 지속 가능성과 발전을 보장합니다.

Learning Strategies

Step 1 교수의 논제를 빠르게 파악한다.

⋯› 교수의 Discussion Topic은 항상 똑같은 길이가 아니라 때로는 짧게, 혹은 길고 장황하게 제시될 수도 있다. 따라서, 후반부를 중점적으로 보고 빠르고 신속하게 주제 파악을 해야 한다.

Step 2 두 학생의 포인트를 간단하게 1–2문장으로 파악한다.

⋯› 토론에 답변하는 두 학생의 의견은 최대한 간단하게 의견(찬성/반대 or 아이디어)만 파악한다. 그 이유는 10분은 답변 작성 시간으로는 정말 짧게 느껴지는 시간이며, 채점관이 중점적으로 보는 부분은 제시된 두 학생의 의견 요약이 아닌 시험 응시자 본인의 개인적 의견과 뒷받침하는 이유이기 때문이다.

Step 3 시간 관리를 철저히 하여 답변을 작성한다.

⋯› 답변은 9분 동안 작성하고, 나머지 1분 동안 작성한 내용을 처음부터 끝까지 훑어보면서 누락된 내용이나 문법적 오류나 오타가 없는지 살펴보며 수정한다. 즉, 답변 작성은 9분, 검토는 1분이 필수이다.

고득점 전략 만점 답변은 약 200단어에 가까운 구체적이고 논리적인 글이다.

Part 1

기초 다지기

◎ Lesson 01   스트레스 관련 표현

◎ Lesson 02   분위기 관련 표현

◎ Lesson 03   사람들과의 관계 관련 표현

◎ Lesson 04   관점의 확장 관련 표현

◎ Lesson 05   조언 관련 표현

◎ Lesson 06   편리함 관련 표현

◎ Lesson 07   시간 활용 관련 표현

유형 1. 찬성/반대

교수의 Discussion 주제 제시 부분 중 후반부를 보면 주제를 바로 파악할 수 있다.

답변 인트로 문장

From my perspective, both made excellent statements, but I'm on the same page as "토론 참여자들 둘 중 한 명."

Q. **Professor:** Participating in organization or club activities can provide many benefits. Do you agree or disagree?
조직 또는 동아리 활동에 참여하는 것은 많은 이점을 제공할 수 있습니다. 찬성하십니까, 반대하십니까?

Jeorge: agree / **April:** disagree
조지: 동의 / 에이프릴: 반대

A. From my perspective, both made excellent statements, but I'm on the same page as Jeorge.
제 관점에서, 두 사람 모두 훌륭한 주장을 했지만 저는 조지와 같은 생각입니다.

예시처럼 답변 인트로 문장을 이용해서 빈칸을 채워 보자.

Q1 **Professor:** When it comes to spending money, some argue that it is better to invest in something long-lasting, like an expensive piece of jewelry, rather than indulging in short-term pleasures, such as a vacation. What are your thoughts on this matter?

- **Jeorge:** jewelry / **April:** vacation
  April과 같은 의견을 가지고 있는 경우의 인트로 문장을 만들어 보자.

A. _____

_____

Q2

Professor: Many cities nowadays are devising plans to improve themselves, yet they are unsure of an optimal solution. When it comes to a city's benefit, some argue that the best way to achieve it is by focusing on constructing new buildings rather than preserving nature. What are your thoughts on this matter?

- **Jeorge:** constructing new buildings / **April:** preserving nature
  April과 같은 의견을 가지고 있는 경우의 인트로 문장을 만들어 보자.

A. _____

_____

Q3

Professor: Some argue that it is more important for parents to spend quality time playing and bonding with their children, rather than focusing solely on academic achievements. What are your thoughts on this statement?

- **Jeorge:** agree / **April:** disagree
  Jeorge와 같은 의견을 가지고 있는 경우의 인트로 문장을 만들어 보자.

A. _____

_____

Q4

Professor: We often hear the saying "Families should have meals together on a regular basis." What are your thoughts on this statement?

- **Jeorge:** agree / **April:** disagree
  Jeorge와 같은 의견을 가지고 있는 경우의 인트로 문장을 만들어 보자.

A. _____

_____

유형 2. 아이디어 말하기

교수의 Discussion 주제 제시 부분 중 후반부를 보면 주제를 바로 파악할 수 있다.

답변 인트로 문장

> From my perspective, both made excellent statements, but I would like to add that "자신의 아이디어."

예시

Q. **Professor:** If you had to select just one class to be mandatory for the school's curriculum, which class would you prioritize?
학교 교육과정의 필수 과목으로 딱 한 과목을 선택해야 한다면, 어떤 과목을 우선시하겠습니까?

Jeorge: a class focusing on personal finance / **April:** a class on critical thinking
조지: 개인 금융에 중점을 둔 과목 / 에이프릴: 비판적 사고에 중점을 둔 과목

A. From my perspective, both made excellent statements, but I would like to add that PE class should be mandatory for the school's curriculum.
제 관점에서, 두 사람 모두 훌륭한 주장을 했지만, 저는 학교 교육 과정에 체육 수업이 필수적이어야 한다는 점을 덧붙이고 싶습니다.

예시처럼 답변 인트로 문장을 이용해서 빈칸을 채워 보자.

Q1 **Professor:** People can benefit from traveling all around the world. Tell me one benefit you can gain from world travel.

- **Jeorge:** relieving stress / **April:** meeting different people
'시야/견문을 확장할 수 있다'란 아이디어로 인트로 문장을 만들어 보자.

A. _____

_____

Q2 **Professor:** Please describe a new experience you have had recently that significantly impacted your life. Explain how this experience has influenced your perspective and personal growth.

- **Jeorge:** volunteer program / **April:** internship at a laboratory
  '작은 회사에서의 인턴십'이란 아이디어로 인트로 문장을 만들어 보자.

A. _____

_____

Q3 **Professor:** Which significant scientific breakthrough or technological innovation from the past two centuries would you select as a crucial advancement?

- **Jeorge:** antibiotics / **April:** computer
  '인터넷'이란 아이디어로 인트로 문장을 만들어 보자.

A. _____

_____

Q4 **Professor:** Technology has made the world a better place to live, so please tell me one aspect that impacts your life.

- **Jeorge:** communication / **April:** gaining information
  '효과적인 시간 관리'란 아이디어로 인트로 문장을 만들어 보자.

A. _____

_____

01 스트레스 관련 표현

'예체능 관련 수업, 취미, 여러 가지 사회적 모임, 여행, 동아리 활동' 관련 주제는 일관된 아이디어로 답변을 전개할 수 있다. 사람들과 즐겁게 보내면서, 또한 재충전을 하면서 기분 전환을 하는 것은 모두 '스트레스 해소'와 관련 있는 내용으로 전개할 수 있기 때문이다. 다음의 표현을 익혀둔다면, 별도의 brainstorming 과정 없이도 관련 주제에 대해서 빠르게 정확한 답변을 기술할 수 있다.

01. alleviate stress (= relieve stress)
스트레스를 완화하다

It's a good way to alleviate stress.
그것은 스트레스를 완화할 수 있는 좋은 방법이다.

02. get stressed out from ~
~때문에 스트레스를 받다

I get stressed out from academic matters.
나는 학업과 관련된 일 때문에 스트레스를 받는다.

03. a pleasant diversion
즐거운 여가/기분 전환

Playing with friends can be a pleasant diversion.
친구들과 노는 것은 즐거운 기분 전환이 될 수 있다.

04. quality time
깊고 의미 있는 시간

My best friend and I spend quality time together by having sincere conversations.
내 가장 친한 친구와 나는 진솔한 대화를 나누는 것으로 깊고 의미 있는 시간을 보낸다.

05. suffer from ~
~로 고통을 겪다

He suffers from severe allergies during the spring.
그는 봄철 심한 알레르기로 고통을 겪는다.

06. stay up all night
밤을 지새우다

They stayed up all night watching movies.
그들은 영화를 보느라 밤을 지새웠다.

07. be exhausted
지치다

After working for 8 hours straight, I was completely exhausted.
8시간 동안 쉬지 않고 일한 후, 나는 완전히 지쳐버렸다.

08. escape from ~
~로부터 탈출하다/ 벗어나다

She needed a vacation to escape from the stress of her work.
그녀는 스트레스를 받는 일에서 벗어나기 위해 휴가가 필요했었다.

09. thanks to ~
~ 덕분에

Thanks to your help, we were able to complete the project on time.
당신의 도움 덕분에, 우리는 프로젝트를 제시간에 완료할 수 있었다.

10. mental state
심리/정신 상태

Regular exercise can help improve one's mental state.
규칙적인 운동은 사람의 정신 상태를 향상하는 데 도움을 줄 수 있다.

Part 1 Academic Discussion Task

Practice

>> 앞에서 학습한 표현들을 활용하여 다음 문장을 영작하시오.

01. 클럽 활동에 참여하는 것은 스트레스를 완화하는 것에 도움을 준다.

_____

_____

02. 요즘 학생들은 그들의 과중한 일과 주변 사람들과의 경쟁 때문에 종종 스트레스를 받는다.

_____

_____

03. 그들은 정신적으로 편안해지기 위한 즐거운 기분 전환이 필요하다.

_____

_____

04. 즐거운 동아리 활동으로 깊고 의미 있는 시간을 보냄으로써, 그들은 결국 휴식을 취하고 그들의 일로 다시 돌아갈 수 있을 것이다.

_____

_____

05. 그는 너무 많은 일(공부)과 중압감으로 고통을 겪곤 했다.

_____

_____

06. 그는 때때로 그의 일을 끝내기 위해 밤을 지새웠다.

_____

_____

07. 이 때문에, 그는 완전히 신체적으로나 정신적으로 지쳐 있었다.

_____

_____

08. 인라인 하키를 하는 것은 그에게 일의 스트레스에서 벗어날 수 있게끔 해 주었다.

_____

_____

09. 이 덕분에 그는 상쾌한 기분으로 다시 일로 돌아갈 수 있었다.

_____

_____

10. 그는 현재 안정되고 자신감 있는 심리상태를 가지고 있다.

_____

_____

Part 1
Academic Discussion Task

02 분위기 관련 표현

'자연 보존, 회사에서의 복장 규율, 학교의 교육과정, 여행, 여러 가지 레저 활동들' 관련 주제는 일관된 아이디어로 답변을 전개할 수 있다. 다양한 활동들에 대한 참여, 각 장소의 분위기에 영향을 받는 것은 모두 'atmosphere의 영향'과 관련 있는 내용으로 전개할 수 있기 때문이다. 다음의 표현을 익혀둔다면, 별도의 brainstorming 과정 없이도 관련 주제에 대해서 빠르게 정확한 답변을 기술할 수 있다.

01. a positive ambiance
긍정적인 분위기

Students can experience a positive ambiance.
학생들은 긍정적인 분위기를 경험할 수 있다.

02. be influenced
영향을 받다

Most students can be influenced by their environment's atmosphere.
대부분의 학생들은 그들의 환경의 분위기에 영향을 받을 수 있다.

03. a lot more important than they might realize
생각(인지)하는 것 이상으로 훨씬 더 중요하다

The influence of the atmosphere is a lot more important than they might realize.
그 분위기의 영향은 그들이 생각(인지)하는 것 이상으로 훨씬 더 중요하다.

04. feel a good atmosphere
좋은 분위기를 느끼다

Students should feel a good atmosphere while they are at school.
학생들은 그들이 학교에 있는 동안에는 좋은 분위기를 느껴야만 한다.

05. competitive and strict
치열하고 엄격한

The workplace used to be very competitive and strict.
그 일터는 매우 치열하고 엄격하곤 했었다.

06. little by little

조금씩

Things changed little by little.

상황이 조금씩 변했다.

07. time and effort

시간과 노력

A lot of time and effort were put into making the city better.

도시를 더 좋게 만들기 위해 많은 시간과 노력이 들어갔다.

08. genuinely appreciate

진심으로 감사해하다

I genuinely appreciate the changed environment.

나는 변화된 환경을 진심으로 감사해하고 있다.

09. top schools with a good reputation

좋은 평판을 가지고 있는 학교들

It made the college one of the top schools with a good reputation.

이는 그 대학을 좋은 평판을 가진 최고의 학교 중 하나로 만들었다.

10. compared to ~

~에 비교해 볼 때

I had a more enjoyable school life compared to my friends.

나는 내 친구들에 비해서 더 즐거운 학교생활을 보냈다.

Practice

>> 앞에서 학습한 표현들을 활용하여 다음 문장을 영작하시오.

01. 학생들은 체육 시간 동안 에너지 넘치는 활동에 몰입하면서 긍정적인 분위기를 경험한다.

_____

_____

02. 대부분의 학생들은 그들의 주변 환경의 분위기에 영향을 받을 수 있다.

_____

_____

03. 그 분위기의 영향은 그들이 생각하는 것보다 훨씬 더 중요하다.

_____

_____

04. 학생들은 그들이 학교에 있는 동안에는 좋은 분위기를 느껴야만 한다.

_____

_____

05. 그 학교는 매우 치열하고 엄격하곤 했었다.

_____

_____

06. 하지만 교장이 분위기를 바꾸려고 노력한 이후 상황이 조금씩 바뀌었다.

07. 더욱더 즐길 수 있는 체육 수업을 통해 교육과정을 개선하기 위해 많은 시간과 노력이 들었다.

08. 우리 학교의 재학생들은 기분 좋고 활기찬 분위기에 진실로 감사해한다.

09. 학교 또한 학생들이 입학하고 싶어 하는 좋은 평판을 얻게 되었다.

10. 나는 솔직히 현재 학교의 모습이 과거와 비교해 볼 때 훨씬 더 바람직하다고 생각한다.

Part 1 Academic Discussion Task

03 사람들과의 관계 관련 표현

부모와 자식, 교수와 학생, 친구들과 관련된 주제는 일관된 아이디어로 답변을 전개할 수 있다. 주제는 다양할지라도 사람들과의 관계에 관련한 공통점만 있다면 모두 'people과의 관계'와 관련 있는 내용으로 전개할 수 있기 때문이다. 다음의 표현을 익혀둔다면, 별도의 brainstorming 과정 없이도 관련 주제에 대해서 빠르게 정확한 답변을 기술할 수 있다.

01. interact with ~
~와 어우러지다 / 소통하다

She likes to interact with her friends on social media.
그녀는 친구들과 소셜 미디어에서 소통하는 것을 좋아한다.

02. optimal condition
최적의 조건

An optimal condition to improve a relationship can be achieved through sincere conversation.
진중한 대화는 관계를 증진하는 최적의 조건이라고 간주된다.

03. share experiences and emotions
경험과 감정을 공유하다

Close friends often share experiences and emotions with each other.
가까운 친구들은 종종 그들의 경험과 감정을 공유한다.

04. sincere conversation
진중한 대화

He had a sincere conversation about his future plans.
그는 그의 미래 계획에 관한 진중한 대화를 가졌다.

05. drift apart
소원해지다 / 사이가 멀어지다

After going to different colleges, they slowly began to drift apart.
서로 다른 대학교를 다니게 된 이후, 그들은 서서히 사이가 멀어지기 시작했다.

06. have a hard time -ing

~하는 데 힘든 시간을 보내다

They have a hard time interacting with each other.
그들은 서로 소통하는 데 힘든 시간을 보냈다.

07. not just ~ but also ~

단순히 ~뿐만 아니라 ~도 역시

We played sports not just to entertain ourselves but also to strengthen our friendship.
우리는 단지 즐거워지기 위해서 뿐만 아니라 우리의 우정을 더 강화하기 위해 스포츠를 했다.

08. awkward at first

처음에는 어색한

Meeting new people can be awkward at first.
새로운 사람들을 만나는 것은 처음에는 어색할 수 있다.

09. get close to ~

~와 가까워지다

It took a long time for him to get close to his friends.
그가 그의 친구들과 가까워지는 데에는 긴 시간이 걸렸다.

10. strong bond

끈끈한 유대/관계

A strong bond was built between them.
그들 사이에 끈끈한 유대가 만들어졌다.

Practice

>> 앞에서 학습한 표현들을 활용하여 다음 문장을 영작하시오.

01. 부모는 그들의 자식들과 같이 놀면서 진정으로 소통할 수 있다.

_____

_____

02. 이것은 그들의 관계를 증진하는 최적의 조건을 만든다.

_____

_____

03. 그들이 같이 놀 때, 그들은 다양한 경험과 감정을 공유할 수 있는 더 많은 기회들을 갖게 된다.

_____

_____

04. 이러한 공유된 경험은 나중에 진중한 대화로 이어질 수도 있을 것이다.

_____

_____

05. 그는 그의 직업 때문에 아들과 관계가 소원했었다.

_____

_____

06. 그는 그의 아들과 소통하는 데 힘든 시간을 보냈다.

_____

_____

07. 그러던 어느 날, 그는 그의 아들과 일주일에 적어도 한 번은 단순히 그의 건강을 유지하기 위해서뿐만 아니라, 그들의 관계를 증진하기 위해서 등산하러 가기로 했다.

_____

_____

08. 그의 아들과 친숙해지는 것이 처음에는 어색해 보였다.

_____

_____

09. 그들이 서로 가까워지는 것은 힘들어 보였다.

_____

_____

10. 그의 아들은 천천히 그에게 마음을 열기 시작했고, 그들 사이에 끈끈한 유대가 만들어졌다.

_____

_____

Part 1
Academic Discussion Task

04 관점의 확장 관련 표현

'세계 여행, 유학, 새로운 경험, 다양한 친구들과의 교류' 관련 주제는 일관된 아이디어로 답변을 전개할 수 있다. 서로 다른 상황들이지만 다름과 새로움을 통해서 가지고 있지 못했던 것들에 노출이 되고, 그것으로 인한 견문의 확장과 관련 있는 내용으로 전개할 수 있기 때문이다. 다음의 표현을 익혀둔다면, 별도의 brainstorming 과정 없이도 관련 주제에 대해서 빠르게 정확한 답변을 기술할 수 있다.

01. gain inspiration 영감을 얻다

She would often travel to new places to gain inspiration.
그녀는 영감을 얻기 위해 새로운 장소를 여행하곤 했다.

02. broaden perspective 시야/관점을 넓히다

Reading diverse books can broaden your perspective.
다양한 책을 읽는 것은 당신의 시야를 넓힐 수 있다.

03. gain exposure 노출을 얻다 / ~에 노출되다

Working in different countries allows you to gain exposure to diverse cultures.
여러 나라에서 일하는 것은 당신이 다양한 문화에 노출되게 한다.

04. valuable insight 가치 있는 통찰력 / 깨달음

His experience gave him valuable insights into leadership.
그의 경험은 그에게 리더쉽에 관한 가치 있는 통찰력을 주었다.

05. unpredictable situation 예측할 수 없는 상황

Life is full of unpredictable situations.
삶은 예측할 수 없는 상황들로 가득하다.

06. numerous experiences

수많은 경험

Traveling to different countries has provided me with numerous experiences.

여러 국가를 여행하는 것은 나에게 수많은 경험을 제공해 주었다.

07. embrace diversity

다양성을 포용하다/받아들이다

It's essential to embrace diversity in the workplace.

일터에서 다양성을 포용하는 것은 필수적이다.

08. keep distance

거리를 유지하다

She keeps her distance from people she doesn't know well.

그녀는 잘 알지 못하는 사람들에게 거리를 유지한다.

09. open-minded

열려 있는 마음가짐의

Being open-minded is important when discussing new ideas.

열려 있는 마음을 가지는 것은 새로운 아이디어를 논의할 때 중요하다.

10. awkward moment

어색한 순간

The awkward moment during the meeting made everyone uncomfortable.

미팅 도중의 어색한 순간은 모든 사람을 불편하게 만들었다.

Part 1

Academic Discussion Task

Practice

>> 앞에서 학습한 표현들을 활용하여 다음 문장을 영작하시오.

01. 전 세계를 여행하는 것은 사람들이 영감을 얻게 한다.

_____

_____

02. 전 세계를 여행하는 것은 사람들이 그들의 시야를 넓힐 수 있게 한다.

_____

_____

03. 여러 장소들을 돌아다니면서, 사람들은 그들이 여태 경험해 보지 못한 다양한 것들에 노출된다.

_____

_____

04. 이는 그들에게 가치 있는 통찰을 제공한다.

_____

_____

05. 이러한 통찰들은 그들이 미래에 예측할 수 없는 상황을 헤쳐 나가는 데 필요로 되어진다.

_____

_____

06. 그는 자주 이사했고, 다수의 많은 경험을 겪었다.

_____

_____

07. 하지만 다양성을 포용하는 방법을 배우는 것은 흥미진진했다.

_____

_____

08. 사실 그와 세계 여행을 하는 동안에, 나는 다른 사람들에게 거리를 두었다.

_____

_____

09. 반면에 그는 다양한 배경을 가진 사람들에게 열린 태도를 보였다.

_____

_____

10. 게다가 그와 다른 사람들 사이에 불편하고 어색한 순간은 없었다.

_____

_____

05 조언 관련 표현

'인턴십, 사회 경험, 자원봉사 활동, 실수를 통한 배움' 관련 주제는 일관된 아이디어로 답변을 전개할 수 있다. 서로 다른 상황이지만 다름과 새로움을 통해서 가지고 있지 못했던 것에 노출이 되고, 그것으로 인한 견문의 확장과 관련 있는 내용으로 전개할 수 있기 때문이다. 다음의 표현을 익혀둔다면, 별도의 brainstorming 과정 없이도 관련 주제에 대해서 빠르게 정확한 답변을 기술할 수 있다.

01. gain a lot of advice
많은 조언을 얻다

Traveling can help you gain a lot of advice.
여행은 많은 조언을 얻는 데 도움이 될 수 있다.

02. a significant impact
지대한 영향

Receiving guidance from my mentor had a significant impact on my decisions.
멘토로부터 지도를 받은 것은 내 결정에 지대한 영향을 미쳤다.

03. valuable advice
가치 있는 조언

She offered me valuable advice on managing stress.
그녀는 스트레스 관리에 관한 가치 있는 조언을 해 주었다.

04. evaluate objectively
객관적으로 평가하다

When giving feedback, it's essential to evaluate objectively for personal growth.
피드백을 줄 때, 개인의 성장을 위해 객관적으로 평가하는 것이 필수적이다.

05. introverted personality
내성적인 성격

For those with an introverted personality, seeking small group interactions can be valuable advice for social growth.
내성적 성격을 가진 사람들에게는 소그룹 상호 작용을 추구하는 것이 사회적 성장을 위한 가치 있는 조언일 수 있다.

06. integrate with new people

새로운 사람들과 어울리다

When starting a new job, the advice to integrate with new people can enhance your professional experience.

새로운 일을 시작할 때, 새로운 사람들과 어울리는 것에 대한 조언은 여러분의 전문적인 경험을 향상시킬 수 있다.

07. learn from real-world experience

실제 경험으로부터 배우다

In pursuing success, valuable advice is to learn from real-world experience.

성공을 추구할 때 소중한 조언은 실제 경험으로부터 배우는 것이다.

08. contemplate matters

문제를 심사숙고하다

When facing challenges, wise advice is to contemplate matters deeply.

도전에 직면했을 때, 현명한 조언은 문제를 심사숙고하는 것이다.

09. practical advice

실용적인 조언

In difficult situations, practical advice can be your guiding light.

어려운 상황에서는, 실용적인 조언이 당신의 길잡이가 될 수 있다.

10. mental growth

정신적인 성장

Seeking diverse experiences contributes to mental growth.

다양한 경험을 추구하는 것은 정신적인 성장에 기여한다.

>> 앞에서 학습한 표현들을 활용하여 다음 문장을 영작하시오.

01. 사람들은 그들의 실무 경험으로부터 많은 조언을 얻는다.

_____

_____

02. 이 경험들은 그들의 삶에 지대한 영향을 미친다.

_____

_____

03. 이 경험들은 또한 그들이 예측할 수 없는 상황을 헤쳐 나가는 데 실용적이고 가치 있는 조언을 제공한다.

_____

_____

04. 이런 순간들을 통해서 사람들은 그들 자신을 객관적으로 평가할 기회를 가지게 되고, 이는 미래에 좀 더 나은 삶으로 이어질 수 있다.

_____

_____

05. 난 내성적인 성격 때문에, 순진하고 사교성이 부족했다.

_____

_____

06. 그의 성격 때문에, 새로운 사람들과 어울리는 것은 그에게 너무나 힘든 일이었다.

_____

_____

07. 처음에는 새로운 사람들과 어울리고 실제 경험으로부터 배우는 것이 불편하고 힘들었다.

_____

_____

08. 하지만 그것에 익숙해지면서, 예전에는 생각해 보지 못했던 일들을 심사숙고하기 시작했다.

_____

_____

09. 이러한 가치 있는 경험은 나에게 실용적인 조언을 해주었다.

_____

_____

10. 이는 또한 나의 정신적인 성장에도 크게 도움을 주었다.

_____

_____

Part 1
Academic Discussion Task

06 편리함 관련 표현

'발명, 인터넷, 컴퓨터, 여러 과학 기술' 관련 주제들은 일관된 아이디어로 답변을 전개할 수 있다. 언급된 모든 것이 편리함을 제공한다는 내용으로 전개할 수 있기 때문이다. 다음의 표현을 익혀둔다면, 별도의 brainstorming 과정 없이도 관련 주제에 대해서 빠르게 정확한 답변을 기술할 수 있다.

01. provide convenience
편리함을 제공하다

Smartphones provide convenience for quick communication.
스마트폰은 빠른 소통을 위한 편리함을 제공한다.

02. replace traditional offline settings
전통적인 오프라인 환경을 대체하다

Online stores have started to replace traditional offline settings for shopping.
온라인 쇼핑은 전통적인 오프라인 환경을 대체하기 시작했다.

03. unnecessary process
불필요한 과정

Eliminating unnecessary processes enhances convenience.
불필요한 과정을 제거하면 편의성이 향상된다.

04. tedious process
번거로운 과정

Completing paperwork by hand can be a tedious process.
손으로 서류 작업을 완료하는 것은 번거로운 과정일 수 있다.

05. online video chat
온라인 화상 채팅

We had an online video chat with our overseas relatives.
우리는 해외에 사는 친척들과 온라인 화상 채팅을 했다.

06. variety of functions   다양한 기능들

The smartphone offers a variety of functions, making life more convenient.

스마트폰은 다양한 기능을 제공하여 삶을 더 편리하게 만든다.

07. useful features   유용한 기능들

The new software update added many useful features.

새로운 소프트웨어 업데이트는 많은 유용한 기능들을 추가했다.

08. communicate on a daily basis   매일 소통하다

My best friend and I communicate on a daily basis.

나의 친한 친구와 나는 매일 소통한다.

09. travel a long distance   장거리를 이동하다

She had to travel a long distance to attend the conference.

그녀는 학회에 참석하기 위해 장거리를 이동해야 했다.

10. inconvenient offline process   불편한 오프라인 과정

Submitting paper applications can be an inconvenient offline process.

종이 신청서를 제출하는 것은 불편한 오프라인 과정일 수 있다.

Practice

>> 앞에서 학습한 표현들을 활용하여 다음 문장을 영작하시오.

01. 인터넷은 사람들과의 소통이란 측면에서 편리함을 제공한다.

_____

_____

02. 이는 전통적인 오프라인 환경을 대체하게 되었다.

_____

_____

03. 인터넷 덕분에, 사람들은 불필요한 과정을 건너뛸 수 있게 되었다.

_____

_____

04. 인터넷의 도움으로, 사람들은 번거로운 과정을 거치지 않게 되었다.

_____

_____

05. 그의 친구가 다른 도시로 이사를 가면서 그는 온라인 화상 채팅 플랫폼에 가입했다.

_____

_____

06. 그것은 다양한 기능을 제공하였다.

_____

_____

07. 그가 웹사이트에 접속했을 때, 그것이 유용한 기능을 가지고 있다는 것을 발견했다.

_____

_____

08. 그것은 그가 매일 친구와 소통할 수 있게 해 줄 수 있었다.

_____

_____

09. 결과적으로, 그는 직접 장거리 이동을 하지 않아도 되었다.

_____

_____

10. 이는 인터넷이 다른 사람들과 소통할 때 불편한 오프라인 과정에서 어떻게 사람들을 해방시켜 줄 수 있는지를 보여 준다.

_____

_____

Academic Discussion Task

Part 1

07 시간 활용 관련 표현

'계획적인 생활, 인터넷을 이용한 정보 습득, 소통 상황' 관련 주제들은 일관된 아이디어로 답변을 전개할 수 있다. 언급된 모든 것이 시간을 효과적으로, 현명하게 활용할 수 있도록 도와주는 수단 / 방법이라고 전개할 수 있기 때문이다. 다음의 표현을 익혀둔다면, 별도의 brainstorming 과정 없이도 관련 주제에 대해서 빠르게 정확한 답변을 기술할 수 있다.

01. effective time management
효과적인 시간 관리

Effective time management increases productivity.
효과적인 시간 관리는 생산성을 증가시킨다.

02. a considerable amount of time
상당한 시간

She saved a considerable amount of time by using the shortcut.
그녀는 지름길을 이용해서 상당한 시간을 절약했다.

03. utilize time efficiently
효율적으로 시간을 이용하다

Learning to prioritize tasks helps you utilize time efficiently.
작업의 우선순위를 정하는 것을 배우는 것은 시간을 효율적으로 활용하는 데 도움이 된다.

04. at a faster pace
빠른 속도로

She completed the project at a faster pace than expected.
그녀는 예상보다 빠른 속도로 프로젝트를 완료했다.

05. outstanding performance
눈에 띄는 성과

Her dedication and hard work led to outstanding performance.
그녀의 헌신과 고된 노력은 눈에 띄는 성과를 이끌었다.

06. teaching assistant

조교

The teaching assistant managed her time effectively.

조교는 그녀의 시간을 효과적으로 관리했다.

07. go smoothly

부드럽게 흘러가다 / 진행되다

The meeting didn't go smoothly due to technical issues.

그 모임은 기술적인 이슈 때문에 부드럽게 진행되지 못했다.

08. in advance

미리

She booked her flight tickets in advance to get a discount.

그녀는 할인을 받기 위해서 미리 비행기 표를 예약했다.

09. end up saving time

결국 시간을 절약하다

Using a shortcut on the commute can end up saving time.

통근길에 지름길을 이용하는 것은 결국 시간을 절약할 수 있다.

10. complete on schedule

예정대로 완료하다

She completed the project on schedule.

그녀는 프로젝트를 예정대로 완료했다.

Practice

>> 앞에서 학습한 표현들을 활용하여 다음 문장을 영작하시오.

01. 미리 구체적인 계획을 세우는 것은 효과적인 시간 관리에 크게 기여할 수 있다.

02. 사람들이 즉흥적인 계획을 세우고 단순하게 그 흐름에 맡길 때 상당한 시간이 낭비된 것은 증명된 사실이다.

03. 구체적인 계획을 갖는 것은 개인들이 더 효율적으로 시간을 활용하는 데 도움이 된다.

04. 이는 일하는 사람들이 더 빠른 속도로 여러 작업을 처리할 수 있게 해 준다.

05. 이는 또한 사람들이 더 잘 집중하고 우수한 성과를 낼 수 있게 한다.

06. 그가 조교로 일했을 때, 그는 교수의 연구를 도와야만 했었다.

_____

_____

07. 모든 것은 순조롭게 진행되었지만 한 가지 문제가 있었다.

_____

_____

08. 어느 날, 그는 미리 구체적인 계획을 세우는 것으로 그의 라이프 스타일을 바꾸기로 했다.

_____

_____

09. 그는 결국 상당한 시간을 절약하게 되었다.

_____

_____

10. 그는 예정대로 조교 업무를 완료했다.

_____

_____

Part 1 Academic Discussion Task

Part 2

실전 굳히기

◎ Lesson 01   스트레스 관련 주제 문단 구성

◎ Lesson 02   분위기 관련 주제 문단 구성

◎ Lesson 03   사람들과의 관계 관련 주제 문단 구성

◎ Lesson 04   관점의 확장 관련 주제 문단 구성

◎ Lesson 05   조언 관련 주제 문단 구성

◎ Lesson 06   편리함 관련 주제 문단 구성

◎ Lesson 07   시간 활용 관련 주제 문단 구성

Academic Discussion Task의 답변은 의견을 뒷받침하는 일반적 사실 진술과 구체화 사례로 구성된다.

◎ 답변 구조

> 주제에 해당하는 일반적인 사실 진술 + 해당 진술에 관련된 구체화 사례

1. 일반적 사실 진술

일반적 사실 진술은 답변을 한결 세련되게 다듬어 준다. 사람들이 일반적으로 알고 있는 사실을 풀어내면 글을 보는 채점관과의 공감을 형성할 뿐만 아니라, 글을 더 논리적으로 쓸 수 있다. 지나치게 전문 지식을 쓰면 채점관조차 이해하기 어려울 수 있으니 보편적인 지식으로 의견을 전개하도록 한다.

2. 해당 진술에 연관된 구체화 사례

개인적 경험은 수험자 본인이나 주변 지인들이 겪은 일을 가리킨다. Academic Discussion Task에서는 자기 생각과 경험을 답변에 자유롭게 쓸 수 있으므로, 주제와 경험을 되살려 앞에서 제시한 일반적 사실 진술을 효과적으로 뒷받침하도록 한다.

| Example

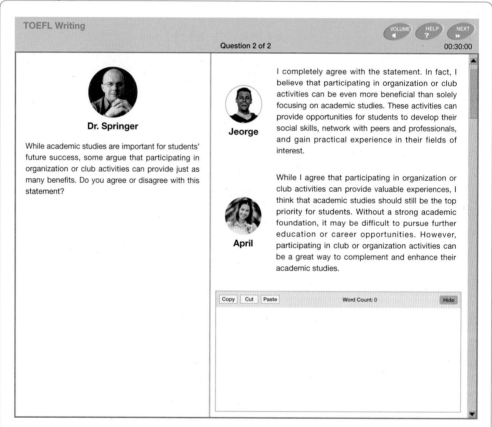

스프린저 교수
스프린저 교수

학문적인 연구는 학생들의 미래 성공에 중요하지만, 일부 사람들은 단체나 동아리 활동에 참여하는 것이 동등한 혜택을 제공할 수 있다고 주장합니다. 이 주장에 찬성하십니까, 반대하십니까?

조지

저는 이 주장에 완전히 찬성합니다. 사실, 저는 단순히 학문에 중점을 두는 것보다 단체나 동아리에 참여하는 것이 더 큰 이점을 제공할 수 있다고 믿습니다. 이러한 활동은 학생들에게 사회적 기술을 개발하고 동료 및 전문가와 네트워킹하며 관심 분야에서 실질적인 경험을 얻을 수 있는 기회를 제공할 수 있습니다.

에이프릴

단체나 동아리에 참여하는 것이 가치 있는 경험을 제공할 수 있다고 동의하지만, 학문적인 연구는 여전히 학생들에게 우선순위여야 한다고 생각합니다. 튼튼한 학문적 기반 없이는 추가 교육이나 진로 기회를 추구하기 어려울 수 있습니다. 그러나 동아리나 단체에 참여하는 것은 학문적인 연구를 보완하고 강화할 수 있는 좋은 방법일 수 있습니다.

◐ 답변 만들기

일반적 진술 From my perspective, both made excellent statements, but I'm on the same page as Jeorge. Simply put, participating in club activities can contribute to alleviating stress. Nowadays, students often get stressed out from their heavy workloads and the competition with those around them, so they need a pleasant diversion to relax mentally. By spending quality time engaging in enjoyable club activities, they will eventually be able to relax and get back to their work.

구체화 사례 A perfect example of this is a close friend of mine. He used to suffer from a huge workload and pressure. He sometimes stayed up all night getting his work done, so he was basically exhausted physically and mentally. Then one day, he joined an inline hockey club. It truly allowed him to escape from all the stressful matters while engaging in this activity. Thanks to this, he now has a relaxed and confident mental state.

일반적 진술 제 관점으로는, 양쪽 모두 훌륭한 진술을 했지만, 저는 조지와 같은 의견입니다. 간단히 말하면, 동아리 활동에 참여하는 것은 스트레스 완화에 큰 도움을 줄 수 있습니다. 요즈음, 학생들은 과도한 일(공부)과 그들 주변 사람들과의 경쟁 때문에 스트레스를 받고 있어 정신적으로 편안해질 수 있는 즐거운 기분 전환이 필요합니다. 즐길 수 있는 동아리 활동이 주는 깊고 의미 있는 시간을 통해서, 그들은 결국 휴식을 취하고 그들의 일로 돌아가게 될 것입니다.

구체화 사례 이에 대한 완벽한 예시는 내 친한 친구 중 한 명입니다. 그는 너무 많은 일(공부)과 중압감으로 고통받았습니다. 그는 때때로 그의 일을 끝내기 위해 밤을 지새웠습니다. 그래서 그는 완전히 신체적으로나 정신적으로 지쳐 있었습니다. 그러던 어느 날, 그는 인라인 하키 동아리에 가입할 기회를 가지게 되었습니다. 그것은 그가 이 활동에 참여하는 동안에, 모든 스트레스 가득한 일로부터 벗어날 수 있게 해 주었습니다. 이 덕분에, 그는 현재 안정되고 자신감 있는 심리 상태를 가지게 되었습니다.

Your professor is teaching a class. Write a post responding to the professor's question.

In your response, you should:
- express and support your opinion
- make a contribution to the discussion

An effective response will contain at least 100 words.
You will have 10 minutes to write it.

Dr. Springer

When it comes to spending money, some argue that it is better to invest in something long-lasting, like an expensive piece of jewelry, rather than indulging in short-term pleasures, such as a vacation. What are your thoughts on this matter?

Jeorge

Personally, I believe that investing in something that lasts, like an expensive piece of jewelry, is a wise decision. Not only does it provide a lasting value, but it can also be seen as an investment that retains or even appreciates in worth over time. Furthermore, owning a valuable piece of jewelry can be a symbol of prestige and accomplishment.

April

While I acknowledge the appeal of long-lasting investments, I believe that spending money on pleasurable experiences, such as a vacation, can be equally valuable. Pleasurable experiences have the potential to create lifelong memories and broaden one's horizons. Additionally, they can contribute to personal growth, cultural understanding, and stress relief, which are all essential aspects of a well-rounded life.

| Copy | Cut | Paste | | Word Count: 0 | Hide |

아웃라인

일반적 진술

short-term pleasure: alleviate stress → stressed from work + competition → quality time enjoying short-term pleasure → relax + get back to work

구체화 사례

example → stressed out from work → "family trip" → relaxed mental state

답변 완성하기

일반적 진술

From my perspective, both made excellent statements, but I'm on the same page as

_____

_____

_____

_____

_____

_____

_____

구체화 사례

A perfect example of this is a close friend of mine.

_____

_____

_____

_____

_____

_____

Practice

Q

Your professor is teaching a class. Write a post responding to the professor's question.

In your response, you should:
- express and support your opinion
- make a contribution to the discussion

An effective response will contain at least 100 words.
You will have 10 minutes to write it.

Dr. Springer

It's interesting to see the differing viewpoints regarding the balance between work-related hobbies and unrelated leisure activities, and the potential benefits they offer for personal well-being and professional growth. Do you agree or disagree with the given statement? Because people spend so much of their time working, it is vital that they use their free time to engage in hobbies that are different from their work.

Jeorge

I agree with the statement. Engaging in hobbies that are different from one's work is crucial for overall well-being and personal growth. Hobbies provide an avenue for individuals to explore their passions, interests, and talents outside the constraints of their professional responsibilities. It allows them to unwind, relax, and recharge, which ultimately improves their productivity and creativity when they return to work.

April

I believe it is equally important to find a balance between work and leisure. In some cases, individuals may find fulfillment in pursuing hobbies related to their work, as it allows them to further develop their expertise and explore new dimensions within their field. Additionally, dedicating time to enhance professional skills during free time can be advantageous for career advancement.

Copy | Cut | Paste   Word Count: 0   Hide

TOEFL Writing

Your professor is teaching a class. Write a post responding to the professor's question.

In your response, you should:
- express and support your opinion
- make a contribution to the discussion

An effective response will contain at least 100 words.
You will have 10 minutes to write it.

Dr. Lucas

When it comes to designing a school's curriculum, there are numerous classes to choose from, each offering its own unique benefits. However, if you had to select just one class to be mandatory for the school's curriculum, which class would you prioritize?

Bobby

Personally, I believe that a class focusing on personal finance and financial literacy should be mandatory for all students. In today's society, financial knowledge is crucial for individuals to navigate the complexities of managing their finances effectively. Such a class would equip students with essential skills like budgeting, saving, and understanding investments, ensuring they have a solid foundation to make informed financial decisions throughout their lives and achieve accomplishments.

Kelly

While I recognize the importance of financial literacy, I would argue that a class on critical thinking and problem-solving should be the mandatory choice. These skills are universally applicable and essential for success in any field. By developing critical thinking abilities, students can learn to analyze and evaluate information, think creatively, and make sound judgments.

| Copy | Cut | Paste | Word Count: 0 | Hide |

아웃라인

일반적 진술

a positive atmosphere in PE class → influence of the atmosphere: important → students should feel a good atmosphere. → PE: makes students feel more cheerful and energetic

구체화 사례

example → competitive and strict atmosphere in the school → the principal's plan to change the atmosphere → a lot of time and effort to provide enjoyable PE class → positive atmosphere in the school

답변 완성하기

일반적 진술

From my perspective, both made excellent statements, but I would like to add that

구체화 사례

A perfect example of this is the high school that I attended.

Practice

Q

Your professor is teaching a class. Write a post responding to the professor's question.

In your response, you should:
- express and support your opinion
- make a contribution to the discussion

An effective response will contain at least 100 words.
You will have 10 minutes to write it.

Dr. Lucas

Many cities nowadays are devising plans to improve themselves, yet they are unsure of the exact answer. When it comes to the city's benefit, some argue that the best way to achieve it is by focusing on constructing new buildings rather than preserving our nature. What are your thoughts on this matter?

Bobby

Personally, I agree with the notion that constructing new buildings can bring financial benefits to the government. The development of infrastructure and new constructions can attract investments, boost the economy, and create job opportunities. These economic gains can then be utilized for various public welfare programs, ultimately benefiting the citizens.

Kelly

While I understand the potential benefits of constructing new buildings, I strongly believe that preserving our natural environment should be a top priority. Our natural resources are invaluable, providing us with clean air, water, and biodiversity. Neglecting environmental preservation can have severe consequences for our planet and future generations.

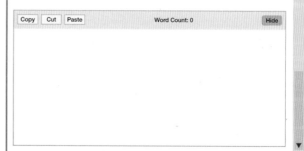

| Copy | Cut | Paste | Word Count: 0 | Hide |

TOEFL Writing

Your professor is teaching a class. Write a post responding to the professor's question.

In your response, you should:
- express and support your opinion
- make a contribution to the discussion

An effective response will contain at least 100 words.
You will have 10 minutes to write it.

Dr. Emilie

Many busy parents struggle to balance their work and family life, and may not have much time to devote to helping their children with schoolwork. Some argue that it is more important for parents to spend quality time playing and bonding with their children, rather than focusing solely on academic achievements. What are your thoughts on this statement?

Oliver

I completely agree with the statement. Spending quality time with your children is essential for building strong relationships and developing their emotional intelligence. Parents who prioritize play-time over academics are sending an important message to their children: that their love and attention are not contingent on academic performance.

Lucy

While I agree that spending quality time with your children is important, I think that academic achievement should not be overlooked. It's important for parents to be involved in their children's education and to provide them with the support they need to succeed in school. This doesn't mean sacrificing play-time, but finding a balance between academic and non-academic activities.

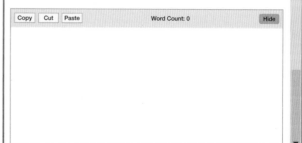

| Copy | Cut | Paste | Word Count: 0 | Hide |

아웃라인

일반적 진술

interaction between parents and children → play together → share experiences and emotions → lead to sincere conversations later

구체화 사례

example → drift apart from his son due to his job → decided to play with his son → awkward and challenging at first → gradually better → a strong bond between father and son

답변 완성하기

일반적 진술

From my perspective, both made excellent statements, but I'm on the same page as

구체화 사례

A perfect example of this is my uncle.

Part 2

Academic Discussion Task

Practice

Q

Your professor is teaching a class. Write a post responding to the professor's question.

In your response, you should:
- express and support your opinion
- make a contribution to the discussion

An effective response will contain at least 100 words.
You will have 10 minutes to write it.

Dr. Emilie

As we discuss the importance of family dynamics, let's delve into the topic of regular family meals. We often hear the saying "Families should have meals together on a regular basis." What are your thoughts on this statement? Does having regular family meals provide significant benefits?

Oliver

Thank you, Professor. I believe that families should indeed prioritize having regular meals together. These shared moments offer more than just nourishment; they provide an opportunity for family members to connect, share their experiences, and strengthen their bonds. It's during these meals that we often engage in meaningful conversations, providing a sense of togetherness and support.

Lucy

I understand the importance of family meals, but I'd like to emphasize the challenges many families face in today's hectic lifestyles. While it's a wonderful idea, the reality is that demanding work schedules, extracurricular activities, and other commitments can make it difficult for everyone to sit down together regularly. Nonetheless, the value of family meals should not be understated, and finding ways to make it work can bring numerous benefits.

| Copy | Cut | Paste | | Word Count: 0 | | Hide |

Lesson
04 관점의 확장 관련 주제 문단 구성

VOLUME | HELP | NEXT

Your professor is teaching a class. Write a post responding to the professor's question.

In your response, you should:
- express and support your opinion
- make a contribution to the discussion

An effective response will contain at least 100 words.
You will have 10 minutes to write it.

Dr. Logan

As we explore the enriching aspects of travel, let's delve into the topic of how people can benefit from traveling from all around the world. We often hear the saying, "People can benefit from traveling from all around the world." What are your thoughts on this statement? Do you believe that travel can provide significant advantages?

Noah

I strongly agree with the statement. Traveling offers a unique opportunity for individuals to broaden their horizons, immerse themselves in different cultures, and gain a deeper understanding of the world. It allows us to break free from our comfort zones, challenge our perspectives, and foster personal growth.

Helen

While I agree that travel can be beneficial, I believe that academic studies should still remain a top priority. Education provides a strong foundation and equips individuals with essential knowledge and skills. However, incorporating travel experiences into one's educational journey can enhance their understanding of diverse cultures and global issues, providing a more holistic and well-rounded education.

| Copy | Cut | Paste | Word Count: 0 | Hide |

일반적 진술

traveling the world: broaden perspectives → exposure to different matters they haven't experienced before → get valuable insights for the future

구체화 사례

example → a friend who often moved + had numerous experiences → not challenging but exciting to learn how to embrace diversity → traveling all over the world with that friend → me: keeping distance from differences → him: open-minded to everything

답변 완성하기

일반적 진술

From my perspective, both made excellent statements, but I'm on the same page as

_____

_____

_____

_____

_____

_____

_____

구체화 사례

A perfect example of this is a close friend of mine.

_____

_____

_____

_____

_____

_____

_____

Practice

Q

Your professor is teaching a class. Write a post responding to the professor's question.

In your response, you should:
- express and support your opinion
- make a contribution to the discussion

An effective response will contain at least 100 words.
You will have 10 minutes to write it.

Dr. Logan

While academic studies are important for a child's education, there is an ongoing debate about whether studying abroad at an early age is beneficial for children. Considering the advantages and potential drawbacks, what factors should parents and educators consider when deciding whether to recommend studying abroad at an early age for children?

Noah

Personally, I believe that studying abroad at an early age can be highly recommended for children. It offers them a unique opportunity to immerse themselves in a different culture, learn a new language, and gain a global perspective. This experience not only enhances their academic knowledge but also helps them develop invaluable life skills, such as adaptability and independence.

Helen

While I understand the potential benefits of studying abroad, I think it's essential to prioritize a child's academic studies. A strong foundation in traditional education provides the necessary skills and knowledge for future success. Although studying abroad can offer cultural exposure, it should not overshadow the importance of a comprehensive academic curriculum.

| Copy | Cut | Paste | Word Count: 0 | Hide |

Lesson 05 조언 관련 주제 문단 구성

Your professor is teaching a class. Write a post responding to the professor's question.

In your response, you should:
- express and support your opinion
- make a contribution to the discussion

An effective response will contain at least 100 words.
You will have 10 minutes to write it.

Dr. Bliss

I'd like you to share your recent experiences that have had a significant impact on your lives. It's remarkable how diverse experiences can shape our perspectives and contribute to personal growth. So, please describe a new experience you have had recently that significantly impacted your life. Explain how this experience has influenced your perspective and personal growth.

James

Recently, I had the opportunity to participate in a volunteer program in a rural community. This experience has had a profound impact on my life. It exposed me to the realities and challenges faced by underprivileged communities, deepening my empathy and understanding of social issues. Interacting with the locals and working together to improve their living conditions sparked a sense of purpose and a desire to contribute positively to society.

Emma

In contrast, my recent experience was completing a research internship at a prestigious laboratory. This opportunity allowed me to work closely with leading scientists in my field of interest. Through this experience, I gained valuable insights into cutting-edge research and acquired practical laboratory skills. It reinforced my passion for scientific inquiry and provided clarity regarding my career path.

Copy   Cut   Paste   Word Count: 0   Hide

일반적 진술

advice from experiences → valuable and practical advice for future → through the experiences, evaluate oneself objectively → better life in the future

구체화 사례

example → me: less sociable → live in my own world → internship as a graduation requirement → challenging to learn from the internship opportunity → get used to the situation → got to contemplate a lot of matters → gained advice + mental growth

답변 완성하기

일반적 진술

From my perspective, both made excellent statements, but I would like to add that

_____

_____

_____

_____

_____

_____

_____

구체화 사례

A perfect example of this is my own experience.

_____

_____

_____

_____

_____

_____

Practice

Q

Your professor is teaching a class. Write a post responding to the professor's question.

In your response, you should:
- express and support your opinion
- make a contribution to the discussion

An effective response will contain at least 100 words.
You will have 10 minutes to write it.

Dr. Bliss

Over time, we've seen numerous cases where people and societies have improved by acknowledging and fixing their errors. Today, we'll discuss a topic that's relevant to people from different cultures and eras: "Do people learn from their mistakes? What's your take on this?"

James

I wholeheartedly agree with this statement. Mistakes are invaluable learning experiences. They teach us important lessons that often can't be gained through success alone. Take, for instance, a student who makes an error in a math problem. That mistake can lead to a deeper understanding of the concept when corrected. Similarly, in life, personal mistakes often lead to self-reflection and personal growth.

Emma

Learning from mistakes is not guaranteed. Some people may repeat the same mistakes without improvement. In certain situations, mistakes can have serious consequences that can't be easily rectified. It's also worth noting that not all lessons need to come from mistakes: guidance, education, and knowledge sharing are proactive ways to learn.

| Copy | Cut | Paste | Word Count: 0 | Hide |

Part 2
Academic Discussion Task

Your professor is teaching a class. Write a post responding to the professor's question.

In your response, you should:
- express and support your opinion
- make a contribution to the discussion

An effective response will contain at least 100 words.
You will have 10 minutes to write it.

Dr. Ethan

Good day, class. Scientific discoveries and technological innovations have been instrumental in shaping the world as we know it. Today, we'll delve into a captivating question: "Which significant scientific breakthrough or technological innovation from the past two centuries would you select as a crucial advancement?" Let's explore the remarkable achievements that have transformed our lives.

Daniel

Thank you, Professor. When considering significant advancements from the past two centuries, I would definitely pick the discovery of antibiotics. When Alexander Fleming stumbled upon penicillin in 1928, it revolutionized medicine and saved countless lives. The ability to treat bacterial infections transformed healthcare, making surgery safer and preventing deaths from once-fatal diseases.

Judy

I understand the importance of antibiotics, but I'd select the development of the computer. Starting from the 1960s, the computer has changed the way we communicate, work, and access information. It has connected people globally, accelerated research and innovation, and transformed industries. Today, it's an integral part of modern life, driving progress in countless fields.

Copy	Cut	Paste	Word Count: 0	Hide

아웃라인

일반적 진술

the Internet: provide convenience → communicate with people anytime → replace traditional offline settings → × go through tedious process

구체화 사례

example → cousin's friend moved → signed up for online video chat → useful features to communicate → × travel a long distance in person

답변 완성하기

일반적 진술

From my perspective, both made excellent statements, but I would like to add that

구체화 사례

A perfect example of this is my cousin.

Part 2

Academic Discussion Task

Practice

Q

Your professor is teaching a class. Write a post responding to the professor's question.

In your response, you should:
- express and support your opinion
- make a contribution to the discussion

An effective response will contain at least 100 words.
You will have 10 minutes to write it.

Dr. Ethan

It is crucial to have access to reliable and comprehensive information in today's society. People have various methods for obtaining the information or data they need. Some individuals acquire information from those around them, while others prefer to visit libraries to gather data. What do you believe is the most effective way to gain information?

Daniel

In my opinion, the Internet is the most effective way to gain information. With its vast resources and convenience, the Internet allows us to access a wide range of information quickly. We can conduct online research, access academic databases, and find reliable sources for our inquiries. Moreover, the Internet provides various multimedia formats, such as videos and interactive tutorials, that enhance our learning experience.

Judy

While I agree that the Internet is a valuable source of information, I believe that a combination of methods is essential for comprehensive knowledge. Libraries, for example, provide access to in-depth books, scholarly journals, and historical archives that may not be readily available online. They offer a quieter and focused environment for studying and conducting research.

| Copy | Cut | Paste | | Word Count: 0 | Hide |

Part 2
Academic Discussion Task

TOEFL Writing

Your professor is teaching a class. Write a post responding to the professor's question.

In your response, you should:
- express and support your opinion
- make a contribution to the discussion

An effective response will contain at least 100 words.
You will have 10 minutes to write it.

Dr. Joanna

It's interesting to see the contrasting viewpoints regarding the benefits of structured plans versus the advantages of being flexible and open to new experiences. Each approach has its merits, and it ultimately depends on individual preferences and circumstances. Some people make a specific plan for their time in advance, while others make instant plans and just go with the flow. Which lifestyle do you prefer?

Justin

Personally, I prefer making specific plans in advance. Having a well-thought-out schedule allows me to prioritize my tasks, manage my time effectively, and stay organized. By planning ahead, I can set clear goals, allocate sufficient time for each activity, and ensure that I make progress towards my objectives. This approach also helps me maintain a sense of discipline and focus, as I have a road map to guide my actions.

Anna

I personally prefer going with the flow. I find that being spontaneous allows me to embrace new opportunities, adapt to unexpected situations, and remain flexible. Sometimes, rigid plans can limit creativity and prevent me from exploring different avenues. By going with the flow, I can seize the present moment, follow my instincts, and embrace serendipity. It allows me to be more open-minded, responsive to changes, and comfortable with uncertainty.

| Copy | Cut | Paste | Word Count: 0 | Hide |

아웃라인

일반적 진술

making specific plan: effective time management → instant plan: time is wasted → specific plan: utilize time efficiently → handle tasks at a faster pace + focus better + outstanding performance

구체화 사례

example → cousin who used to make instant plans + go with the flow → assist professor as T.A. → x enough time for T.A. work → change lifestyle by making specific plans → save time + complete T.A. work on schedule

답변 완성하기

일반적 진술

From my perspective, both made excellent statements, but I'm on the same page as

구체화 사례

A perfect example of this is my cousin,

Practice

Q

Your professor is teaching a class. Write a post responding to the professor's question.

In your response, you should:
- express and support your opinion
- make a contribution to the discussion

An effective response will contain at least 100 words.
You will have 10 minutes to write it.

Dr. Joanna

It's evident that technology has brought about significant benefits, but it's important to consider the potential challenges and societal implications as well. I would like to share your insights on the impact of technology on our world. Technology has made the world a better place to live. Do you agree or disagree?

Justin

I agree with the statement. Technology has revolutionized various aspects of our lives, leading to significant improvements in many areas. For instance, advancements in healthcare technology have enhanced medical treatments, increased life expectancy, and improved the overall well-being of individuals.

Anna

While I acknowledge the benefits of technology, I also believe that it has its drawbacks. One of the major concerns is the impact of technology on social interactions. With the rise of smartphones and social media, people are becoming more isolated and less engaged in face-to-face interactions. There is a risk of losing genuine human connections and fostering a sense of loneliness.

| Copy | Cut | Paste | Word Count: 0 | Hide |

Test

Q1

Your professor is teaching a class. Write a post responding to the professor's question.

In your response, you should:
- express and support your opinion
- make a contribution to the discussion

An effective response will contain at least 100 words.
You will have 10 minutes to write it.

Dr. Liam

Today, we will explore a topic that revolves around the different modes of communication. Our focus will be on the statement that face-to-face communication is superior to other forms, such as letters, emails, or telephone calls. We will examine the reasons and details behind this assertion. Do you agree or disagree that face-to-face communication is superior to other types of communication? Support your answer with specific reasons and details.

Jacob

I strongly agree with the statement. Face-to-face communication allows for nonverbal cues, such as facial expressions and body language, which enhance understanding and build stronger connections between individuals. It also enables immediate feedback and promotes active listening, leading to more effective and meaningful interactions.

Bella

While I acknowledge the benefits of face-to-face communication, I believe that other forms of communication can be equally valuable. In today's fast-paced world, digital communication offers convenience, allowing people to connect regardless of physical distance. Additionally, written communication provides a permanent record and allows for careful articulation of thoughts, which can be especially important in professional settings.

Copy Cut Paste   Word Count: 0   Hide

Q2

Your professor is teaching a class. Write a post responding to the professor's question.

In your response, you should:
- express and support your opinion
- make a contribution to the discussion

An effective response will contain at least 100 words.
You will have 10 minutes to write it.

Dr. Catherine

Today, our discussion will revolve around the importance of maintaining friendships. Specifically, we will explore the statement that the ability to maintain friendships with a small number of people over a long period of time is more crucial for happiness than the ability to easily make many new friends. Do you agree or disagree that the ability to maintain long-term friendships is more crucial for happiness than the ability to make many new friends easily? Provide specific reasons and examples to support your viewpoint.

Isaac

I completely agree with the statement. Long-term friendships provide a sense of deep connection, trust, and support that is essential for lasting happiness. These friendships often involve shared experiences, memories, and a deep understanding of one another, which cannot be easily replicated in new friendships.

Dorothy

While I agree that long-term friendships have their value, I believe that the ability to make new friends easily is equally important. As life evolves, circumstances change, and new opportunities arise, having the flexibility to connect with new individuals can expand our perspectives, introduce us to diverse experiences, and provide fresh sources of happiness.

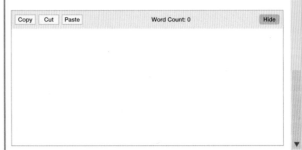

Actual Test

Actual Test 1

Actual Test 2

Actual Test 1

In the late 14th century, an unknown poet from the Midlands composed four poems titled *Pearl*, *Sir Gawain and the Green Knight*, *Patience*, and *Cleanness*. This collection of poems is referred to as *Cotton Nero A.x* and the author is often referred to as the Pearl Poet. Up to this day, there have been many theories regarding the identity of this poet, and these are three of the most popular ones.

The first theory is that the author's name was Hugh, and it is based on the *Chronicle of Andrew of Wyntoun*. In the chronicle, an author called Hucheon (little Hugh) is credited with writing three poems, one of which is about the adventures of Gawain. Not only that, but all three poems are written in alliterative verse, as are all four of the poems in *Cotton Nero A.x*. Since they are written in the same style and one poem from each set concerns Gawain, some people contend that all of the *Cotton Nero A.x* poems were written by Hugh.

The second theory is that John Massey was the poet, and it is supported by another poem called *St. Erkenwald* and penmanship. Although the actual authorship of *St. Erkenwald* is unknown, John Massey was a poet who lived in the correct area and time for scholars to attribute it to him. This manuscript was written in very similar handwriting to that of the Pearl Poet, which indicates that one person is likely the author of all five of the poems.

The third theory is that the poems were actually written by different authors from the same region of England. This comes from the fact that there is little linking the poems to each other. Two are concerned with the Arthur legends, but the only link connecting the other two is that they describe the same area of the countryside. They also seem to be written in the same dialect. Taken together, these facts indicate that they were written in the same region, but they probably were not written by the same person.

🎧 AT1

TOEFL Writing

Question 1 of 2

Directions : You have 20 minutes to plan and write your response. Your response will be judged on the quality of your writing and on how well your response presents the points in the lecture and the relationship to the reading passage. Typically, an effective response will be 150 to 225 words.

Questions : Summarize the points made in the lecture. Be sure to explain how they oppose the specific points made in the reading passage.

In the late 14th century, an unknown poet from the Midlands composed four poems titled *Pearl*, *Sir Gawain and the Green Knight*, *Patience*, and *Cleanness*. This collection of poems is referred to as *Cotton Nero A.x* and the author is often referred to as the Pearl Poet. Up to this day, there have been many theories regarding the identity of this poet, and these are three of the most popular ones.

The first theory is that the author's name was Hugh, and it is based on the *Chronicle of Andrew of Wyntoun*. In the chronicle, an author called Hucheon (little Hugh) is credited with writing three poems, one of which is about the adventures of Gawain. Not only that, but all three poems are written in alliterative verse, as are all four of the poems in *Cotton Nero A.x*. Since they are written in the same style and one poem from each set concerns Gawain, some people contend that all of the *Cotton Nero A.x* poems were written by Hugh.

The second theory is that John Massey was the poet, and it is supported by another poem called *St. Erkenwald* and penmanship. Although the actual authorship of *St. Erkenwald* is unknown, John Massey was a poet who lived in the correct area and time for scholars to attribute it to him. This manuscript was written in very similar handwriting to that of the Pearl Poet, which indicates that one person is likely the author of all five of the poems.

The third theory is that the poems were actually written by different authors from the same region of England. This comes from the fact that there is little linking the poems to each other. Two are concerned with the Arthur legends, but the only link connecting the other two is that they describe the same area of the countryside. They also seem to be written in the same dialect. Taken together, these facts indicate that they were written in the same region, but they probably were not written by the same person.

Your professor is teaching a class. Write a post responding to the professor's question.

In your response, you should:
- express and support your opinion
- make a contribution to the discussion

An effective response will contain at least 100 words.

You will have 10 minutes to write it.

Dr. Michael

Good day, class. As we navigate through the intricacies of resource allocation in universities, a pressing question emerges: "Should universities give the same amount of money to their students' sports activities as they give to their university libraries?" This topic invites us to consider the equilibrium between physical and intellectual development. In the pursuit of a comprehensive discussion, let's explore the dynamics of funding priorities.

Ian

Thank you, Professor. I find merit in the idea that universities should allocate equal funding to sports activities and libraries. While libraries are crucial for academic pursuits, sports play a pivotal role in students' holistic development. Investing in sports fosters physical well-being, teamwork, and a sense of community. These aspects contribute significantly to a student's overall educational experience.

Linda

I appreciate Ian's perspective, but I lean towards a different stance. I believe that universities should prioritize allocating funds based on academic needs rather than equal distribution. Libraries are the heart of academic resources, supporting research, study, and intellectual growth. While sports are valuable for physical well-being, the primary mission of a university is academic excellence. Therefore, a greater allocation to libraries aligns more closely with the core educational mission of universities.

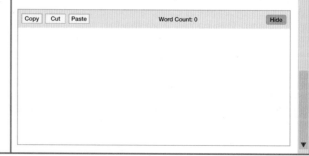

Actual Test 2

Researchers have found that wind turbines kill hundreds of thousands of bats every year. This mostly happens because many migrating bat species fly through areas where wind farms are built, but even non-migrating species are being killed. For this reason, it is important to develop ways to protect bats from wind turbines. Here are three strategies that could help to protect bats.

First, the most basic solution is to avoid building wind turbines in areas where bats are common. Since migrating bats follow the same paths every year, it is easy to figure out where they usually fly and not build in those areas. Bat species that do not migrate usually sleep in caves, and these are also easy to locate and avoid. By carefully researching where bats live and fly, we can build wind farms in areas where they will have little effect on bats.

Second, power companies can protect bats by changing their operating schedules. They can shut down their turbines at night, when bats are most active. If the turbines are not moving, the bats can safely fly around them. This would have little effect on the power companies since the demand for electricity is much lower at night. In fact, one wind power company in the U.S. tested out this method, and they reported far fewer bat deaths with only a tiny loss in annual power generation.

Third, the power companies can use radar to discourage the bats from coming near the turbines. Bats dislike radar waves, which is why they usually avoid areas where radar is used, like airports. So if radar emitters are installed in wind farms and on wind turbines, that will make the bats avoid the area. This method would be ideal, since it keeps the bats safe and allows the wind turbines to operate at any time.

AT2

TOEFL Writing

VOLUME ◄   HELP ?   NEXT ►►

Directions : You have 20 minutes to plan and write your response. Your response will be judged on the quality of your writing and on how well your response presents the points in the lecture and the relationship to the reading passage. Typically, an effective response will be 150 to 225 words.

Questions : Summarize the points made in the lecture. Be sure to explain how they oppose the specific points made in the reading passage.

Copy Cut Paste Undo Redo   Hide Word Count 0

Researchers have found that wind turbines kill hundreds of thousands of bats every year. This mostly happens because many migrating bat species fly through areas where wind farms are built, but even non-migrating species are being killed. For this reason, it is important to develop ways to protect bats from wind turbines. Here are three strategies that could help to protect bats.

First, the most basic solution is to avoid building wind turbines in areas where bats are common. Since migrating bats follow the same paths every year, it is easy to figure out where they usually fly and not build in those areas. Bat species that do not migrate usually sleep in caves, and these are also easy to locate and avoid. By carefully researching where bats live and fly, we can build wind farms in areas where they will have little effect on bats.

Second, power companies can protect bats by changing their operating schedules. They can shut down their turbines at night, when bats are most active. If the turbines are not moving, the bats can safely fly around them. This would have little effect on the power companies since the demand for electricity is much lower at night. In fact, one wind power company in the U.S. tested out this method, and they reported far fewer bat deaths with only a tiny loss in annual power generation.

Third, the power companies can use radar to discourage the bats from coming near the turbines. Bats dislike radar waves, which is why they usually avoid areas where radar is used, like airports. So if radar emitters are installed in wind farms and on wind turbines, that will make the bats avoid the area. This method would be ideal, since it keeps the bats safe and allows the wind turbines to operate at any time.

Your professor is teaching a class. Write a post responding to the professor's question.

In your response, you should:
- express and support your opinion
- make a contribution to the discussion

An effective response will contain at least 100 words.
You will have 10 minutes to write it.

Dr. Irene

Greetings, class. Today, our focus is on the belief that early exposure to studying abroad is essential for broadening horizons and personal development. The question before us is simple yet profound: Do you agree or disagree with this perspective? Studying overseas at an early age is crucial for evolving as individuals. As we embark on this exploration, let's delve into the dynamics of studying abroad and its potential effects on personal development.

Henry

Thank you, Professor. I wholeheartedly agree with the idea that studying abroad at an early age is crucial for personal development. Experiencing different cultures, meeting diverse people, and navigating unfamiliar environments offer unparalleled opportunities for self-discovery. The challenges and joys of studying abroad shape individuals in ways that traditional education might not.

Lottie

While I acknowledge the benefits Henry highlights, I find myself leaning towards disagreement. Not everyone has the privilege or inclination to study abroad early in life. Moreover, local education can also foster personal development through exposure to diverse perspectives and cultures. The emphasis should be on creating a globally aware curriculum locally, ensuring that all students, regardless of their ability to study abroad, can develop as individuals.

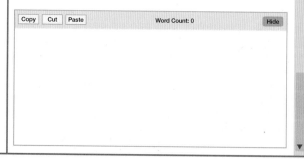

Copy | Cut | Paste   Word Count: 0   Hide

PAGODA TOEFL 80+ Writing

3rd Edition

파고다교육그룹 언어교육연구소, 안병남(Bobby Ahn) | 저

PAGODA
TOEFL

80+
Writing

해설서

PAGODA Books

PAGODA TOEFL

3rd Edition

파고다교육그룹 언어교육연구소, 안병남(Bobby Ahn) I 저

80+
Writing

해설서

PAGODA Books

Q1

Reading

Many scientists advocate substituting species to support ecosystems where an important contributor to the ecology has disappeared or gone extinct. They argue that the balance must be maintained or the entire ecosystem could collapse. However, there are many flaws with this line of thinking.

Firstly, the loss of a species from an ecosystem is not necessarily a disaster. In many cases, other species have altered their feeding habits to exploit that vacancy and thereby become stronger. This is referred to as species substitution, and it occurs naturally, so if we intervene, we are preventing nature from taking its course. We should study the ecosystem to see if any species are filling in the gap. If none are, then maybe we should start to consider substituting another species, but we must do so carefully.

The most serious outcome of introducing a new species is that it may become invasive. Many species that have been introduced to new ecosystems have wreaked havoc upon their new homes. Some of these species introductions were accidental like the zebra mussel, which outcompetes similar shellfish and causes industrial problems. Others were intentional like the cane toad, which was introduced to Australia to control insect populations. Cane toads have no natural predators there, so their population has exploded as they devour many species other than the intended insects.

Species substitution could also disrupt the entire ecosystem. Some experts believe the problems of invasive species can be solved by introducing animals from different populations of the same species. This sounds ideal, but since they are from a different population, they may behave differently and could have a negative effect on the ecosystem as well. For instance, in their native habitat, they may have more competition than in the new area. With less competition, they may overburden the local food chain and cause irreversible damage.

많은 과학자들은 생태에 중요한 기여를 하는 존재가 사라졌거나 멸종된 생태계를 지원하기 위해 종을 대체하는 것을 지지한다. 그들은 균형이 유지되어야 하며, 그렇지 않으면 생태계 전체가 붕괴될 수도 있다고 주장한다. 그러나 이런 식의 논리에는 많은 결함이 있다.

먼저, 생태계에서 한 종의 멸종이 반드시 재난인 것은 아니다. 많은 경우에 다른 종들은 그 빈자리를 이용하기 위해 먹이 섭취 습성을 바꾸었으며 그로 인해 더 강해졌다. 이것을 '종 대체'라고 하는데, 이는 자연스럽게 일어나는 현상으로, 만약 우리가 개입한다면 자연이 순리대로 흘러가는 것을 방해하는 것이다. 우리는 어떤 종이 그 공백을 메우고 있는지 확인하기 위해 생태계를 살펴보아야 한다. 만약에 공백을 메우는 종이 없다면 그때는 또 다른 종으로 대체하는 것을 고려하기 시작해야겠지만, 그 과정에서 신중해야 한다.

새로운 종 유입의 가장 심각한 결과는 그 종이 급속히 퍼질지도 모른다는 것이다. 새로운 생태계에 유입되었던 많은 종들은 그들의 새로운 서식지에 큰 피해를 입혀왔다. 그 종들의 유입 중 일부는 얼룩말 홍합처럼 우연히 이루어진 것이었는데, 이 홍합은 유사한 조개류와의 경쟁에서 이겨 산업 문제를 초래하고 있다. 다른 종들은 수수두꺼비처럼 의도적인 것이었는데, 이 두꺼비는 곤충의 개체 수를 통제하기 위해 호주로 유입되었던 종이다. 그곳에는 수수두꺼비의 천적이 없어서 목표로 했던 곤충 이외의 많은 종들을 먹어 치우면서 그 개체 수는 폭발적으로 증가했다.

종 대체는 또한 생태계 전체에 혼란을 줄 수 있다. 몇몇 전문가들은 같은 종의 다른 개체군에서 동물을 들여옴으로써 외래종으로 인한 문제들을 해결할 수 있다고 생각한다. 이것은 이상적으로 들리지만, 그 동물들이 다른 개체군에서 온 것이기 때문에 다른 행동 양식을 보일지도 모르는데 이 또한 생태계에 부정적인 영향을 미칠 수 있다. 예를 들어, 그들의 토착 서식지는 새로운 지역보다 경쟁이 치열했을지도 모른다. 경쟁이 줄어들면서 그들은 현지의 먹이 사슬에 과도한 부담을 주어 돌이킬 수 없는 피해를 입힐 수도 있다.

어휘 advocate ▾ 지지하다, 옹호하다 | substitute ▾ 대신하다, 교체하다 | contributor ⋂ 기여자, 공헌자 | ecology ⋂ 생태(계), 생태학 | go extinct 멸종하다 | flaw ⋂ 결함 | not necessarily 반드시 ~은 아닌 | alter ▾ 변경하다 | feeding habit 먹이 섭취 습성 | exploit ▾ 이용하다, 착취하다 | vacancy ⋂ 공석, 빈자리 | intervene ▾ 개입하다 | take one's course 자연히 되어가다 | fill in the gap 공백[틈]을 메우다 | invasive 급속히 퍼지는 | wreak ▾ (큰 피해 등을) 입히다, 가하다 | havoc ⋂ 대파괴, 큰 혼란 | accidental 우연한 | zebra mussel 얼룩말 홍합 | outcompete ▾ 경쟁자보다 더 잘하다 | shellfish ⋂ 조개류 | intentional 의도적인 | cane toad 수수두꺼비 | predator ⋂ 포식자 | devour ▾ 걸신 들린 듯이 먹다 | substitution ⋂ 대체, 바꾸기 | disrupt ▾ 방해하다, 혼란스럽게 하다 | habitat ⋂ 서식지 | overburden ▾ 과중한 부담을 주다 | food chain ⋂ 먹이 사슬 | irreversible 되돌릴 수 없는

When scientists are dealing with disappearing species, one of the methods that they can use to stabilize an ecosystem is species substitution. The author of the reading maintains that this practice tends to do more harm than good. However, while these claims are indeed important issues to consider, substitutions must sometimes be made to prevent irreparable damage to the ecosystem.

The author's first point is that species substitution is unnecessary because other species typically adapt to fill the vacancy left by an extinct species. This does occur in nature, but the process can take a very long time. Considering how rapidly species are becoming extinct due to human influence, relying on this natural process alone is impractical because the niches would remain unfilled for too long.

Invasive species are a serious threat that should not be underestimated. However, the majority of deliberate introductions that have led to negative results were due to a lack of diligence. The species were not monitored and were allowed to spread freely throughout their new environment. For example, cane toads were introduced to Australia by merely setting them free in the wild. If a test group had been monitored in a contained area, researchers could have predicted such an outcome and chosen a different species to introduce.

According to the author, the introduction of members of the same species from a different population could cause irreversible damage as well. However, we should keep in mind that the animals that cause the most disruption to an ecosystem are usually large predators like lions and wolves. They can easily be monitored by scientists who have attached tracking devices to them. So, if they cause problems for the ecosystem, they can be captured and relocated.

과학자들이 종이 멸종되는 문제를 다룰 때 생태계를 안정시키기 위해 사용할 수 있는 방법 중 하나가 종의 대체입니다. 읽기 지문의 저자는 이런 실행이 득보다 실이 많다고 주장합니다. 그러나 이런 주장들이 실제로 고려해봐야 할 중요한 사안이긴 하지만 생태계에 돌이킬 수 없는 피해를 주는 것을 막기 위해 때로는 종 대체가 이루어져야 하죠.

저자의 첫 번째 요점은 다른 종들이 일반적으로 멸종된 종에 의해 남겨진 빈자리를 메우는 데 적응하기 때문에 종 대체가 불필요하다는 것입니다. 이것은 자연에서 실제로 일어나는 일이지만 그 과정은 매우 오랜 시간이 걸리죠. 인간의 영향으로 인해 종들이 얼마나 빠르게 멸종되는지를 생각해본다면 그 빈자리들이 너무 오랫동안 채워지지 않은 채로 남아 있을 것이기 때문에 이런 자연 과정에만 의지하는 것은 비현실적입니다.

급증하는 외래종은 과소평가해서는 안 될 심각한 위협입니다. 그러나 부정적인 결과로 이어졌던 의도적인 유입의 대다수는 성실함 부족이 그 원인이었어요. 종들은 추적 관찰되지 않았고, 새로운 환경 곳곳에 자유롭게 퍼져 살게 내버려 두었죠. 예를 들어, 수수두꺼비는 그저 야생으로 풀려나서 호주에 유입되었습니다. 실험군이 있었던 지역에서 추적 관찰이 이루어졌다면, 연구원들은 이런 결과를 예상하고 다른 종을 유입하기로 결정했을 것입니다.

저자에 따르면 다른 개체군에서 같은 종의 동물들을 유입하는 것 또한 되돌릴 수 없는 피해를 야기할 수 있습니다. 그러나 생태계에 최대의 혼란을 초래하는 동물들은 보통 사자나 늑대와 같은 큰 포식자라는 것을 명심해야 하죠. 그 동물들은 그들에게 추적 장치를 부착한 과학자들이 쉽게 관찰할 수 있어요. 따라서 그 동물들이 생태계에 문제를 초래한다면 포획하거나 이동시킬 수 있습니다.

어휘 stabilize ⓥ 안정시키다 | do more harm than good 득보다 실이 많다 | irreparable ⓪ 회복할 수 없는 | impractical ⓪ 비현실적인, 비실용적인 | niche ⓝ 틈새, 적소 | underestimate ⓥ 과소평가하다 | deliberate ⓪ 의도적인 | diligence ⓝ 근면, 성실 | disruption ⓝ 분열, 혼란 | tracking device 추적 장치 | capture ⓥ 포획하다 | relocate ⓥ 이동시키다

강의에서 제시한 요점을 요약하시오. 읽기 지문의 요점에 대해 강의에서 어떻게 반박하는지 설명하시오.

The reading and the lecture both talk about the necessity of substituting species to support ecosystems. The author contends that species substitutions have more disadvantages than advantages, but the lecturer points out that the reading's arguments are ill founded.

Firstly, the author mentions the possibility that another species will adapt to fill that position when an ecological

읽기 지문과 강의에서는 모두 생태계를 지원하기 위해 종을 대체하는 것의 필요성에 대해 이야기한다. 저자는 종 대체가 장점보다 단점이 더 많다고 주장하지만 강의자는 지문의 주장이 근거 없는 것이라고 지적한다.

먼저, 저자는 생태계의 틈새가 생기면 또 다른 종이 그 자리를 채우기 위해 적응할 가능성을 언급한다. 그

niche becomes vacant. However, the lecturer says that this is an unrealistic idea because the natural species succession mentioned in the reading is likely to take too long.

Secondly, the reading states that when different species are introduced to the environment, they may become invasive because there are no natural predators. While the lecturer admits that this can be a serious problem, he argues that we can minimize side effects if the substitution is done with great care and continually monitored.

Thirdly, the reading concludes that even though locally extinct animals are replaced with the same species from another area, they can irreversibly damage the ecosystem. The lecturer, however, contradicts this idea by suggesting that these substitute animals can be easily monitored and controlled. This is because the animals that cause problems are more likely to be large species.

러나 강의자는 읽기 지문에서 언급된 자연스러운 종 천이가 너무 오랜 시간이 걸릴 가능성이 높다며 이것이 비현실적인 생각이라고 말한다.

둘째로, 읽기 지문에서는 다른 종들이 환경으로 유입되면 그곳에 천적이 없기 때문에 급속히 퍼질지도 모른다고 언급한다. 강의자는 이것이 심각한 문제일 수 있다는 것을 인정하면서도 대체가 매우 조심스럽게 이루어지고 지속해서 관찰된다면 부작용을 최소화할 수 있다고 주장한다.

세 번째로, 읽기 지문에서는 어떤 지역에서 멸종된 동물들이 또 다른 지역에서 온 같은 종으로 대체된다고 하더라도 그들이 생태계를 돌이킬 수 없을 정도로 파괴할 수 있다고 결론짓는다. 그러나 강의자는 이런 대체 동물들을 쉽게 관찰하고 통제할 수 있다는 것을 시사하며 이 의견에 반박한다. 이는 문제를 일으키는 동물들이 커다란 종일 가능성이 더 높기 때문이다.

어휘 ill founded 근거 없는 I ecological **adj** 생태계의 I vacant **adj** 비어 있는 I minimize **v** 최소화하다 I side effect 부작용 I continually **adv** 계속해서, 지속적으로, 끊임없이 I irreversibly **adv** 돌이킬 수 없을 정도로 I contradict **v** 반박하다, 이의를 제기하다

Q2

Your professor is teaching a class. Write a post responding to the professor's question.

In your response, you should:
- express and support your opinion
- make a contribution to the discussion

An effective response will contain at least 100 words.
You will have 10 minutes to write it.

Dr. Harlow: Hello, everyone. Today, let's discuss the notion that teaching kids nowadays is trickier due to their extensive engagement with video games, phone chats, and social media updates. We need to consider how these advanced technologies influence children's learning and how we can strike a balance in utilizing technology for education without causing issues.

The question is: Do you believe these new technologies make it more challenging for kids to learn? Let's delve into this and examine how modern gadgets impact their education.

Alex: Thanks, Professor. I totally think that dealing with advanced technology is a big challenge in educating kids today. Video games and constant phone use can distract them from studying. We need to figure out how these distractions affect their learning and development.

Sara: While I agree with Alex about the challenges, I also see some good sides. Instead of just thinking about the problems,

당신의 교수님께서 강의 중입니다. 교수님의 질문에 답하는 글을 쓰세요.

- 당신의 의견을 표현하고 뒷받침하세요
- 토론에 기여하세요

효과적인 답변은 최소한 100단어를 포함할 것입니다.
당신은 10분 동안 글을 작성할 수 있습니다.

할로우 교수: 안녕하세요, 여러분. 오늘은 요즘 어린이들을 가르치는 것이 비디오 게임, 핸드폰 채팅, 그리고 소셜 미디어 업데이트에 영향을 받아 더 어려워진다는 개념에 대해 이야기해봅시다. 우리는 어떻게 이러한 첨단 기술들이 어린이들의 학습에 영향을 미치는지 고려하고 교육을 위해 기술을 활용할 때 문제를 일으키지 않고 균형을 맞출 수 있는지 생각해야 합니다.

이 질문은 다음과 같습니다: 여러분은 이러한 새로운 기술들이 어린이들에게 학습이 더 어렵게 만든다고 생각하십니까? 이 문제에 대해 깊이 들어가서, 이 기술들이 어린이들의 교육에 어떻게 영향을 미치는지 살펴봅시다.

알렉스: 감사합니다. 교수님. 저는 완전히 첨단 기술과 관련된 문제를 다루는 것이 오늘날 어린이 교육에서 큰 도전이라고 생각합니다. 비디오 게임과 지속적인 핸드폰 사용은 공부에 집중하는 것을 방해할 수 있습니다. 우리는 이러한 방해가 그들의 학습과 발전에 어떤 영향을 미치는지 알아내야 합니다.

we should see how using technology in education can make learning fun for kids. Plus, the skills they learn from using gadgets can be helpful in the future.

사라: 알렉스의 도전에 동의하는 한편, 저는 몇 가지 긍정적인 면도 보고 있습니다. 문제에 대해 생각하는 대신 교육에서 기술을 사용하는 것이 어린이들에게 학습을 즐겁게 만들 수 있는 방법을 찾아보아야 합니다. 게다가, 기기 사용으로 얻는 기술은 미래에 도움이 될 수 있습니다.

어휘 extensive **adj** 광범위한 ㅣ utilize **v** 활용하다 ㅣ challenging **adj** 도전적인 ㅣ gadget **n** 도구, 장치 ㅣ constant **adj** 지속적인 ㅣ distract **v** 산만하게 하다 ㅣ examine **v** 조사하다 ㅣ figure out 해결하다 ㅣ challenge **n** 도전

예시 답변

From my perspective, both made excellent statements, but I'm on the same page as April. Simply put, students experience a positive atmosphere when participating in classes that integrate video games and online chat sessions. This is primarily because most students are significantly influenced by the atmosphere of their surroundings. The impact of the atmosphere is more crucial than they might recognize. Classes incorporating technology make students so cheerful and energetic that they like to enjoy their classes even more. A perfect example of this is my high school experience. The school used to be highly competitive and strict. However, things changed little by little after the school principal aimed to change the atmosphere. A lot of time and efforts were put into making the school curriculum better with classes that integrate engaging video games and online chat sessions. Now, current students at my school genuinely value the enjoyable atmosphere.

제 시각에서는 둘 다 훌륭한 주장을 했지만, 나는 사라와 동일한 의견을 가지고 있습니다. 간단히 말하면 학생들은 비디오 게임과 온라인 채팅 세션을 통합한 수업에 참여할 때 긍정적인 분위기를 경험합니다. 이는 대부분의 학생들이 주변 환경의 분위기에 큰 영향을 받기 때문입니다. 분위기의 영향은 그들이 인식할 것보다 훨씬 중요합니다. 기술을 통합한 수업은 학생들을 기쁘고 활기차게 만들 뿐만 아니라 수업을 더 즐겁게 만듭니다. 이와 관련된 완벽한 예시는 내가 다녔던 고등학교입니다. 학교는 이전에 매우 경쟁적이고 엄격했습니다. 그러나 학교 교장이 분위기를 변화시키기 위해 조금씩 변화를 시도한 후에 상황이 변했습니다. 학교 교육과정을 향상시키기 위해 흥미로운 비디오 게임과 온라인 채팅 세션을 통합한 수업을 도입하는 데 많은 시간과 노력이 투입되었습니다. 지금은 학교에 다니는 현재 학생들이 그 즐거운 분위기를 진심으로 감사하고 있습니다.

Part 1 Integrated Task

I. Integrated Task   Part 1. 기초 다지기

Lesson 01 노트테이킹

1. Practice
본서 P. 35

Q1

Many large companies have cafeterias where their employees can eat their lunches. This has many benefits. Employees do not have to use their break to travel to and from restaurants. Thus, they have more time to relax and enjoy their meals. Additionally, they can talk to their coworkers about non-work topics and form closer relationships.

많은 대기업들은 직원이 점심을 먹을 수 있는 구내식당을 갖추고 있다. 여기에는 많은 이점이 있다. 직원들은 식당을 찾아 왔다 갔다 하는 일에 휴식 시간을 쓸 필요가 없다. 따라서 쉬면서 식사를 즐길 시간이 더 있다. 또한, 동료들과 일이 아닌 주제에 관해 이야기하며 더 친밀한 관계를 쌓을 수도 있다.

노트

주제	company cafeteria's benefits
	1. X waste time finding restaurants → relax & enjoy meal
	2. talk to coworkers → closer relationships

회사 구내식당의 이점
1. 식당을 찾는 데 시간 낭비 X → 휴식 & 식사 즐김
2. 동료들과 이야기 → 더 친밀한 관계

PART 1 Lesson 01. 노트테이킹 **5**

어휘   cafeteria **n** 구내식당 ǀ employee **n** 직원 ǀ break **n** 휴식 시간 ǀ relax **v** 휴식을 취하다, 쉬다 ǀ additionally **adv** 추가적으로 ǀ coworker **n** 동료 ǀ relationship **n** 관계

Q2

The governments of many countries invest millions of dollars in space exploration every year. However, many editorials have been published that say this is a complete waste of money. Most people do not see any profit gained from space exploration, but they pay for it with their taxes. Not only that, but searching the galaxy for planets that are Earth-like but unreachable is a pointless exercise.

많은 나라의 정부에서 매년 우주 탐사에 수백만 달러를 투자한다. 그러나 이것이 완전히 돈 낭비라고 말하는 많은 사설들이 게재되었다. 대부분의 사람들이 우주 탐사에서 어떤 이윤도 찾지 못하고 있지만, 이를 위해 자신들의 세금으로 돈을 내고 있다. 그뿐 아니라 지구와 비슷하지만 도달할 수 없는 행성을 은하계에서 찾는 것은 무의미한 일이다.

노트

주제	invest $ on space exp. = waste of $	우주 탐사에 돈 투자 = 돈 낭비
	1. no profit gained → tax wasted	1. 얻는 것 없음 → 세금 낭비됨
	2. Earth-like planets → can't go anyway	2. 지구와 같은 행성 → 어차피 못 감

어휘   invest **v** 투자하다 ǀ exploration **n** 탐사 ǀ editorial **n** 사설 ǀ publish **v** 게재하다, 출간하다, 출판하다 ǀ complete **adj** 완전한 ǀ profit **n** 이윤 ǀ tax **n** 세금 ǀ galaxy **n** 은하계 ǀ unreachable **adj** 도달할 수 없는 ǀ pointless **adj** 무의미한, 할 가치가 없는

Q3

Many people choose to take package tours when they go on vacation, but that is not recommended. People on package tours spend most of their time crammed into tour buses, so they cannot enjoy the scenery. Moreover, when they arrive at a tourist attraction, they are hurried through the experience so they cannot really enjoy any aspect of their trip.

많은 사람들이 휴가를 갈 때 패키지여행을 선택하지만 그건 추천할 만하지 않다. 패키지여행을 하는 사람들은 관광버스에 구겨 넣어진 채 대부분의 시간을 보내기 때문에 풍경을 즐길 수가 없다. 게다가 관광지에 도착하면 서둘러서 관광해야 하기 때문에 여행의 어떤 측면도 진정 즐길 수 없다.

노트

주제	package tour → X recommend	패키지 여행 → 추천 안 함
	1. spend time in the bus → can't enjoy scenery	1. 버스에서 시간 보냄 → 경치 못 즐김
	2. tourist att. → have to hurry	2. 관광지 → 서둘러야 함

어휘   recommend **v** 추천하다 ǀ cram into ~에 쑤셔 넣다 ǀ scenery **n** 풍경 ǀ tourist attraction 관광지, 관광 명소 ǀ experience **n** 경험 ǀ aspect **n** 측면, 양상

Q4

Cities that host professional sports teams can receive two major benefits. First, the team's stadium creates hundreds of new jobs, and the ticket sales, refreshments, and team merchandise all bring in revenue to the city. Second, the team brings attention to the city, which can make it more prominent on the national level and attract sports fans and other tourists to the city.

프로 스포츠팀을 유치하는 도시들은 두 가지 중요한 이익을 얻을 수 있다. 첫 번째로, 팀의 경기장이 수백 개의 새로운 일자리를 창출하고, 티켓 판매와 간식, 팀 상품 등이 모두 도시에 수익을 가져온다. 두 번째로, 팀이 도시에 대한 관심을 불러일으켜 국가적으로 이 도시를 더 유명하게 할 것이고, 스포츠 팬들과 다른 관광객들을 도시로 끌어들일 것이다.

노트

주제	cities hosting pro. sports teams → profit	프로 스포츠팀 유치 도시 → 이익
	1. stadium → create many jobs → revenue	1. 경기장 → 많은 일자리 창출 → 수익
	2. attention to city → sports fans & tourists visit	2. 도시에 관심 → 스포츠 팬 & 관광객 방문

어휘   host **v** 주최하다, 주인 노릇을 하다 ǀ professional **adj** 프로의, 전문적인, 직업의 ǀ refreshment **n** 가벼운 음식 ǀ revenue **n** 수익 ǀ prominent **adj** 중요한, 유명한 ǀ national **adj** 국가의 ǀ attract **v** 끌다, 끌어들이다

Q5

Many cultures practice arranged marriage in the past, but that tradition has faded from much of the world. However, some studies indicate that they were more successful than love marriages. For example, the rate of divorce has only increased as arranged marriage has been abandoned. This is because the family is less involved. Moreover, love marriages are often based on passion instead of compatibility, which means that they are destined to fail while arranged marriages are more likely to last.

많은 문화가 과거에 중매 결혼을 했지만, 그 전통은 세계 많은 지역에서 점차 사라졌다. 그러나 일부 연구는 중매 결혼이 연애 결혼보다 더 성공적이었음을 보여준다. 예를 들어, 이혼율은 사람들이 중매 결혼을 그만둔 후 증가하기만 했다. 왜냐하면 가족이 덜 관여되었기 때문이다. 게다가 연애 결혼은 두 사람의 화합 대신 열정에 자주 기반하는데, 이는 중매 결혼이 오래 지속될 가능성이 높은 반면 연애 결혼은 실패할 수밖에 없다는 의미다.

> **노트**
>
> | 주제 | arranged marriage = better than love m.? | 중매 결혼 = 연애 결혼보다 낫다? |
> |---|---|---|
> | | 1. divorce ↑ after arr. m. was abandoned | 1. 중매 결혼 그만둔 후 이혼 증가 |
> | | 2. love m. = passion/arr. m. = compatibility | 2. 연애 결혼 = 열정/중매 결혼 = 화합 |

어휘 practice ⓥ 행하다, 실천하다 | arranged marriage 중매 결혼 | tradition ⓝ 전통 | fade ⓥ 사라지다 | successful ⓐⓓⓙ 성공적인 | rate of divorce 이혼율 | abandon ⓥ 그만두다, 버리다 | be involved 관계되다, 연루되다 | passion ⓝ 열정 | compatibility ⓝ 적합성, 화합성 | be destined to ~할 운명이다, ~할 수밖에 없다 | fail ⓥ 실패하다

Q6

Although fast food restaurants serve convenient, inexpensive, and tasty meals and snacks, people should not visit these establishments. Fast food poses many health risks. The menu items can cause many health problems due to their high salt and sugar content. Not only that, but they can make people overweight if they eat them too often. They contain a lot of fat and empty calories, which quickly become fat deposits in the body.

패스트푸드 식당은 편리하고 값이 싸며 맛있는 식사와 간식을 제공하지만, 사람들은 이러한 가게에 가면 안 된다. 패스트푸드는 많은 건강상의 위험을 일으킨다. 메뉴에 있는 제품들이 높은 염분과 당분 함유량 때문에 건강 문제를 야기할 수 있다. 그뿐 아니라 너무 자주 먹으면 사람들을 과체중으로 만들 수도 있다. 지방 과다에 영양 없는 빈 칼로리가 많이 들어있는데, 이것은 체내에서 금세 지방으로 축적된다.

> **노트**
>
> | 주제 | don't buy fast food = many health risks | 패스트푸드를 사면 안 됨 = 많은 건강 문제 |
> |---|---|---|
> | | 1. ↑ salt & sugar content | 1. 높은 염분 & 당분 |
> | | 2. overweight = fat & empty calories | 2. 과체중 = 지방 & 빈 칼로리 |

어휘 convenient ⓐⓓⓙ 편리한 | tasty ⓐⓓⓙ 맛있는 | establishment ⓝ 시설, 점포 | pose ⓥ 제기하다 | risk ⓝ 위험 | content ⓝ 함유량 | overweight ⓐⓓⓙ 과체중인 | contain ⓥ 함유하다, ~이 들어있다 | fat ⓝ 지방 | fat deposit 지방 축적

Q7

Although watching movies that are produced within your own culture may be easier because of shared language and ideas, watching movies from other cultures can be very rewarding. Watching a movie that is in another language requires a level of concentration that people often don't apply to movie watching. So they get more involved in the story. In addition, you may be exposed to new ideas and values that do not exist in your own culture that can enrich your understanding of the world.

자신의 문화권에서 제작된 영화를 보는 것이 공유된 언어와 생각 때문에 더 쉬워질지 몰라도, 다른 문화의 영화를 보는 것은 아주 보람 있을 수 있다. 다른 언어로 된 영화를 보는 일은 사람들이 영화를 볼 때 흔히 적용하지 않는 수준의 집중이 필요하다. 그래서 사람들은 이야기에 더 집중하게 된다. 또한, 세상을 더 풍부하게 이해할 수 있게 해주는, 자신의 문화권에는 존재하지 않는 새로운 아이디어나 가치에 노출될 수도 있다.

> **노트**
>
> | 주제 | watching movie from other cultures = rewarding | 다른 문화의 영화 보기 = 보람 있음 |
> |---|---|---|
> | | 1. another lang. = requires concentration → more involved in the story | 1. 다른 언어 = 집중이 필요함 → 이야기에 더 집중 |

| 2. exposed to new ideas & values | 2. 새로운 아이디어 & 가치에 노출됨 |

어휘 produce ☑ 제작하다 | rewarding adj 보람 있는 | require ☑ 요구하다 | concentration ⓝ 집중 | expose ☑ 노출하다 | value ⓝ 가치 | exist ☑ 존재하다 | enrich ☑ 질을 높이다, 풍요롭게 하다

Q8

Most drivers on the roads today rely on GPS navigation systems to find their way. These devices are useful, but people should not become dependent upon them for several reasons. First, people do not learn the routes that they are taking as they would if they studied a map before leaving. Not learning the route makes people rely completely on their GPS map system. Second, the devices constantly need to be updated, so people can easily become lost or have accidents if they do not question their instructions.

오늘날 주행 중인 운전자들 대부분이 길을 찾기 위해 GPS 내비게이션 시스템에 의존한다. 이 장치는 유용하지만 사람들은 몇 가지 이유에서 그것에 의존하면 안 된다. 먼저, 사람들은 출발하기 전에 지도를 살펴볼 때만큼이나 자기가 가야 하는 길을 잘 배우지 못한다. 길을 익히지 못하면 사람들은 GPS에 전적으로 의존하게 된다. 두 번째로, 장치는 지속해서 업데이트되어야 하기에 사람들이 장치의 지시에 의문을 품지 않으면 쉽게 길을 잃거나 사고가 날 수도 있다.

노트

주제	X depend on GPS navi.	내비에 의존하면 안 됨
	1. ppl do not learn the routes → rely too much on GPS	1. 사람들이 길을 익히지 못함 → GPS에 너무 의존
	2. GPS → need to be updated or lost/accident	2. GPS → 업데이트 안 하면 길을 잃거나 사고

어휘 rely on ~에 의지하다 | device ⓝ 장치 | dependent adj 의지하는 | route ⓝ 루트, 길 | completely adv 완전히 | constantly adv 계속, 지속적으로 | accident ⓝ 사고 | question ☑ 의문을 가지다 | instructions ⓝ 지시

Q9

Many lesser crimes are punished by making the person complete community service. This is an effective method because it forces the person to become involved in society instead of hiding them from it like a prison. They must work to help other people while they contemplate their own wrongdoing. Furthermore, it is much more effective than imposing a fine, since some people are happy to pay a fine and continue to break the law.

많은 경범죄는 범죄자가 지역 봉사 활동을 완수하도록 함으로써 체벌한다. 이는 감옥처럼 그 사람을 사회에서 보이지 않게 감추는 대신 사회에 관여할 수밖에 없도록 하므로 효과적인 방법이다. 이들은 스스로의 범죄를 생각하면서 다른 사람을 돕기 위해 일해야 한다. 게다가 어떤 이들은 벌금을 기꺼이 내고 계속 법을 어기기 때문에 그 방법이 벌금보다 훨씬 더 효과적이다.

노트

주제	lesser crime → punishment : comm. service = effective	경범죄 → 벌: 지역 봉사활동 = 효율적
	1. ppl get involved in society, not hiding → think about their crime	1. 숨지 않고 사회에 관여 → 자신의 범죄를 생각함
	2. better than fine – ppl just pay $ and break laws	2. 벌금보다 나음 – 사람들은 그냥 벌금을 내고 법을 어김

어휘 lesser crime 경범죄 | punish ☑ 벌을 주다 | complete ☑ 완수하다, 끝내다 | community service 지역 봉사 활동 | effective adj 효과 있는 | force ☑ 강제하다 | contemplate ☑ 숙고하다 | wrongdoing ⓝ 범법 행위, 악행 | impose ☑ 시행하다, 부과하다 | fine ⓝ 벌금

Q10

Parents often require their children to do chores around the house. Although some people question the wisdom of this practice, it actually has many benefits for the children. First of all, having children take part in chores prepares them for later in their lives when they will have to do such work alone. Also, it teaches them how to share responsibility, which will help them to interact better with roommates and coworkers when they are older.

부모들은 자주 아이들에게 집에서 심부름하게 한다. 어떤 사람들은 이 관행의 지혜를 의심하지만, 이는 아이들에게 많은 이익을 준다. 먼저, 아이들이 일에 참여하게 하는 것은 아이들이 나중에 이러한 일을 혼자 해야 할 때 준비가 되도록 해준다. 또한 책임을 공유하는 법을 가르쳐서 더 나이가 들었을 때 룸메이트, 동료와 더 잘 교류할 수 있게 도와준다.

노트

주제	children doing house chores = beneficial	아이들이 집안일을 함 = 이로움
	1. prepare children for future – when doing it alone	1. 미래를 위해 아이들을 준비 – 혼자 할 때
	2. learn how to share responsibility → interact better when older	2. 책임을 공유하는 법을 배움 → 나이가 들었을 때 더 잘 소통

어휘 require ⓥ 요구하다 l chore ⓝ 심부름, 자질구레한 일 l wisdom ⓝ 지혜 l practice ⓝ 관행 l take part in ~에 참여하다 l prepare ⓥ 준비하다 l responsibility ⓝ 책임, 책임감 l interact ⓥ 소통하다, 교류하다 l coworker ⓝ 동료

---

2. Practice
본서 P. 41

Q1

I would like to suggest hiking as a great hobby with many benefits. First, it is obviously good for people to get low-impact exercise and fresh air. In addition, walking alone or with friends in the forest is very relaxing and a great way to alleviate stress.

나는 하이킹이 많은 이점이 있는 훌륭한 취미라고 생각합니다. 먼저, 하이킹은 사람들이 충격이 적은 운동을 하고 신선한 공기를 마시는 데 분명 좋습니다. 또한 혼자 또는 친구들과 숲을 걷는 것은 마음을 아주 느긋하게 해주며, 스트레스를 완화하기에 매우 좋은 방법입니다.

노트

주제	hiking = beneficial	하이킹 = 이로움
	1. low-impact exercise & fresh air	1. 충격이 적은 운동 & 신선한 공기
	2. walking in the forest = relaxing & get rid of stress	2. 숲에서 걷기 = 휴식 & 스트레스 없애줌

어휘 obviously ⓐⓓⓥ 분명히, 명백히 l low-impact ⓐⓓⱼ 충격이 적은, 영향을 덜 미치는 l relaxing ⓐⓓⱼ 편한, 마음을 느긋하게 해주는 l alleviate ⓥ 완화하다, 덜다

Q2

As you read, some people think that a universal minimum wage is a good idea, but I think it would do much more harm than good. Many people would rather not work at all if they would still get paid. It would also take money away from other important government programs.

읽은 것처럼 어떤 사람들은 보편적인 최저 시급이 좋은 생각이라고 생각하지만, 나는 장점보다는 단점이 더 많다고 생각해요. 많은 사람들이 여전히 돈을 받게 된다면 일을 하지 않으려 할 것입니다. 이는 또한 다른 중요한 정부 프로그램을 위한 자금을 빼앗을 거예요.

노트

주제	universal min. wage = bad idea	보편적 최저 시급 = 안 좋은 생각
	1. ppl X work – still get paid	1. 사람들이 일을 안 함 – 여전히 돈 받음
	2. take $ from other import. gov't programs	2. 정부의 다른 중요한 프로그램을 위한 돈을 빼앗음

어휘 universal ⓐⓓⱼ 보편적인 l minimum wage 최저 시급

Q3

Some professors like to give their students essays to write at home as their final exam, but I don't think that is a good idea. First, it allows the students to do all of their research on one day instead of studying like they should. Second, an exam is supposed to make the students perform under pressure, and writing an essay at home does not give students that kind of pressure at all.

일부 교수들은 기말시험으로 학생들이 집에서 리포트를 써 오게 하는 것을 좋아하지만 나는 그것이 좋은 생각이라고 보지 않아요. 먼저, 이는 학생들이 해야만 하는 공부를 하게 하는 대신 하루에 자료 조사를 전부 하게 만듭니다. 두 번째로, 시험은 학생들이 중압감을 느끼면서 치러야 하는 것이며, 집에서 리포트 쓰는 학생들에게 그러한 압박을 전혀 주지 않습니다.

노트

주제	essay @ home = final exam → bad idea	집에서 리포트 = 기말시험 → 안 좋은 생각
	1. do all research on one day – X study	1. 하루 만에 자료 조사 – 공부 안 함
	2. exam = should perform under pressure	2. 시험 = 중압감을 느끼며 치러야 함

어휘 be supposed to ~해야 하다, ~하기로 되어있다 I perform **v** 해내다, 실시하다 I pressure **n** 압박

Q4

Now, I believe that doctor residency programs are valuable, but they need to be restructured. First, the residents are required to work very long shifts that make mistakes much more likely. Second, the extreme stress of working in that environment can permanently damage their health.

나는 의사 레지던트 프로그램이 가치 있다고 믿지만, 그 프로그램은 개혁해야 합니다. 먼저, 레지던트들은 교대 근무 시간이 매우 길어 실수할 가능성이 훨씬 커집니다. 둘째로, 그런 환경에서 일하는 극한의 스트레스가 그들의 건강을 영구적으로 해칠 수 있습니다.

노트

주제	doctor resi. program → restructure	의사 레지던트 프로그램 → 개혁
	1. long shift → chance of mistakes ↑	1. 긴 근무 시간 → 실수 가능성 높아짐
	2. extreme stress → permanent health damage	2. 극한의 스트레스 → 영구적인 건강 손상

어휘 residency program (의사) 레지던트 프로그램 I restructure **v** 개혁하다, 구조를 조정하다 I shift **n** 교대 근무 시간 I extreme **adj** 극단적인 I permanently **adv** 영구적으로 I damage **v** 손상을 입히다

Q5

Even though many people believe that the world is overpopulated, this is not the case for the following reasons. First, the world's natural resources will be sufficient for the current population since people are putting more efforts into sharing them properly. Second, although the populations of some nations are increasing, many others are actually shrinking.

많은 사람이 세계가 인구 과잉이라고 믿지만, 그것은 다음의 이유로 사실이 아닙니다. 먼저, 세계의 천연자원은 사람들이 자원을 적절히 공유하기 위해 더 많은 노력을 하고 있으므로 현재의 인구에 충분할 겁니다. 두 번째로, 일부 국가의 인구가 늘고 있기는 하지만 다른 많은 나라들의 인구는 사실 줄고 있습니다.

노트

주제	world = overpopulated? No	세계 = 인구 과잉? 아니다
	1. natural resources: sufficient if shared properly	1. 천연자원: 제대로 공유하면 충분함
	2. many nations' pop. ↓	2. 많은 나라의 인구가 줄어듦

어휘 overpopulated **adj** 인구 과잉의 I natural resource 천연자원 I sufficient **adj** 충분한 I population **n** 인구 I properly **adv** 적절히 I shrink **v** 줄어들다

Q6

Despite their popularity, ride sharing services are not a great idea. For one thing, the services cannot do thorough background checks on the drivers that want to participate, so it can be dangerous for the passengers. For another thing, the drivers themselves are not paid much, so they tend to be very picky about where they will drive.

그 인기에도 불구하고 차량 공유 서비스는 좋은 생각이 아닙니다. 한 이유로, 이 서비스는 참여하고 싶어 하는 운전자의 신원 조회를 철저하게 할 수 없기 때문에 승객에게 위험할 수도 있어요. 다른 이유로, 운전자들이 돈을 많이 받지 못하기 때문에, 목적지에 관해 아주 까다로운 경향이 있습니다.

노트

주제	ride sharing service = not good	차량 공유 서비스 = 안 좋음
	1. backgr. check X sufficient = dangerous	1. 신원 조회 불충분 = 위험

2. drivers X paid much → picky about location

2. 운전자들 돈 많이 못 받음 → 목적지에 대해 까다로움

어휘   popularity ⓝ 인기 I ride sharing service 탈것(차량) 공유 서비스 I thorough 【adj】 철저한 I background check 신원 조사 I participate 【v】 참여하다, 참가하다 I passenger ⓝ 승객 I picky 【adj】 까다로운

Q7

So, today, let's examine the positive aspects of joining a tutoring program. For one, it allows you to help other students by sharing your knowledge and experience. For another, it also requires you to revisit topics from earlier in your university career that you might need a refresher on.

그럼, 오늘은 개인 교습 프로그램 참여의 긍정적인 면을 살펴봅시다. 한 가지 면은 자신의 지식과 경험을 공유하여 다른 학생들을 돕게 해준다는 것입니다. 또 다른 면은 다시 상기해야 할 필요가 있을지 모르는, 대학에서 이전에 배웠던 주제들을 다시 볼 수밖에 없도록 합니다.

노트

주제	tutoring program = positive	개인 교습 프로그램 = 긍정적
	1. help others = share knowledge & exp.	1. 다른 이들을 도움 = 지식 & 경험 공유
	2. revisit topics that need a refresher on	2. 상기해야 하는 주제 다시 보기

어휘   examine 【v】 살펴보다, 관찰하다 I positive 【adj】 긍정적인 I join 【v】 참가하다, 참여하다 I knowledge ⓝ 지식 I experience ⓝ 경험 I revisit 【v】 다시 방문하다 I refresher ⓝ 환기시키는 것

Q8

Now, I know that many students prefer true or false questions because they are very simple. But that is exactly why they are not a good way to evaluate a student's knowledge. First of all, a student can simply guess at the answer and they still have a 50% chance of being correct. In addition, they rarely test a student's understanding of the course material, which is the point of a test.

옳고 그름 문제가 아주 간단하기 때문에 많은 학생들이 이 문제를 선호한다는 것을 알고 있습니다. 하지만 바로 그래서 그런 문제가 학생의 지식을 평가하기에 좋지 않은 거예요. 먼저, 학생은 그냥 답을 찍기만 해도 맞힐 가능성이 50%나 됩니다. 게다가 이 문제들은 수업 내용에 관한 학생의 이해도를 시험할 때가 드문데, 그게 바로 시험의 목적이죠.

노트

주제	T/F q. = X evaluate student knowledge	옳고 그름 문제 = 학생의 지식을 평가하지 못함
	1. can guess = 50% chance	1. 찍기 가능 = 50% 가능성
	2. can't really test understanding of course m.	2. 수업 내용에 대한 이해도를 제대로 시험할 수 없음

어휘   exactly 【adv】 정확히 I evaluate 【v】 평가하다 I knowledge ⓝ 지식 I correct 【adj】 옳은, 맞는 I rarely 【adv】 거의 ~하지 않는, 드물게

Q9

I am sure that some of you will disagree, but I think that the voting age should be kept at 18. First, it should not be raised because the voting age and the age to serve in the military are the same. If 18 is old enough to serve in the military, then those people should be allowed to vote. Second, it should not be lowered because high school students are too immature to understand the issues during elections.

여러분 일부는 분명 동의하지 않겠지만, 투표 연령은 18세로 유지해야 한다고 생각합니다. 먼저, 투표 연령과 군 복무 연령이 같기 때문에 나이를 올려서는 안 됩니다. 만약 18세가 군에 복무하기에 충분한 나이라면 이 사람들은 투표도 할 수 있어야 해요. 두 번째로, 고등학생들은 선거에서 다루는 문제들을 이해하기에 너무 미성숙하기 때문에 낮춰서는 안 됩니다.

노트

주제	keep voting age at 18	투표 연령을 18세로 유지하기
	1. ↑X: 18 old enough to serve military	1. 높이면 안 됨: 18세는 군에 복무하기에 충분한 나이
	2. ↓X: high school stu. too immature	2. 낮추면 안 됨: 고등학생은 너무 미성숙함

어휘 voting age 투표 연령 | raise ▣ 높이다, 올리다 | valid ▣ 유효한, 정당한 | serve in the military 군복무하다 | lower ▣ 낮추다 | immature ▣ 미성숙한 | election ▣ 선거

Q10

As I am sure you have noticed, we live in a society where antibacterial products are commonplace. However, this practice has many negative results. Firstly, if people are not exposed to diseases, they cannot build up natural immunity. So the diseases will always be a threat. Second and more importantly, bacteria are very adaptable, so attacking them with such chemicals unnecessarily allows them to build up a defense.

여러분도 알아차렸겠지만, 우리는 항균 제품이 흔한 사회에 살고 있습니다. 그러나 이런 관행은 많은 부정적 결과를 야기해요. 첫째, 만약 사람들이 질병에 노출되지 않으면 자연 면역을 키울 수가 없습니다. 그래서 질병은 항상 위험이 될 거예요. 두 번째로 더 중요한 점이 있다면, 박테리아가 아주 적응을 잘하므로 그런 화학 물질로 박테리아를 불필요하게 공격하면 그들이 방어 체계를 구축하게 될 겁니다.

노트

주제	antibacterial use → negative result	항균 제품 사용 → 부정적 결과
	1. X exposed to disease → X natural immunity	1. 병에 노출 안 됨 → 자연 면역 없음
	2. bacteria = adapt & build up a defense	2. 박테리아 = 적응하고 방어 체계 구축함

어휘 notice ▣ 알아차리다 | antibacterial ▣ 항균성의 | product ▣ 제품 | commonplace ▣ 흔한 | practice ▣ 관행 | negative ▣ 부정적인 | expose ▣ 노출하다 | disease ▣ 질병 | natural immunity 자연 면역 | threat ▣ 위협 | adaptable ▣ 적응할 수 있는 | attack ▣ 공격하다 | chemical ▣ 화학 물질 | unnecessarily ▣ 불필요하게 | defense ▣ 방어

Lesson 02 요약하기

1. Practice

본서 P. 49

Q1

Many people like to drink soft drinks with their meals instead of water. Unfortunately, this is bad for your health in a number of ways. For example, soft drinks contain a lot of sugar and they are very acidic, which means that they can damage your teeth. On top of that, they offer nothing good to your body. They contain very few nutrients so the calories they provide are basically empty. Unneeded calories often lead to weight gain.

많은 사람들이 식사할 때 물 대신 청량음료를 마시는 걸 좋아한다. 안타깝게도 이는 많은 이유에서 건강에 좋지 않다. 예를 들어, 청량음료는 당이 많이 함유되어 있고 산성이 강해 치아에 손상을 입힐 수 있다. 게다가 몸에 좋은 점이 하나도 없다. 영양가는 거의 없어서 이들이 제공하는 칼로리는 기본적으로 빈 칼로리이다. 불필요한 칼로리는 흔히 체중 증가로 이어진다.

노트

주제	soft drinks → bad for health	청량음료 → 건강에 나쁨
	1. sugar and acid → damage teeth	1. 당분과 산성 → 치아 손상
	2. nutrition X/empty calories → gain weight	2. 영양가 없음/빈 칼로리 → 체중 증가

Q. According to the passage, why is drinking soft drinks not recommended?

지문에 따르면, 청량음료를 마시는 것은 왜 권고되지 않는가?

First, soft drinks are bad for your health because they are full of sugar and acid. They can damage your teeth. In addition, they contain very little nutrition and are mostly empty calories that can make people gain weight if they regularly drink them.

먼저, 청량음료는 당과 산 성분으로 가득해서 건강에 나쁘다. 치아에 손상을 입힐 수 있다. 그리고 영양분은 거의 함유하고 있지 않고 대부분 빈 칼로리라 자주 마시면 살이 찌게 한다.

어휘 soft drink 청량음료 | unfortunately ▣ 안타깝게도 | a number of 많은 | contain ▣ 함유하다, 포함하다, ~가 들어있다 | sugar ▣ 설탕, 당 | acidic ▣ 산성의 | damage ▣ 손상을 입히다 | on top of that 게다가, 그뿐 아니라 | nutrient ▣ 영양분 | basically ▣ 기본적으로 | unneeded ▣ 불필요한 | weight ▣ 체중 | gain ▣ 증가 ▣ 늘리다

Q2

Avocados are unique fruit that provides many health benefits. One, it is very nutritious and contains important vitamins like B, C, E, and potassium. In addition, avocados are also a rich source of monounsaturated fat, which is very good for the heart and arterial health.

아보카도는 많은 건강상의 이점을 제공하는 독특한 과일이다. 한 가지 이점으로 이 과일은 영양분이 아주 많으며 비타민 B, C, E 같은 중요 비타민과 칼륨을 함유하고 있다. 게다가, 아보카도는 불포화 지방도 많이 함유하고 있는데, 이는 심장과 동맥 건강에 아주 좋다.

노트

주제	avocado – benefits	아보카도 – 이점
	1. important vitamins & potassium	1. 중요한 비타민 & 칼륨
	2. fat = good for heart	2. 지방 = 심장에 좋음

Q. According to the passage, how are avocados beneficial?

지문에 따르면, 아보카도는 어떻게 이로운가?

Avocados are very nutritious and contain many important vitamins. Also, they contain a lot of fat that is good for the heart.

아보카도는 영양분이 아주 많으며 중요한 비타민을 많이 함유하고 있다. 또한, 심장에 좋은 지방이 많이 들어 있다.

어휘　unique adj 독특한 | nutritious adj 영양가가 있는 | potassium n 칼륨 | monounsaturated fat 불포화 지방 | arterial adj 동맥의

Q3

It is a widely held belief that children who begin studying foreign languages early in their life generally reach and maintain a higher level of fluency. Research has proven this idea to be correct for a few reasons. Children appear to have a preexisting mental ability to understand and use grammar easily. Second, they constantly mimic the speech of others, which allows them to adopt new words freely.

조기에 외국어를 공부하기 시작하는 아이들은 일반적으로 더 높은 수준의 유창함에 도달하고 유지한다는, 널리 퍼진 믿음이 있다. 연구는 이 생각이 몇 가지 이유로 옳다고 증명했다. 아이들은 쉽게 문법을 이해하고 사용하는 기존의 정신적 능력을 갖춘 것으로 보인다. 두 번째로, 아이들은 다른 사람들의 말을 계속 따라 하며, 이는 새로운 단어를 자유롭게 쓰게 해 준다.

노트

주제	study foreign language early – high level	일찍 외국어 공부 – 높은 수준
	1. innate ability to learn grammar	1. 선천적인 문법 학습 능력
	2. repeat what others say	2. 다른 사람들이 하는 말 반복

Q. According to the passage, why does starting to learn languages early in life allow people to become more fluent?

지문에 따르면, 일찍 언어 공부를 시작하는 것은 왜 사람들을 더 유창하게 만드는가?

First, children have an innate ability to learn grammar. Second, they repeat what they hear others say.

먼저, 아이들은 선천적인 문법 학습 능력을 갖고 있다. 두 번째로, 아이들은 다른 사람들이 하는 말을 듣고 반복한다.

어휘　generally adv 일반적으로 | fluency n 유창함 | correct adj 옳은 | pre-existing adj 이미 존재하는 | grammar n 문법 | constantly adv 계속, 지속적으로 | mimic v 흉내 내다, 따라 하다 | adopt v 쓰다, 취하다, 채택하다

Q4

Sleep is very beneficial for people's health. First of all, it provides the body with down time to relax and repair itself. That is why sleep is an important part of recovering from an illness. On top of that, it also gives the brain time to process new information and create new mental pathways. This is what happens during dreaming.

잠은 사람의 건강에 매우 이롭다. 먼저, 몸이 쉬고 치유할 휴식 시간을 준다. 그래서 잠은 병에서 회복하는 데 중요한 부분이다. 또한, 잠은 뇌가 새 정보를 처리하고 새로운 정신 경로를 만들 시간을 준다. 이것이 꿈을 꾸는 동안 일어나는 일이다.

Q. According to the passage, what are the benefits of sleeping? ┊ 지문에 따르면, 잠의 이점은 무엇인가?

Sleep helps your body to relax and repair itself. It helps you to recover when you are sick. In addition, dreaming helps your mind to deal with new data.

잠은 몸이 쉬고 자신을 보수하는 것을 돕는다. 아플 때 회복하는 것을 돕는다. 그리고 꿈은 정신이 새로운 정보를 처리하는 것을 돕는다.

어휘 beneficial **adj** 이익이 되는 I down time 휴식 시간 I relax **v** 쉬다 I repair **v** 회복하다, 치료하다 I recover **v** 회복하다 I illness **n** 병 I process **v** 처리하다 I pathway **n** 진로, 경로

Q5

Most school districts rely upon standardized tests to determine what level of academic achievement students have reached. Unfortunately, these tests are flawed for a number of reasons. One is that such tests only measure a small part of cognitive abilities. Another is that some people cannot perform well when tested in this way. Therefore, standardized tests are not a viable way to assess achievement.

대부분의 학군은 학생들이 어떤 수준의 학문적 성과에 도달했는지 알아내기 위해 표준화된 시험에 의존한다. 안타깝게도, 이 시험들은 몇 가지 이유로 결함이 있다. 하나는 이 시험들이 인지 능력의 작은 부분만을 측정한다는 점이다. 또 다른 점은 일부 사람들은 이런 방식으로 시험을 보면 능력을 잘 발휘할 수가 없다는 점이다. 따라서 표준화된 시험은 성과를 평가하기에 실용적인 방법이 아니다.

Q. According to the passage, why are standardized tests flawed? ┊ 지문에 따르면, 표준화된 시험은 왜 결함이 있는가?

For one thing, standardized tests only test a small part of mental ability. For another thing, they do not account for people who are bad at test taking. Hence, they are not a good way to assess academic achievement.

우선, 표준화된 시험은 인지 능력의 작은 부분만 시험할 뿐이다. 또한, 시험을 잘 못 보는 사람들을 설명해주지 못한다. 따라서, 학업 성과를 평가하기에 좋은 방법이 아니다.

어휘 school district 학군 I standardized **adj** 표준화된 I determine **v** 알아내다 I academic **adj** 학문적인 I achievement **n** 성취, 달성 I unfortunately **adv** 불행히도 I flawed **adj** 결함이 있는 I measure **v** 측정하다 I cognitive **adj** 인지의 I viable **adj** 실행 가능한, 실용적인 I assess **v** 평가하다

Q6

Although many students and parents question whether playing team sports at school is necessary, it actually has many benefits for children. Obviously, playing sports provides students with regular exercise, which is important for their health. Team sports also require them to work together toward a common goal. This is a skill that will be very valuable to them throughout their lives.

많은 학생과 부모가 학교에서 팀 스포츠를 하는 것이 필요한지 아닌지에 대해 의문을 품지만, 사실 이는 아이들에게 많은 이점을 준다. 분명, 스포츠를 하면 규칙적으로 운동을 하게 되는데, 이는 건강에 중요하다. 팀 스포츠는 또한 공통된 목표를 향해 학생들이 함께 노력하게 한다. 이는 살아가는 동안 무척 소중히 여기게 될 능력이다.

1. make students exercise 2. work together → achieve tasks = life skill	1. 학생들이 운동하게 함 2. 함께 노력함 → 목표 이룸 = 삶의 기술

Q. According to the passage, why should students be required to play team sports at school?

지문에 따르면, 왜 학생들은 학교에서 팀 스포츠를 해야 하는가?

First, playing team sports regularly makes students exercise. Second, it forces them to work together with people they don't know well to achieve a task. This is a life skill that they need.

첫 번째로, 팀 스포츠를 규칙적으로 하면 학생들은 운동하게 된다. 두 번째로, 이것은 학생들이 과업을 달성하기 위해 잘 모르는 사람들과 협력하게 한다. 이는 학생들에게 필요한 삶의 기술이다.

어휘 question ⓥ 의문을 갖다 | obviously adv 분명히, 확실히 | regular adj 정기적인, 규칙적인 | common adj 공통의 | valuable adj 가치 있는 | throughout prep 쭉, 내내

Q7

One of the methods suggested for controlling global warming is to plant entire forests of trees. This has many advantages for people and the planet. As most people know, trees take in carbon dioxide and release oxygen. This reduces CO_2 levels in the atmosphere, and CO_2 is an important greenhouse gas. What people may not realize is that they also pull water out of the ground and release it through their leaves as water vapor. This can form into low level clouds that block the Sun's rays.

지구 온난화 통제를 위해 제안된 방법들 중 하나는 나무로 가득한 숲을 조성하는 것이다. 이는 사람과 지구에 많은 이점을 준다. 대부분의 사람들이 알고 있듯 나무는 이산화탄소를 흡수하고 산소를 내뿜는다. 이는 중요한 온실가스인 이산화탄소의 대기 중 농도를 줄인다. 사람들이 깨닫지 못할지도 모르는 점은 나무가 땅에서 물을 끌어올려 잎을 통해 수증기로 내보낸다는 것이다. 이는 태양 광선을 막아주는 하층운을 형성할 수 있다.

노트

주제 control global w. → plant trees
   1. CO_2(greenhouse gas) out
   2. draw water out of ground → release into air → cloud
      → block Sun's rays
	지구 온난화 통제 → 나무 심기
	1. 이산화탄소(온실가스) 줄임
	2. 땅에서 물 끌어올림 → 대기로 내보냄 → 구름
	   → 태양 광선 차단

Q. According to the passage, how does planting trees help fight global warming?

지문에 따르면, 나무를 심는 것은 어떻게 지구 온난화를 막는데 도움을 주는가?

First, trees pull CO_2 out of the air, and it is a major greenhouse gas. Next, they draw water out of the ground and release it into the air to form clouds and block the Sun's rays. Both of these actions can help control global warming.

먼저, 나무는 이산화탄소를 대기에서 끌어내는데, 이는 주된 온실가스이다. 다음으로, 나무는 땅에서 물을 끌어올려 대기로 내뿜고 구름을 만들어 태양 광선을 막는다. 이 두 활동은 지구 온난화를 통제하는 데 도움을 줄 수 있다.

어휘 global warming 지구 온난화 | entire adj 전체의 | carbon dioxide 이산화탄소 | release ⓥ 방출하다 | reduce ⓥ 줄이다, 감소시키다 | atmosphere ⓝ 대기 | realize ⓥ 깨닫다 | pull ⓥ 끌어당기다 | water vapor 수증기 | ray ⓝ 광선

Q8

In many countries, students do not have to pay tuition to attend university. This system has many advantages for both students and society. On the one hand, charging tuition makes it impossible for many qualified students to attend university. Placing a financial barrier in front of students promotes inequality in society. On the other hand, having a well educated population makes society function better as a whole. Therefore, making university free apart from fees would make society better.

많은 나라에서 학생은 대학을 다니기 위해 등록금을 낼 필요가 없다. 이 시스템은 학생과 사회 둘 다에 많은 이점을 준다. 한편으로 등록금 부과는 자격 있는 많은 학생들이 대학에 다니는 것을 불가능하게 한다. 학생 앞에 경제적 장벽을 치는 것은 사회에서 불평등을 부추긴다. 다른 한편으로, 교육을 잘 받은 인구가 있으면 사회는 전체적으로 더 잘 기능하게 된다. 따라서 입학금 외에 대학을 무상으로 하는 것은 사회를 더 낫게 만들어줄 것이다.

노트

주제	no tuition for univ. → beneficial	대학 등록금 안 냄 → 이로움
	1. tuition prevent qualified stud. from attending univ. = unequal society	1. 등록금은 자격 있는 학생이 대학에 다니는 것을 막음 = 불평등한 사회
	2. educated pop. = stronger society	2. 교육받은 인구 = 더 강한 사회

Q. According to the passage, why should universities not charge tuition?

지문에 따르면, 왜 대학들은 등록금을 부과해서는 안 되는가?

First, charging students tuition prevents many qualified students from attending university, which makes society more unequal. Second, an educated population makes society stronger.

첫 번째로, 학생들에게 등록금을 받는 것은 많은 자격 있는 학생들이 대학에 다니는 것을 막으며 이는 사회를 더 불평등하게 만든다. 두 번째로, 교육을 받은 인구는 사회를 더 강하게 만든다.

어휘 tuition n 등록금 | attend v (학교 등에) 다니다 | charge v 요금을 부과하다 | qualified adj 자격을 갖춘 | financial adj 재정적인 | barrier n 장벽 | promote v 장려하다 | population n 인구 | function v 기능하다

Q9

In general, teachers in the United States are not paid well, and this needs to change for many reasons. For one thing, paying teachers a low salary reduces their motivation to teach, which means that their students are not getting the best education possible. For another thing, a low salary forces teachers with families to take on additional work to pay their bills. This causes a lot of stress that can damage both their physical and mental health.

일반적으로, 미국의 교사들은 급여를 많이 받지 못하며 이는 많은 이유에서 바뀌어야 한다. 한 가지 이유로는, 교사들에게 낮은 급여를 주는 것은 이들이 가르칠 열의를 떨어뜨리는데, 이는 학생들이 가능한 한 최고의 교육을 받지 못할 것이라는 의미다. 다른 이유로는, 낮은 급여는 가족이 있는 교사들이 공과금을 내기 위해 추가로 일을 하게 만든다. 이는 교사의 신체적, 정신적 건강 둘 다 피해를 입히는 큰 스트레스를 야기한다.

노트

주제	teachers not paid well → change	교사들이 급여를 많이 못 받음 → 바뀌어야 함
	1. small salary = motivation ↓	1. 적은 봉급 = 열의 떨어짐
	2. get other jobs → stress level ↑	2. 다른 일을 함 → 스트레스 높아짐

Q. According to the passage, why should teachers in the Unites States receive more pay?

지문에 따르면, 왜 미국의 교사들은 더 많은 봉급을 받아야 하는가?

First, getting paid a small salary for difficult work lowers teachers' motivation to work. Second, teachers often have to get other jobs, which increases their stress levels.

먼저, 어려운 일에 대해 적은 봉급을 받는 것은 일하고자 하는 교사들의 열의를 떨어뜨린다. 두 번째로, 교사들은 자주 다른 일을 추가로 해야 하고 이는 이들의 스트레스 수치를 높인다.

어휘 salary n 급여, 봉급 | motivation n 열의, 동기 부여 | additional adj 추가의, 부가적인 | bill n 요금, 고지서 | damage v 피해를 입히다 | physical adj 신체적인, 물리적인 | mental adj 정신적인

Q10

Many people say that people should become vegetarians because it is better for the environment and people's health. However, there are many disadvantages to such a diet. First, some vegetarian alternative foods like almond milk require huge amounts of water, which can harm the environment. Second, many nutrients that are easily gotten from animal products

많은 사람들은 채식주의자가 되는 것이 환경과 건강에 더 좋기 때문에 채식주의자가 되어야 한다고 한다. 그러나 그런 식습관에는 많은 단점이 있다. 먼저, 아몬드 우유 같은 채식주의용 대체 식품은 엄청나게 많은 물을 필요로 하며 이는 환경을 해칠 수 있다. 두 번째로, 동물성 제품에서 쉽게 얻을 수 있는 많은 영양분은 식물에서 얻기 어렵기에

are difficult to get from plants, so people are forced to take supplements to stay healthy.

사 람들은 건강을 유지하기 위해 억지로 보충제를 먹어야 한다.

| 노트 |

주제	vegetarian diet = beneficial?
	1. neg. affect on envi.
	2. X nutrients like animal products → have to take pills

채식 식습관 = 이로움?
1. 환경에 부정적 영향
2. 동물성 제품과 같은 영양분 X → 보충제를 먹어야 함

Q. According to the passage, what are the disadvantages of a vegetarian diet?

지문에 따르면, 채식주의 식습관의 단점은 무엇인가?

Firstly, vegetarians eat many alternative foods that can negatively affect the environment. Secondly, the diet does not provide many nutrients that animal products do, so people have to take pills.

먼저, 채식주의자들은 환경에 부정적인 영향을 줄 수 있는 많은 대체 식품들을 먹는다. 두 번째로, 이 식습관은 동물성 제품이 주는 많은 영양분을 제공하지 않아서 사람들은 보충제를 먹어야 한다.

어휘 vegetarian **n** 채식주의자 **adj** 채식주의의, 채식의 ㅣ environment **n** 환경 ㅣ diet **n** 식습관, 식생활 ㅣ alternative **adj** 대안의, 대체의 ㅣ harm **v** 해치다, 손상을 입히다 ㅣ nutrient **n** 영양분 ㅣ supplement **n** 보충제

2. Practice

Q1

Let's take a critical look at pet ownership. Many people talk about the advantages this can have for people, but it has many disadvantages for the animals themselves. People buy pets to keep them company at home, but that often means that the animals spend most of the day alone. Loneliness can affect animals, too. People also say that owning pets teaches responsibility, but people often do the bare minimum to take care of their pets. Feeding and cleaning up after an animal is important, but they need exercise and socialization as well.

반려동물 소유를 비판적인 시각으로 봅시다. 많은 사람들이 이것이 사람에게 주는 이점에 관해 이야기하지만, 사실 동물에게는 단점이 많아요. 사람들은 집에서 함께하기 위해 반려동물을 구입하지만, 그것은 그 동물들이 거의 온종일 혼자 보내야 한다는 뜻일 때가 많습니다. 외로움은 동물들에게도 영향을 줄 수 있어요. 사람들은 또한 반려동물을 소유하는 것이 책임감을 가르쳐준다고 하지만 사람들은 반려동물을 돌보는 데 가장 기본적인 최소한의 일만 하는 경우가 많습니다. 동물에게 먹이를 주고 용변을 치워주는 것도 중요하지만 동물은 운동과 사회화 또한 필요로 해요.

| 노트 |

주제	pet ownership = bad for pets
	1. alone most of the day → lonely
	2. ppl don't do much → pets don't get things they need

반려동물 소유 = 반려동물에게 나쁨
1. 거의 온종일 혼자 있음 → 외로움
2. 사람들이 많은 일을 안 함 → 반려동물이 필요한 것을 얻지 못함

Q. According to the passage, why is pet ownership bad for the pets themselves?

지문에 따르면, 왜 반려동물 소유는 반려동물에게 나쁜가?

First, the pets are often left alone most of the day, which makes them feel lonely. Next, people don't do much to take care of their animals, so pets don't get things that they need.

첫 번째로, 반려동물은 거의 온종일 혼자 남겨질 때가 많아서 외롭다. 다음으로, 사람들은 동물을 돌보기 위해 그다지 많은 일을 하지 않아서 반려동물은 필요한 것을 얻지 못한다.

어휘 critical **adj** 비판적인 ㅣ ownership **n** 소유 ㅣ company **n** 동반자, 벗 ㅣ loneliness **n** 외로움 ㅣ affect **v** 영향을 주다 ㅣ responsibility **n** 책임, 책임감 ㅣ bare **adj** 가장 기본적인 ㅣ minimum **n** 최소 한도 ㅣ feed **v** 먹이를 주다 ㅣ socialization **n** 사회화

PART 1 Lesson 02. 요약하기 17

Q2

I want to address a common misconception about catching colds. Many people think that being exposed to cold, wet weather can make you sick, but that is only an indirect factor. The common cold is caused by a virus, so weather does not cause the illness. However, such weather does weaken the immune system, which makes it easier for a virus to infect a person. In addition, the cold virus is passed between people quite easily, and cold weather often makes people stay inside. The more people you have in an enclosed space, the easier it is to spread disease.

저는 감기에 걸리는 것과 관련된 흔한 오해를 짚어 보려고 합니다. 많은 사람들이 춥고 습한 날씨에 노출되는 것이 사람을 병들게 한다고 생각하지만, 이는 간접 요인에 불과해요. 평범한 감기는 바이러스 때문에 야기되는 것이라 날씨가 병을 불러오진 않습니다. 하지만 이러한 날씨가 면역 체계를 약화시켜 바이러스에 더 쉽게 감염되게 하죠. 또한, 감기 바이러스는 사람들 사이에서 쉽게 전염되고, 추운 날씨는 사람들이 자주 실내에 머물도록 합니다. 닫힌 공간에 사람이 더 많을수록 질병이 퍼지기는 더 쉽죠.

노트

주제	cold weather & catching cold	추운 날씨 & 감기 걸림
	1. weaken immune system → easy to get sick	1. 면역력 약화 → 병들기 쉬워짐
	2. ppl stay inside w. others → easy to catch cold	2. 사람들이 다른 이들과 실내에 있음 → 감기 걸리기 쉬워짐

Q. According to the passage, how does cold weather indirectly make people sick?

지문에 따르면, 추운 날씨는 간접적으로 어떻게 사람들을 아프게 만드는가?

First, cold weather can weaken your immune system, which makes it easier to get sick. Second, it makes people stay inside with other people, making it easier to catch a cold.

첫 번째로, 추운 날씨는 면역 체계를 약화시킬 수 있는데, 그러면 병들기 쉬워진다. 두 번째로, 사람들이 다른 사람과 실내에 있게 하므로 감기에 걸리기 더 쉬워진다.

어휘 address v 다루다, 이야기하다 | common adj 흔한, 평범한 | misconception n 오해, 잘못된 생각 | catch (a) cold 감기에 걸리다 | expose v 노출하다 | indirect adj 간접적인 | weaken v 약화시키다 | immune system 면역 체계 | infect v 감염시키다 | enclosed adj 닫힌 | disease n 질병

Q3

The Internet may have its drawbacks, but its intended purposes far outweigh any negative aspects. First, it facilitates communication in a way that no other method can rival. It allows people to send a message to anyone with Internet access anywhere in the world at any time. Furthermore, it allows people to access information quickly and easily. Before it existed, one had to talk to an expert or go to a library.

인터넷은 단점이 있을 수도 있지만, 겨냥하는 목표는 모든 부정적인 면보다 더 큽니다. 먼저, 인터넷은 그 어떤 방법도 필적할 수 없는 방식으로 소통을 가능하게 해요. 언제든, 세계 어느 곳에 있든 인터넷 접속이 가능한 누구에게나 메시지를 보낼 수 있게 해 줍니다. 게다가, 사람들이 정보를 빠르고 쉽게 이용할 수 있게 해요. 인터넷이 존재하기 전에 사람들은 전문가와 이야기하거나 도서관에 가야만 했습니다.

노트

주제	Internet's benefits	인터넷의 이점
	1. communicate w/o restrictions & limit	1. 제한 & 한계 없이 소통
	2. access info quickly & easily	2. 빠르고 쉽게 정보를 얻음

Q. According to the passage, what are the benefits of the Internet?

지문에 따르면, 인터넷의 이점은 무엇인가?

First, it allows people to communicate without restrictions. Second, it allows people to access information quickly and easily.

먼저, 인터넷은 사람들이 제한 없이 소통하게 해준다. 두 번째로, 사람들이 정보를 빠르고 쉽게 얻도록 해준다.

어휘 drawback n 단점 | intended adj 의도된 | purpose n 목적 | outweigh v ~보다 더 크다 | negative adj 부정적인 | facilitate v 가능하게 하다, 용이하게 하다 | rival v 필적하다, 경쟁하다 | instantly adv 즉시 | furthermore adv 뿐만 아니라, 더욱이 | exist v 존재하다 | expert n 전문가

Q4

Now, many people believe that boys and girls benefit from attending single-sex schools, but the actual data does not back up this claim. Research has shown that students that attend single-sex schools do not perform any better on tests than their counterparts at regular schools. Not only that, but the researchers stated that the children who attend co-ed schools are much better at socializing with members of the other gender. So, single-sex schools may actually be hindering their social development.

많은 사람들이 남자와 여자가 한쪽의 성만으로 구성된 학교에 다니면 이점이 있다고 믿지만, 실제 자료는 이 주장을 뒷받침하지 않습니다. 연구자들은 공학이 아닌 학교에 다니는 학생들이 일반 학교에 다니는 상대편 학생들보다 시험 결과가 더 좋은 건 아니라는 점을 보여주었습니다. 그뿐 아니라, 연구자들은 남녀공학에 다니는 학생들이 반대 성별의 학생들과 더 잘 어울린다고 주장했어요. 그래서 공학이 아닌 학교가 사실 학생들의 사회적 발달에 방해가 될 수도 있다는 겁니다.

노트

주제	single-sex schools – drawbacks	한 성별만 다니는 학교 – 단점
	1. students don't perform better	1. 학생들이 더 좋은 성적을 받지 않음
	2. prevents learning to socialize	2. 사회화 학습을 방해함

Q. According to the passage, what are the drawbacks of single-sex schools?

지문에 따르면, 한 성별만 있는 학교들의 단점은 무엇인가?

Research has shown that students at single-sex schools do not get a better education. It also showed that it prevents them from learning to socialize properly.

연구는 한 성별만 있는 학교에 다니는 학생들이 더 나은 교육을 받지 못한다는 것을 보여주었다. 또한, 학생들이 제대로 사회화하는 법을 배우지 못하게 한다는 점을 보여주었다.

어휘 attend ⓥ (학교 등을) 다니다 | single-sex adj 한쪽 성만을 위한 | back up 뒷받침하다 | claim ⓝ 주장 | counterpart ⓝ 대응 관계에 있는 사람(것), 상대 | co-ed adj 남녀 공학의 | socialize ⓥ 어울리다, 사귀다 | hinder ⓥ 방해하다, 저해하다 | development ⓝ 발달

Q5

Many people play the lottery because they think it will make their life perfect. However, in many cases it has had the opposite effect. First of all, when you win a large amount of money, the government will take a huge chunk out of it in taxes. Second, since many lotteries require the winner to publicly receive their prize, everyone knows that you have won. So, people will constantly be asking you for money.

많은 사람들이 복권이 삶을 완벽하게 만들어주리라는 생각으로 복권을 삽니다. 하지만 많은 경우 복권은 반대의 효과를 불러오죠. 먼저, 큰 액수에 당첨되면 정부가 그중 상당액을 세금으로 떼어갈 겁니다. 두 번째로, 대다수는 복권 당첨자가 공개적으로 상금을 수령하도록 요구해서 모두가 당첨자를 알게 됩니다. 그래서 사람들이 항상 당첨자에게 돈을 요구할 거예요.

노트

주제	lottery – not good	복권 – 안 좋음
	1. win → pay a lot in tax	1. 당첨 → 세금을 많이 냄
	2. get prize publicly → ppl will ask for $	2. 공개적으로 수령 → 사람들이 돈을 달라고 할 것

Q. According to the passage, what are the negative aspects of winning a lottery?

지문에 따르면, 복권에 당첨되는 것의 부정적인 측면은 무엇인가?

First, lottery winners will have to pay a lot of their money in taxes. Second, lottery winners often have to get their prize publicly, so many people will ask them for money.

먼저, 복권 당첨자들은 상당액을 세금으로 내야만 한다. 두 번째로, 복권 당첨자들은 공개적으로 상금을 타야 하는 경우가 많으므로 많은 사람들이 이들에게 돈을 달라고 할 것이다.

어휘 lottery ⓝ 복권 | opposite adj 반대의 | chunk ⓝ 상당히 많은 양 | tax ⓝ 세금 | publicly adv 공개적으로 | prize ⓝ 상금 | constantly adv 계속, 지속적으로

Q6

Many people believe that people should have to wear a uniform or obey a dress code at their work. However, a recent study has shown that this is actually a bad idea. The typical clothing that men and women wear to look professional is often uncomfortable, which can distract them from doing their work. In addition, being forced to conform to a standard can stifle people's creativity, so their work will be lower in quality.

많은 사람들이 직장에서 제복을 입거나 복장 규정을 따라야 한다고 믿습니다. 하지만 최근의 연구는 이것이 사실 안 좋은 생각이라는 것을 보여주죠. 전문적으로 보이기 위해 남성과 여성이 입는 일반적인 옷은 불편할 때가 많으며, 이는 일하는 데 방해가 될 수 있습니다. 또한, 기준에 순응하라고 강요받는 것은 사람들의 창조성을 억누를 수 있어서 작업의 질이 저하될 거예요.

노트

주제	uniform @ work = X good idea	직장에서 제복 = 안 좋은 생각
	1. uncomfortable = hard to work	1. 불편 = 일하기 힘듦
	2. forced to conform → make ppl less creative	2. 순응을 강요 → 사람들을 덜 창의적으로 만듦

Q. According to the passage, why is wearing a uniform at work a bad idea?

지문에 따르면, 직장에서 제복을 입는 것은 왜 안 좋은 생각인가?

First, the clothing that people usually wear for work is often uncomfortable, which makes it hard to work. Second, being forced to conform can make people less creative.

먼저, 사람들이 일하기 위해 보통 입는 옷은 불편할 때가 많으며 이는 일을 하기 어렵게 한다. 두 번째로, 순응하도록 강요받는 것은 사람들의 창의성을 떨어뜨린다.

어휘 uniform ⓝ 제복, 교복 I obey ⓥ 따르다 I dress code 복장 규정 I recent ⓐⓓⓙ 최근의 I typical ⓐⓓⓙ 일반적인 I professional ⓐⓓⓙ 전문직의 I uncomfortable ⓐⓓⓙ 불편한 I distract ⓥ 방해하다 I conform ⓥ 순응하다 I stifle ⓥ 억누르다, 억압하다 I creativity ⓝ 창조성

Q7

You may not have noticed this before, but most eye doctors who have vision problems have not had corrective surgery. There are two main reasons for this. Firstly, the techniques for correcting vision surgically have not been perfected yet, so they prefer to wait. Moreover, if there is an accident during the surgery, they could lose their vision altogether, which would ruin their career.

전에는 이것을 알아차리지 못했을지도 모르지만, 시력 문제가 있는 대부분의 안과 의사들은 교정 수술을 받지 않았습니다. 여기에는 두 가지 주된 이유가 있어요. 먼저 수술로 시력 교정을 하는 기술이 아직 완벽하지 않아서 기다리려는 것입니다. 게다가 만약 수술하는 동안 사고가 생기면 완전히 시야를 잃을 수도 있어서 의사들의 경력을 망가뜨릴 거예요.

노트

주제	eye doctor – X get corrective surgery	안과 의사 – 교정 수술 받지 않음
	1. methods are not perfect at the moment	1. 방법이 현재 완벽하지 않음
	2. X want to risk career – potential for accidents	2. 경력을 위험에 빠뜨리고 싶지 않음 – 사고 가능성

Q. According to the passage, why do eye doctors not get corrective surgeries?

지문에 따르면, 안과 의사들은 왜 교정 수술을 받지 않는가?

First, the methods for fixing a person's eyesight are still being improved. Second, they don't want to risk their careers due to the potential for accidents.

첫 번째로, 사람의 시력을 교정하는 방법들은 여전히 발전하고 있다. 두 번째로, 의사들은 사고 가능성 때문에 커리어를 위험에 빠뜨리고 싶지 않은 것이다.

어휘 notice ⓥ 알아차리다 I vision ⓝ 시력 I corrective ⓐⓓⓙ 교정의 I surgery ⓝ 수술 I surgically ⓐⓓⓥ 수술적으로, 외과적으로 I perfect ⓥ 완벽하게 하다 I accident ⓝ 사고 I altogether ⓐⓓⓥ 완전히, 전적으로 I ruin ⓥ 망가뜨리다

Q8

Despite their usefulness, the introduction of computers into the classroom has had some unexpected side effects. The obvious

그 유용함에도 불구하고 교실에 컴퓨터를 도입한 것은 예기치 못한 일부 부작용을 불러왔습니다. 명백한 부작용은

one is that children who are used to typing everything tend to have pretty bad handwriting. But another less obvious effect is that the children have weaker hands. The muscles that are strengthened by writing with a pencil are not being exercised.

모든 것을 키보드로 타이핑하는 데 익숙한 아이들은 상당히 심한 악필이 되는 경향이 있다는 것이죠. 하지만 덜 명백한 다른 부작용은 아이들의 손이 더 약해졌다는 겁니다. 연필을 잡고 글씨를 써서 강화되는 근육이 단련되지 않아서죠.

노트

주제	computers in classroom → side effect
	1. worse hand writing
	2. weaker hands – don't exercise properly

주제	교실 내의 컴퓨터 → 부작용
	1. 글씨체 더 안 좋아짐
	2. 더 약한 손 – 제대로 단련 안 함

Q. According to the passage, what are the side effects of using computers in a classroom?

지문에 따르면, 교실에서 컴퓨터를 사용하는 것의 부작용은 무엇인가?

The speaker says that children have worse hand writing, which isn't really surprising. But they also have weaker hands because they do not exercise them properly.

화자는 아이들의 필체가 나빠졌다고 하는데, 이는 놀라운 일이 아니다. 그러나 아이들은 또한 손을 제대로 쓰지 않기 때문에 손이 더 약해졌다.

어휘 usefulness n 유용함 l introduction n 도입 l unexpected adj 예기치 못한 l side effect 부작용 l obvious adj 명백한, 분명한 l hand writing n 필체, 글씨 l muscle n 근육 l strengthen v 강화하다

Q9

When people discuss hibernation, they often use bears as an example of this habit. But they really shouldn't because they do not actually hibernate. Firstly, animals that hibernate enter a sleeplike state that they do not wake until spring. But bears often wake up and leave their dens to feed. Not only that, but their internal body temperature does not change, which is an important aspect of hibernation.

사람들은 동면을 논의할 때 이 습성의 예로 곰을 자주 듭니다. 하지만 사실 곰은 동면을 하지 않기 때문에 그래선 안 돼요. 먼저, 동면하는 동물들은 봄까지 잠에서 깨지 않는 유사 수면 상태에 들어갑니다. 하지만 곰은 자주 깨어나서 먹이를 먹으러 굴 밖으로 나와요. 그뿐만 아니라, 곰의 체내 온도는 변하지 않는데, 이는 동면의 중요한 측면입니다.

노트

주제	bear = hibernation? No
	1. don't sleep continuously – leave den
	2. internal temp. = X ↓

주제	곰 = 동면? 아니다
	1. 계속 잠을 자는 것이 아님 – 굴을 떠남
	2. 체내 온도 = 떨어지지 않음

Q. According to the passage, why is bear not a hibernating animal?

지문에 따르면, 곰은 왜 동면을 하는 동물이 아닌가?

Firstly, they do not sleep continuously and often leave their den. Secondly, their internal temperature does not go down, which is an important part of hibernation.

먼저, 곰은 계속 잠을 자지 않으며 굴에서 자주 나온다. 두 번째로, 곰의 체내 온도는 내려가지 않는데, 이는 동면의 중요한 부분이다.

어휘 discuss v 논의하다 l hibernation n 동면, 겨울잠 l habit n 습성, 습관, 버릇 l hibernate v 동면하다, 겨울잠을 자다 l sleeplike adj 잠을 자는 것 같은 l state n 상태 l den n 굴 l internal adj 내부의

Q10

Many parents would disagree with me on this point, but playing video games is actually quite beneficial for children. First of all, playing video games improves children's problem solving abilities as they figure out puzzles and how to win the games. On top of that, it also helps to develop their eye-hand coordination as they react to what happens in the games.

많은 부모들이 이 점에 대해 동의하지 않겠지만, 비디오 게임을 하는 것은 사실 아이들에게 상당히 유익합니다. 먼저, 비디오 게임은 아이들이 퍼즐을 푸는 법과 게임에서 이기는 법을 알아내려고 하는 과정에서 문제 해결 능력을 향상시킵니다. 게다가, 아이들이 게임에서 일어나는 일에 반응하는 동안 눈과 손의 조정력 발달에 도움을 줍니다.

주제	video game = beneficial to children	비디오 게임 = 아이들에게 이로움
	1. prob. solving ability ↑	1. 문제 해결 능력 높아짐
	2. eye-hand coordination ↑	2. 눈-손 조정력 높아짐

Q. According to the passage, how is playing video games beneficial for children?

지문에 따르면, 비디오 게임을 하는 것은 아이들에게 왜 유익한가?

First, children have to use their problem solving abilities to play the games. Second, playing the games can improve their eye-hand coordination.

첫 번째로, 아이들은 게임을 하려면 문제 해결 능력을 이용해야 한다. 두 번째로, 게임을 하는 것은 아이들의 눈-손 조정력을 향상할 수 있다.

어휘 beneficial **adj** 유익한, 이로운 I improve **v** 향상시키다 I figure out 알아내다 I coordination **n** 조정력 I react **v** 반응하다

I. Integrated Task　　Part 2. 실전 굳히기

Lesson 01 정리하기

1. Practice

본서 P. 66

Q1

As the saying goes, "Two heads are better than one." Completing a project as a team is better than doing it alone. Having a group of people divide work can help save time and effort, so many companies and schools focus more on group work. Teamwork brings several benefits.

First, one of the benefits that teamwork brings is that working as a team helps to carry out work more efficiently. A group of people has various abilities. If a team member in a group is skillful at statistics, the group will have expertise in dealing with data. The abilities that each member has help to complete a given task more efficiently.

Second, group work allows team members to come up with various creative ideas. Each team member can talk freely in the process of making a group decision. As various ideas are suggested, there is a high possibility that the group will have creative solutions to problems they have to tackle. For example, when writing an essay, an individual can face limitations in brainstorming for ideas. But a group of people can think of more various and creative ideas than a single individual.

Another benefit of having a group of people tackle a problem is that teamwork can make team members actively participate in the work. This is because team members will feel more responsible for what they do in the group, and they will work harder to achieve positive results. They know that the others are depending on them, so they have more reason to perform.

옛말에도 있듯 '백지장도 맞들면 낫다.' 팀으로 하나의 과제를 완성하는 것은 혼자 하는 것보다 낫다. 한 무리의 사람들에게 일을 나누게 하면 시간과 노력을 절약할 수 있기에 많은 기업과 학교가 그룹 활동에 더 초점을 맞춘다. 팀 활동은 여러 이점을 가져다준다.

먼저, 팀워크가 주는 장점 중 하나는 팀으로 협력하는 것이 일을 더 효율적으로 하도록 돕는다는 것이다. 한 집단의 사람들은 다양한 능력을 갖추고 있다. 만약 그룹의 구성원 중 한 명이 통계학에 능숙하다면 그 그룹은 자료를 처리하는 데 전문성을 갖게 된다. 각 구성원이 가진 능력은 주어진 업무를 더 효율적으로 완수하게 돕는다.

두 번째로, 그룹 활동은 팀 구성원이 다양하고 창의적인 아이디어를 떠올리게 해 준다. 그룹이 결정을 내리는 과정에서 팀 구성원 각자가 자유롭게 이야기할 수 있다. 다양한 생각들이 제안되기 때문에 그룹은 해결해야 할 문제에 대한 창의적인 해결 방안을 얻을 가능성이 높다. 예를 들면, 논문을 쓸 때 한 개인은 아이디어를 떠올리는 데 한계에 부딪힐 수 있다. 하지만 한 무리의 사람들은 한 명의 개인보다 더 다양하고 독창적인 아이디어를 생각해 낼 수 있다.

한 무리의 사람들에게 문제를 해결하게 하는 또 다른 이점은 팀 구성원이 적극적으로 활동에 참여하게 할 수 있다는 것이다. 왜냐하면 팀 구성원들은 그 그룹에서 자신들이 하는 일에 더 많은 책임감을 느낄 것이고, 긍정적인 성과를 내기 위해 더 열심히 작업할 것이기 때문이다. 다른 사람들이 의지하고 있다는 것을 알기 때문에 잘해야 하는 이유가 더 있는 것이다.

주제	project: team > alone	프로젝트: 팀 > 혼자

주제 project: team > alone
    1. work more efficiently
       - each individual has different abilities
    2. more creative ideas
       - various ideas are suggested → creative solutions
    3. members actively participate
       - more responsibility → work harder

프로젝트: 팀 > 혼자
1. 더 효율적으로 일함
   − 개인이 서로 다른 능력을 갖추고 있음
2. 더 창의적인 아이디어
   − 다양한 아이디어 제시 → 창의적 해결책
3. 팀원들이 적극적으로 참여
   − 더 많은 책임감 → 더 열심히 일함

어휘 Two heads are better than one. 백지장도 맞들면 낫다. | complete ⓥ 완료하다, 끝마치다 | save time and effort 시간과 노력을 줄이다 | focus on ~에 초점을 맞추다 | carry out 수행/이행하다 | be skillful at ~에 능숙하다 | statistics ⋒ 통계, 통계 자료 | expertise in ~에 대한 전문 지식 | deal with 다루다, 처리하다, 해결하다 | come up with ~을 떠올리다, 생각해내다 | tackle ⓥ 해결하다 | face limitations in ~하는 데 한계에 부딪히다 | brainstorm for ideas (여러 가지) 아이디어를 생각해내다 | participate ⓥ 참여하다 | achieve ⓥ 달성하다, 해내다 | perform ⓥ (일, 과제 등을) 해내다

Q2

Many animals and plants have been imported intentionally or by accident to new areas. These new species transported to new environments often have negative effects. Let us take a look at these negative consequences.

First, a new species always upsets the local ecological balance. A new species is never just added to the native ecosystem. It always competes with some native ecosystems. The damage does not end with the displacement of native competitors as the new species is often unsuitable as food for species further up the food chain. The negative effects thus spread through the whole ecosystem.

Second, the introduction of new species often destroys the local environment. For example, the cane toad, native to South Africa, was introduced to Australia, where it has spread at an alarming speed and has had harmful effects on the local environment. The cane toad, a natural predator, has killed a large number of native species in Australia. In addition to this, its poison sometimes poses a direct threat to children and pets when touched.

Finally, the negative impact caused by the introduction of new species often leads to economic burdens. For example, mesquites, a shrub native to America, were introduced to Africa. After the introduction of mesquites, commonly planted for land restoration and as a source of wood, they started to displace native species in Africa. As a result, African governments are forced to commit economic and bureaucratic resources to control the replacement of native species by mesquites.

많은 동식물이 의도적으로 혹은 우연히 새로운 지역으로 반입된다. 새로운 환경으로 옮겨진 이러한 새로운 종들은 흔히 부정적인 영향을 미친다. 이러한 부정적인 결과를 살펴보자.

첫 번째로, 새로운 종은 항상 지역 생태계의 균형을 깨뜨린다. 새로운 종은 고유한 생태계에 단순히 추가되는 것이 결코 아니다. 그것은 항상 일부 생태계와 경쟁한다. 새로운 종은 흔히 먹이 사슬 위에 있는 종에게 먹이로 적합하지 않기에 피해는 현지 경쟁자의 대체로 끝나지 않는다. 따라서 부정적인 영향은 생태계 전체로 퍼지게 된다.

두 번째로, 새로운 종의 유입은 지역 환경을 파괴하는 경우가 많다. 예를 들면, 원래 남아프리카에 서식하는 사탕수수 두꺼비가 호주에 유입되었고, 이곳에서 놀라운 속도로 퍼져 지역 환경에 해로운 영향을 끼치게 되었다. 자연 포식자인 사탕수수 두꺼비는 호주에서 많은 재래종을 죽였다. 이뿐 아니라 이 두꺼비의 독은 때때로 아이나 애완동물과 접촉할 때 직접적인 위협이 되기도 한다.

마지막으로 새로운 종의 유입으로 인한 부정적인 영향은 종종 경제적 부담으로 이어진다. 예를 들면, 미국이 원산지인 관목의 일종인 메스키트가 아프리카로 유입되었다. 토지 복원을 위해, 그리고 목재의 원천으로서 흔히 심는 메스키트의 유입 이후 이들은 아프리카의 재래종을 대체하기 시작했다. 그 결과 아프리카 정부들은 메스키트로 인한 재래종의 교체를 통제하는 데 경제적, 관료적 자원을 투입해야 한다.

노트

주제 new species in new envi. → negative effect
    1. upset local ecology's balance
       - compete w/ natives
       - mess up the food chain → upset whole eco.

새 환경의 새로운 종 → 부정적 영향
1. 지역 생태계 균형 무너뜨림
   − 토착종들과 경쟁
   − 먹이 사슬 망가뜨림 → 생태계 전체를 무너뜨림

Part 2
Integrated Task

2. destroy local envi.
- new species kill native species
- poisonous ones can even harm humans
3. economic burden
- gov't have to invest money to control the spread of new species

2. 지역 환경 파괴
– 새 종이 토착종을 죽임
– 독이 있는 것들은 인간도 해칠 수 있음
3. 경제적 부담
– 정부가 새 종의 확산을 통제하기 위해 돈을 투자해야 함

어휘 intentionally **adv** 의도적으로 | by accident 우연히 | transport **v** 이동시키다, 옮기다 | consequence **n** 결과 | upset **v** 뒤엎다, 망치다 | native ecosystem 재래 생태계, 고유 생태계 | compete **v** 경쟁하다 | displacement **n** (제자리에서 쫓겨난) 이동, 대체 | further up 더 위쪽의 | food chain 먹이 사슬 | cane toad 사탕수수 두꺼비 | alarming **adj** 놀라운, 걱정스러운 | native species 재래종 | in addition to ~뿐만 아니라 | pose a threat 위협이 되다 | mesquite **n** 메스키트(콩과 식물의 일종) | shrub **n** 관목 | restoration **n** 회복, 복구 | commit **v** (시간, 돈 등을) 쓰다 | bureaucratic **adj** 관료의, 관료주의적인

Q3

In England before the Industrial Revolution of the late 18th century, manufactured goods such as cloth and thread were produced manually at homes and small workshops. This so-called "putting-out system" developed into the factory system. There are several reasons why the development of the factory system was first made possible in England.

First, the advent of new technologies resulted in the accelerated development of the factory system. The development of steam engines played an especially pivotal role in the spread of the factory system. The introduction of steam engines to factories made it possible to generate a considerable amount of energy that individual workers at home could not create.

Second, the development of the factory system in England was the result of the introduction of property rights. Stable and strict rules of law that protected private property encouraged property holders to develop their property and efficiently allocate resources based on the operation of the market. This, in turn, caused property owners to invest more in new factories.

Finally, this system helped factory owners reduce production costs, especially transportation costs. Before the advancement of the system, raw materials and equipment had been supplied for workers who worked at home. This would have cost business owners considerable amounts of money for transportation. In this case, naturally, they preferred the factory system in which they could reduce the cost of transporting raw materials and goods.

18세기 후반 산업혁명 이전의 영국에서 천이나 섬유 같은 제조 상품은 집이나 작은 작업장에서 수작업으로 생산되었다. 이러한 소위 '선대제'라고 불리는 것이 공장제로 발달했다. 공장제가 영국에서 처음으로 가능했던 데에는 몇 가지 이유가 있다.

첫째, 새로운 기술의 출현이 공장제의 발전을 가속화하는 결과를 가져왔다. 증기 기관의 발달이 공장제 확산에 특히 중추적 역할을 했다. 증기 기관의 공장 도입으로 집에서 개개인의 근로자들이 만들 수 없었던 상당한 양의 에너지가 만들어질 수 있었다.

두 번째로, 영국에서 공장제의 발달은 사유 재산권 도입의 결과였다. 사유 재산을 보호해 주는 안정적이고 엄격한 법 규정은 재산을 가진 사람들이 재산을 늘리고 시장의 운용에 기초해 자원을 효율적으로 배분하도록 장려했다. 이것은 결과적으로 재산을 가진 사람들이 새로운 공장에 더 많이 투자하게 했다.

마지막으로, 이러한 시스템은 공장 소유주가 생산 비용, 특히 운송비를 줄이도록 도와주었다. 이 시스템의 발전 이전에는 원자재와 장비가 집에서 일하는 노동자들에게 공급되었다. 이것이 사업주에게 상당한 운송 비용을 초래했을 것이다. 이러한 상황에서 이들은 자연스럽게 원자재와 상품을 운송하는 비용을 줄일 수 있는 공장제를 선호했다.

노트

주제 development of factory system in England
1. new technologies
- steam engines: huge energy generation
2. intro. of property rights
- protect property holders
- invest more in new factories
3. owners: reduce production costs, esp. trans. costs
- cost for transp. raw materials & equipment ↓

영국의 공장 시스템 발달
1. 새로운 기술
– 증기 기관: 엄청난 에너지 생산
2. 사유 재산권 도입
– 사유 재산 소유자를 보호
– 새 공장에 더 투자
3. 소유주: 생산 비용, 특히 운송비 절감
– 원자재 & 장비 운송 비용 줄임

Q4

It is well known that fossil fuels will not power the world for much longer. In fact, hydrogen fuel will most likely replace fossil fuels as the main source of global energy in a very short period of time. There are many reasons why hydrogen fuel will replace fossil fuels.

First of all, hydrogen is not only more abundant than fossil fuels, but also renewable. One day, the world will use up fossil fuel reserves and be forced to use alternative energy sources. Hydrogen is one of the most abundant elements in the universe and is therefore much more readily available than fossil fuels. This means hydrogen can be used as a potential source of energy and the world will never run out of hydrogen.

Another point is the problem of pollution. When we burn fossil fuels to generate energy, carbon dioxide, a greenhouse gas, builds up in the atmosphere. As the amount of carbon dioxide in the air increases, global temperatures rise. However, the only byproduct of hydrogen fuel engines is water. This in no way harms the environment and seems to be the most logical choice for the world's next energy supply.

Finally, as the cost of acquiring and maintaining hydrogen fuel cell engines decreases, consumers will have no reason not to use them. Already, hydrogen fuel cell engines cost less to maintain than combustion engines since hydrogen fuel engines malfunction much less often. As the engines operated by hydrogen become cheaper to buy, they will turn out to be the best replacement for combustion engines.

화석 연료가 전 세계에 오랫동안 동력을 공급하지 못할 것이라는 점은 잘 알려져 있다. 실제로 수소 연료는 아주 짧은 시일 내에 전 세계의 주요 에너지원으로 화석 연료를 대체할 것으로 보인다. 왜 수소 연료가 화석 연료를 대체할 것인지에 대한 이유는 많다.

먼저, 수소는 화석 연료보다 더 풍족할 뿐 아니라 재생할 수 있다. 언젠가 세계는 화석 연료 비축분을 다 소모할 것이며 대체 에너지원을 사용해야 할 것이다. 수소는 우주에서 가장 풍부한 원소 중 하나이며, 따라서 화석 연료보다 훨씬 더 쉽게 이용할 수 있다. 이는 수소가 잠재적 에너지원으로 사용될 수 있고 이 세상에서 결코 수소가 고갈되지 않을 거라는 의미다.

또 다른 점은 오염 문제다. 에너지를 만들기 위해 화석 연료를 태우면 온실가스인 이산화탄소가 대기에 쌓인다. 대기에 이산화탄소의 양이 증가하면서 지구의 온도는 올라간다. 그러나 수소 연료 엔진의 유일한 부산물은 물이다. 이는 결코 환경에 해를 끼치지 않고, 세계의 다음 에너지 공급원으로 가장 합리적인 선택으로 보인다.

마지막으로, 수소 연료 전지 엔진을 입수하고 유지하는 비용이 감소하면서 소비자는 그것을 사용하지 않을 이유가 없을 것이다. 이미 수소 연료 전지 엔진은 오작동이 훨씬 덜하기 때문에 연소 엔진보다 적은 유지 비용이 든다. 수소로 작동하는 엔진이 구매비가 더 싸지면서 연소 엔진을 대신하는 최고의 대체물이 될 것이다.

노트

주제	hydrogen fuel will replace fossil f.	수소 연료가 화석 연료를 대체할 것
	1. hydrogen = abundant & renewable	1. 수소 = 풍부함 & 재생 가능
	- world will never run out of hydro.	– 수소가 고갈될 일은 없음
	2. pollution X	2. 오염 X
	- fossil f. → CO_2, temp. ↑	– 화석 연료 → 이산화탄소, 온도 올라감
	- hydro. fuel's only byproduct = water	– 수소 연료의 유일한 부산물 = 물
	3. costs less	3. 비용 덜 듦
	- hydrogen f.'s cost is ↓ (engine, maintaining…)	– 수소 연료 비용이 더 낮음 (엔진, 유지비…)

어휘   fossil fuel 화석 연료 l power ⓥ 전력을 공급하다 l hydrogen fuel 수소 연료 l abundant ⓐⓓⓙ 풍부한, 풍족한 l renewable ⓐⓓⓙ 재생 가능한 l use up ~을 다 써버리다, 고갈시키다 l reserve ⓝ 비축(물) l be forced to ~하도록 강요받다 l alternative ⓐⓓⓙ 대체 가능한, 대안이 되는 l element ⓝ 원소, 성분 l readily ⓐⓓⓥ 손쉽게, 순조롭게 l potential ⓐⓓⓙ 잠재적인 l run out of ~을 다 써버리다, 바닥내다 l generate ⓥ 만들다, 생산하다 l carbon dioxide 이산화탄소 l greenhouse gas 온실가스 l byproduct ⓝ 부산물 l in no way 결코 ~하지 않는 l acquire ⓥ 얻다, 획득하다 l combustion ⓝ 연소, 불에 탐 l malfunction ⓥ 오작동하다, 고장 나다

Q5

Many people think that increasing energy prices is the most effective way to save limited sources of energy. They believe that if gasoline prices increase because of raising gas taxes, gasoline can be conserved. However, the policy of increasing gas taxes cannot be a solution to saving energy, especially gasoline. There are several reasons why this policy is inefficient and problematic.

Firstly, one reason why this policy is inefficient is that people will not stop consuming gasoline even if gasoline prices increase. For example, even though the government raised the price of cigarettes from $2 to $4, a 100% increase, smokers who could not find a substitute for cigarettes did not reduce their consumption of cigarettes by 100%. Likewise, no matter how much gasoline prices increase, people will not give up using it.

Secondly, increasing gas taxes can put a financial burden on people. In particular, this increase may burden poor families that live on the outskirts of the city because of high housing prices. The families have to commute to work by car, so they would have to spend too much money on buying gasoline if prices of gasoline increased.

Thirdly, there are much better ways of conserving gasoline like making cars more fuel efficient. Governments should make car manufacturers develop cars that use less gasoline, such as hybrid gas-electric vehicles that can be operated partially by electricity. Without raising the prices of gasoline, governments can easily achieve their goal of conserving gasoline.

많은 사람들은 유가를 올리는 것이 제한된 에너지원을 절약하는 가장 효과적인 방법이라고 생각한다. 그들은 만약 주유세 인상 때문에 휘발유 가격이 오른다면 휘발유는 보존될 수 있다고 믿는다. 그러나 주유세를 인상하는 정책은 연료, 특히 휘발유를 절약하는 해결책이 될 수 없다. 이 정책이 비효율적이고 문제가 있는 이유는 여러 가지다.

첫 번째로, 이 정책이 비효율적인 이유는 사람들이 휘발유 가격이 오르더라도 휘발유 소비를 멈추지 않을 것이라는 점이다. 예를 들면, 정부가 담배 가격을 2달러에서 4달러로 100% 인상했어도 담배의 대체재를 찾을 수 없던 흡연자들은 100%까지 담배 소비를 줄이지 않았다. 이와 마찬가지로 휘발유 가격이 얼마나 오르든 사람들은 휘발유 사용을 중단하지 않을 것이다.

두 번째로, 주유세를 올리는 것은 사람들에게 재정적인 부담을 줄 수 있다. 특히, 이러한 증가는 높은 집값 때문에 도시 교외 지역에 사는 가난한 가정들에게 부담을 줄지 모른다. 이 가정들은 자동차로 통근을 해야 해서 만약 휘발유 가격이 오르면 휘발유를 사는 데 너무 많은 돈을 지출해야 할 것이다.

세 번째로, 연비가 더 높은 차량을 만드는 등 휘발유를 아끼는 데 훨씬 더 좋은 방법들이 있다. 정부는 자동차 제조업자들이 부분적으로 전기로 운행할 수 있는 휘발유-전기 하이브리드 자동차처럼 휘발유를 적게 쓰는 차를 개발하도록 해야 한다. 정부는 휘발유 가격을 올리지 않고도 휘발유를 보존하려는 목표를 쉽게 달성할 수 있다.

노트

주제	↑ energy price = saving source of energy? No	유가 올리기 = 에너지원 절약? 아니다

주제 ↑ energy price = saving source of energy? No
1. ppl won't stop consuming gas
   - ppl will not give up b/c there's no substitute
2. financial burden
   - esp. poor families living on the outskirts
   - commuting by car = too much $
3. better ways
   - making fuel-efficient cars(hybrid ones)

유가 올리기 = 에너지원 절약? 아니다
1. 사람들은 휘발유 소비를 멈추지 않을 것
   – 대체재가 없기 때문에 사람들은 중단하지 않을 것임
2. 재정적 부담
   – 특히 교외에 사는 가난한 가정들
   – 차로 통근 = 너무 많은 돈이 듦
3. 더 나은 방법
   – 연비가 높은 차 개발(하이브리드 자동차)

어휘 effective **adj** 효과적인, 실질적인 ׀ limited **adj** 제한된, 한정된 ׀ gas tax 주유세, 석유세 ׀ conserve **v** 보존하다, 절약하다 ׀ inefficient **adj** 비효율적인 ׀ problematic **adj** 문제가 되는, 문제를 일으키는 ׀ substitute **n** 대체재, 대체물 ׀ likewise **adv** 이와 마찬가지로, 이와 같이 ׀ no matter how much 얼마나 간에, 얼마든 상관없이 ׀ give up -ing ~하는 것을 그만두다, 포기하다 ׀ burden **n** 부담, 짐 **v** 부담을 주다 ׀ outskirts **n** 교외, 변두리 ׀ commute **v** 통근하다 ׀ manufacturer **n** 제조사 ׀ electric **adj** 전기의, 전기를 이용하는 ׀ vehicle **n** 차량 ׀ operate **v** 운전하다, 조작하다 ׀ partially **adv** 부분적으로

Q6

Due to the lack of written history documenting England during the Dark Ages, debate has arisen as to the true origins of the English people who now inhabit the country. Some contend that they are descended from the tribes who lived there long before the Roman

암흑시대의 잉글랜드가 기록된 역사가 부족하다는 이유로 현재 그 나라에 거주하는 잉글랜드인들의 진정한 기원에 관한 논쟁이 일어났다. 일부는 그들이 로마 점령 전 오랫동안 그곳에 살았던 켈트족으로 알려진 종족의 후손이

occupation, known as the Celts. Others claim that most people are descended from the people who invaded soon after, referred to as Anglo-Saxons. However, the majority of the evidence suggests that the latter is true.

Firstly, the arrival of Anglo-Saxons into the British Isles was not the result of exploration or trade. It was actually a mass migration from what is now North Central Europe. Constant pressure and invasions from the East forced the majority of the Angles and the Saxons to flee their homeland. When they arrived in England, they quickly displaced the Celtic population, forcing them into the farthest corners of the land. The Anglo-Saxons rapidly became the dominant population.

Secondly, the language of England is directly derived from the Anglo-Saxons. Modern English can be clearly traced back to their Germanic languages and not those of the Celts. Indeed, apart from a few terms that were adopted by the invaders, there is no evidence of Celtic languages in England. Rather, Celtic tongues survive in Wales, Ireland, and Scotland, clearly supporting the theory that the people of modern day England are Anglo-Saxons.

Thirdly, a recent genetic study of the DNA of people living in the eastern portion of England has provided compelling proof. The mapping of the human genetic code has made determining people's background easier and much more accurate. The DNA profiles of the people sampled were virtually identical to the profiles of people living in modern day Germany and Denmark, which is the area from which the Anglo-Saxons came.

라고 주장한다. 다른 이들은 대부분의 사람들이 그 직후에 침략한 앵글로색슨족이라고 불리는 사람들의 후손이라고 주장한다. 그러나 대부분의 증거는 후자가 사실임을 시사한다.

첫째로, 앵글로색슨족의 영국 제도 출현은 탐사나 무역의 결과가 아니었다. 그것은 사실상 지금의 북중 유럽으로부터의 집단 이주였다. 동쪽 지방으로부터의 계속되는 압박과 침략으로 대다수의 앵글족과 색슨족은 고향을 떠나 피난을 가야 했다. 잉글랜드에 도착했을 때 그들은 빠르게 켈트족 인구를 대체하며 그들을 잉글랜드의 가장 먼 끄트머리로 몰아냈다. 앵글로색슨족은 급속도로 지배 인구가 되었다.

둘째로, 잉글랜드의 언어는 앵글로색슨 언어에서 직접 유래했다. 현대 영어는 켈트족의 언어가 아니라 게르만 언어에서 분명 그 유래를 찾아볼 수 있다. 실제로 이 침략자들이 채택한 몇 가지 용어 외에 잉글랜드에서 켈트어의 증거는 없다. 오히려 켈트어는 웨일스, 아일랜드와 스코틀랜드에 남아 있는데, 이는 현대 잉글랜드 사람들이 앵글로색슨인이라는 이론을 명확하게 뒷받침한다.

셋째로, 잉글랜드의 동쪽 지역에 사는 사람들의 DNA에 관한 최근의 한 유전자 연구가 강력한 증거를 제공하고 있다. 인간의 유전 암호 지도는 더 쉽고 정확하게 사람들의 출신을 알아내게 해 주었다. 표본 집단의 DNA 프로필은 오늘날 독일과 덴마크에 사는 사람들의 프로필과 사실상 동일했는데, 그곳은 앵글로색슨족의 출신지다.

노트

주제	origins of English ppl = Anglo-Saxons?

주제 origins of English ppl = Anglo-Saxons?
　　1. mass migration
　　　- invasion → Angles & Saxons ran away from homeland
　　　- arrived in England → displaced Celtic
　　2. language
　　　- directly from Anglo-Saxons
　　　- no evidence of Celtic lang. in England
　　3. DNA study
　　　- almost identical to Germany/Denmark ppl
　　　= where Anglo-Saxons came from

잉글랜드인들의 기원 = 앵글로색슨?
1. 집단 이주
　- 침략 → 앵글족 & 색슨족이 고국에서 도망
　- 영국 도착 → 켈트인들을 대체
2. 언어
　- 앵글로색슨족에서 직접 유래
　- 잉글랜드에 켈트족 언어의 증거가 없음
3. DNA 연구
　- 독일/덴마크 사람들과 거의 일치
　　= 앵글로색슨인들의 출신지

어휘 document ⓥ 기록하다 | arise ⓥ 발생하다, 생기다 | inhabit ⓥ 살다, 거주하다 | contend ⓥ 주장하다 | be descended from ~의 후손/자손이다 | occupation ⓝ 점령 | claim ⓥ 주장하다 | referred to as ~로 불리다 | mass migration 집단 이주 | flee ⓥ 피하다, 도망치다 | displace ⓥ 대체하다, 쫓아내다 | dominant ⓐⓓⓙ 우세한, 지배적인 | be derived from ~에서 유래되다, 파생되다 | trace back to ~에서 유래하다 | apart from ~외에도 | term ⓝ 용어 | adopt ⓥ 쓰다, 택하다, 취하다 | tongue ⓝ 언어 | compelling ⓐⓓⓙ 강력한, 설득력 있는 | sample ⓥ 표본 조사를 하다 | virtually ⓐⓓⓥ 사실상, 거의 | identical ⓐⓓⓙ 동일한

Q7

The Everglades is a large area of wetlands in southern Florida that contain abundant plant and animal life. However, recent

에버글레이즈는 풍부한 식물과 동물이 사는 플로리다 남쪽에 위치한 거대한 습지이다. 하지만 최근 환경 문제가

environmental issues have threatened the unique ecology of the region. If these issues are not addressed, the Everglades may disappear.

One serious issue for the Everglades is invasive species, which are plants and animals that have been introduced from other parts of the world. One such species is the paperbark tree from Australia. The tree's native habitat is very similar to the Everglades, which allows it to spread rapidly. Paperbark trees take over the sawgrass marshes that comprise most of the Everglades, turning them into swamp.

An even more serious problem for the region is water pollution. The two main pollutants are chemical fertilizers used in farming and mercury released from power plants burning fossil fuels. The fertilizers change the chemical composition of the soil, killing marsh grasses and encouraging other plants like cotton tails to grow. Mercury builds up in animals' bodies as they feed on each other. This eventually kills many animals and makes fish unsafe to eat.

The most serious threat to the Everglades is its decreased water supply. Wetlands need a large supply of slow moving water to exist. Dams and canals were built to prevent flooding and divert water for farming and residential areas. This led to insufficient water flow to the area. So, large sections of the Everglades are simply drying up, removing the habitat from the plants and animals that depend upon it.

이 지역 고유의 생태계를 위협하고 있다. 만약 이러한 문제가 해결되지 않는다면 에버글레이즈는 사라질 것이다.

에버글레이즈의 한 가지 심각한 문제는 전 세계의 다른 지역에서 유입된 동식물인 외래종이다. 이러한 종들 중 하나가 호주에서 온 페이퍼바크 나무이다. 이 나무의 원래 서식지가 에버글레이즈와 매우 유사해서 급속히 확산되고 있다. 페이퍼바크 나무는 에버글레이즈의 대부분을 차지하는 억새풀 습지를 장악하고 동시에 그것을 늪으로 바꿔버린다.

이 지역의 더 심각한 문제는 수질 오염이다. 두 가지 주된 오염 물질은 농사에 쓰이는 화학 비료와 화석 연료를 태우는 발전소에서 방출된 수은이다. 비료는 토양의 화학적 구성을 바꿔 여러해살이풀을 죽이고, 코튼테일 같은 다른 식물이 자라게 한다. 수은은 동물들이 서로를 먹이로 삼으면서 체내에 쌓인다. 이는 결과적으로 많은 동물을 살상하고 어류 섭취를 위험하게 한다.

에버글레이즈에 가장 심각한 위협은 물 공급 감소이다. 습지가 존재하려면 천천히 흐르는 많은 양의 물 공급이 필요하다. 댐과 운하는 범람을 막고 농지와 주거 지역의 우회수로를 위해 건설되었다. 그 결과 그 지역에 흐르는 물이 부족해졌다. 그래서 에버글레이즈의 넓은 지대가 말라가고 있으며 거기에 의존하는 동식물의 서식지를 없애고 있다.

노트

주제	issues threatening the Everglades → they may disappear	에버글레이즈를 위협하는 문제 → 사라질지도 모름

1. invasive plants & animals
- paperbark tree → take over sawgrass marshes → swamp
2. water pollution
- chemical fertilizer & mercury
3. ↓ water supply
- wetlands need water but dams & canals…
- large sections are drying up

1. 외래종 식물 & 동물
 – 페이퍼바크 나무 → 억새풀 습지 장악 → 늪
2. 수질 오염
 – 화학 비료 & 수은
3. 물 공급 감소
 – 습지는 물이 필요하지만 댐 & 운하는…
 – 많은 부분이 말라가고 있음

어휘 wetlands n 습지 l ecology n 생태(계) l address v (문제 등을) 다루다, 해결하다 l invasive species 외래종 l habitat n 서식지 l sawgrass n 억새풀 l marsh n 습지 l comprise v 구성하다, 차지하다 l swamp n 늪 l pollutant n 오염원, 오염 물질 l fertilizer n 비료 l mercury n 수은 l composition n 구성 l build up 쌓이다 l feed on ~을 먹다 l canal n 운하 l divert v 방향을 돌리다, 우회시키다 l residential adj 주거의 l insufficient adj 불충분한 l dry up 마르다, 말라붙다

Q8

Sometimes, the introduction of new species can result in several negative consequences, so the government is considering a law to restrict importing, buying, and selling of non-native species of animals. However, this law should not be implemented for the following reasons.

때때로 새로운 종의 유입은 몇 가지 부정적 결과를 초래할 수 있기에 정부는 외래종 동물의 수입, 구매, 판매를 제한하기 위한 법을 고려하고 있다. 하지만 다음 이유로 이 법은 시행되어서는 안 된다.

First of all, the law might be used to force pet owners to give up ownership of their pets. This law could have an immediate effect on pet owners who currently have non-native species animals since they have to worry about their pets being taken away. Most of these animals are kept inside the owner's homes, so they rarely come into contact with native species. Since they are not much of a threat, their owners should be allowed to keep them.

Second, implementing the law is expensive because conducting studies to find out whether non-native species cause damage when they are released to the wild requires a lot of money. A variety of new animals, ranging from a marine species, such as the zebra mussel, to pets, have been introduced or transported to the US intentionally or accidentally, and it costs a lot to investigate the consequences of their release to the wild.

Another reason to oppose this law is that the law is not reasonable because it applies a single standard to the entire country. For example, South American rabbits cannot survive long in northern parts of the US simply because the regions are too cold for them to survive. Therefore, it is unreasonable to apply the law to the entire US.

무엇보다도, 이 법은 반려동물 주인이 반려동물에 대한 권리를 포기하도록 강요하는 데 이용될 수 있다. 이 법은 현재 외래종 동물을 소유한 반려동물 주인들이 반려동물을 빼앗길까 봐 걱정해야 하므로 이들에게 즉각적인 영향을 줄 수 있다. 이 동물들 대부분은 주인의 집에서 기르는 것이므로 토착종과 접촉할 일이 거의 없다. 그다지 위협이 되지 않기에 주인들은 이 동물들을 계속 키울 수 있어야 한다.

두 번째로, 외래종이 야생에 풀렸을 때 피해를 야기하는지 아닌지를 알아내기 위한 연구를 하는 데에는 많은 돈이 필요하기 때문에 그 법을 시행하는 데는 큰 비용이 든다. 얼룩말 홍합 같은 해양 종부터 반려동물에 이르기까지 다양한 새로운 동물들이 의도적이든 우연이든 미국으로 유입되거나 옮겨졌고, 이것들이 야생에 방사되어 일어난 결과를 조사하는 일에는 비용이 많이 든다.

이 법에 반대하는 또 다른 이유는 이 법이 하나의 기준을 국가 전체에 적용하기 때문에 합리적이지 않다는 점이다. 예를 들어, 남아메리카 토끼가 살아남기에는 미국 북부 지역이 너무 춥기 때문에 이곳에서 오래 생존할 수 없다. 따라서 이 법을 미국 전역에 적용하는 것은 합리적이지 않다.

노트

| 주제 | gov't law = restrict importing/buying/selling non-native species
→ shouldn't be implemented
1. pet owners will give up their pets
　- non-native species as pets = should be allowed to keep them
2. cost
　- conducting studies of non-native species damage to the wild will be $$$
3. not reasonable
　- single standard to the entire country? | 정부 법 = 토착종이 아닌 동물의 수입/구매/판매 제한
→ 시행되어서는 안 됨
1. 반려동물 소유주가 반려동물을 포기할 것
　– 토착종이 아닌 반려동물 = 계속 키울 수 있어야 함
2. 비용
　– 토착종 아닌 종이 야생에 끼치는 피해를 연구하는 데는 많은 비용이 들 것임
3. 합리적이지 않음
　– 나라 전체에 하나의 기준? |

어휘　restrict ⓥ 제한하다, 규제하다 l non-native adj 재래종이 아닌, 외래종의 l implement ⓥ 시행하다 l conduct a study 연구를 하다 l a variety of 다양한 l range from A to B A에서 B에 이르다 l marine adj 바다의, 해양의 l zebra mussel 얼룩말 홍합 l introduce ⓥ (식물, 동물 등을) 들여오다, 도입하다 l transport ⓥ 이동시키다 l investigate ⓥ 조사하다 l reasonable adj 합리적인 l apply ⓥ 적용하다 l standard ⓝ 규범, 기준 l unreasonable adj 비합리적인, 불합리한

Q9

Scattered across the Atlantic coast of the United States there are shallow, round depressions in the land. They are called Carolina bays, and the bay part of their name comes from a type of tree that is commonly found in them and not the fact that they often hold water. The origin of the bays remains undetermined, but many scientists think that they may have been created by large meteors that exploded above the ground for the following reasons.

First, the depressions that form the bays are shaped in a way

미국 대서양 연안에는 얕고 동그랗게 팬 지형들이 흩어져 있다. 이것들은 캐롤라이나만이라고 불리는데, '만'이라는 이름은 그곳에 종종 물이 차 있다는 사실에서 비롯된 것이 아니라 그 지역에서 흔히 발견되는 나무의 한 종류에서 유래한 것이다. 그 만의 기원은 분명치 않은 채로 남아 있으나, 많은 과학자들은 다음의 이유로 그 지역이 지상에서 폭발했던 커다란 유성들에 의해 형성되었을지도 모른다고 생각한다.

첫 번째로, 그 만을 형성하는 움푹 팬 땅은 지면에서 폭발

that is consistent with impact craters created by fragments of meteors that exploded above the ground. When that happens, most of the fragments strike the ground at an angle, which makes an oval crater with one side deeper than the other. The deeper side will have fine, crushed material piled high on its edge. The bays are ovals that lie in a northwest to southeast direction, their southeastern rim is higher, and it is usually made of white sand. This suggests that they were likely formed in this way.

Second, the sand contained in the bays is different from the sand found in the Atlantic coastal region. The normal sand has a coating of iron compounds, but the sand in the bays lacks this coating. The absence of iron can be explained by the intense heat that would result from a meteor impact. This heat would have melted the iron, causing it to vaporize and be blown away. So, as the meteor fragments created the bays, they could have left behind sand that does not have the usual iron coating.

Third, scientists have found buckyballs in some of the bays, which may point to an object from space striking the Earth. Buckyballs are unique carbon structures that are composed of 60 tightly interconnected carbon atoms. They are made when carbon is exposed to intense heat and pressure. These conditions can be created during a meteor strike. So the meteor fragments that made the bays could have also created the buckyballs that were found in them.

했던 유성 파편에 의해 형성된 충돌 분화구와 일치하는 모양이다. 이때, 대부분의 파편은 지면에 비스듬히 부딪히는데, 이는 한쪽 면이 다른 쪽보다 더 깊은 타원형의 분화구를 만든다. 더 깊은 쪽의 가장자리에는 입자가 고운 부서진 물질이 높이 쌓이게 될 것이다. 이 만은 북서에서 남동 방향으로 펼쳐진 타원형으로, 남동쪽 가장자리가 더 높은데 이곳은 주로 흰 모래로 구성되어있다. 이는 이 만들이 이런 식으로 형성되었을 가능성이 높다는 것을 보여준다.

두 번째로, 이 만에 있는 모래는 대서양 연안 지역에서 발견되는 모래와 다르다. 그 지역의 전형적인 모래는 철 화합물로 뒤덮여 있지만, 이 만의 모래는 이런 막이 없다. 이렇게 철이 없는 것은 유성 충돌로 인한 강한 열기로 설명될 수 있다. 이 열기가 철을 녹여서 이를 증발시켜 날려버렸을 것이다. 유성 파편들이 이 만을 형성했기 때문에 흔히 볼 수 있는 철로 된 막이 없는 모래를 남겼을 수도 있다.

세 번째로, 과학자들은 이 만의 곳곳에서 버키볼을 발견했는데, 이는 지구와 충돌한 우주의 물체를 나타내는 것일 수 있다. 버키볼은 서로 단단히 연결된 60개의 탄소 원자들로 구성된 독특한 탄소 구조물이다. 버키볼은 탄소가 강한 열과 압력에 노출될 때 만들어진다. 이런 환경은 유성이 충돌하는 동안에 조성될 수 있다. 따라서 이 만을 형성한 유성 파편들이 그곳에서 발견된 버키볼 또한 만들었을 수 있다.

노트

주제	Carolina bays – their origin = large meteors?	캐롤라이나 만 – 기원 = 거대 유성?

주제 Carolina bays – their origin = large meteors?
1. depressions' shape
   - similar to impact craters created by meteors
   - oval shape
2. sand is different
   - not found in Atlantic coast
   - absence of iron = meteor impact's intense heat
3. buckyballs
   - carbon structures that can be made from meteor strike
   - found in some of the bays

캐롤라이나 만 – 기원 = 거대 유성?
1. 움푹 팬 땅의 모양
   – 유성으로 만들어진 충돌 분화구와 유사
   – 타원형
2. 모래가 다름
   – 대서양 연안에서 발견되지 않음
   – 철이 없음 = 유성 충돌의 엄청난 열기
3. 버키볼
   – 유성 충돌로 생겨날 수 있는 탄소 구조물
   – 일부 만에서 발견됨

어휘 scattered [adj] 드문드문 있는, 흩어져 있는 | depression [n] 오목한 곳, 움푹한 땅 | undetermined [adj] 미확인의, 분명치 않은 | meteor [n] 유성, 별똥별 | consistent with ~와 일치하는 | impact crater 충돌 분화구 | fragment [n] 조각, 파편 | at an angle 비스듬히 | oval [adj] 타원형의 | rim [n] 가장자리, 테두리 | iron compound 철 화합물 | intense [adj] 극심한, 강렬한 | vaporize [v] 증발하다 | blow away 불어 날리다, 날려 보내다 | buckyball [n] 버키볼(60개의 탄소 원자로 구성된 공 모양의 분자) | be composed of ~로 구성되다 | interconnected [adj] 서로 연결된

Q10

In the densely populated Northeastern Unites States, many cities have been linked by express trains for decades, and high-speed rail service has been operating since 2000 linking Boston, NYC, Philadelphia, and Washington DC. This type of transportation system has many advantages, and for those reasons, the next

인구가 밀집한 미국 북동부 지역에서는 수십 년간 여러 도시들이 급행열차로 연결되었으며, 보스턴, 뉴욕, 필라델피아, 워싱턴 DC를 잇는 고속철도 서비스는 2000년 이래로 운행되어 왔다. 이런 유형의 대중교통 체계에는 많은 이점이 있으며, 그러한 이점 때문에 이 서비스를 도입하는

area to receive this kind of service should be California, between San Francisco and Los Angeles.

Firstly, railroad tracks are cheaper and easier to maintain than roads. Asphalt roads must frequently be repaired due to damage from the vehicles that use them and the weather, so they are a constant drain on the economy. This is extremely expensive and uses up a large portion of the government's budget for infrastructure. By comparison, railways are much easier to maintain and need to be repaired far less often. Since the tracks are made from steel and they are attached to concrete, they are much more durable than asphalt.

Secondly, creating a high-speed rail system will help to relieve traffic congestion. The streets and highways in the Los Angeles area have some of the worst traffic congestion in the whole country, and it is only getting worse. If they were provided with an alternative way to travel, many people would prefer to use that. A high-speed rail system would provide them with such an alternative. So, if people can ride trains, there will be fewer cars on the road, which would mean less congestion on the road.

Thirdly, a high-speed rail system is an environmentally friendly form of transportation. High-speed trains use far less energy to transport people than cars. Since cars travel much more slowly than high-speed trains, they must use a lot more energy to cover the same distance. This means that they also produce more emissions than the high-speed trains do. So, high-speed trains are more energy-efficient, and they produce far less pollution than a highway full of cars.

다음 지역은 캘리포니아의 샌프란시스코와 로스앤젤레스 사이여야 한다.

첫 번째로, 철로는 도로보다 저렴하고 유지하기가 더 쉽다. 아스팔트 도로는 도로를 이용하는 차량들과 날씨로 인한 훼손 때문에 자주 보수해야 하므로, 끊임없이 경제를 고갈시킨다. 이는 엄청나게 비싸고 사회 기반 시설을 위한 정부 예산의 상당 부분을 소진하는 일이다. 그에 비해 철로는 관리하기가 훨씬 쉬우며 보수하는 경우도 훨씬 드물다. 철로는 강철로 만들어졌으며 콘크리트에 부착되어 있기 때문에 아스팔트보다 훨씬 더 내구성이 뛰어나다.

두 번째로, 고속 철도망을 만드는 것은 교통 혼잡을 완화하는 데 도움이 될 것이다. 로스앤젤레스 지역의 거리와 고속도로는 전국에서 최악의 교통 혼잡 현상을 보이는 곳들이며, 이는 점점 악화할 뿐이다. 만약 대체 이동 수단이 있다면 많은 사람들은 그것을 이용하고 싶어 할 것이다. 고속 철도망은 그들에게 그런 대안을 제공해 줄 것이다. 따라서, 사람들이 기차를 탈 수 있다면 도로에 차가 줄어들 것이며, 이는 교통 혼잡이 덜할 것을 의미한다.

세 번째로, 고속 철도망은 환경친화적인 교통수단이다. 고속 열차는 차보다 사람들을 실어 나르는 데 훨씬 더 적은 연료를 사용한다. 자동차가 고속 열차보다 훨씬 더 느리게 이동하므로 같은 거리를 가는 데 훨씬 더 많은 연료를 사용해야 한다. 이는 자동차가 또한 고속 열차보다 많은 배기가스를 만들어 낸다는 의미다. 따라서, 고속 열차는 연비가 더 높으며, 차로 가득 찬 고속도로보다 오염 물질을 훨씬 덜 배출한다.

노트

주제	high-speed trains = advantages → California
	1. cheaper & easier to maintain than roads
	- asphalt repair too frequent → $$$
	- railways repair = less often, more durable
	2. relieve traffic congestion
	- provide alternative way to travel
	- ppl use more → less traffic
	3. environ. friendly
	- use less energy than cars

고속 철도 = 이점 → 캘리포니아
1. 도로보다 싸고 유지하기 쉬움
– 아스팔트 보수 너무 잦음 → 비용 많이 듦
– 철길 보수 = 빈도 덜함, 더 오래감
2. 교통 혼잡 완화
– 이동할 대체 방법 제공
– 사람들이 더 많이 이용 → 교통 줄어듦
3. 환경친화적
– 자동차보다 연료를 덜 사용함

어휘 densely populated 인구가 밀집한 I express train 급행열차 I railroad track 철로 I drain ⓝ 고갈시키는/잡아먹는 것 I budget ⓝ 예산 I infrastructure ⓝ 사회 기반 시설 I durable adj 내구성이 있는 I relieve ⓥ 덜어 주다, 완화하다 I traffic congestion 교통 혼잡 I alternative adj 대체 가능한, 대안이 되는 ⓝ 대안 I environmentally friendly 환경친화적인 I emission ⓝ 배기가스, 배출 I energy-efficient adj 에너지 효율이 좋은

---

2. Practice

본서 I P. 78

Q1

Okay, class. Yes, I know "Two heads are better than one." It

자, 여러분. 네, 저는 '백지장도 맞들면 낫다.'라는 말을 알

seems right to argue that teamwork leads to better results, but in fact there are more problems that people fail to notice when working together as a team. These problems far outweigh the benefits. Let me explain.

Contrary to the reading's claim that teamwork helps people to work more efficiently, a group of people takes more time to do a project. This is because all of the group members have to reach a consensual agreement. Each member has to adjust their schedule to decide when they are going to meet. This is pretty time-consuming.

Second, the reading indicates that teamwork will help team members come up with creative ideas. But in reality, this is not true. The reason for this is that one or two influential people in a group will dominate the group's decision making process. Thus, group members will be forced to follow the ideas that the leader suggests.

Finally, I do not think group work will make members work harder. This is because of the free rider problem. The free riding problem in a group makes it more difficult for the group to produce efficient results. Humans are selfish. They will gladly reap the good results other teammates have produced rather than exert themselves. Eventually, this free riding problem will make all team members reluctant to participate actively in any work. No one will work hard in a situation in which someone next to them just sits back and relaxes.

고 있습니다. 팀 활동이 더 나은 결과를 가져다준다고 주장하는 것이 옳은 것처럼 보이지만, 사실 사람들이 팀을 이뤄 일할 때 보지 못하는 문제점이 더 많습니다. 이러한 문제점들은 이점보다 훨씬 더 많죠. 설명하도록 하겠습니다.

팀 활동이 사람들이 일을 더 효율적으로 하도록 도와준다는 지문의 주장과는 반대로 한 그룹의 사람들이 어떤 프로젝트를 하는 데에는 시간이 더 걸립니다. 그룹 구성원들 모두가 합의점에 도달해야 하기 때문이죠. 언제 만날지 결정하기 위해 팀원들 각자 일정을 조정해야 해요. 이건 꽤 시간이 걸리는 일입니다.

두 번째로, 지문은 팀 활동이 팀의 구성원들이 창의적인 아이디어를 생각해내도록 도와준다고 말합니다. 하지만 이것은 사실이 아니에요. 그 이유는 한 그룹에서 영향력 있는 한두 명이 그 그룹의 의사 결정 과정을 장악할 것이기 때문입니다. 그러므로 그룹의 구성원들은 리더가 제안하는 생각을 따를 수밖에 없을 거예요.

마지막으로, 나는 구성원들이 그룹 활동이라고 해서 더 열심히 할 것으로 생각하지 않아요. 왜냐하면 무임승차자 문제 때문이죠. 한 그룹 내의 무임승차 문제는 그 그룹이 효율적인 성과를 내는 것을 더 어렵게 합니다. 인간은 이기적이에요. 자신이 노력하기보다는 팀의 다른 구성원들이 만들어낸 좋은 결과를 기꺼이 거둡니다. 결국 이러한 무임승차 문제는 모든 팀 구성원들이 어떤 활동이든 적극적으로 참여하는 것을 꺼리게 할 겁니다. 옆에 있는 누군가가 그저 편히 앉아서 쉬고 있는 상황에서는 누구도 열심히 일하지 않을 거예요.

노트

주제 working as a team = not good	팀으로 일하는 것 = 안 좋음
1. not efficient 　- always have to reach an agreement 　- time-consuming 2. creative ideas? no 　- 1 or 2 ppl will lead the group 　- other ppl have to follow leaders 3. ppl don't work harder in a group 　- a free rider → everyone will lose motivation	1. 효율적이지 않음 　- 항상 합의에 이르러야 함 　- 시간이 걸림 2. 창의적 아이디어? 아니다 　- 한두 사람이 무리를 이끌 것 　- 다른 사람들은 리더를 따라야 함 3. 사람들은 무리에서 더 열심히 일하지 않는다 　- 무임승차자 → 모두가 의욕을 잃을 것

어휘　fail to ~하지 못하다, ~하는 데 실패하다 | outweigh **v** ~보다 더 크다 | consensual **adj** 합의하는, 합의에 의한 | adjust **v** 조절하다, 조정하다 | time-consuming **adj** (많은) 시간이 걸리는 | come up with 생각해내다, 떠올리다 | influential **adj** 영향력 있는 | dominate **v** 압도하다, 지배하다 | free riding 무임승차 | selfish **adj** 이기적인 | reap **v** 거두다, 수확하다 | exert oneself 노력하다 | reluctant **adj** 꺼리는, 망설이는

Q2

Some species that have been introduced to new regions of the world are believed to cause harm. However, new species do not necessarily cause only bad effects. Rather, depending on what specific aspects you look at, the impact of the introduction of new species can be interpreted differently.

First, the argument that the introduction of new species disturbs

세계의 새로운 지역에 유입된 일부 종은 피해를 야기하는 것으로 여겨집니다. 하지만 새로운 종이 반드시 해로운 영향만 야기하는 것은 아니에요. 오히려 어떤 특정 관점으로 보는지에 따라 새로운 종 유입의 영향은 다르게 해석될 수 있습니다.

첫 번째로, 새로운 종의 유입이 생태계의 균형을 어지럽힌

the ecological balance seems to be quite exaggerated. The introduction of some species makes a great contribution to local communities without upsetting the local ecological balance. For example, a new type of wheat was introduced to Kansas because of favorable conditions for wheat production, and it resulted in high-yield production. This has made it possible to supply a large quantity of wheat as an essential food source for animals as well as humans.

Second, although it can be argued that some introduced new species would degrade the overall quality of the environment, the impact of a new species depends on which part of the environment you look at. For instance, the cane toad was initially introduced for the biological control of agricultural pests, and it has successfully reduced the number of garden insects and rats. As a result, the introduction of that new species has in some ways helped the local environment.

Finally, as for economic burdens brought about by the introduction of new species, their impact also depends on which part of the economy you look at. For example, economic burdens that mesquites cause should be compared with the benefits that they generate. This is because they serve as a source of valuable products such as firewood and high-quality timber. Therefore, given that these economic benefits have a significant effect on local economies, the economic burdens they cause should be reconsidered.

다는 주장은 상당히 과장된 것으로 보입니다. 일부 종의 유입은 그 지역의 생태적 균형을 깨뜨리지 않고 지역 사회에 크게 기여할 수 있어요. 예를 들면, 밀 생산에 적합한 조건 때문에 캔자스 주에 유입된 새로운 종류의 밀은 높은 생산량이라는 결과를 가져왔습니다. 이는 인간뿐 아니라 동물에게도 중요한 식량 원천으로 많은 양의 밀 공급을 가능하게 했어요.

두 번째로, 새로 유입된 일부 종이 전체적인 환경의 질을 저하시킬 거라고 주장할 수는 있겠지만, 새로운 종의 영향은 환경의 어떤 부분을 볼 것인가에 달려 있습니다. 예를 들면, 사탕수수 두꺼비는 처음에 농작물 해충들의 생물학적 통제를 위해 도입되었으며 정원의 곤충과 쥐의 개체수를 성공적으로 감소시켰어요. 그 결과, 이 새로운 종의 도입은 지역 환경에 어느 정도 도움을 주었습니다.

마지막으로, 새로운 종의 유입으로 야기된 경제적 부담의 경우, 그들의 영향 또한 경제의 어떤 부분을 보는가에 달렸습니다. 예를 들면, 메스키트가 초래하는 경제적 부담은 그것이 창출한 이점과 비교되어야 해요. 왜냐하면 그것이 장작이나 양질의 목재 등 가치 있는 생산물의 원천 역할을 하기 때문입니다. 따라서, 이러한 경제적 이익이 지역 경제에 중대한 영향을 미치는 것을 고려할 때, 이들이 일으킨 경제적 부담은 재검토되어야 합니다.

노트

주제	new species in a new envi. cause problems? No

1. disturb ecology? Not really
   - can contribute to local comm. (e.g. ↑ yield production)
2. destroy the natives?
   - No. e.g. = cane toad ↓ # of insects and rats
   - can be helpful to local envi.
3. economic burden?
   - they can also generate benefits

새 환경에서 새 종이 문제를 야기한다? 아니다
1. 생태계 교란? 그렇지 않다
   – 지역 사회에 일조할 수 있음(예: 생산량 높아짐)
2. 토착종 파괴?
   – 아니다. 예 = 사탕수수 두꺼비가 곤충, 쥐 숫자를 감소시킴
   – 지역 환경에 도움을 줄 수 있음
3. 경제적 부담?
   – 이윤도 창출할 수 있음

어휘 species n 생물의 종 | not necessarily 반드시 ~는 아닌 | aspect n 관점, 측면 | interpret v 해석하다 | disturb v 어지럽히다 | exaggerate v 과장하다 | contribution n 기여, 이바지 | wheat n 밀 | favorable adj 적합한, 유리한 | degrade v (질적으로) 저하시키다, 저해하다 | initially adv 처음에 | pest n 해충 | serve as ~로서 역할을 하다 | firewood n 장작 | timber n 목재 | given that ~을 고려하면 | significant adj 중대한, 상당한 | reconsider v 다시 생각/검토하다

Q3

Okay, class, I'd like to continue to discuss the emergence of the factory system in the beginning of the Industrial Revolution. Now, the article that I gave you to read over the weekend seems to imply that there were three strong factors that affected the rise of the factory system in England, but in fact, um, there are some problems… well, with the reasons mentioned in the reading.

좋아요, 여러분, 산업 혁명 초기의 공장제 출현에 관해 이야기를 계속하겠습니다. 자, 주말 동안 읽으라고 여러분에게 준 글은 영국에서 공장제의 발달에 영향을 미친 세 가지 강력한 요인들이 있다고 암시하는 것처럼 보이지만, 사실, 음, 지문에서 언급된 이유에는… 몇 가지 문제점이 있어요.

First of all, contrary to the suggestion of the reading, there were not many noticeable breakthroughs. For example, steam engines were not used that much because the engines often broke down and had a high risk of explosion. So at that time, workers used almost the same machines that they used before and kept the same manufacturing process, with several fellow workers at home or at a small workshop.

Second, property rights introduced by the English government are generally thought of as a main factor in the creation of the factory system. However, property rights do not necessarily contribute to the rise of a factory system. For example, we could hardly find the advancement of the system in Germany even though the government made a great effort to protect individual property rights.

Finally, yes, it is true that factory owners could reduce the costs of transporting raw materials and goods. But they had to spend the same amount of money on managing their factories as they saved. For instance, they had to build a factory and hire someone who could supervise the factory laborers.

먼저, 지문이 제시하는 내용과는 반대로 주목할 만큼 획기적인 발전은 많지 않았습니다. 예를 들면, 증기 기관은 엔진이 자주 고장 났고 폭발의 위험이 컸기 때문에 그렇게 많이 사용되지 않았어요. 그래서 당시 노동자들은 전에 쓰던 것과 거의 같은 기계를 사용했고, 몇 명의 동료 노동자들과 집이나 작은 작업장에서 같은 제조 과정을 고수하며 일했습니다.

두 번째로, 영국 정부가 도입한 재산권은 일반적으로 공장제 탄생의 중요한 요소로 여겨집니다. 하지만 재산권은 딱히 공장제의 성공에 기여하지 않아요. 예를 들면, 독일 정부는 개인의 재산권을 지키기 위해 엄청난 노력을 기울였지만, 독일에서는 공장제의 발전을 찾아보기 어렵습니다.

마지막으로, 네, 공장 소유주가 원자재와 상품의 운송 비용을 줄일 수 있었던 것은 사실이에요. 하지만 아낀 돈을 공장을 관리하는 데 써야만 했습니다. 예를 들면, 공장을 짓거나 공장 근로자들을 감독하는 누군가를 고용해야만 했죠.

주제	3 reasons for the rise of factory system in England → problems	영국 공장 시스템 성공의 세 가지 이유 → 문제점들

	1. many breakthroughs? no
	  - steam engine → not used much
	  - workers used same machines
		1. 획기적인 발전 많음? 아니다
		  - 증기 기관차 → 많이 사용되지 않음
		  - 노동자들은 같은 기계 사용

	2. property rights X contribute
	  - German gov't did the same → nothing really happened
		2. 재산권이 기여 X
		  - 독일 정부도 똑같이 함 → 아무 일도 일어나지 않음

	3. cost ↓ X
	  - had to spend same $ for managing factories
		3. 비용 절감 X
		  - 공장 관리에 그만큼의 비용을 써야 했음

어휘 emergence ⓝ 출현, 도래 l rise ⓝ 성공, 상승, 증가 l noticeable adj 주목할 만한, 주요한 l breakthrough ⓝ 획기적인 변화, 발전 l break down 망가지다 l explosion ⓝ 폭발 l property rights 재산권 l contribute to ~에 기여하다 l advancement ⓝ 발전 l make a great effort to ~에 큰 노력을 기울이다 l transport ⓥ 운송하다 l raw material 원자재, 원료 l good ⓝ 재화(상품) l manage ⓥ 운영하다, 관리하다 l supervise ⓥ 감독하다, 감시하다

Q4

Okay, class. Yes, I know hydrogen is a cleaner energy source than fossil fuels, but the article is simply too optimistic about the possibility that hydrogen fuel will replace fossil fuels anytime soon. I think the possibility seems very low. Let's look at the key points discussed in the reading.

Even though it is true that hydrogen gas is renewable and very abundant, the kind of hydrogen that is used in hydrogen fuel engines is highly artificial and requires a very complicated process to create. The gas is processed into a liquid state that must be kept at a constant temperature of -253 degrees Celsius in specially designed containers. This means it is very hard to

자, 여러분. 그래요, 수소가 화석 연료보다 깨끗한 에너지라는 것은 알지만, 지문은 수소 연료가 화석 연료를 조만간 언제든 대체할 것이라는 가능성에 그저 너무 긍정적입니다. 저는 그 가능성이 매우 낮다고 생각해요. 지문에서 논의된 요점들을 살펴봅시다.

수소 가스가 재생할 수 있고 매우 풍부하다는 것은 사실이지만, 수소 연료 엔진에 사용되는 종류의 수소는 매우 인공적이고 만드는 데 아주 복잡한 과정을 필요로 합니다. 이 기체는 특별히 고안된 용기에서 섭씨 영하 253도의 일정한 온도로 유지되어야 하는 액체 형태로 처리되죠. 이는 이러한 유형의 액체 형태를 만드는 일이 매우 복

create hydrogen that can be used as an energy source because generating this liquid form is very complex.

Next, the article mentions pollution. Yes, it is true that the only byproduct generated when using hydrogen as an energy source is water. But, the article fails to discuss the process used to create that type of hydrogen. In order to create the liquid hydrogen used in fuel cells, a very large amount of fossil fuels, such as coal, must be burned. So, you see that, even though no pollution is given off when hydrogen is used for energy, there is a lot of pollution added to the atmosphere when generating it.

And last, I can't see why the reading would say that hydrogen fuel cell engines will become more cost-effective. These engines require platinum. As you all know, platinum is a very rare and very expensive metal. Without platinum, the engines used in hydrogen fuel cells cannot complete the chemical reactions to achieve energy creation. So, without this very expensive metal, these engines can't make the energy move a vehicle.

잡기 때문에 에너지원으로 사용될 수 있는 수소를 만드는 것은 매우 어렵다는 뜻입니다.

다음으로, 지문은 오염을 언급합니다. 그래요, 수소를 에너지원으로 사용할 때 만들어지는 유일한 부산물이 물이라는 것은 사실입니다. 하지만 지문은 그러한 유형의 수소를 만드는 데 사용되는 과정을 논의하지 않아요. 연료 전지에 사용되는 액체 수소를 만들기 위해서는 석탄 같은 매우 많은 양의 화석 연료를 태워야 합니다. 그래서 수소가 에너지로 사용될 때는 아무런 오염물을 배출하지 않는다고 해도 수소를 만들어 낼 때는 대기가 크게 오염된다는 걸 알 수 있죠.

그리고 마지막으로, 저는 왜 수소 연료 전지 엔진이 비용 대비 효과가 더 클 것이라고 지문에서 말했는지 이해할 수 없군요. 이러한 엔진에는 백금이 필요합니다. 여러분 모두 알다시피, 백금은 매우 희귀하고 아주 비싼 금속입니다. 백금 없이는 수소 연료 전지에 사용되는 엔진이 에너지를 생성시키기 위한 화학 반응을 온전히 일으킬 수 없어요. 그래서 이 비싼 금속이 없으면 이러한 엔진은 자동차를 움직이게 만드는 에너지를 생성해 낼 수 없습니다.

노트

주제	hydrogen fuel can replace fossil f. soon? No	수소 연료가 곧 화석 연료를 대체? 아니다

1. not that simple
 - the kind of H. used for H. fuel engines is artificial & complicated to make
2. No pollution?
 - byproduct = water, true
 - but the process of making that H. requires fossil f. too → pollution
3. cost effective?
 - H. fuel engine = platinum = rare & expensive

1. 그렇게 간단하지 않음
 – 수소 연료 엔진에 사용되는 수소는 인공적 & 만들기 복잡함
2. 오염 없음?
 – 부산물 = 물, 사실
 – 그러나 그 수소를 만드는 과정에서도 화석 연료가 사용됨 → 오염
3. 비용 효율적?
 – 수소 연료 엔진 = 백금 = 귀함 & 비쌈

어휘 optimistic adj 낙관적인, 긍정적인 I renewable adj 재생 가능한 I abundant adj 풍부한 I artificial adj 인공적인, 인위적인 I complicated adj 복잡한 I liquid adj 액체의 I state n 상태 I constant adj 지속적인, 일정한 I designed adj 고안된, 만들어진 I container n 용기, 그릇 I byproduct n 부산물 I fail to ~하지 못하다 I coal n 석탄 I give off 발산하다, 내뿜다 I cost-effective adj 비용 효율적인 I platinum n 백금 I rare adj 드문, 희귀한 I chemical reaction 화학 반응

Q5

I know many people assume that high gasoline prices caused by a gas tax increase would not make energy consumers restrain themselves from using gas. But, in reality, this policy of increasing gas taxes is greatly helpful in saving gasoline. I will explain to you how this policy is efficient.

First, people will reduce their consumption of gasoline. The reading mentions cigarette prices to support the idea that if there were nothing to replace gasoline, people still would not reduce consumption. But if it becomes too expensive to use commodities, the first thing people will do is attempt to use them economically. For example, people will not drive their car to travel a short distance.

많은 사람들이 주유세 인상으로 인한 높은 휘발유 가격이 에너지 소비자들의 휘발유 소비를 자제하게 하지 못할 것이라고 생각한다는 것을 알고 있습니다. 하지만 현실적으로는 주유세를 인상하는 이 정책이 휘발유를 절약하는 데 매우 큰 도움이 됩니다. 이 정책이 어떻게 효율적인지 여러분에게 설명하죠.

첫째로, 사람들이 휘발유 소비를 줄일 겁니다. 지문은 만약 휘발유를 대체할 것이 아무것도 없으면 사람들이 여전히 소비를 줄이지 않을 것이라는 견해를 뒷받침하기 위해 담배 가격을 언급합니다. 하지만 만약 상품을 사용하는 비용이 너무 비싸지면 사람들은 첫 번째로 그것을 알뜰하게 사용하려고 노력할 거예요. 예를 들면, 짧은 거리를 이동

Second, this policy will not financially burden people. I know many people live on the outskirts because of skyrocketing housing prices. But, the reading says that the families who live in these areas use only private cars for commuting. But as we all know, a well-developed public transportation system, such as buses, subways, and trains, is available for people to use. Also, they can carpool as a means of reducing gasoline consumption.

Third, increasing gas taxes is a better way to encourage car makers to develop fuel-efficient cars. This policy can accelerate the development of more fuel-efficient vehicles by automakers because consumers will push car companies to develop those cars through a gradual rise in the demand for the cars. Consumers will demand fuel-efficient cars. This change in demand will force car companies to develop more fuel-efficient cars.

하기 위해 차를 몰지 않을 겁니다.

두 번째로, 이 정책은 사람들에게 재정적으로 부담을 주지 않을 겁니다. 많은 사람들이 치솟는 집값 때문에 교외 지역에 살고 있다는 점은 알아요. 하지만 지문은 이 지역에 사는 가족들이 통근을 위해 자가용만 이용한다고 말합니다. 그러나 우리 모두 알다시피 사람들은 버스와 지하철, 기차 같은 잘 발달한 대중교통 시설을 이용할 수 있어요. 휘발유 소비를 줄이려는 수단으로 카풀을 할 수도 있죠.

세 번째로, 주유세 인상은 자동차 제조업체들이 연료 효율이 좋은 자동차를 개발하도록 장려하는 데 더 좋은 방법입니다. 이 정책은 자동차 제조업체들이 더 연료 효율이 좋은 차를 개발하는 것을 가속화할 수 있는데, 소비자들이 그런 차에 대한 점진적인 수요 증가를 통해 자동차 회사들에 그런 차를 개발하도록 압박할 것이기 때문입니다. 소비자들은 연료 효율이 좋은 차를 요구할 거예요. 이러한 수요 변화는 자동차 회사를 압박해 연비가 더 뛰어난 자동차를 개발하게 만들 겁니다.

노트

주제 ↑ energy price = saving source of energy? Yes	에너지 가격 올리기 = 에너지원 절약? 맞다
1. ppl will ↓ consuming gas - use gas economically(e.g. X drive a short distance) 2. financial burden X - we have public transp.(bus, subway, train…) - ppl can carpool too 3. better ways - encourage making more fuel-efficient cars - ppl will demand these cars	1. 사람들이 휘발유 소비를 줄일 것 – 가솔린 알뜰하게 사용(예: 짧은 거리를 운전하지 않음) 2. 재정적 부담 없음 – 대중교통이 있음(버스, 지하철, 기차…) – 카풀도 할 수 있음 3. 더 좋은 방법 – 연비가 더 좋은 자동차 제조를 장려 – 사람들이 이런 차를 원할 것

어휘 assume **v** 가정하다, 추정하다 I restrain **v** 자제하다 I commodity **n** 상품 I attempt **v** 노력하다, 시도하다 I economically **adv** 경제적으로 I financially **adv** 재정적으로 I skyrocketing **adj** 치솟는, 급격히 증가하는 I well-developed **adj** 잘 발달된 I public transportation system 대중교통 시설 I carpool **v** 카풀을 하다 I fuel-efficient **adj** 연료 효율이 좋은 I accelerate **v** 가속화하다 I gradual **adj** 점차적인, 점진적인

Q6

The arguments provided in your reading do seem logical at first, but upon closer examination there are many weak points. When one takes the time to examine the facts from a larger perspective, there is no clear evidence to suggest that most of the modern population of England is actually descended from the Anglo-Saxons. Allow me to demonstrate.

Firstly, it is true that the Anglo-Saxons had good reason to leave their homes, and did so in large numbers. However, the author did not take into account the actual size of the Celtic population. Historical studies have shown that the Celtic population vastly outnumbered the invading Anglo-Saxons. So, while they may have gained political control of the country, it seems very doubtful that they could displace so many people.

Secondly, simply because English became the official language

지문에서 제시된 주장들은 처음에는 논리적인 것 같지만 엄밀히 보면 많은 허점들이 있어요. 좀 더 큰 관점에서 진위를 들여다볼 시간을 가지면 현대 잉글랜드 인구 대부분이 사실 앵글로색슨족의 후손이라는 것을 시사하는 명백한 증거는 없습니다. 제가 설명해보죠.

첫째로, 앵글로색슨족이 고국을 떠날 타당한 이유가 있었고, 많은 인구가 떠났다는 것은 사실입니다. 그러나 저자는 켈트족 인구의 실제 규모를 고려하지 않았어요. 여러 역사 연구는 침략한 앵글로색슨족보다 켈트족 인구가 훨씬 더 많았다는 점을 보여줍니다. 그래서 잉글랜드를 정치적으로 지배할 수 있었을지는 모르지만, 그 많은 사람들을 쫓아낼 수 있었다는 점은 매우 의심스러워요.

둘째로, 단순히 영어가 그 나라의 공식어가 됐다고 해서 반드시 앵글로색슨족이 인구의 다수를 차지하게 되었다

of the country, it does not necessarily mean that the population became largely Anglo-Saxon. Conquered people often take the language of their new rulers as their own. For example, the greatest empire in European history was Rome, and it stretched from Spain to the Middle East. Many of the nations within their empire adopted Latin as their language, but this hardly means that their populations were replaced with ethnic Romans. Therefore, it seems very likely that the Celts simply adopted the Anglo-Saxon language and remained the majority of the population.

Thirdly, the genetic study mentioned in the passage has a fatal flaw. The flaw is that the English people sampled in the study live in a small area in the Eastern section of the country. This area was where the invaders would have arrived and set up their own villages and towns early on. I mean the majority of the populations living in this area originated from the Anglo-Saxons, so the DNA profiles of the people sampled have such a strong Anglo-Saxon background. As a result, the results of the DNA testing cannot be applied to the rest of the country.

는 의미는 아닙니다. 정복당한 사람들은 새로운 통치자들의 언어를 자신의 언어로 받아들여요. 예를 들면, 유럽 역사에서 가장 거대한 제국은 로마였고 이 제국은 스페인에서 중동까지 뻗어 나갔습니다. 제국 내의 많은 나라들이 라틴어를 언어로 채택했지만, 이는 그 인구가 로마 민족으로 대체되었다는 의미는 아니죠. 따라서 켈트족이 단순히 앵글로색슨족의 언어를 채택하고 인구의 대다수로 남았을 가능성이 커 보입니다.

셋째로, 지문에서 언급된 유전 연구는 치명적인 오류를 가지고 있어요. 그 오류는 그 연구에서 표본이 된 잉글랜드인들이 잉글랜드 동부의 작은 지역에 산다는 겁니다. 이 지역은 침략자들이 도착해서 초기에 마을과 도시를 세웠을 지역입니다. 그러니까, 이 지역에 사는 인구의 대다수가 앵글로색슨족에서 기원했기에 표본의 DNA형에서 앵글로색슨족의 비중이 매우 높은 것이죠. 결과적으로, 이 DNA 검사 결과는 잉글랜드의 나머지 지역에 적용될 수가 없습니다.

노트

주제	origins of English ppl = Anglo-Saxons? Not clear

1. mass migration
   - displaced Celtic? No, Celtics # too large
   - can't displace that many ppl
2. language
   - conquered ppl often use their ruler's language too
   - Celts adopting Anglo-Saxon language? Not really…
3. DNA study
   - DNA samples came from a small area where Anglo-Saxons would have arrived

잉글랜드인들의 기원 = 앵글로색슨족? 확실치 않음
1. 집단 이주
   - 켈트족을 대체? 아니다. 켈트족의 숫자가 너무 많았다.
   - 그렇게 많은 사람을 대체할 수는 없음
2. 언어
   - 정복당한 사람들은 정복자의 언어도 흔히 사용함
   - 켈트족이 앵글로색슨 언어를 사용? 그다지…
3. DNA 연구
   - DNA 표본은 앵글로색슨인들이 도착했을 작은 지역에서 얻은 것

어휘 perspective 🅝 관점, 시각 | take into account ~을 고려하다 | outnumber 🆅 ~보다 수가 더 많다, ~을 수적으로 압도하다 | stretch 🆅 뻗어 있다, 펼쳐지다 | ethnic 🄰🄳🄹 민족의 | genetic 🄰🄳🄹 유전의, 유전학의 | flaw 🅝 결함, 오류 | set up 세우다 | early on 초기에

Q7

The Everglades have been extensively damaged by many factors, but the reading creates the impression that there is little that can be done to save the region. However, the problems affecting the Everglades can and are being dealt with several solutions. There is hope for the Everglades.

First, the introduction of invasive species is a serious problem, but the main problem with many of them is that their natural enemies are not present. The paperbark tree was purposefully introduced to drain wetlands, which people later realized was a mistake. It was chosen because it was well-suited to the climate. There are insects in Australia that limit the growth and spread of paperbark trees by eating their leaves and flowers. So, one of the measures

에버글레이즈는 많은 요인 때문에 광범위한 피해를 보았지만, 지문은 이 지역을 구하기 위해 할 수 있는 일은 거의 없다는 인상을 심어 줍니다. 하지만 에버글레이즈에 영향을 끼치는 문제들은 몇 가지 방법을 통해 해결될 수 있고, 또 해결되고 있어요. 에버글레이즈에 희망은 있습니다.

첫째, 외래종의 유입은 심각한 문제이지만, 그 외래종들 중 다수의 주된 문제는 이들의 천적이 존재하지 않는다는 겁니다. 페이퍼바크 나무는 의도적으로 습지의 물을 빼기 위해 도입되었고 사람들은 이후에 이것이 실수였다는 것을 깨달았죠. 그것은 기후에 잘 맞았기 때문에 선택되었습니다. 호주에는 이 나무들의 잎과 꽃을 먹어 치워 성장과 확산을 제한하는 곤충들이 있어요. 그래서 외래종들을 통

that have been taken to control them is to release those insects into the Everglades.

Second, while pollutants are a serious problem for the Everglades, the damage is reversible. To solve this problem, the government passed an act limiting fertilizer use. Farmers are forced to use less fertilizer, which immediately lowers levels downstream. They also created strict emission standards for fossil fuel burning facilities. Together, these measures can drastically reduce both fertilizer and mercury levels in the wetlands.

Third, I know the drought conditions affecting the Everglades are severe. However, since the causes are manmade, they are not difficult to correct. Many of the dams and canals that were built to reduce flooding are being removed. This allows rivers and wetlands to return to their natural state. Also, less rainwater is being diverted to residential areas, so water levels have begun returning to normal. Given enough time to recover, the wetlands should be able to reclaim their former territory.

제하기 위해 취하고 있는 조치 중 하나는 에버글레이즈에 그런 곤충을 풀어놓는 것입니다.

두 번째로, 오염 물질이 에버글레이즈에 심각한 문제인 반면 그 피해는 되돌릴 수 있어요. 이 문제를 해결하기 위해 정부는 비료 사용을 제한하는 법안을 통과시켰습니다. 농부들은 비료를 덜 쓸 수밖에 없고 이는 즉시 하류 수준으로 낮춰 주죠. 또한, 화석 연료를 태우는 시설들에 관해 엄격한 배출 기준을 만들었습니다. 이러한 조치들은 비료와 습지의 수은 수치를 모두 급격하게 줄일 수 있어요.

세 번째로, 에버글레이즈에 영향을 주는 가뭄의 수준이 심각하다는 사실을 알고 있습니다. 하지만 그 원인이 인공적이기 때문에 바로잡는 것은 어렵지 않아요. 홍수를 줄이기 위해 지어졌던 많은 댐과 운하가 제거되고 있습니다. 이는 강과 습지가 자연적인 상태로 되돌아가게 해 주죠. 또한 더 적은 빗물이 주거 지역으로 우회되고 있어서 물 수위가 정상으로 돌아오기 시작했습니다. 회복을 위한 충분한 시간이 주어지면 습지는 기존의 영역을 되찾을 수 있을 거예요.

노트

| 주제 | issues threatening the Everglades → there is hope | 에버글레이즈를 위협하는 문제 → 희망은 있다 |

1. invasive plants & animals
    - introduce natural enemies that eat those invasive plants
2. water pollution
    - chemical fertilizer & mercury → gov't passed laws
3. ↓ water supply
    - dams & canals are being removed
    - water levels are returning to normal → recover

1. 외래종 식물 & 동물
    – 이 외래종 식물을 먹는 천적을 도입
2. 수질 오염
    – 화학 비료 & 수은 → 정부가 법안을 통과시킴
3. 물 공급 감소
    – 댐 & 운하 제거되는 중
    – 수위 원래대로 돌아오는 중 → 회복

어휘 extensively adv 광범위하게 | natural enemy 천적 | purposefully adv 고의적으로 | drain v 물을 빼내다 | reversible adj (원상태로) 되돌릴 수 있는 | act n 법률 | downstream adv 하류로 | emission n 배출 | drastically adv 급격히, 대폭 | drought n 가뭄 | manmade adj 인공적인 | divert v 우회시키다, 방향을 바꾸다 | reclaim v 되찾다

Q8

It is undeniable that laws that restrict trade can have undesirable results. The arguments in the reading against a law restricting the importation of non-native species may seem plausible at first glance. However, the reasons mentioned in the reading are not all that convincing; in fact, the law is a very good idea.

First of all, the reading says that this law could force pet owners to give up their animals. However, this law has almost no effect on pet owners because the law is applied to only additional imports and sales, I mean, in the future, people will not be allowed to purchase non-native species of animals. But, this does not mean that the law affects pet owners who now own these animals. So, there is no need for the pet owners to worry about this law.

Yes, it is true that it costs a lot of money to conduct environmental studies, but you know, these studies are worth conducting because this research can prevent further financial loss from

교역을 제한하는 법이 원치 않는 결과를 불러올 수 있다는 것은 부정할 수 없습니다. 외래종 수입을 제한하는 법에 반대하는 지문의 주장들은 처음 봤을 때는 이치에 맞는 것처럼 보일 수 있어요. 하지만 지문에서 언급된 이유들은 그다지 설득력이 있지 않습니다. 사실, 이 법은 아주 좋은 생각이에요.

먼저, 지문은 반려동물 주인들이 이 법 때문에 자기 동물을 포기하게 만들 수 있다고 말합니다. 하지만 이 법은 추가적인 수입과 판매에만 적용되기 때문에 반려동물 주인에게는 거의 효력을 발휘하지 못해요. 내 말은, 미래에 사람들이 외래종 동물을 구입하지 못하게 될 겁니다. 하지만 이것이 지금 이 동물들을 소유한 소유주들에게 영향을 준다는 뜻은 아니에요. 그래서 반려동물 주인들이 이 법을 걱정할 필요는 없습니다.

그래요. 환경 연구를 하는 데는 많은 돈이 드는 것이 사실

non-native species. For instance, huge snakes called the Burmese pythons were imported from Asia as pets, and they have devastated native species in Florida. The cost of restoring damage that these non-native species do to native species would be far greater than that of doing research on the suitability of a species.

I do not agree with the reading's argument that single standards should not be applied to the whole country. This is because non-native species can be dangerous to native species everywhere. The South American rabbits mentioned in the reading brought the myxoma virus to the UK. This virus can be transmitted by fleas and mosquitoes, which can take it anywhere. It killed 99% of the native rabbits. Even though a species cannot live in a cold habitat, that doesn't mean that the virus can't spread there.

이지만 이 연구는 외래종이 야기하는 더 큰 경제적 손실을 방지할 수 있기 때문에 시행할 가치가 있습니다. 예를 들어, 버마왕뱀이라고 불리는 거대한 뱀이 아시아에서 반려동물로 들어왔고 플로리다에서 토착종을 완전히 몰아냈어요. 이 외래종이 토착종에 끼친 피해를 복구하는 비용은 특정 종의 적합성을 연구하는 데 드는 비용보다 훨씬 더 클 겁니다.

저는 하나의 기준이 나라 전체에 적용되어서는 안 된다는 지문의 주장에 동의하지 않습니다. 왜냐하면 외래종은 모든 곳의 토착종에게 위험할 수 있기 때문이죠. 지문에서 언급된 남아메리카 토끼는 영국에 점액종 바이러스를 들여왔습니다. 이 바이러스는 벼룩과 모기로 전염될 수 있으며 이것들은 바이러스를 어디로든 옮길 수 있죠. 바이러스는 토착종 토끼의 99%를 살상했습니다. 특정 종이 추운 서식지에서 생존할 수 없다고 해서 바이러스가 그곳에서 퍼지지 못한다는 의미는 아니에요.

노트

| 주제 | gov't law = restrict importing / buying / selling non-native species
→ good idea
1. pet owners will give up their pets
　- the law X apply to current pets → no worries
2. cost
　- conducting studies is $$$, but worth
　- prevent further financial loss from non-native species
3. not reasonable?
　- non-native species can be dangerous to native species everywhere / virus can still spread | 정부 법 = 토착종이 아닌 동물의 수입 / 구매 / 판매 제한
→ 좋은 생각
1. 반려동물 소유주가 반려동물을 포기할 것
　- 법은 지금의 반려동물에 적용 안 됨 → 걱정 안 해도 된다
2. 비용
　- 연구 비용은 많이 들지만 가치가 있다
　- 토착종이 아닌 종으로 인한 더 이상의 재정 손실을 막음
3. 합리적이지 않다?
　- 토착종이 아닌 종은 어디서든 토착종에게 위험할 수 있다 / 바이러스는 여전히 퍼질 수 있다 |

어휘　undeniable **adj** 부정할 수 없는 ǀ restrict **v** 제한하다 ǀ undesirable **adj** 원하지 않는, 달갑지 않은 ǀ argument **n** 주장 ǀ importation **n** 수입 ǀ plausible **adj** 타당한, 이치에 맞는 ǀ at first glance 처음에는, 언뜻 보기에 ǀ convincing **adj** 설득력 있는 ǀ additional **adj** 추가의 ǀ purchase **v** 구입하다 ǀ conduct **v** 진행하다, 실시하다 ǀ prevent **v** 방지하다 ǀ financial **adj** 재정적인 ǀ devastate **v** 완전히 파괴하다 ǀ restore **v** 복구하다 ǀ suitability **n** 적합함, 어울림 ǀ transmit **v** 전염시키다, 전달하다 ǀ flea **n** 벼룩 ǀ mosquito **n** 모기

Q9

Carolina bays are definitely interesting geological features, but nothing about them points to an extraterrestrial origin. The reading provides three pieces of evidence that support the idea that the bays were created by meteors exploding in the air. However, these arguments are unconvincing, and there are other natural processes that can explain the evidence cited in the reading.

First, the reading contends that the shape of the bays shows that they were created by meteor fragments. However, ocean currents and wind can also produce similarly-shaped features. The area where the bays are found used to be underwater, and a steady current that flows in one direction for a long time can

캐롤라이나만은 분명히 흥미로운 지질학 특징입니다만, 외계의 기원을 암시하는 건 아무것도 없습니다. 지문에서는 그 만이 공중에서 폭발한 유성에 의해 형성되었다는 주장을 뒷받침하는 세 가지 증거를 제시합니다. 그러나 이런 주장들은 설득력이 없으며, 지문에서 언급된 증거를 설명할 수 있는 다른 자연적 과정들이 있어요.

먼저, 지문에서는 캐롤라이나만의 형태가 그곳이 유성 파편들로 인해 형성되었다는 것을 보여준다고 주장하죠. 그렇지만 해류와 바람도 비슷한 모양의 특징들을 만들어낼 수 있습니다. 그 만이 발견되는 지역은 예전에 물속에 잠겨 있었고, 오랜 시간 동안 지속적으로 한 방향으로 흐르는 해류는 해저에 이와 같이 움푹 팬 지형을 만들 수 있어

create depressions like these on the sea floor. When ocean levels lowered, the bays were exposed to the air, and wind action could have continued to sculpt them into the shapes we see today.

Second, the reading mentions that the sand contained in the bays lacks the iron coating that sand in the region usually has. The author blames this on the intense heat that a meteor strike would have caused. However, the intense heat would also have melted the sand into glass, and no glass has been found in the bays. There is a much simpler explanation: water can chemically react with the iron compounds when it fills the bays, and the iron is then carried away when the water level drops.

Third, the reading states that buckyballs have been found in some of the bays, and they can be created by meteor strikes. This is true, but it is by no means the only way that buckyballs can form. They can also be created by lightning strikes during thunderstorms. If the buckyballs were created by meteor impacts, then they should be present in most of the bays, but they only exist in a few. Therefore, it is more likely that lightning created them.

요. 바닷물의 수위가 낮아졌을 때 그 만은 공기에 노출되었으며, 이어서 바람의 작용이 그곳을 우리가 오늘날 보는 형태로 만들어 낼 수 있었죠.

두 번째로, 지문에서는 그 만에 있는 모래에는 그 지역 모래가 대개 가지고 있는 철로 된 막이 없다고 말합니다. 저자는 이것을 유성 충돌로 인해 야기되었을 강한 열 때문이라고 보고 있죠. 그렇지만 강한 열은 또한 모래를 녹여 유리로 만들었을 텐데, 이 만에서는 유리가 전혀 발견되지 않습니다. 여기서 훨씬 더 간단한 설명이 가능하죠. 만에 바닷물이 가득 차면 물은 철 화합물과 화학적으로 반응하고, 바닷물의 수위가 떨어질 때 물이 철을 휩쓸어갑니다.

세 번째로, 지문에서는 버키볼이 이 만의 일부에서 발견되었으며, 이들이 유성과의 충돌로 만들어졌을 수도 있다고 주장하죠. 이것은 사실이지만 버키볼이 오직 이 방법으로만 형성될 수 있는 것은 결코 아닙니다. 이들은 폭풍우가 칠 때 떨어진 번개에 의해 생성될 수도 있어요. 만약 버키볼이 유성 충돌로 생겨난다면 만의 거의 모든 곳에 있어야 하지만, 이것들은 몇 군데에서만 존재하죠. 따라서 이것들은 번개가 만들었을 가능성이 더 큽니다.

노트

주제	Carolina bays – their origin = large meteors?	캐롤라이나만 – 기원 = 거대 유성?
	1. depressions' shape	1. 움푹 팬 땅의 모양
	- ocean currents & wind can also make similar bays	– 해류와 바람 또한 유사한 만을 만들 수 있음
	2. sand is different	2. 모래가 다름
	- this heat would've melted sand too → glass	– 이 열은 모래도 녹였을 것 → 유리가 됨
	- No glass found	– 유리가 발견되지 않음
	3. buckyballs	3. 버키볼
	- they can also be formed by lightning strikes	– 번개로도 만들어질 수 있음
	- only found in a few bays	– 일부 만에서만 발견됨

어휘 geological adj 지질학(상)의, 지질의 I extraterrestrial adj 외계의 I unconvincing adj 설득력이 없는 I contend v 주장하다 I ocean current n 해류 I sea floor n 해저 I sculpt v 조각하다, 형태를 만들다 I chemically adv 화학적으로 I by no means 결코 ~이 아닌 I thunderstorm n 뇌우, 폭풍우

Q10

In the reading, the author talks about the benefits of high-speed rail systems and the advantages that they could have for California. However, while high-speed trains have enjoyed some success in the Northeastern United States, they are not suitable for California. The advantages that he lists are true for some areas, but they do not apply in that region.

The author first talks about how high speed rail lines are more cost efficient than highways. Highways constantly need repairs, which makes them a serious drain on government funds. This is true, but we should not ignore the massive costs involved in constructing a high-speed rail system. Building a system in California would cost upwards of 100 billion dollars, which would be over 75% of the state's annual tax revenue. The state simply

읽기 지문에서 필자는 고속 철도망의 혜택과 캘리포니아에 철도망을 구축했을 때의 장점에 관해 이야기합니다. 그러나 고속 열차가 미국 북동부 지역에서 어느 정도 성공을 거두긴 했지만 캘리포니아에는 적합하지 않아요. 그가 열거하는 장점들은 일부 지역에서는 사실이지만 해당 지역에는 적용되지 않습니다.

필자는 맨 먼저 고속철도가 얼마나 고속도로보다 비용 효율이 더 높은지 이야기합니다. 고속도로는 끊임없이 보수해야 하고, 이로 인해 정부 자금을 심각하게 고갈시킵니다. 이것은 사실이지만, 고속 철도망을 건설하는 데 드는 막대한 비용을 간과해서는 안 됩니다. 캘리포니아에 철도망을 건설하는 데에는 1천억 달러 이상의 비용이 소요될 것이며, 이는 캘리포니아주 연간 세수의 75%를 웃도는 금

cannot afford to undertake such a building project, especially with its current economic condition.

The author next discusses how a high-speed rail system will ease traffic congestion. Of course, the system that was built on the East Coast achieved this goal, but it was successful for two key reasons. The large cities of the East Coast are relatively close together, and they all have good public transportation systems. However, there are very few large cities between San Francisco and Los Angeles, and the public transportation system is poor. This means that most people would still have to drive their cars to reach the train stations, so traffic congestion would not be alleviated much.

The author finishes by pointing out that high-speed rail is more environmentally friendly than traveling by car. However, it would not work that way in California because that is true only if the high-speed trains can maintain a constant speed. Since the trains would often have to run on older tracks, they would not travel at a steady speed, but would have to repeatedly adjust their speed depending on what section of track they are using. This means that the trains could not run efficiently, using more energy and producing more pollution.

액이에요. 이 주는 특히 지금과 같은 경제 상황에서 그런 건설 프로젝트에 착수할 여유가 전혀 없습니다.

필자는 다음으로 고속 철도망이 어떻게 교통 혼잡을 완화할 것인지 말합니다. 물론 동부 해안에 건설되었던 철도망으로 이 목표를 달성하긴 했지만, 그것이 성공할 수 있었던 데에는 두 가지 이유가 있었어요. 동부 해안의 대도시들은 상대적으로 서로 가까이에 있으며, 모두 대중교통 시설이 잘 갖추어져 있죠. 그러나 샌프란시스코와 로스앤젤레스 사이에는 대도시가 거의 없으며, 대중교통 시설도 형편없습니다. 이는 대부분의 사람들이 기차역에 가기 위해서는 여전히 차를 운전해야 한다는 뜻이므로, 교통 혼잡이 크게 완화되지 않을 것을 의미합니다.

필자는 고속철도가 차를 타고 이동하는 것보다 더 환경친화적이라고 지적하며 마무리를 짓습니다. 그러나 이는 고속 열차가 일정한 속도를 유지할 수 있을 때만 사실이기 때문에 캘리포니아에서는 그런 효과가 없을 것입니다. 열차들은 종종 오래된 선로 위를 달려야 하므로 일정한 속도로 운행되지 않을 것이며, 그들이 이용하는 선로의 구간에 따라 속도를 여러 차례 조정해야 할 거예요. 이는 열차가 더 많은 에너지를 사용하고 더 많은 오염 물질을 배출하며 효율적으로 운행될 수 없음을 의미합니다.

노트

주제	high-speed trains = advantages → California X	고속 철도 = 이점 → 캘리포니아는 안 좋음

high-speed trains = advantages → California X
  1. cheaper & easier to maintain than roads
     - building this railway system in Cali → 100 billion
  2. relieve traffic congestion
     - worked in East since cities are close together
     - in Cali, few large cities & public transp. poor → ppl need to drive to train stations
  3. environ. friendly
     - need to maintain a constant speed → X in Cali

고속 철도 = 이점 → 캘리포니아는 안 좋음
  1. 도로보다 싸고 유지하기 쉬움
     – 이 철도 시스템을 캘리포니아에 건설 → 천억 달러
  2. 교통 혼잡 완화
     – 도시들이 서로 가까워서 동부에서는 효과 있었음
     – 캘리포니아는 대도시가 소수 & 대중교통이 열악 → 사람들이 기차역까지 운전해서 가야 함
  3. 환경친화적
     – 일관된 속도를 유지해야 함 → 캘리포니아에서는 안 됨

어휘 cost efficient 비용 효율적인 | massive **adj** 막대한, 엄청난 | upwards of ~의 이상 | annual **adj** 연간의, 연례의 | tax revenue 세수(입) | undertake **v** 착수하다 | alleviate **v** 완화하다 | adjust **v** 조정하다

Lesson 02 노트 & 답변 연결하기

Practice

본서 P. 88

Q1 Reading

The top priority for any company is to increase its profits. In order to do so, companies must regularly assess their performance in the market and find new strategies suitable for rapidly changing their economic circumstances. Such strategies often involve releasing new products onto the market, and this can be done in three ways.

어떤 기업이든 최우선순위는 이익을 증대하는 것이다. 그러기 위해 기업들은 시장에서 거둔 성과를 정기적으로 평가하고, 그들의 경제적 상황을 빠르게 변화시키기에 알맞은 새로운 전략을 찾아야 한다. 이러한 전략들에는 시장에 새 제품을 출시하는 것이 흔히 포함되며, 이는 세 가지 방법으로 행할 수 있다.

One strategy for increasing a company's sales is to develop an entirely new product by using the company's image. For example, if a renowned car company develops a motorcycle, the company can use its popularity to sell the product. Consumers who intend to buy a motorcycle will probably choose this particular motorcycle because of the company's image. Consumers will naturally think that the motorcycles will be just as good as the cars the company produces, so they will buy its motorcycles without any doubt.

The second strategy for raising a company's sales is to make a new version of an existing product. For example, if a soft drink company that is famous for its cola creates a version with an added fruit flavor, the company can easily increase sales. Consumers who love the original cola drink will be inclined to try this variation of the original product. The new cola benefits from both the familiarity that customers have with the old version and their curiosity about the newer one.

The final strategy is to make a partnership with another company. For example, if a company that makes chocolate forms a partnership with an ice cream company, the two companies can easily produce chocolate ice cream products together. In this case, both companies can increase their sales in a short period of time because they both receive a percentage of the new sales of the new chocolate ice cream. The brand images of both companies contribute to those sales.

회사의 매출을 올리는 한 가지 전략은 회사의 이미지를 이용하여 아예 새로운 제품을 개발하는 것이다. 예를 들어, 유명한 자동차 회사가 오토바이를 개발하면 그 회사는 제품을 판매하기 위해 회사의 인기를 이용할 수 있다. 오토바이를 사려고 하는 소비자들은 아마도 그 회사의 이미지 때문에 이 특정 오토바이를 선택할 것이다. 소비자들은 그 회사에서 생산하는 자동차만큼 그 오토바이 역시 좋을 거라고 자연스럽게 생각할 것이기에 의심하지 않고 오토바이를 구매할 것이다.

회사의 매출을 증가시키는 두 번째 전략은 기존 제품의 새로운 버전을 만드는 것이다. 예를 들어, 만약 콜라로 유명한 청량음료 회사가 과일 맛이 추가된 버전의 콜라를 만든다면 그 회사는 쉽게 매출을 올릴 수 있다. 원래의 콜라를 좋아하는 소비자들이 원래 제품의 다른 버전인 이 제품을 마셔보고 싶어 할 것이다. 새 콜라는 소비자들이 기존 버전에 대해 가진 익숙함과 새 제품에 대한 호기심 둘 다에서 덕을 본다.

마지막 전략은 다른 회사와 제휴를 맺는 것이다. 예를 들어, 만약 초콜릿을 생산하는 어떤 회사가 아이스크림 회사와 제휴를 맺는다면 두 회사는 쉽게 같이 초콜릿 아이스크림 제품을 생산할 수 있다. 이 경우 두 회사가 새 초콜릿 아이스크림의 판매에서 오는 수익의 일부를 가져가게 되므로 두 회사 모두 짧은 기간에 매출을 증가시킬 수 있다. 두 회사의 브랜드 이미지가 매출에 기여한다.

어휘 priority **n** 우선순위 ǀ profit **n** 이윤 ǀ regularly **adv** 정기적으로 ǀ assess **v** 평가하다 ǀ strategy **n** 전략 ǀ suitable **adj** 적합한 ǀ release **v** 출시하다 ǀ entirely **adv** 완전히 ǀ renowned **adj** 유명한 ǀ popularity **n** 인기 ǀ intend **v** 의도하다 ǀ particular **adj** 특정한 ǀ consumer **n** 소비자 ǀ doubt **n** 의심 ǀ existing **adj** 기존의, 존재하는 ǀ flavor **n** 맛 ǀ variation **n** 변형 ǀ familiarity **n** 익숙함, 낯익음 ǀ curiosity **n** 호기심 ǀ partnership **n** 제휴, 동업 ǀ percentage **n** 수익의 일부 ǀ contribute **v** 기여하다, 일조하다

Listening

Okay, class. Today, I am going to talk about different ways that companies try to expand their product lines. The article I gave to you yesterday introduced three common strategies that companies often use, but I do not think such strategies always bring benefits. In fact, those strategies often cause companies serious problems. Let me explain.

The first strategy that the reading mentions is creating an entirely new product that the company will market using its existing positive image. But, this strategy can have the opposite effect and harm its image instead. For example, what if the motorcycles mentioned in the reading turn out to be not as good as the company's cars? Then the car company's image will be damaged, and this will end up lowering the sales of its cars as well as the motorcycles.

Next, making a new version of an existing product may seem effective at first glance. But this strategy can actually cause a company to lose its long-time loyal customers. For example, the

자, 여러분. 오늘은 회사가 제품군을 확장하는 다른 방법들에 관해 이야기하겠습니다. 어제 여러분에게 준 글은 기업들이 자주 사용하는 세 가지 흔한 전략을 소개하지만, 나는 그 전략들이 항상 이익을 가져온다고 생각하지는 않아요. 사실, 그 전략들은 기업에게 자주 심각한 문제를 야기합니다. 설명하도록 하죠.

지문이 언급하는 첫 번째 전략은 그 기업이 기존에 가진 긍정적 이미지를 이용해서 광고해 아예 새로운 제품을 만드는 겁니다. 하지만 이 전략은 반대의 효과를 불러 이미지를 훼손할 수 있어요. 예를 들어, 만약 지문에서 언급된 오토바이가 이 회사의 자동차만큼 좋지 않다면 어떻게 될까요? 그러면 자동차 회사의 이미지가 손상을 입을 것이고, 이는 결국 오토바이 매출뿐 아니라 자동차 매출까지 하락하게 할 겁니다.

다음으로, 기존 제품의 새로운 버전을 만드는 것은 언뜻 보면 효율적으로 보일지 모릅니다. 하지만 이 전략은 사실 기업이 오래된 충성 소비자들을 잃게 할 수도 있어요. 예

soft drink company mentioned in the reading developed a new version of an existing cola drink. Consumers who have bought the original cola drink for a long time may doubt the quality of the drink that they have trusted. They may think the company made the new fruit flavored version because the quality of the original cola drink declined. These consumers may not purchase the original product or the new version.

Lastly, let's talk about a partnership between two companies. Forming a partnership is a very dangerous strategy because one partner could violate the deal. The ice cream company mentioned in the reading may decide to steal the chocolate company's recipe to make chocolate ice cream products on its own. This would result in undesirable consequences for the chocolate company, and it could lead to an expensive legal battle.

를 들어, 지문에서 언급된 청량음료 회사는 기존 콜라 제품의 새 버전을 개발했습니다. 오랫동안 원래의 콜라를 구매했던 소비자들은 자신들이 믿었던 음료의 품질에 의심을 가질 수 있어요. 원래 콜라의 품질이 하락해서 새 과일 맛 버전을 만들었다고 생각할지도 모릅니다. 이 소비자들은 원래 제품도, 새 버전도 구매하지 않을 수 있어요.

마지막으로, 두 기업의 제휴에 관해 이야기합시다. 제휴를 맺는 것은 한 파트너가 거래를 위반할 수도 있기 때문에 매우 위험한 전략입니다. 지문에서 언급된 아이스크림 회사가 직접 초콜릿 아이스크림 제품을 만들기 위해 초콜릿 회사의 제조법을 훔치기로 결심할 수도 있어요. 이는 초콜릿 회사에 원치 않는 결과를 야기할 것이고, 큰 비용이 드는 법적 싸움으로 이어질 수 있습니다.

어휘 expand ☑ 확장하다 ｜ article ⓝ 글, 기사 ｜ introduce ☑ 소개하다 ｜ opposite adj 반대의 ｜ harm ☑ 해를 끼치다 ｜ effective adj 효과적인 ｜ loyal adj 충성스러운 ｜ decline ☑ 하락하다, 쇠퇴하다, 감소하다 ｜ violate ☑ 위반하다, 어기다 ｜ deal ⓝ 거래, 협정 ｜ steal ☑ 훔치다 ｜ undesirable adj 원하지 않는, 바람직하지 않은 ｜ consequence ⓝ 결과 ｜ legal adj 법적인, 법의

Reading 노트

주제 　↑ profit by releasing new products, 3 ways
　　　1. develop an entirely new pro. by using the comp's image
　　　　- consumers buy b/c the comp's image
　　　2. new v. of existing pro.
　　　　- consumers' familiarity & curiosity
　　　3. partnership w. another comp.
　　　　- 2 comps → new product
　　　　- brand images of both comps

새 제품을 출시하여 이익 증대하기, 3가지 방법
1. 회사의 이미지를 이용해 완전히 새로운 제품 개발
　　 – 소비자가 회사 이미지 때문에 구매
2. 기존 제품의 새로운 버전
　　 – 소비자의 익숙함 & 호기심
3. 다른 회사와의 제휴
　　 – 두 회사 → 새 제품
　　 – 두 회사의 브랜드 이미지

Listening 노트

주제 　↑ profit by releasing new products, 3 ways?
　　　1. develop an entirely new pro. by using the comp's image?
　　　　- new product not as good? → hurt the company's image and lower the sales of existing pro.
　　　2. new v. of existing pro.?
　　　　- comp. might lose long-time customers
　　　　- they will think the original one's quality is ↓
　　　3. partnership w. another comp.?
　　　　- one partner could violate the deal
　　　　- lead to expensive lawsuit

새 제품을 출시하여 이익 증대하기, 3가지 방법?
1. 회사의 이미지를 이용해 완전히 새로운 제품 개발?
　　 – 새 제품이 전처럼 좋지 않으면? → 회사의 이미지를 훼손하고 기존 제품 매출을 하락시킴
2. 기존 제품의 새로운 버전?
　　 – 회사가 오래된 고객을 잃을 수 있음
　　 – 기존 제품의 품질이 떨어졌다고 생각할 것
3. 다른 회사와의 제휴?
　　 – 한 파트너가 거래를 깰 수도 있음
　　 – 값비싼 소송으로 이어짐

노트 & 답변 연결

주제

읽기 The reading and the lecture both talk about strategies companies can use to raise profits by producing new products. The reading says that there are three strategies that companies can use.

지문과 강의 모두 새 제품을 만들어 이익을 증대하기 위해 기업들이 이용할 수 있는 전략에 관해 이야기한다. 지문은 회사들이 이용할 수 있는 세 가지 전략이 있다고 말한다.

Part 2
Integrated Task

요점 1

읽기 Firstly, the reading states that making a new product by using the company's positive image is a good strategy. The author gives the example of a car company producing motorcycles and relying on the company image for sales.

듣기 On the contrary, the lecturer claims that if the quality of the motorcycles proves to be not as good as the cars it makes, the company can end up damaging its image instead. And eventually, the company's sales will drop significantly.

먼저, 지문은 기업의 긍정적 이미지를 이용해 새 제품을 만드는 것이 좋은 전략이라고 주장한다. 필자는 오토바이를 생산하고 판매를 위해 회사의 이미지에 의존하는 한 자동차 회사의 예시를 든다.

그와 반대로, 강의자는 만약 오토바이의 품질이 이 회사에서 만드는 자동차만큼 좋지 않은 것으로 밝혀질 경우 회사는 오히려 스스로의 이미지에 손상을 입힐 수 있다고 주장한다. 그리고 결국 회사의 매출은 크게 감소할 것이다.

요점 2

읽기 Secondly, in the reading, the author argues that making a new version of an existing product is a good strategy. He provides the example of a soft drink company producing a new version of its popular cola.

듣기 However, the lecturer says that making a new version may cause the company to lose its loyal customers. Consumers who have trusted the soft drink company may think that the company developed the new fruit flavored version because the quality of the original cola declined. This means that the company cannot sell the original product or the new version.

두 번째로, 지문에서 필자는 기존 제품의 새 버전을 만드는 것이 좋은 전략이라고 주장한다. 그는 인기 많은 콜라의 새 버전을 만든 한 청량음료 회사의 예를 제시한다.

그러나, 강의자는 새로운 버전을 만들 경우 기업이 충성 고객들을 잃을 수도 있다고 한다. 그 청량음료 회사를 신뢰했던 소비자들은 원래 콜라의 품질이 떨어졌기 때문에 새로운 과일 맛 버전을 개발했다고 생각할 수도 있다. 이는 이 회사가 원래 제품도, 새 버전도 판매할 수 없다는 의미이다.

요점 3

읽기 Thirdly, the reading goes on to say that forming a partnership is a good strategy. For example, a chocolate company can establish a partnership with an ice cream company to increase sales.

듣기 However, the lecturer contradicts this opinion, arguing that this strategy is very dangerous because one partner might break the deal. The ice cream company could steal the chocolate company's know-how for making chocolate and sell their own chocolate ice cream products. This could cause an expensive legal fight.

세 번째로, 지문은 이어서 제휴를 맺는 것이 좋은 전략이라고 말한다. 예를 들어, 한 초콜릿 회사에서 판매량 증가를 위해 아이스크림 회사와 제휴를 맺을 수 있다.

하지만 강의자는 이 의견에 반박하며 한 파트너가 거래를 깰 수도 있기 때문에 아주 위험한 전략이라고 주장한다. 아이스크림 회사에서 초콜릿 회사가 초콜릿을 만드는 노하우를 훔쳐 스스로 초콜릿 아이스크림 제품을 판매할 수도 있다. 이는 비용이 많이 드는 법적 싸움을 야기할 수 있다.

어휘 negative adj 부정적인 | positive adj 긍정적인 | significantly adv 상당히, 크게 | establish v 설립하다, 수립하다 | contradict v 반박하다, 부인하다, 모순되다

Q2 Reading

Intentionally setting a forest fire, called prescribed fire or controlled burning, is widely used in national parks across America. Prescribed fire is widely used because of the benefits that it brings to all of the organisms that live in the forest.

'지정 화재' 또는 '통제 소각'이라고 불리는, 고의로 낸 산불은 미국 전역의 국립 공원에서 널리 활용되고 있다. 지정 화재는 숲에 사는 모든 생물에게 가져다주는 이점 때문에 널리 활용되고 있다. 그러나 숲을 태우는 것의 이점

However, there are disadvantages far outweigh the benefits of burning forests.

First, in the process of burning forests on a regular basis, many animals are killed. Some argue that animals can escape from the fire. However, what about the young animals that cannot get away from these fires? For example, young birds are not able to fly and therefore will be trapped and die. And even adult animals can become trapped as forest fires spread very rapidly.

Second, like all fires, prescribed fire releases harmful greenhouse gases into the air. The carbon dioxide that is emitted when trees burn is one of the gases that contributes to global warming. As we all know, global warming has a detrimental impact on the planet. For example, global warming makes many areas arid and this harms the forests.

Third, prescribed fire is a waste of time and resources. That is because naturally occurring fire happens in areas where prescribed fire has already been carried out. This happens because of occasional lightning strikes, camping accidents, or just senseless acts of arson. Either way, firefighters and residents must work to put out these fires again, which means that prescribed fire is a waste of time and resources.

을 훨씬 넘어서는 단점들이 있다.

첫째로, 정기적으로 숲을 태우는 과정에서 많은 동물이 죽는다. 어떤 사람들은 동물들이 그 불을 피할 수 있다고 주장한다. 하지만 이러한 불에서 도망칠 수 없는 어린 동물들은 어떤가? 예를 들면, 어린 새들은 날 수가 없어 갇혀서 죽게 될 것이다. 그리고 심지어 다 자란 동물도 산불이 아주 빠르게 퍼지기 때문에 갇힐 수 있다.

둘째로, 모든 불과 마찬가지로 지정 화재는 공기 중으로 해로운 온실가스를 방출한다. 나무가 타면서 방출되는 이산화탄소는 지구 온난화에 일조하는 가스 중 하나다. 우리 모두 알고 있듯이 지구 온난화는 지구에 해로운 영향을 끼친다. 예를 들어, 지구 온난화는 많은 지역을 메마르게 하고 이는 숲에 해를 끼친다.

세 번째로, 지정 화재는 시간과 자원 낭비다. 왜냐하면 지정 화재가 이미 행해진 장소에서는 자연적으로 발생하는 화재가 일어나기 때문이다. 이는 가끔 일어나는 낙뢰나 캠핑 사고, 몰상식한 방화 행위 때문에 발생한다. 어떤 식으로든 소방관과 주민들을 이 불을 다시 진화하기 위해 애써야 하는데, 이는 지정 화재가 시간과 자원 낭비라는 뜻이다.

어휘 intentionally **adv** 의도적으로, 고의로 | prescribed **adj** 미리 정해진, 지정의 | outweigh **v** ~보다 더 크다 | on a regular basis 정기적으로 | trap **v** 가두다 | spread **v** 퍼지다 | release **v** 방출하다 | emit **v** 내뿜다 | detrimental **adj** 해로운, 유해한 | arid **adj** 건조한, 메마른 | lightning strike 낙뢰 | senseless **adj** 몰상식한, 지각없는, 무분별한 | arson **n** 방화 | put out (불 등을) 끄다

Listening

The reading states that prescribed fire is not beneficial for various reasons. However, the arguments are not convincing because prescribed fire isn't as harmful or inefficient as the reading says. Let me explain.

The point in the reading about trapping animals is way off. For a certain period of time during the year, animals reproduce and raise their young. Prescribed fires can be executed during the months when animals don't breed and there wouldn't be any offspring to worry about. All that has to be considered is to make the timing of the fire coincide with the time of the year when animals are not reproducing.

Another point made in the reading is that carbon dioxide from the smoke will pollute the air, but this is also a false statement. Carbon dioxide released into the air from fires is absorbed by nearby vegetation. Plants normally take in carbon dioxide during photosynthesis. Moreover, the young plants that grow after the fire also absorb the excess carbon dioxide from the air, so there won't be as much pollution as was stated in the reading.

Finally, I don't think prescribed fire is a waste of time and resources. Natural fires that happen after would be less intense due to prescribed fire. This is because prescribed fire decreases

지문은 지정 화재가 여러 이유에서 이롭지 않다고 주장합니다. 하지만 지정 화재가 지문이 말하는 것만큼 해롭거나 비효율적이지 않기 때문에 이 주장은 설득력이 없어요. 설명하겠습니다.

동물들이 갇히는 것에 관한 지문의 주장은 완전히 잘못되었습니다. 한 해의 일정 기간 동안 동물들은 새끼를 낳고 기릅니다. 지정 화재는 동물들이 새끼를 낳지 않아서 걱정할 만한 새끼 동물들이 없는 달에 시행될 수 있어요. 유일하게 고려해야 할 점은 동물들이 번식하지 않는 그 시기와 화재 시점이 맞아떨어지게 하는 겁니다.

지문의 또 다른 주장은 연기에서 나오는 이산화탄소가 공기를 오염시킨다는 것이지만, 이 또한 틀린 주장입니다. 산불로 인해 공기 중으로 방출되는 이산화탄소는 근처의 식물들에 흡수돼요. 식물들은 보통 광합성을 하면서 이산화탄소를 흡수합니다. 게다가 화재 이후 자라는 어린 식물 또한 대기로부터 잉여 이산화탄소를 흡수하기에 지문에서 말하는 것만큼의 오염은 없을 거예요.

마지막으로, 나는 지정 화재가 시간과 자원 낭비라고 생각하지 않습니다. 지정 화재 뒤에 일어나는 자연발생적 화재는 지정 화재 때문에 정도가 덜합니다. 왜냐하면 지정 화재가 숲 바닥에 남아 있던 죽은 관목과 나무를 제거하여

the possibility of great forest fires by eliminating the excess dead shrubs or trees on the forest floor. So people will not need to allocate much time and money to trying to put out these fires.

큰 산불의 가능성을 낮추기 때문이죠. 그래서 사람들은 이러한 불을 끄는 데 많은 시간과 돈을 할애하지 않아도 됩니다.

어휘 inefficient **adj** 비효율적인 I reproduce **v** 생식하다, 번식하다 I execute **v** 실행하다 I breed **v** 새끼를 낳다 I offspring **n** 자손, (동물의) 새끼 I coincide with ~와 동시에 일어나다 I pollute **v** 오염시키다 I absorb **v** 흡수하다 I vegetation **n** 식물, 초목 I photosynthesis **n** 광합성 I excess **adj** 잉여의, 여분의, 초과한 I intense **adj** 극심한, 강렬한 I eliminate **v** 제거하다 I shrub **n** 관목 I allocate **v** 할당하다, 할애하다

Reading 노트

주제 prescribed fire – disadvantages 〉 benefits
 1. animals are killed
  - can't escape easily
 2. harmful greenhouse gas
  - CO_2 → global warming
 3. waste of time & resources
  - natural fire occurs in the same area anyway → have to put out

지정 화재 – 단점 〉 장점
 1. 동물들이 죽음
  – 쉽게 탈출 못 함
 2. 해로운 온실가스
  – 이산화탄소 → 지구 온난화
 3. 시간 & 자원 낭비
  – 자연발생적 화재가 같은 지역에서 일어남 → 불을 꺼야 함

Listening 노트

주제 prescribed fire – disadvantages 〉 benefits?
 1. animals are killed?
  - set fire when animals are not reproducing
 2. harmful greenhouse gas?
  - CO_2 → absorbed by nearby vegetation
 3. waste of time & resources?
  - natural fire = easy to put out since prescribed f. clears forest floor

지정 화재 – 단점 〉 장점?
 1. 동물들이 죽음?
  – 동물들이 번식하지 않는 시기에 불을 놓음
 2. 해로운 온실가스?
  – 이산화탄소 → 근처 식물에 흡수됨
 3. 시간 & 자원 낭비?
  – 자연발생적 화재 = 지정 화재가 숲 바닥을 깨끗하게 정리하므로 끄기 쉬움

노트 & 답변 연결

주제

읽기 The reading and the lecture both talk about prescribed fire. The article says that such artificial fire leads to several negative consequences.
듣기 However, the lecturer argues that prescribed fire is not as harmful or inefficient as the reading argues.

지문과 강의 둘 다 지정 화재에 대해서 말한다. 지문은 그런 인위적인 화재가 몇 가지 부정적인 결과를 가져온다고 말한다.
하지만 강의자는 지정 화재가 지문이 주장하는 만큼 해롭거나 비효율적이지 않다고 주장한다.

요점 1

읽기 Firstly, the reading states that prescribed fire kills animals in the forest like young animals that cannot escape from the flames.
듣기 However, according to the lecturer, prescribed fire can be implemented during the months when animals don't breed. This means that prescribed fire would not kill many animals, nor would it be dangerous to young animals in particular.

첫째로, 지문은 지정 화재가 불길에서 탈출할 수 없는 어린 동물들과 같은 숲속의 동물들을 죽인다고 말한다.

그러나 강의자의 말에 따르면, 지정 화재는 동물들이 번식하지 않는 시기에 시행될 수 있다. 이는 지정 화재가 많은 동물들을 죽이지 않을 뿐만 아니라, 특히 어린 동물들에게 위험하지 않을 거라는 의미다.

읽기 Secondly, in the reading, the author argues that prescribed fire releases harmful gases, such as carbon dioxide, which pollutes the air.

듣기 In contrast, the lecturer claims that the carbon dioxide that is released by fires is absorbed by nearby vegetation. He goes on to say that the young plants that grow after the fire also absorb the carbon dioxide in the atmosphere.

두 번째로, 지문에서 저자는 지정 화재가 대기를 오염시키는 이산화탄소 등의 해로운 가스를 배출한다고 주장한다.
이와 반대로 강의자는 화재에서 방출되는 이산화탄소가 근처의 식물에 흡수된다고 주장한다. 강의자는 이어서 화재 뒤에 자라는 어린 식물들 또한 대기 중의 이산화탄소를 흡수한다고 말한다.

읽기 Thirdly, the reading goes on to say that prescribed fire is a waste of time and resources because fires occur naturally or intentionally in areas where prescribed fire has already been implemented.

듣기 However, the lecturer contradicts this opinion by stating that people will spend less money and time on extinguishing these fires. According to the lecture, the fires will be less intense because materials on the forest floor that can make fires intense, like dead trees, have been eliminated beforehand by prescribed fire.

세 번째로, 지문은 이어서 지정 화재가 이미 시행된 지역에서도 화재는 자연적으로나 의도적으로 일어나기 때문에 지정 화재는 시간과 자원 낭비라고 말한다.

하지만 강의자는 사람들이 이러한 화재를 진압하기 위해 돈과 시간을 덜 쓸 것이라고 말하며 이 의견을 반박한다. 강의에 따르면 화재를 키울 수 있는 죽은 나무 같은 숲속 바닥의 물질들이 지정 화재로 미리 제거되었기 때문에 화재 규모가 덜할 것이다.

어휘 implement **v** 이행하다, 시행하다 | extinguish **v** (불을) 끄다 | beforehand **adv** 전에, 미리

Q3 Reading

Recycling is useful in that it reuses materials in the creation of new products without the need to gather as many new raw materials. Single-stream recycling is a process that allows recyclable materials to be thrown away in one bag without any sorting. Sorting is done at a single-stream recycling center by a machine that automatically separates the collected materials. However, this method has been shown to have many disadvantages.

First, single-stream recycling is dangerous. The sorting machine at a single-stream recycling center is responsible for separating paper, glass, and plastic. Though the sorting machine at the recycling plant sorts materials automatically, it frequently breaks glass bottles. Employees at the plant have to manually remove these broken pieces of glass and are at risk of causing serious injury to their hands.

Second, this method also leads to a waste of valuable resources. This method of sorting various materials in one bag is far from perfect. Sometimes, broken glass will get mixed in with collected paper. This may contaminate paper so that it cannot be used for its intended purpose. In this case, high-quality paper has to be used for making cheap boxes instead. This clearly shows precious materials can be wasted.

A third problem is that single-stream recycling is too expensive. The cost of building a single-stream recycling center is up to

재활용은 새로운 재료를 되도록 많이 모을 필요 없이 새로운 제품을 만드는 데 재료를 재사용한다는 점에서 유용하다. 단일 흐름 재활용은 재활용 가능한 재료들을 분류하지 않고 한 주머니에 버리게 하는 과정이다. 분류는 단일 흐름 재활용 센터에서 모은 재료를 자동으로 나누는 기계에 의해 이루어진다. 하지만 이 방법은 많은 단점이 있다는 것으로 드러났다.

먼저, 단일 흐름 재활용은 위험하다. 단일 흐름 재활용 센터의 분류 기계는 종이, 유리, 플라스틱을 분류하는 일을 맡고 있다. 재활용 공장의 분류 기계는 자동으로 재료를 분류하지만, 유리병을 자주 깨뜨린다. 공장에 있는 근로자들이 이 부서진 유리 조각을 손으로 제거해야 하기에 이들의 손은 치명적인 부상의 위험에 놓여있다.

두 번째로, 이 방법은 또한 귀중한 자원의 낭비로 이어진다. 다양한 재료를 한 주머니에 분류하는 이 방법은 완벽과 거리가 멀다. 때때로 깨진 유리가 모은 종이와 함께 섞일 것이다. 이것은 종이를 더럽혀서 의도된 목적을 위해 쓰이지 못할 수도 있다. 이 경우 좋은 질의 종이가 대신 싸구려 상자를 만드는 데 사용되어야 한다. 이는 귀중한 재료가 낭비될 수 있다는 점을 명백히 보여준다.

세 번째 문제점은 단일 흐름 재활용이 너무 돈이 많이 든다는 것이다. 단일 흐름 재활용 센터를 짓는 비용은 옛 방식의 재활용 공장을 짓는 비용의 3배 이상까지 든다. 많은

Part 2 Integrated Task

three times higher than the cost of building a traditional recycling plant. Many cities have very limited budgets to use for such facilities. For cities that already have a working recycling system, it is unreasonable to switch to a single-stream recycling solution.

도시에서는 그러한 시설을 위해 사용할 예산이 매우 제한되어있다. 이미 가동 중인 재활용 시스템을 갖춘 도시의 경우 단일 흐름 재활용 해결책으로 바꾸는 것은 비합리적이다.

Listening

There is no question that people must recycle to conserve natural resources, and one popular way to do that is single-stream recycling. According to the reading I gave you, it would seem that single-stream recycling has a lot of disadvantages. But you know single-stream recycling is actually the most realistic way to recycle. I want to talk about why it's actually the best method.

First, some would have you think that it's hazardous. But it is not dangerous at all because there are many ways to avoid danger. For one thing, plants provide safety training that helps to reduce the potential dangers of using a single-stream recycling process. Another thing is to issue protective equipment, like thick gloves, to make sure that employees don't cut their hands on glass.

Another argument is that single-stream recycling wastes too much potential recyclable material. Well, the traditional method of recycling meant that families had to presort their waste. It was a hassle, so many families didn't participate. But in single-stream recycling, families can just throw everything away in one bag. It's very convenient, so more families are likely to participate. Even though a small amount may get contaminated, I think this is negligible because there's more trash to recycle since more families contribute.

And one final point, while I acknowledge that building a single-stream recycling plant is more expensive than building a traditional plant, remember a traditional plant needs separate trucks to pick up the trash from a single family. For example, a truck for recycling plastic, another truck for bottles, etc. However, if single-stream recycling is used, we need only one truck that picks up every kind of trash at one time. That will save money in terms of lower fuel and labor costs.

천연자원을 보존하기 위해 사람들이 재활용해야 하는 것은 당연하며, 그렇게 하는 한 가지 인기 있는 방법은 단일 흐름 재활용입니다. 여러분에게 준 지문에 따르면 단일 흐름 재활용이 단점을 많이 가진 것처럼 보일 거예요. 하지만 단일 흐름 재활용은 사실 가장 현실적인 재활용 방법입니다. 왜 이게 실제로 최고의 방법인지 말하도록 하죠.

먼저, 여러분은 일부 사람들 때문에 이것이 위험하다고 생각할 겁니다. 하지만 위험을 피할 방법은 많이 있기 때문에 이것은 전혀 위험하지 않아요. 우선 공장들은 단일 흐름 재활용 과정을 사용하는 데 있어 잠재적 위험을 줄이는 안전 교육을 제공합니다. 또 다른 것은 근로자들이 유리에 손을 베이지 않도록 두꺼운 장갑 같은 보호 장비를 지급하는 거예요.

또 다른 주장은 단일 흐름 재활용이 잠재적으로 재활용 가능한 재료를 너무 많이 낭비한다는 것입니다. 음, 전통적인 재활용 방식은 가정에서 쓰레기를 미리 분류해야 한다는 의미였어요. 이는 귀찮은 일이라 많은 가정이 참여하지 않았습니다. 하지만 단일 흐름 재활용은 가정에서 그냥 하나의 주머니에 모든 것을 버릴 수 있죠. 매우 편리해서 더 많은 가정이 참여할 거예요. 비록 소량은 오염될지 몰라도, 더 많은 가정이 기여하기에 재활용할 쓰레기가 더 많아지므로 이것은 무시해도 될 정도라고 생각합니다.

그리고 마지막 요점이 있죠. 단일 흐름 재활용 공장을 짓는 것이 전통 방식 공장을 짓는 것보다 더 비용이 많이 든다는 점은 인정하지만, 전통 공장은 한 가정에서 나온 쓰레기를 수거하기 위해 개별 트럭들이 필요하다는 점을 기억해야 합니다. 예를 들면, 재활용 플라스틱을 위한 트럭, 병을 위한 트럭 등등이요. 하지만 만약 단일 흐름 재활용이 사용되면 모든 쓰레기를 한 번에 수거할 단 한 대의 트럭만 필요해요. 이는 연료비와 인건비가 더 적게 든다는 측면에서 돈을 절약해 줄 겁니다.

Reading 노트

주제	single-stream recycling(recycle together w/o sorting) → sort by a machine = many disadvantages	단일 흐름 재활용(분류하지 않고 함께 재활용) → 기계로 분류 = 단점 많음

single-stream recycling(recycle together w/o sorting)
→ sort by a machine = many disadvantages
   1. dangerous
      - sorting machine → sort paper, glass, plastic…
        → can hurt employees
   2. waste of valuable resources
      - sorting = X perfect(glass get mixed w. paper, etc.)
        → paper X used for intended purpose
   3. $$$
      - 3 X more $$$ than building a traditional recycling plant
      - cities have limited budgets

단일 흐름 재활용(분류하지 않고 함께 재활용)
→ 기계로 분류 = 단점 많음
   1. 위험함
      – 분류 기계 → 종이, 유리, 플라스틱 분류…
        → 직원을 다치게 할 수 있음
   2. 가치 있는 자원 낭비
      – 분류 = 완벽하지 않음(유리가 종이와 섞이는 등)
        → 종이가 의도한 목적으로 사용될 수 없음
   3. 비용
      – 기존 재활용 공장을 짓는 것보다 3배 더 큰 비용
      – 도시들의 제한된 예산

Listening 노트

주제 single-stream recycling(recycle together w/o sorting)
→ sort by a machine = many disadvantages?
   1. not dangerous
      - plants provide safety training & protective equipment
   2. waste of valuable resources? No
      - many ppl didn't recycle because sorting was a hassle
      - now they will participate more → more things to recycle
   3. $$$?
      - building a single-s. plant itself is more $$$, but trad. ones require separate trucks → more fuel & labor costs

단일 흐름 재활용(분류하지 않고 함께 재활용)
→ 기계로 분류 = 단점 많음?
   1. 위험하지 않음
      – 공장에서 안전 교육 & 보호 장비 제공
   2. 귀중한 자원 낭비? 아니다
      – 많은 사람이 분류가 귀찮아서 재활용을 안 했음
      – 이제 더 많이 참여할 것 → 재활용할 것들이 더 많음
   3. 비용?
      – 단일 흐름 재활용 공장 건설 자체는 돈이 많이 들지만, 전통적인 공장은 별도의 트럭들이 필요함 → 더 많은 연료비 & 인건비

노트 & 답변 연결

주제

읽기 The reading and the lecture both talk about single-stream recycling. The article says that this method results in many disadvantages.
듣기 However, the lecturer argues that the method is the best way to recycle.

지문과 강의는 둘 다 단일 흐름 재활용에 관해 말한다. 지문은 이 방법이 많은 단점을 낳는다고 한다.

하지만 강의자는 그 방법이 재활용하기에 가장 좋은 방법이라고 주장한다.

요점 1

읽기 Firstly, the reading says that this system is very dangerous because of things like broken glass.
듣기 On the contrary, the lecturer disagrees with this argument. She claims that there are ways to avoid dangers. She gives safety training and protective equipment as examples. Providing proper training and equipment can help employees reduce the chances of hurting themselves in the process of recycling.

첫 번째로, 지문은 이 시스템이 깨진 유리 등의 물질 때문에 매우 위험하다고 말한다.
반대로, 강의자는 이 주장에 동의하지 않는다. 위험을 피할 방법이 있다고 주장한다. 예시로 안전 교육과 보호 장비를 든다. 적절한 교육과 장비를 제공하면 재활용 과정에서 직원들이 다칠 위험을 낮추도록 도울 수 있다.

읽기 Secondly, in the reading, the author argues that this system is wasteful because some materials may get contaminated. In contrast, the lecturer makes an opposing point to this claim.

듣기 The lecturer's point is that this method encourages people to actively participate in recycling because it is convenient. She goes on to say that although some materials may get contaminated, more trash will be recycled overall because recycling participation will be higher.

두 번째로, 지문에서 저자는 일부 물질이 오염될 수 있기 때문에 이 시스템이 낭비적이라고 주장한다. 반면에 강의자는 이 주장에 반대 의견을 제시한다.

강의자의 요점은 이 방법이 편리하기 때문에 사람들이 적극적으로 재활용에 참여하게 만들 수 있다는 것이다. 더 나아가 비록 일부 물질이 오염될지 몰라도 재활용 참여율이 더 높을 것이기 때문에 더 많은 쓰레기가 재활용될 것이라고 한다.

읽기 Thirdly, the reading goes on to say that this system is very expensive.

듣기 Although the lecturer admits that the cost of building a single-stream recycling plant is higher than the cost of building an ordinary plant, she claims that this method can save a lot of money. The reason for this is that in this system, only one truck is needed to pick up every kind of trash, so fuel and labor costs become lower.

세 번째로, 지문은 이 시스템이 매우 비싸다고 말한다.

강의자는 단일 흐름 재활용 공장을 짓는 비용이 통상적인 공장을 짓는 비용보다 비싸다는 것을 인정하지만 이 방법이 많은 돈을 절약하게 해줄 수 있다고 주장한다. 그 이유는 이 시스템에서는 오로지 한 대의 트럭이 모든 쓰레기를 수거하는 데 필요하기에 연료비와 인건비가 낮아지기 때문이다.

어휘 disadvantage **n** 단점 l hurt oneself 다치다

Q4 Reading

Hydroelectric dams change the power of falling water into electricity, and they are the most realistic means of generating power. A hydroelectric dam extracts energy from a reusable source of energy, water, which is stored in a large reservoir behind a dam. Compared to other methods of power generation, hydroelectric dams are the most efficient.

The cost of operating a hydroelectric dam is very low compared to the cost of operating traditional power plants that burn fossil fuels. The reason for this is that the dams do not require much money to generate power. If there are enough rainfall and water flow, the amount of energy produced by hydroelectric dams can be tremendous. Because of these relatively low dam operation costs, hydroelectric energy is seen as a low-cost renewable energy source.

Another advantage of hydroelectric dams is environmental friendliness. Hydroelectric dams do not harm the environment. Since hydroelectric dams do not burn fossil fuels, the dams do not emit carbon dioxide, which means that the dams do not release greenhouse gases that directly devastate the environment.

Finally, hydroelectric dams do not harm wildlife either, especially river wildlife. Hydroelectric dams use fish ladders, which are structures designed to allow fish to pass dams. So for example, salmon can reach their spawning grounds by swimming across dams safely through these fish ladders.

수력 발전 댐은 떨어지는 물의 힘을 전기로 바꾸며, 동력을 만들어내는 가장 현실적인 방법이다. 수력 발전 댐은 댐 뒤의 큰 저장소에 저장된 재사용 가능한 에너지원, 즉 물에서 에너지를 추출한다. 다른 전력 생산 방법들과 비교하면 수력 발전 댐이 가장 효율적이다.

수력 발전 댐을 운영하는 비용은 화석 연료를 태우는 기존의 발전소 운영 비용보다 아주 낮다. 그 이유는 이 댐이 전력을 생산하는 데 많은 돈이 필요하지 않기 때문이다. 충분한 강우와 유수량만 있다면 수력 발전 댐에서 만들어내는 에너지의 양은 엄청날 수 있다. 이렇게 상대적으로 낮은 댐 가동 비용 때문에 수력 발전 에너지는 비용이 낮은 재생 가능 에너지원으로 보인다.

수력 발전 댐의 또 다른 장점은 친환경적이라는 점이다. 수력 발전 댐은 환경에 해를 입히지 않는다. 수력 발전 댐은 화석 연료를 태우지 않기 때문에 이산화탄소를 방출하지 않으며, 이는 댐이 환경을 직접적으로 파괴하는 온실가스를 배출하지 않는다는 의미이다.

마지막으로, 수력 발전 댐은 야생 동물, 특히 강에 사는 야생 동물에게 해를 입히지 않는다. 수력 발전 댐은 물고기가 댐을 지나갈 수 있게 고안된 구조물인 어제(魚梯)를 사용한다. 그래서 예를 들면 연어는 이 어제를 통해 댐을 안전하게 헤엄쳐 지나가서 산란하는 곳에 도착할 수 있다.

어휘 **hydroelectric** adj 수력 발전의, 수력 전기의 I **change A into B** A를 B로 바꾸다 I **realistic** adj 현실적인 I **generate** v 만들어내다, 발생시키다 I **extract** v 뽑다, 추출하다 I **reusable** adj 재사용 가능한 I **reservoir** n 저수지, 저장소(댐 뒤에 물을 담아두는 곳) I **operate** v 운영하다, 가동하다 I **power plant** 발전소 I **fossil fuel** 화석 연료 I **rainfall** n 강우 I **tremendous** adj 엄청난 I **relatively** adv 상대적으로 I **renewable** adj 재생 가능한 I **environmental friendliness** 환경 친화성, 친환경적임 I **emit** v 방출하다 I **directly** adv 직접적으로 I **devastate** v 황폐화하다 I **harm** v 해를 입히다 I **wildlife** n 야생 동물 I **fish ladder** 어제(魚梯)(댐 한쪽에 계단 등을 만들어 물고기가 지나다닐 수 있게 만든 장치) I **structure** n 구조, 구조물 I **salmon** n 연어 I **spawning** n (물고기 등의) 산란

Listening

You just read some pretty good arguments about why hydroelectricity is the most effective method of generating power, and they're good arguments, but they're not complete. I think that hydroelectric dams are not perfect like the reading argues. Let's talk about the points made in the reading.

First, operation costs for hydroelectric dams are very low. But you know, as far as other costs spent on hydroelectric dams are concerned, the dams are not cost-effective. First of all, initial research on geologically appropriate locations must be carried out before building the dams. In addition to this initial cost, the cost of dam construction is higher than one might expect. For example, constructing great reservoirs to hold the water needed to create great amounts of electricity costs a lot.

Second, I doubt that hydroelectricity is harmless to the environment. You know, actually, hydroelectric dams release the same amount of the greenhouse gases as plants operated by fossil fuels. Hydroelectric dams need large reservoirs that can store huge amounts of water. However, in order to create these reservoirs, large areas must be flooded. And when these areas are flooded, plants in the water decompose, resulting in the formation of methane, which is a greenhouse gas. Therefore, hydroelectric dams do in fact harm the environment.

Next, the reading says that with the help of fish ladders, hydroelectric dams do not harm wildlife. Yes, salmon are strong enough to use these ladders, but other species of fish such as shad are not strong enough to ascend vertically through fish ladders. So the population of shad has been reduced.

Part 2 / Integrated Task

여러분은 방금 왜 수력 발전이 동력을 발생시키는 가장 효과적인 방법인가에 관한 꽤 좋은 의견을 읽었는데, 그것은 좋은 주장이지만 완벽하지는 않습니다. 나는 수력 발전 댐이 지문에서 주장하는 것처럼 완벽하지 않다고 생각해요. 지문에서 언급된 주장들에 대해 말해봅시다.

첫째로, 수력 발전 댐의 운영 비용은 아주 낮습니다. 하지만 수력 발전 댐에 드는 다른 비용을 고려하면 비용 효율적이지 않아요. 무엇보다 댐을 짓기 전에 지질학적으로 적합한 지역에 관한 초기 연구가 수행되어야 합니다. 이 초기 비용 외에도 댐 건설 비용이 예상보다 많이 들어요. 예를 들면 많은 양의 전기를 만들기 위한 물을 비축할 거대한 저장소를 짓는 데 비용이 많이 들죠.

두 번째로, 수력 전기가 환경에 무해한지 의심스럽습니다. 사실 수력 발전 댐은 화석 연료로 가동되는 발전소와 비슷한 양의 온실가스를 배출합니다. 수력 발전 댐은 많은 양의 물을 저장할 수 있는 큰 저장소들이 필요하죠. 그러나 이러한 저장소들을 만들기 위해서는 넓은 지역이 침수되어야 합니다. 그리고 이러한 장소들이 침수되면 물속의 식물들이 부패하며 온실가스인 메탄이 만들어지죠. 그래서 수력 발전 댐은 사실 환경에 해를 입힙니다.

다음으로, 지문은 어제(魚梯)의 도움으로 수력 발전 댐이 야생 동물에 해를 끼치지 않는다고 말합니다. 그래요, 연어는 이 사다리를 이용할 만큼 강하지만 전어 같은 다른 종의 물고기들은 어제를 통해 수직으로 올라갈 만큼 강하지 않아요. 그래서 전어의 수가 감소했죠.

어휘 **as far as ~ is concerned** ~에 관한 한 I **cost-effective** adj 비용 효율적인 I **geologically** adv 지질학적으로 I **construction** n 건설, 건축 I **harmless** adj 무해한 I **flood** v 침수시키다 I **decompose** v 부패되다, 썩다 I **methane** n 메탄 I **shad** n 전어, 준치 I **ascend** v 오르다, 올라가다 I **vertically** adv 수직으로

Reading 노트

주제	hydroelectric dams = the most efficient power generator

1. operation cost ↓
   - < than fossil fuel power plants
   - just need rainfall & water flow to generate energy
2. envi. friendly
   - don't burn fossil fuel → No CO$_2$
3. don't harm wildlife
   - use fish ladder → fish can pass dams

수력 발전 댐 = 가장 효율적인 발전기
1. 운영 비용 낮음
   – 화석 연료 발전소보다 더 낮음
   – 전력 생산에 빗물 & 유수량만 필요
2. 환경친화적
   – 화석 연료 태우지 않음 → 이산화탄소 없음
3. 야생 동물 해치지 않음
   – 어제 사용 → 물고기가 댐을 지나갈 수 있음

주제	hydroelectric dams = not that perfect	수력 발전 댐 = 그다지 완벽하지 않음

주제   hydroelectric dams = not that perfect

1. operation cost ↓, but…
    - other costs(initial cost on location research, reservoir construction, etc…) $$$
2. envi. friendly?
    - to make huge reservoir, area must be flooded → plants decompose → generate harmful gas
3. don't harm wildlife?
    - fish like salmon can use the ladder, but other fish can't → their # ↓

수력 발전 댐 = 그다지 완벽하지 않음

1. 운영 비용이 낮긴 하지만…
    – 다른 비용(장소 물색, 저수지 건설 등의 초기 비용)이 많이 듦
2. 환경친화적?
    – 거대 저수지를 만들기 위해 지역을 침수시켜야 함 → 식물이 부패함 → 해로운 가스 생성
3. 야생 동물을 해치지 않는다?
    – 연어 같은 물고기는 사다리 사용 가능, 그러나 다른 물고기들은 사용 못 함 → 개체 수 감소

노트 & 답변 연결

주제

읽기 The reading and the lecture both talk about hydroelectric dams. The article says that these dams bring several benefits.
듣기 However, the lecturer argues that the dams have negative effects in those respects.

지문과 강의 둘 다 수력 발전 댐에 관해 말한다. 지문은 이 댐이 몇 가지 이점이 있다고 말한다.
그러나 강의자는 그 댐이 그 점에 있어서 부정적인 영향을 준다고 주장한다.

요점 1

읽기 Firstly, the reading argues that hydroelectric dams reduce operation costs.
듣기 Although the lecturer admits that operation costs are low, he claims that when considering other costs spent on the construction of dams, the dams are not cost-effective. The reasons for this are that the costs of doing research on finding geologically appropriate locations are high, and constructing dams costs a lot.

첫째로, 지문은 수력 발전 댐이 운영 비용을 줄여준다고 주장한다.
강의자는 운영 비용이 낮다는 것은 인정하지만 댐을 짓는 데 드는 다른 비용들을 고려했을 때 비용 효율적이지 않다고 주장한다. 그 이유는 지리적으로 알맞은 장소를 찾는 조사를 하는 비용이 많이 들고 댐을 건설하는 데 비용이 많이 든다는 것이다.

요점 2

읽기 Secondly, the reading claims that hydroelectric dams do not damage the environment because they do not burn fossil fuels.
듣기 However, the lecturer's point is that the dams still emit a large amount of greenhouse gases. A hydroelectric dam needs a reservoir that stores a huge amount of water, which causes land to be flooded. When the plants there decompose, they release methane, a greenhouse gas. Thus, the lecturer concludes that hydroelectric dams cause damage to the environment.

두 번째로, 지문은 수력 발전 댐이 화석 연료를 태우지 않기 때문에 환경에 해를 입히지 않는다고 주장한다.
그러나 강의자의 의견은 댐이 여전히 많은 양의 온실가스를 배출한다는 것이다. 수력 발전 댐은 엄청난 양의 물을 저장하는 저장소가 필요하며 이는 땅을 침수시킨다. 그곳의 식물들이 부패하면 온실가스인 메탄을 방출한다. 그래서 강의자는 수력 발전 댐이 환경에 해를 야기한다는 결론을 내린다.

요점 3

읽기 Thirdly, the reading goes on to explain that hydroelectric dams do not have negative effects on wildlife. For example, salmon can pass dams by using fish ladders.
듣기 Even though the lecturer agrees that some fish like salmon can use these ladders, he states that there are many

세 번째로, 지문은 수력 발전 댐이 야생 동물에 부정적인 영향을 미치지 않는다고 설명한다. 예를 들면, 연어는 어제를 통해 댐을 지나갈 수 있다.
강의자는 연어 같은 몇몇 물고기들이 이 사다리를 이용할 수 있다는 점에 동의하지만, 어제를 통과할 만큼

other species that are not strong enough to pass through the ladders.

강하지 않은 다른 많은 종들이 있다고 주장한다.

어휘 respect **n** 점, 측면 I do research on ~에 대해 연구하다 I have an effect on ~에 영향을 미치다

Q5 Reading

The Internet seems to benefit society as a whole. Further, through the Internet, users share information on a global scale. It is becoming increasingly clear that the Internet offers us waves of opportunities. There is no doubt that the Internet brings several benefits.

First, the information that the Internet provides is useful and valuable. If you enter any topic on a search engine, a huge amount of useful information related to it would instantly come up. This is much faster and easier than going to a library, where it could take hours to find the information that you need. Thanks to the Internet, you do not need to look up the information in the library any more.

Second, the Internet allows ordinary people to access a lot of information that they could not in the past. Before the Internet, a few groups monopolized information. If someone wanted to obtain specific information, he or she had to pay for it. However, today, even poor people who cannot afford to attend college can get specific information or knowledge easily on the Internet.

Finally, the Internet increases the rate at which information or ideas are shared. Many Internet users are willing to share what they know. For example, if someone knows how to travel around Europe in economical ways, they will post the information on their website so that many people can obtain the information.

인터넷은 사회 전체를 이롭게 하는 것처럼 보인다. 게다가 인터넷을 통해 이용자들은 세계적인 규모로 정보를 공유한다. 인터넷을 통해 기회의 물결이 밀려든다는 점은 점점 더 명백해지고 있다. 인터넷이 우리에게 몇 가지 이점을 제공한다는 사실에는 의심의 여지가 없다.

첫째로, 인터넷이 제공하는 정보는 유용하고 가치가 있다. 만약 검색 엔진에 어떤 주제든 입력하면 그와 관련된 엄청난 양의 유용한 정보가 즉시 뜬다. 이는 필요한 정보를 찾는 데 몇 시간이 걸릴 수도 있는 도서관에 가는 것보다 훨씬 더 빠르고 쉽다. 인터넷 덕분에 더 이상 도서관에서 정보를 찾지 않아도 된다.

두 번째로, 인터넷은 일반인들이 과거에는 접근할 수 없었던 많은 정보에 접근하게 해준다. 인터넷이 생기기 전에는 소수의 집단이 정보를 독점했다. 만약 특정 정보를 얻고 싶다면 돈을 지불해야 했다. 그러나 오늘날에는 대학에 다닐 형편이 안 되는 가난한 사람들도 인터넷에서 쉽게 특정 정보나 지식을 얻을 수 있다.

마지막으로, 인터넷은 정보나 아이디어가 공유되는 속도를 증가시킨다. 많은 인터넷 사용자들이 기꺼이 아는 것을 공유하려고 한다. 예를 들어, 만약 누군가가 유럽을 알뜰하게 여행하는 방법을 안다면 많은 사람이 그 정보를 얻을 수 있도록 자기 웹사이트에 그 정보를 올릴 것이다.

어휘 increasingly **adv** 점점 더, 갈수록 더 I a wave of ~의 물결 I valuable **adj** 가치 있는, 귀중한 I enter **v** 입력하다 I instantly **adv** 즉시 I look up 정보를 찾아보다 I monopolize **v** 독점하다 I obtain **v** (노력하여) 얻다 I specific **adj** 특정한, 구체적인 I rate **n** 속도, 비율 I be willing to 기꺼이 ~하다 I economical **adj** 알뜰한, 절약하는 I post **v** (정보, 그림, 사진 등을) 올리다, 게시하다

Listening

Okay, class. Some may say that the effects that the Internet has on society are really great and always positive. But, you know, the Internet does not necessarily offer benefits; in fact, it sometimes causes some problems we might fail to notice. Let me explain.

First, not all information on the Internet is useful or valuable. For example, children can be exposed to sexually explicit content such as pornography. They can easily log on to harmful websites using their parents' IDs. Further, some users may obtain dangerous information online, such as how to design or use explosives.

Well, it seems plausible to say that every user can access all the information on the Internet. But you know, it is still hard for

좋아요, 여러분. 어떤 사람은 인터넷이 사회에 미친 영향이 매우 훌륭하고 언제나 긍정적이라고 말할지 모릅니다. 하지만 인터넷이 반드시 이로운 점만을 제공하지는 않으며 사실 때때로 우리가 알아차리지 못할 수 있는 몇 가지 문제점을 야기합니다. 설명하죠.

첫째로, 인터넷에 있는 모든 정보가 유용하거나 가치가 있는 것은 아닙니다. 예를 들면, 아이들은 음란물 같은 성적으로 노골적인 내용에 노출될 수 있어요. 부모님의 아이디를 이용해 해로운 웹사이트에 쉽게 접속할 수 있죠. 게다가 일부 이용자들은 폭발물을 설계하고 사용하는 방법 같은 위험한 정보를 인터넷에서 얻을 수도 있습니다.

음, 모든 사용자가 인터넷에 있는 모든 정보에 접근할 수

the poor to get information from the Internet. For one thing, it costs a lot to use the Internet. They would have to not only buy a computer but also pay a monthly fee to an Internet service provider.

Finally, the Internet keeps people from coming up with new and innovative ideas that benefit society as a whole. This is because Internet users can use someone else's work for free and illegally. For example, an Internet user can pirate a computer vaccine program that someone else developed. Consequently, the program developer might not be given credit for making the anti-virus program. So, fewer people will try hard to make original movies, music, or software because their work can be downloaded illegally.

있다고 말하는 것은 그럴듯해 보입니다. 하지만 가난한 사람들이 인터넷에서 정보를 얻는 것은 여전히 힘들어요. 우선 인터넷을 사용하는 데 비용이 많이 듭니다. 컴퓨터를 사야 할 뿐 아니라 인터넷 서비스 회사에 매달 비용도 지불해야 해요.

마지막으로, 인터넷은 사회 전체에 이로운 새롭고 창조적인 아이디어를 사람들이 생각해내지 못하게 합니다. 왜냐하면 인터넷 사용자들이 무료로, 그리고 불법으로 다른 사람의 작업물을 이용할 수 있기 때문입니다. 예를 들어 어떤 인터넷 사용자가 다른 사람이 개발한 컴퓨터 바이러스 백신 프로그램을 불법 복제할 수 있어요. 결과적으로 그 프로그램 개발자는 백신 프로그램을 만든 것에 대한 공로를 인정받을 수 없게 될지도 모릅니다. 그래서 작업물이 불법적으로 다운로드될 수 있기 때문에 사람들은 점차 독창적인 영화나 음악, 소프트웨어를 만들려고 하지 않을 겁니다.

어휘 not necessarily 반드시 ~한 것은 아닌 | be exposed to ~에 노출되다 | explicit **adj** 음란한, 노골적인 | pornography **n** 음란물 | log on to ~에 접속하다 | explosive **n** 폭탄, 폭발물 | plausible **adj** 그럴듯한, 타당한 것 같은 | come up with (아이디어 등을) 생각해 내다 | for free 공짜로, 돈을 내지 않고 | pirate **v** 불법 복제하다 | consequently **adv** 결과적으로 | be given credit for ~에 대해 공로를 인정받다 | download **v** (데이터를) 다운로드하다

Reading 노트

| 주제 | Internet brings benefits to society. | 인터넷은 사회를 이롭게 한다. |

1. info. = useful & valuable
   - enter a keyword → instant info.
   - X need to go to library
2. access info. that ppl couldn't in the past
   - past: had to pay for the info.
3. info. & idea share speed ↑
   - ppl are willing to share what they know

1. 정보 = 유용 & 가치 있음
   – 키워드 입력 → 즉각적인 정보
   – 도서관 갈 필요 없음
2. 과거에 사람들이 얻지 못했던 정보 얻음
   – 과거: 정보를 위해 돈을 내야 했음
3. 정보 & 아이디어 공유 속도 증가
   – 사람들이 아는 것을 기꺼이 공유함

Listening 노트

| 주제 | Internet brings benefits to society? → sometimes causes problems | 인터넷은 사회에 이익을 준다? → 때로는 문제를 일으킨다 |

1. info. = useful & valuable?
   - what about children exposed to harmful info?
   - ppl can obtain dangerous info too
2. access info. that ppl couldn't in the past
   - ppl still have to pay to use the Internet
3. new & innovative idea X
   - ppl can use others' work online
   - piracy → discourages ppl from making movies, music, etc…

1. 정보 = 유용 & 가치 있음?
   – 해로운 정보에 노출된 아이들은?
   – 사람들이 위험한 정보까지 얻을 수 있다
2. 과거에 사람들이 얻지 못했던 정보 얻음
   – 사람들은 여전히 인터넷을 이용하기 위해 돈을 내야 함
3. 새롭고 혁신적인 아이디어를 생각하지 못하게 함
   – 사람들이 온라인에서 다른 사람들의 작업물을 사용할 수 있음
   – 저작권 침해 → 사람들이 영화와 음악 등을 만들려는 의욕을 꺾음

주제

읽기 The reading and the lecture both talk about the usefulness of the Internet. The article says that the Internet brings several benefits.

듣기 However, the lecturer argues that the Internet does not necessarily offer benefits but rather causes some problems.

지문과 강의 둘 다 인터넷의 유용함에 관해 이야기한다. 지문은 인터넷이 몇 가지 이로운 점을 가져다준다고 말한다.

하지만 강의자는 인터넷이 반드시 이로운 점을 제공하는 것은 아니며 오히려 몇 가지 문제점을 야기한다고 주장한다.

요점 1

읽기 Firstly, the reading says that the Internet offers users useful information.

듣기 On the contrary, the lecturer claims that the Internet does not always provide useful and valuable information. She takes pornography as an example. Children may be exposed to this harmful content. She goes on to mention dangerous information that can be obtained on the web such as instructions for making explosives.

첫째로, 지문은 인터넷이 사용자들에게 유용한 정보를 제공한다고 말한다.

반대로 강의자는 인터넷이 항상 유용하고 가치가 있는 정보를 제공하는 것은 아니라고 주장한다. 그녀는 음란물을 한 예로 든다. 아이들이 이런 해로운 내용에 노출될 수 있다. 이어서 강의자는 폭발물을 만드는 방법처럼 웹에서 얻을 수 있는 위험한 정보를 언급한다.

요점 2

읽기 Secondly, in the reading, the author argues that the Internet lets poor people access much more information.

듣기 In contrast, the lecturer says that poor people have to pay a certain amount of money for using the Internet. For example, they have to buy a computer and pay a monthly fee to an Internet service provider.

두 번째로, 지문에서 저자는 인터넷이 가난한 사람들이 더 많은 정보에 접근하게 해 준다고 주장한다.

그에 반해 강의자는 가난한 사람들은 인터넷을 사용하는 데 일정한 돈을 지불해야 한다고 말한다. 예를 들어, 컴퓨터를 사야 하고, 인터넷 서비스 회사에 매달 요금을 지불해야 한다.

요점 3

읽기 Thirdly, the reading goes on to explain that the Internet helps users share information or ideas more quickly.

듣기 On the other hand, the lecturer argues that the Internet prevents users from coming up with new and creative ideas. This is because some users may steal someone else's work, which will make people reluctant to post what they have on the Internet.

세 번째로, 지문은 이어서 인터넷이 정보나 아이디어를 사용자들이 더 빨리 공유하도록 돕는다고 설명한다.

한편 강의자는 인터넷은 사용자들이 새롭고 창의적인 아이디어를 생각해 내지 못하게 한다고 주장한다. 왜냐하면 일부 사용자가 다른 누군가의 작업물을 훔칠 수 있으며, 이는 사람들이 자기가 가진 것을 인터넷에 게시하는 일을 망설이게 할 것이기 때문이다.

어휘 prevent(= keep) someone from V-ing …가 ~하는 것을 막다 l reluctant to ~하는 것을 꺼리는

Q6 Reading

Menhaden are small but important fish that have been disappearing from the Chesapeake Bay in Virginia. The government has recommended that the fishing industry drastically limit the amount of menhaden that is harvested from the bay in order to protect the fishing industry and the species. There are some reasons why this is not the best solution.

First, it is better to remove a predator to prevent the decrease in a fish population because they are not careful about which

청어는 버지니아주의 체사피크만에서 사라지고 있는, 작지만 중요한 물고기이다. 정부는 어업과 이 종을 보호하기 위해 체사피크만의 청어 포획량을 어업에서 철저히 제한하는 것을 권고했다. 이것이 최고의 해결책이 아닌 이유가 몇 가지 있다.

첫째로, 포식자는 자신이 어떤 물고기를 잡는지 신경을 쓰지 않기 때문에 물고기 개체 수의 감소를 막기 위해서는 포식자를 제거하는 것이 더 낫다. 어부들은 개체 수가 계

fish they catch. Fishermen do not take very young fish so that the population can continue to grow. Some scientists say that the striped bass plays a major role in reducing the number of menhaden. This means a main cause of the extinction of these fish is the bass, so removing the bass would be more effective.

Second, the government's proposal would have a negative effect on agriculture. Menhaden are used as an important source of protein for animal feed that is given to livestock and poultry. If the government limits the amount of menhaden caught, the agriculture industry will suffer greatly. Their animals will not consume enough protein, which will slow down their growth.

Third, reducing the amount of menhaden caught would cause many people to lose their jobs in the fishing industry. The government's proposal would affect the fishing industry directly, but it would also affect the whole economy in the end. For example, if many people became unemployed because of the government's proposal, consumer spending in the local area would drop significantly. This would make the local economy become sluggish.

속 늘어날 수 있도록 아주 어린 물고기는 잡지 않는다. 일부 과학자들은 줄무늬 농어가 청어 숫자 감소에 주된 역할을 한다고 말한다. 이는 이 물고기 멸종의 주된 원인이 줄무늬 농어라는 의미이며, 그래서 이 농어를 없애는 것이 더 효과적일 것이다.

두 번째로, 정부의 제안은 농업에 부정적인 영향을 미칠 것이다. 청어는 가축과 가금류에 주어지는 동물의 먹이에 중요한 단백질 공급원으로 사용된다. 만약 정부가 청어 포획량을 제한하면 농업이 큰 피해를 볼 것이다. 동물이 충분한 단백질을 섭취하지 못할 것이고, 이는 동물들의 성장을 저해할 것이다.

세 번째로, 청어 포획량을 줄이면 어업에 종사하는 많은 사람들이 실직하게 될 것이다. 정부의 제안은 어업에 직접 영향을 미치겠지만, 결국 경제 전체에 영향을 줄 것이다. 예를 들어, 만약 정부의 제안으로 많은 사람들이 실직하게 되면 그 지역의 소비자 지출이 많이 감소할 것이다. 이는 지역 경제가 침체되게 할 것이다.

어휘   menhaden n 청어의 일종 I drastically adv 철저하게, 급격히 I harvest v 수확하다, 거두다 I predator n 포식자 I bass n 농어 I play a role in ~에서 역할을 하다 I extinction n 멸종 I proposal n 제안 I protein n 단백질 I livestock n 가축 I poultry n 가금류 I become unemployed 실직하다 I consumer spending 소비자 지출, 개인 소비 I sluggish adj 부진한, 침체한

Listening

Okay, class, it seems logical to say that the policy of restricting the amount of menhaden that may be caught could have very negative effects. However, I think the reasons mentioned in the reading are not reasonable and the government's proposal is the best solution. Allow me to explain why that is the case.

The reading first suggests that eliminating predators would be more effective than limiting fishing. However, the idea of eliminating the bass is very dangerous. This is because the bass is a part of nature. The bass is not only a predator of menhaden, but also an important prey of other species. So reducing the bass population would disrupt the food chain and upset the balance of the ecosystem.

Then the reading states that limiting fishing would have a strong effect on agriculture. It is true that menhaden are used as an important source of protein for livestock and poultry, but you know, it is not the only available protein. I mean, for instance, soybeans are a great replacement that is high in protein that can be used for livestock and poultry feed.

Lastly, the reading says that the government's proposal would affect the economy, and not just the fishing industry. Yes, some may lose their jobs, but this is quite temporary. The fishing restrictions are only intended for the short term. If menhaden populations recover naturally, the local economy will flourish

네, 여러분. 잡을 수 있는 청어의 양을 제한하는 정책이 아주 부정적인 영향을 야기할 수 있다고 말하는 것은 논리적으로 보입니다. 하지만 나는 지문에서 언급한 이유들이 합리적이지 않다고 생각하고, 정부의 제안이 가장 좋은 해결책이라고 봐요. 왜 그렇게 생각하는지 설명하겠습니다.

지문은 먼저 포식자 제거가 물고기를 잡는 것을 제한하는 것보다 더 효과적일 거라고 제시합니다. 그러나 농어를 제거한다는 생각은 아주 위험해요. 왜냐하면 농어는 자연의 일부이기 때문입니다. 농어는 청어의 포식자일 뿐 아니라 다른 종들의 중요한 먹이입니다. 그래서 농어 개체 수를 줄이는 것은 먹이 사슬을 교란하고 생태계의 균형을 어지럽힐 거예요.

지문은 그 다음 물고기 잡기를 제한하는 것이 농업에 큰 영향을 줄 거라고 주장합니다. 청어가 가축과 가금류를 위한 중요한 단백질 원천으로 사용되는 것은 사실이지만, 사용 가능한 단백질은 이뿐만이 아닙니다. 내 말은, 예를 들어 콩이 가축과 가금류에게 먹이로 주는 데 사용될 수 있는 고단백질의 좋은 대체물이죠.

마지막으로, 지문은 정부의 제안이 어업뿐만 아니라 경제에 영향을 줄 거라고 말합니다. 네, 어떤 사람들이 일자리를 잃을 수도 있지만, 이는 일시적인 겁니다. 어업 제한은 단기적인 것으로 의도되었어요. 만약 청어 개체 수가 자연적으로 회복되면 지역 경제는 다시 살아날 겁니다. 따라서

again. Thus, in the long term, this decision should not have much of an effect on the whole economy.

장기적으로 이 결정은 경제 전체에 그다지 큰 영향을 주지 않을 거예요.

어휘 logical **adj** 논리적인 | policy **n** 정책 | restrict **v** 제한하다 | reasonable **adj** 합리적인 | eliminate **v** 제거하다 | prey **n** 먹이, 사냥감 | disrupt **v** 방해하다, 교란하다 | upset **v** 어지럽히다 | available **adj** 이용 가능한 | soybean **n** 콩, 대두 | replacement **n** 대체(물) | temporary **adj** 일시적인, 임시의 | flourish **v** 번영하다, 번창하다 | in the long term 장기적으로

Reading 노트

주제	menhaden fish disappearing → gov't solution = limit harvesting → NOT a good solution
	1. better to remove predator
	   - striped bass is a major threat
	2. neg. effect on agriculture
	   - menhaden = important protein for livestock & poultry
	   - menhaden ↓ = agriculture industry will suffer
	3. many ppl will lose jobs
	   - fishing industry ↓ → local economy ↓
		청어가 사라지고 있음 → 정부의 해결책 = 포획 제한 → 좋은 해결책이 아님
		1. 포식자 제거가 더 나음
		   – 줄무늬 농어가 주된 위협이다
		2. 농업에 부정적 영향
		   – 청어 = 가축과 가금류에게 중요한 단백질
		   – 청어 줄어듦 = 농업계가 힘들어질 것
		3. 많은 사람이 일자리를 잃을 것이다
		   – 어업 침체 → 지역 경제 침체

Listening 노트

주제	menhaden fish disappearing → gov't solution = limit harvesting → It IS a good solution
	1. removing the bass is dangerous
	   - will upset the balance of the food chain & ecosystem
	2. neg. effect on agriculture?
	   - menhaden is not the only protein source
	   - soybean can be used too
	3. some may lose jobs, but…
	   - temporary = restriction is only for the short term
	   - menhaden # back → economy will flourish too
		청어가 사라지고 있음 → 정부의 해결책 = 포획 제한 → 좋은 해결책이다
		1. 농어 제거는 위험하다
		   – 먹이 사슬 & 생태계의 균형을 어지럽힐 것
		2. 농업에 부정적 영향?
		   – 청어가 유일한 단백질원은 아니다
		   – 콩도 사용될 수 있음
		3. 일부는 일자리를 잃겠지만…
		   – 일시적임 = 제한은 단기적이다
		   – 청어 개체 수 회복 → 경제도 살아날 것

노트 & 답변 연결

주제

읽기 The reading and the lecture both talk about a government's policy of limiting the amount of menhaden caught. The article says that there are three reasons why this policy should not be implemented.
듣기 However, the lecturer argues that the reasons mentioned in the reading are not convincing and that this is the best solution.

지문과 강의 모두 청어 포획량을 제한하는 정부의 정책에 관해 이야기한다. 지문은 이 정책이 시행되어서는 안 되는 세 가지 이유가 있다고 말한다.

하지만 강의자는 지문에서 언급된 이유들이 설득력 있지 않으며, 이것이 최고의 해결책이라고 주장한다.

요점 1

읽기 Firstly, the reading claims that reducing the population of the striped bass, a predator of the menhaden, is better than limiting the amount of menhaden caught. The author supports this by saying that unlike fishermen, the bass catch all sizes of fish.

첫째로, 지문은 청어의 포식자인 줄무늬 농어 개체 수를 줄이는 것이 청어 포획량을 제한하는 것보다 더 낫다고 주장한다. 필자는 어부와 달리 농어는 모든 크기의 물고기를 잡기 때문이라고 이 주장을 뒷받침한다.

| 듣기 | According to the lecture, however, getting rid of the bass would be a very bad idea. That is because it would disrupt the ecosystem since the bass is also a prey animal that is important to other species. | 그러나 강의에 따르면, 농어를 없애는 것은 아주 좋지 않은 생각일 것이다. 왜냐하면 농어 또한 다른 종들에게 중요한 먹이라서 생태계를 교란할 것이기 때문이다. |

요점 2

| 읽기 | Secondly, in the reading, the author says that this policy would be responsible for harming the local agriculture. That is because farmers would lose an important source of protein for their animal feed.
듣기 On the other hand, the lecturer argues that there are other sources of protein for agriculture. He supports his point by stating that soybeans are rich in protein that can be used for livestock and poultry farming. | 두 번째로, 지문에서 필자는 이 정책이 지역 농업에 피해를 입히게 될 것이라고 한다. 왜냐하면 농부들이 동물의 먹이가 될 중요한 단백질원을 잃게 될 것이기 때문이다.
반면에 강의자는 농업을 위한 다른 단백질원이 있다고 주장한다. 가축과 가금류를 기르는 데 고단백인 콩이 사용될 수 있다고 하며 자신의 주장을 뒷받침한다. |

요점 3

| 읽기 | Thirdly, the reading goes on to say that this policy may damage the whole economy in Virginia. That is because fishermen would lose their jobs, and they would not contribute to the economy.
듣기 Although the lecturer agrees that this policy may make some jobs temporarily unavailable, he claims that in the long term, it will not affect the whole economy. That is because the recovery of menhaden populations will make the local economy flourish again. | 세 번째로, 지문은 이어서 이 정책이 버지니아 전체의 경제에 피해를 줄 수도 있다고 한다. 왜냐하면 어부들이 직업을 잃을 것이고, 그래서 경제에 기여하지 못하게 될 것이기 때문이다.
강의자는 이 정책이 일부 직업을 일시적으로 없앨 거라는 점에 동의하긴 해도 장기적으로 경제 전체에 영향을 주지 않을 거라고 주장한다. 왜냐하면 청어 개체 수 회복이 지역 경제가 다시 번창하도록 할 것이기 때문이다. |

어휘   get rid of 없애다, 제거하다 | unavailable [adj] 획득할 수 없는, 존재하지 않는 | recovery [n] 회복

Q7 Reading

Since the first pterosaur fossils were discovered, there has been much debate as to whether or not these creatures were capable of powered flight like birds and bats are today. As flying reptiles, their body shape does bear similarities to modern bird species, and their wing structure is similar to that of bats. However, there are many factors that indicate that they couldn't actually have flown under their own power, but may have glided instead.

Firstly, pterosaurs would have had too low of a metabolism for flight. They were an order of reptiles, and as such they would have been cold-blooded. Reptiles depend upon their environment for warmth, so they are only capable of short bursts of energy. Considerable energy is required for taking off from the ground and flapping wings to maintain altitude and increase speed. However, this energy expenditure would have been impossible for organisms with such a slow metabolism.

Secondly, the body structure of pterosaurs would have made them far too heavy for flight. When compared to modern bats and birds, they had uniformly heavier bone structure. In addition,

최초의 익룡 화석이 발견된 이래 이 생명체가 오늘날의 새와 박쥐처럼 동력 비행을 할 수 있는지 여부에 대해 많은 논쟁이 있었다. 날아다니는 파충류인 그들의 체형은 현대의 조류와 유사하며 그들의 날개 구조는 박쥐의 날개와 유사하다. 그러나 그들이 실제로는 자력으로 날지 못했을 것이며 대신에 활공했을지 모른다는 것을 보여주는 많은 요인들이 있다.

먼저, 익룡들이 날기에는 그들의 신진대사가 너무 저조했을 것이다. 그들은 파충류 목이었으며, 그렇기에 냉혈 동물이었을 것이다. 파충류는 환경에 의지해서 온기를 유지하므로 에너지를 짧게 분출하는 것만 가능하다. 땅에서 날아오르거나 고도를 유지하고 속도를 높이기 위해 날개를 퍼덕이는 것에는 상당한 에너지가 필요하다. 그러나 그렇게 신진대사가 느린 생물들에게는 이런 식의 에너지 소모가 불가능했을 것이다.

둘째로, 익룡들의 신체 구조상 날기엔 너무 무거웠을 것이다. 현대의 박쥐나 새와 비교해 보면 그들은 한결같이 더 무거운 뼈 구조를 가지고 있었다. 게다가 몇몇 종의 익룡

some species of pterosaurs were truly massive, with estimated wingspans of over 10 meters. Such huge bodies would have made them extremely heavy. So heavy that their wings could not have generated enough downward thrust to take off.

Thirdly, the feeble hind legs of pterosaurs would not have been capable of launching their bodies into the air. For an animal to begin flying under its own power, it must be able to leap off of the ground high enough to flap its wings. However, pterosaurs had short legs that were not muscular enough to propel them into the air. Their wings would have collided with the ground, thwarting any attempt at powered flight.

들은 날개폭이 10미터 이상이라고 추정될 정도로 정말로 거대했다. 그런 거대한 몸집은 그들을 극도로 무겁게 만들었을 것이다. 몸이 너무 무거워서 그들의 날개는 날아오를 수 있을 정도의 하향 추진력을 만들어낼 수 없었다.

셋째로, 아주 약한 익룡의 뒷다리는 그들의 몸을 공중으로 떠오르게 할 수 없었을 것이다. 동물이 자력으로 날기 시작하려면 날개를 파닥일 수 있을 정도로 땅에서 높이 뛰어오를 수 있어야 한다. 그러나 익룡들은 공중으로 날아오를 수 있을 만큼 근육이 발달하지 못한 짧은 다리를 가지고 있었다. 그들의 날개는 지면과 충돌했을 것이고, 동력 비행을 하려는 모든 시도를 좌절시켰을 것이다.

어휘 pterosaur **n** 익룡 | powered flight 동력 비행 | reptile **n** 파충류 | bear a similarity 비슷하다, 닮다 | under one's own power 혼자서, 자력으로 | glide **v** 활공하다 | metabolism **n** 신진대사 | order **n** 동식물 분류상의 목(目) | cold-blooded **adj** 냉혈의 | burst **n** 분출 | considerable **adj** 상당한 | take off 이륙하다 | flap **v** (날개를) 퍼덕거리다 | altitude **n** 고도 | expenditure **n** 소모 | wingspan **n** 날개 길이(폭) | thrust **n** 추진력 | feeble **adj** 아주 약한 | hind leg **n** 뒷다리 | muscular **adj** 근육이 발달한, 근육의 | propel **v** 추진시키다 | thwart **v** 좌절시키다

Listening

As the author of the reading stated, there has been much debate regarding the flying ability of pterosaurs. He provides evidence to support the idea that they were not capable of powered flight and could only glide. However, recent research suggests that each of his points is inaccurate, and that many of the pterosaur species may indeed have been capable of flying like birds and bats do today.

The reading first points out that pterosaurs were reptiles and therefore cold-blooded, which would mean that their metabolism could not generate enough energy for flight. However, some fossils show that many pterosaurs had bodies covered in hair-like growths that are analogous to mammalian fur. These fur-like coats show that they were conserving internal warmth, which means that they were warm-blooded and had high metabolisms that could have supported flight.

The second argument the reading gives is that pterosaur fossils show that they would have been too heavy for flight. While their bones were large and some species were gigantic, their bones were hollow much like those of birds today. In addition, their skeletal structure also shows that they probably had air sacs that would have reduced their overall bone density. This means that pterosaurs would have been much lighter than previously estimated.

The third point in the reading states that the legs of pterosaurs were too weak for them to have been able to jump into the air and take off from the ground. This argument only stands up if they were bipedal, but their tracks show that they actually used all four legs to move around. Instead of folding their wings onto their backs like birds, they folded them to their side and used their

지문의 필자가 언급했듯 익룡의 비행 능력에 관해 많은 논쟁이 있었죠. 그는 익룡들이 동력 비행을 할 수 없었고 활공만을 할 수 있었다는 견해를 지지하는 증거를 제시합니다. 그렇지만 최근의 연구에서는 그의 주장 하나하나가 부정확한 것이며, 많은 익룡 종이 사실 오늘날의 새와 박쥐처럼 날 수 있었을지도 모른다는 점을 보여주고 있어요.

지문에서는 맨 먼저 익룡들이 파충류였고 따라서 냉혈 동물이었다고 지적하는데, 이는 그들의 신진대사로는 날 수 있을 만한 충분한 에너지를 생산할 수 없었다는 것을 의미합니다. 그러나 일부 화석을 보면 많은 익룡들이 포유류의 털과 유사한 털 같은 것으로 뒤덮인 신체를 가지고 있었다는 것을 알 수 있어요. 이런 털 같은 가죽은 그들이 체내의 온기를 유지하고 있었다는 것을 보여주는데, 이는 그들이 온혈 동물이며 비행을 지원할 수 있었을 정도로 신진대사가 활발했다는 것을 의미하죠.

지문에서 제기하는 두 번째 주장은 화석을 보면 익룡들이 날기에는 너무 무거웠을 거라는 것입니다. 그들의 뼈는 컸으며 몇몇 종들은 거대했지만, 그들의 뼈는 마치 오늘날의 조류처럼 속이 비어 있었어요. 게다가 그들의 골격 구조 또한 그들이 전체적인 골밀도를 감소시켰을 공기주머니를 가지고 있었을지 모른다는 것을 보여줍니다. 이는 익룡이 앞서 추정했던 것보다 훨씬 더 가벼웠으리라는 것을 의미하죠.

지문의 세 번째 주장에서는 익룡의 다리가 너무 약해서 공중으로 뛰어올라 지면에서 이륙할 수 없었다는 것을 언급합니다. 이 주장은 오직 그들이 두 발 보행하는 경우에만 유효합니다만 그들의 발자국을 보면 실제로 이동하는 데 네 다리를 모두 사용했다는 것을 알 수 있죠. 그들

forelegs for walking. This would have allowed them to use their flying muscles to launch themselves into the air.

은 새처럼 날개를 등 위쪽으로 접지 않고 날개를 옆구리 쪽으로 접고 앞다리를 사용해서 걸었습니다. 이는 그들이 비행용 근육을 사용하여 스스로 공중으로 날아오를 수 있도록 해주었을 것입니다.

어휘 growth 🅝 (수염, 손톱 등의) 생장물, 발생물 ∣ analogous 🅐🅳🅹 유사한 ∣ mammalian 🅐🅳🅹 포유류의 ∣ conserve 🆅 유지하다, 보존하다 ∣ warm-blooded 🅐🅳🅹 온혈의 ∣ hollow 🅐🅳🅹 속이 빈 ∣ skeletal structure 골격 구조 ∣ air sac 공기주머니 ∣ bone density 골밀도 ∣ stand up 여전히 유효하다 ∣ bipedal 🅐🅳🅹 두 발로 걷는 ∣ track 🅝 발자국 ∣ foreleg 🅝 앞다리

Reading 노트

주제 pterosaur – was it able to fly like birds & bats? No, they glided.
  1. ↓ metabolism
    - reptiles = cold-blooded, short bursts of energy
    - flying not possible b/c metabolism too slow
  2. body structure
    - too heavy to fly
    - some species' wingspan = 10 m.
  3. feeble hind legs
    - can't launch body into the air = can't leap off
    - legs too short

익룡 – 새나 박쥐처럼 날 수 있었나? 아니다. 활공했다.
1. 저조한 신진대사
  – 파충류 = 냉혈, 에너지를 짧게 분출
  – 신진대사가 너무 느려 나는 것이 불가능
2. 신체 구조
  – 날기에 너무 무겁다
  – 일부 종의 날개폭 = 10미터
3. 약한 뒷다리
  – 공중으로 몸을 떠오르게 할 수 없음 = 뛰어오르지 못함
  – 다리가 너무 짧음

Listening 노트

주제 pterosaur – was it able to fly like birds & bats? Possibly
  1. ↓ metabolism?
    - no, fossils show that they had fur-like coats → internal warmth
    - warm-blooded = high metabolism → can fly
  2. body structure
    - too heavy to fly? bones were hollow
    - had air sacs = bone density ↓
  3. feeble hind legs?
    - actually used all 4 legs instead of 2
    - folded wings to side & used forelegs
      → can use flying muscles

익룡 – 새나 박쥐처럼 날 수 있었나? 가능성 있음
1. 저조한 신진대사?
  – 아니다. 화석은 이들이 털과 비슷한 가죽을 갖고 있었다는 것을 보여줌 → 체내 온기
  – 온혈 = 높은 신진대사 → 날 수 있음
2. 신체 구조
  – 날기에 너무 무겁다? 뼈가 비어 있었음
  – 공기주머니가 있었음 = 골밀도 감소
3. 약한 뒷다리?
  – 실제로는 두 다리 대신 네 다리 모두 사용
  – 옆으로 날개를 접고 앞다리를 사용함
    → 비행용 근육 사용 가능

노트 & 답변 연결

주제

읽기 The reading and the lecture both talk about the flying ability of pterosaurs. The author maintains that they were not able to fly under their own power and could only glide.
듣기 However, the lecturer provides evidence to show that they were capable of powered flight like birds and bats are today.

지문과 강의는 모두 익룡의 비행 능력에 대해 이야기하고 있다. 지문 필자는 그들이 자력으로 날 수 없었으며 활공만 할 수 있었다고 주장한다.
그러나 강의자는 그들이 오늘날의 새와 박쥐처럼 동력 비행을 할 수 있었다는 것을 보여주는 증거를 제시한다.

요점 1

읽기 Firstly, the reading states that pterosaurs were reptiles and therefore cold-blooded animals. The author suggests that

첫째로, 지문은 익룡들이 파충류였으며 따라서 냉혈 동물이었다고 말한다. 필자는 그들의 신진대사가 너

their metabolism must have been too low to produce enough energy for flight.

[듣기] However, the lecturer contends that many of them had fur-like coats to help them keep warm. This shows that pterosaurs could have had a metabolism high enough to support flight.

무 낮아 비행을 위한 충분한 에너지를 생산하지 못했을 것이라고 말한다.

그러나 강의자는 다수의 익룡들에게는 체온을 유지하는 데 도움이 되는 털 같은 가죽이 있었다고 주장한다. 이것은 익룡들의 신진대사가 비행을 뒷받침할 수 있을 만큼 높았을 수 있다는 것을 보여준다.

요점 2

[읽기] Secondly, the reading maintains that pterosaurs would have been too heavy to fly because their body structure was massive and dense.

[듣기] However, the lecturer refutes this idea by saying that they would have been relatively light considering their body size. This is because their bones were hollow and had air sacs to decrease overall bone density.

두 번째로, 지문에서 익룡들은 신체 구조가 거대하며 조밀했기 때문에 너무 무거워서 날지 못했을 것이라고 말한다.

그러나 강의자는 신체 크기를 감안한다면 그들은 비교적 가벼운 편이었을 것이라고 말하며 이 의견에 반박한다. 이는 그들의 뼈가 속이 비어 있었으며 전체 골밀도를 감소시키는 공기주머니를 가지고 있었기 때문이다.

요점 3

[읽기] Thirdly, the reading states that pterosaurs could not have taken off from the ground because their hind legs were too short and poorly muscled.

[듣기] However, the lecturer points out that this argument is valid only if they used just their hind legs to jump up. According to her, they could have folded their wings to their side and used their four legs to take a flying leap into the air.

세 번째로, 지문에서는 익룡들의 뒷다리가 너무 짧고 근육이 빈약했기 때문에 그들이 지면에서 이륙하지 못했을 것이라고 말한다.

그러나 강의자는 이 주장이 익룡들이 뛰어오르는 데 그들의 뒷다리만을 사용했을 경우에 한해 유효하다고 지적한다. 강의자에 따르면 익룡들은 날개를 옆구리 쪽으로 접고 네 다리로 도움닫기를 하여 공중으로 뛰어오를 수 있었을 것이다.

어휘 refute [v] 반박하다 I valid [adj] 유효한 I flying leap 도움닫기를 한 도약

Q8 Reading

White nose syndrome is an infection caused by a fungus that grows on the snouts and wings of bats. The infection causes the bats to wake up frequently when they are hibernating during the winter. This increases their metabolism when they cannot feed to replenish their fat stores, slowly starving them to death. Since it is a serious threat to the bat population of North America, scientists have proposed several possible ways to combat the fungus.

Some scientists have suggested that the fungus is being spread by humans, so people should be prevented from entering caves with large bat populations. First detected in a cave in New York, the fungus spread to 25 states and 5 Canadian provinces in just 8 years. Since the fungus can survive on clothing, human visitors would appear to explain its rapid spread. Therefore, people, and tourists in particular, should be barred from entering infected caves.

Another way to help the afflicted bats is to study European bat populations that seem to be resistant to the fungus. It is believed

흰코증후군은 박쥐의 코와 날개에서 자라는 균에 의해 발생하는 전염병이다. 이 전염병은 박쥐가 겨울에 동면할 때 자주 깨어나게 만든다. 이는 박쥐가 먹이를 먹어 저장 지방을 보충할 수 없을 때 그들의 신진대사를 증가시키며 서서히 굶겨 죽인다. 이것은 북미의 박쥐 개체군에 심각한 위협 요소이기 때문에 과학자들은 이 균을 퇴치하기 위한 몇 가지 가능한 방법들을 제시했다.

일부 과학자들은 이 균이 인간들에 의해 확산되고 있으며, 따라서 사람들이 박쥐 개체 수가 많은 동굴에 들어가지 못하도록 해야 한다고 주장했다. 뉴욕에 있는 한 동굴에서 처음 발견된 후로 이 균은 단 8년 만에 25개 주와 캐나다의 5개 지방으로 확산되었다. 이 균은 옷감을 먹고 살 수 있기 때문에 인간 방문객들이 그 급속한 확산의 원인으로 볼 수 있다. 그러므로 사람들, 특히 관광객들이 감염된 동굴에 들어가는 것은 금지되어야 한다.

이 증후군에 걸린 박쥐들을 도울 수 있는 또 다른 방법은 그 균에 저항력이 있는 것 같은 유럽의 박쥐 개체군을 연

that the fungus was most likely introduced to North America from Europe. According to the scientists, while the fungus is already widespread in Europe, most of the infected European bats are healthy. If the reason behind their resistance can be determined, perhaps it could be utilized to save their North American cousins.

Yet another way of addressing the issue lies in a limitation of the fungus. The organism is psychrophilic, which means that it prefers cooler conditions to grow in. In fact, if it is exposed to temperatures over 20 degrees centigrade, it cannot survive. So, if the air temperature in infected caves could be raised slightly, that would cause it to die off. This solution would not be simple to implement, but it could have a dramatic effect on the spread of the syndrome.

구하는 것이다. 그 균은 아마도 유럽에서 북미로 유입되었을 것으로 여겨진다. 과학자들에 따르면 유럽에는 그 균이 이미 널리 퍼져있는데도 감염된 유럽 박쥐들 대부분이 건강하다고 한다. 그 저항력 이면에 있는 이유를 밝혀낼 수 있다면 그것은 아마 북미의 동족들을 구하는 데 활용될 수 있을 것이다.

그리고 이 사안을 해결하는 또 다른 방법은 그 균을 제한하는 것이다. 그 생물은 호냉성으로, 이는 차가운 생장 환경을 선호한다는 의미이다. 사실 섭씨 20도 이상의 온도에 노출된다면 이 생물은 살아남지 못한다. 따라서 감염된 동굴 내부의 기온을 약간 올릴 수 있다면 멸균할 수 있을 것이다. 이 해결책은 시행하기가 간단하지 않을지 몰라도 그 증후군의 확산에 극적인 영향을 미칠 수 있을 것이다.

어휘 syndrome ⓝ 증후군 | infection ⓝ 전염병, 감염 | fungus ⓝ 균류, 곰팡이류 | snout ⓝ 코, 주둥이 | hibernate ⓥ 동면하다 | metabolism ⓝ 신진대사 | replenish ⓥ 보충하다 | starve somebody to death 굶겨 죽이다 | combat ⓥ 싸우다 | detect ⓥ 발견하다 | bar ⓥ 금지하다 | afflicted adj (병으로) 괴로워하는, 고통받는 | resistant adj 저항력 있는, ~에 잘 견디는 | psychrophilic adj 호냉의 | implement ⓥ 시행하다

Listening

As the article you read stated, white nose syndrome is spreading rapidly through North America and leaving millions of bats dead in its wake. This fungal infection is a serious threat to the further existence of many bat species, so we have ample reason to find a solution. However, the suggestions in the article for resolving the situation would not be effective for significant reasons.

Firstly, the article suggests that the fungus's rapid proliferation is due to it being spread by people who are visiting the caves where the bats hibernate. While the fungus most likely was imported to the Americas by people from Europe since bats do not migrate between the continents, there is little evidence that humans have continued to contribute to its spread. In fact, the direction and speed from the original site of infection in New York correspond to normal bat movement patterns. It doesn't spread over long distances as it would if people were transporting it.

Secondly, the author states that European bat species should be studied since they appear to be resistant to the fungus. He implies that the European bats may be immune to the fungus due to prolonged exposure, which cannot be ruled out. However, there may be other environmental factors that inhibit the fungus's spread which are wholly unrelated to the bats. If we focus our search too narrowly, we may miss important information that could lead to positive results.

Finally, he explains that some scientists have suggested attacking the fungus more directly by increasing the temperature in the bats' caves. Since the fungus is cold-loving, raising the temperature above its habitable range for a sustained period would most likely kill it. However, the fungus kills the bats by disturbing their hibernation cycle, which raising the temperature

여러분이 읽은 글에 나와 있듯이 흰코증후군은 북미 전역에 빠르게 확산 중이며 그 결과 수백만 마리의 박쥐를 죽음으로 몰아넣고 있죠. 이 균류에 의한 전염병은 많은 박쥐 종의 앞으로의 생존에 심각한 위협 요소이므로 우리에겐 해결책을 찾아야 할 충분한 이유가 있습니다. 그러나 그 글에 있는 문제 해결 방안들은 중요한 이유들로 인해 효과적이지 않을 것입니다.

먼저, 글에서는 균의 급격한 확산이 박쥐가 동면하는 동굴을 방문하는 사람들에 의해 전파되기 때문이라고 주장합니다. 박쥐는 대륙 간을 이동하지 않기 때문에 그 균은 사람들에 의해 유럽에서 미 대륙으로 옮겨 왔을 가능성이 높지만, 사람들이 계속해서 그 확산에 기여해왔다는 증거는 거의 없어요. 사실, 뉴욕에 있는 최초 감염지로부터 그 병이 확산된 방향과 속도는 일반적인 박쥐의 이동 경로와 일치합니다. 그것은 사람들이 옮길 경우에 가능할 만한 먼 거리에 걸쳐 확산되지 않죠.

두 번째로, 필자는 유럽의 박쥐 종들이 그 균에 저항력이 있는 것으로 보이기 때문에 연구해야 한다고 말합니다. 그는 유럽의 박쥐들이 장기적인 노출로 인해 그 균에 면역이 생겼을 것이라고 암시하는데, 이런 주장을 배제할 수는 없죠. 그렇지만 박쥐와 완전히 무관하면서 균의 확산을 저해하는 다른 환경적인 요인들이 있을 수 있습니다. 우리가 조사 범위를 너무 좁게 잡는다면 긍정적인 결과로 이어질 수 있는 중요한 정보를 놓칠 수도 있어요.

마지막으로, 그는 몇몇 과학자들이 박쥐 동굴의 온도를 높임으로써 균을 더 직접적으로 공격하는 것을 제안했다고 설명합니다. 그 균은 추운 곳을 좋아하므로 일정 기간 동안 생존 가능한 범위 이상으로 온도를 높이면 그것을 죽일 수 있을 것입니다. 그러나 그 균은 박쥐의 동면 주기를

in a cave would also do. Therefore, this method would probably increase the number of deaths rather than lower it.

교란시켜 박쥐를 죽음에 이르게 하는데, 동굴 내부의 온도를 높이는 것 또한 이 같은 결과를 낳을 수 있죠. 그러므로 이런 방식은 아마도 죽는 박쥐의 수를 낮추기보다는 늘리게 될 것입니다.

어휘 in one's wake ~에 뒤이어 | fungal **adj** 균류에 의한 | proliferation **n** 급증, 확산 | migrate **v** 이동하다 | correspond **v** 일치하다 | transport **v** 수송하다, 이동시키다 | immune **adj** 면역이 된 | prolonged **adj** 장기적인 | rule out 제외시키다, 배제하다 | inhibit **v** 저해하다 | habitable **adj** 살 수 있는, 주거의

Reading 노트

주제 white nose syndrome – fungus on bats' snouts & wings, make them wake up during winter → population ↓ → solutions?
  1. fungus spread by humans
     - keep ppl from entering bat caves
  2. study European bats
     - they seem to be resistant to this fungus
  3. fungus limitation
     - can't survive over 20℃
     - ↑ air temp. → kill the fungus

흰코증후군 – 박쥐의 코와 날개에 균이 자라서 박쥐가 겨울에 깨어나게 함 → 개체 수 감소 → 해결책은?
  1. 인간이 옮긴 균
     – 사람들이 박쥐 굴에 들어가지 못하게 막는다
  2. 유럽 박쥐 연구
     – 이 균에 저항력을 가진 것으로 보인다
  3. 균 제한
     – 섭씨 20도 이상에서는 생존하지 못한다
     – 공기 온도 높임 → 균 죽임

Listening 노트

주제 white nose syndrome – fungus on bats' snouts & wings, make them wake up during winter → population ↓ → solutions = X effective
  1. fungus spread by humans? Not really
     - little evidence
     - original site = showed normal bat movement patterns
  2. study European bats?
     - there could be other envi. factors
     - can't search too narrowly, might miss import. info.
  3. fungus limitation?
     - ↑ air temp. will also disturb bats & kill them

흰코증후군 – 박쥐의 코와 날개에 균이 자라서 박쥐가 겨울에 깨어나게 함 → 개체 수 감소 → 해결책 = 효과 X
  1. 인간이 균을 옮긴다? 아니다
     – 증거 적음
     – 근원지 = 일반적인 박쥐 이동 패턴을 보임
  2. 유럽 박쥐 연구?
     – 다른 환경적 요인이 있을 수도 있음
     – 너무 좁게 조사하면 중요한 정보를 놓칠지도 모름
  3. 균 제한?
     – 공기 온도를 높이면 박쥐들을 교란시켜 죽일 것

노트 & 답변 연결

주제

읽기 The reading and the lecture both discuss white nose syndrome, which threatens the bat population of North America. According to the reading, there are three ways to fight off the fungus that causes the syndrome.
듣기 However, the lecturer argues that these methods are not as effective as the author says.

지문과 강의는 모두 북미의 박쥐 개체군을 위협하는 흰코증후군에 대해 논하고 있다. 지문에 따르면 이 증후군을 유발하는 균을 퇴치하는 세 가지 방법이 있다. 그러나 강의자는 이런 방법들이 필자가 말하는 것처럼 효과적이지 않다고 주장한다.

요점 1

읽기 First of all, the reading states that humans should not be allowed to visit the caves where the bats hibernate because the fungus is likely to be spread by them.

우선, 지문에서는 인간들이 박쥐가 동면하는 동굴에 방문하는 것을 허용하지 말아야 한다고 말하는데, 이는 그 균이 인간들에 의해 확산될 가능성이 높기 때문

듣기 However, the lecturer argues that even though people brought it over to the Americas from Europe, there is no concrete evidence that they have continued contributing to its proliferation.

이다.
그러나 강의자는 사람들이 그 균을 유럽에서 미주로 들여오긴 했지만, 사람들이 그 확산에 계속해서 기여했다는 구체적인 증거는 없다고 주장한다.

요점 2

읽기 Next, the author claims that we can find a solution for the North American bats by studying European species which already seem to be resistant to the fungus.
듣기 On the other hand, the lecturer points out that there could be other crucial factors that influence the spread of the fungus. If we only focus on the European bats, this research will be biased.

다음으로, 필자는 이미 그 균에 대한 저항력이 있는 것으로 보이는 유럽의 종을 연구함으로써 북미의 박쥐들을 위한 해결책을 찾을 수 있다고 주장한다.
반면에 강의자는 균의 확산에 영향을 주는 다른 중요한 요인들이 있을 수 있다고 지적한다. 우리가 유럽의 박쥐들에게만 초점을 맞춘다면 이 연구는 편향될 것이다.

요점 3

읽기 Finally, the reading passage suggests that it is possible to effectively get rid of the fungus by raising the air temperature in infected caves. This is because it cannot survive at over 20 degrees centigrade.
듣기 However, the lecturer undermines this idea by saying that changing the temperature would also kill the bats by disturbing their hibernation cycle.

마지막으로, 읽기 지문에서는 감염된 동굴 내의 기온을 올림으로써 균을 효과적으로 제거하는 것이 가능하다고 말한다. 이는 균이 섭씨 20도 이상에서는 살아남지 못하기 때문이다.
그러나 강의자는 온도를 바꾸는 것이 박쥐의 동면 주기를 교란시켜 박쥐들까지 죽일 수 있다고 말하며 이 견해를 일축한다.

어휘 fight off ~와 싸워 물리치다 I biased **adj** 편향된, 선입견이 있는 I undermine **v** 약화시키다

Q9 Reading

According to various ancient records, there once existed a fabulously wealthy kingdom called Ophir that traded with the Eastern Mediterranean. They supplied huge amounts of luxury goods including sandalwood, gems, gold, and ivory. However, the documents provide little information regarding its location. For the following reasons, many scholars think that the Kingdom of Ophir was located somewhere in South Asia.

Firstly, South Asia seems to have been a likely location for Ophir when looking at the goods that were imported to the Eastern Mediterranean. Gold and gems could be imported from anywhere, but sandalwood trees are native to India and Pakistan in South Asia, and they were the only suppliers of the trees until fairly recently. In addition, Asian elephants have been a source of ivory for thousands of years. Therefore, Ophir is likely to have been located in South Asia because most of its goods originated from South Asia.

Secondly, the Kingdom of Ophir was located quite far from its trading partners in the Eastern Mediterranean. The records say that merchant ships of the Eastern Mediterranean returned from Ophir every three years full of trade goods. Some scientists suggest that Ophir was located in the Middle East or Africa, but

여러 고대 기록에 따르면 예전에 지중해 동부 지역과 교역을 하던 오빌이라는 엄청나게 부유한 왕국이 있었다. 그 나라는 백단유, 보석, 금, 상아를 포함한 엄청난 양의 사치품을 공급했다. 그러나 문서에 그곳의 위치에 관한 정보는 거의 나와 있지 않다. 다음과 같은 이유들로 많은 학자들은 오빌 왕국이 남아시아의 어딘가에 위치해있었다고 생각한다.

첫째로, 지중해 동부 지역으로 수입되었던 상품들을 살펴보았을 때, 오빌은 남아시아에 위치해 있었을 것으로 보인다. 금과 보석은 어디에서나 수입할 수 있지만 백단나무는 남아시아의 인도와 파키스탄이 원산지이며 꽤 최근까지 그 나라들이 그 나무의 유일한 공급지였다. 게다가 아시아 코끼리들은 수천 년 동안 상아의 공급원이었다. 따라서 오빌의 상품들 대부분이 남아시아에서 난 것이었으므로 그곳은 남아시아에 위치해있었을 가능성이 높다.

두 번째로, 오빌 왕국은 지중해 동부 지역에 있는 교역 상대국들로부터 꽤 멀리 떨어진 곳에 위치해 있었다. 기록에 따르면 지중해 동부의 상선들이 오빌에서 교역품을 가득 싣고 3년마다 돌아왔다고 한다. 일부 과학자들은 오빌이 중동이나 아프리카에 위치했다고 추측하지만, 그 지역들은 너무 가깝다. 항해하여 지중해 동부 지역으로 돌아오

those areas are far too close. It must have been much farther away for the voyage to take three years to return to the Eastern Mediterranean.

Thirdly, according to the records, the terms that were used for the trade goods from Ophir are the same as or very similar to the names they had in South Asia. Some of the imported goods were quite exotic, so no local terms existed for them in the Eastern Mediterranean. It is still common practice today to borrow words for new things from the culture that introduced them. A prime example of this is the many words that English has adopted from other languages for new things or ideas.

는 데 3년이 걸리려면 그곳은 훨씬 더 멀리 떨어진 지역 이었을 것이다.

세 번째로, 기록에 따르면 오빌에서 온 교역품에 사용되었 던 용어들은 남아시아에서 사용했던 명칭과 같거나 매우 유사하다. 일부 수입품들은 상당히 이국적이었으므로 지 중해 동부 지역에는 그것들을 칭하는 현지의 용어가 존재 하지 않았다. 새로운 것을 칭하기 위해 이를 들여온 문화 권의 말을 차용하는 관행은 오늘날에도 아직 흔히 있는 일 이다. 이것의 전형적인 예로는 새로운 것이나 사상을 위해 다른 언어로부터 영어가 채택한 많은 단어들이 있다.

어휘 fabulously `adv` 엄청나게 | sandalwood `n` 백단유 | regarding `prep` ~에 관하여 | fairly `adv` 꽤, 상당히 | originate `v` 비롯되다, 유래하다 | merchant ship 상선 | voyage `n` 여행, 항해 | exotic `adj` 외국의, 이국적인 | a prime example of ~의 전형적인 예

Listening

Ancient documents and archaeological finds indicate that the Kingdom of Ophir really existed. However, no one knows where it was actually located. The reading passage contends that the Kingdom of Ophir was somewhere in South Asia. While this may indeed be true, the arguments that it provides are far from convincing.

First, the reading contends that the goods that were imported from Ophir indicate that it was in South Asia. Yes, sandalwood is native to that region, and Asian elephants are a traditional source of ivory. However, this doesn't necessarily mean that Ophir and South Asia were the same place. Their presence in Ophir may only mean that it was a trade center. Goods from South Asia may have been brought to Ophir and then traded with merchants from the Eastern Mediterranean. So, this is not a very convincing argument.

Next, the reading says that ships from the Eastern Mediterranean that went to Ophir only returned every three years. This shows that South Asia was a likely location considering how far away it is. However, navigation techniques and maps were very poor in the ancient world. So, ships had to follow the coastline to avoid being lost at sea, which would make any trip take much longer than it would be today. Just because it takes a long time to get somewhere doesn't necessarily mean that it is far away.

Finally, the author states that the names used for the trade goods imported to the Eastern Mediterranean are quite similar to those used in South Asia. So, he supposes that South Asia must be where Ophir was located. However, South Asia could have had earlier contact with the Kingdom of Ophir than the Eastern Mediterranean did. I mean, we cannot conclude that the terms originated in South Asia, let alone that they are the same place.

고대의 문헌 및 고고학 발견물에서는 오빌 왕국이 실제로 존재했다는 것을 보여줍니다. 그렇지만 그것이 실제로 어 디에 위치해있었는지는 아무도 모릅니다. 읽기 지문은 오 빌 왕국이 남아시아의 어딘가에 있었다고 주장하고 있습 니다. 이것이 정말 사실일지도 모르긴 하지만 지문에서 제 시하고 있는 주장들은 전혀 설득력이 없어요.

먼저, 지문에서는 오빌에서 수입된 상품들에서 그곳이 남 아시아였다는 것을 알 수 있다고 주장하고 있죠. 그래요, 백단유는 그 지역이 원산지이며 아시아 코끼리들은 상아 의 전통적인 공급원입니다. 그렇지만 이것이 반드시 오빌 과 남아시아가 같은 장소였음을 의미하는 것은 아니에요. 오빌에 그 상품들이 있었다는 것은 단지 그곳이 교역의 중심지였음을 의미하는 것일 수도 있어요. 남아시아에서 온 상품들이 오빌로 들어온 후에 지중해 동부 지역에서 온 상인들과 거래가 되었을 수도 있습니다. 따라서 이것은 그리 설득력 있는 주장이 아닙니다.

다음으로, 지문에서는 오빌로 가던 지중해 동부 지역의 배 들이 3년마다 돌아왔다고 말하고 있어요. 이는 멀리 떨어 져 있는 정도를 고려했을 때 남아시아가 소재지일 가능성 이 높다는 것을 보여줍니다. 그렇지만 고대의 항해 기술 과 지도는 매우 형편없었어요. 따라서 배들은 바다에서 실 종되지 않기 위해 해안선을 따라다녀야만 했고, 이 때문에 항해 시 오늘날보다 훨씬 더 오랜 시간이 걸렸을 것입니 다. 어딘가에 가는 데 오랜 시간이 걸린다는 것이 반드시 멀리 떨어져 있음을 의미하지는 않지요.

마지막으로, 필자는 지중해 동부 지역으로 수입된 교역품 에 사용된 명칭들이 남아시아에서 사용하던 것들과 매우 유사하다고 말합니다. 따라서 그는 오빌이 남아시아에 위 치해있었을 것으로 추측하죠. 그러나 남아시아가 지중해 동부 지역보다 더 일찍 오빌 왕국과 접촉했을 수도 있어 요. 다시 말해서, 그들이 같은 장소라는 것은 고사하고 그 용어들이 남아시아에서 유래했다고 단정할 수 없다는 것 이죠.

어휘 archaeological **adj** 고고학의 I contend **v** 주장하다 I convincing **adj** 설득력 있는 I conclude **v** 결론짓다, 주장하다 I let alone ~은 고사하고

Reading 노트

주제 ancient kingdom named Ophir – was in S. Asia?
  1. imported goods
    - sandalwood trees from India & Pakistan
    - ivory of Asian elephants
  2. far from trading partners in E. Mediterranean
    - records say ships returned every 3 yrs
  3. terms were similar
    - trade goods' terms were similar to the names in S. Asia

오빌이라는 고대의 왕국 – 남아시아에 있었다?
1. 수입된 상품
  − 인도 & 파키스탄에서 온 백단나무
  − 아시아 코끼리의 상아
2. 지중해 동부의 교역 상대국들과 멀었음
  − 기록은 배가 3년마다 돌아왔다고 함
3. 용어가 비슷했음
  − 교역 상품 용어들이 남아시아의 이름과 비슷했음

Listening 노트

주제 ancient kingdom named Ophir – was in S. Asia? Not convincing…
  1. imported goods?
    - they don't mean that Ophir = S. Asia
    - sandalwood & ivory may have been just traded in Ophir
  2. far from trading partners in E. Mediterranean?
    - navigation tech. & maps were poor
    - any trip could take really long
  3. terms were similar?
    - S. Asia may have contacted Ophir earlier than E. Med.
    - no evidence to show that the words originated from S. Asia

오빌이라는 고대의 왕국 – 남아시아에 있었다? 설득력이 없음…
1. 수입된 상품?
  − 그렇다고 오빌이 남아시아라는 의미는 아님
  − 백단나무 & 상아가 단순히 오빌에서 거래되었던 것일 수 있음
2. 지중해 동부의 교역 상대국들과 멀었음?
  − 항해 기술 & 지도가 좋지 않았다
  − 어떤 여정이든 엄청나게 오래 걸릴 수 있었음
3. 용어가 비슷함?
  − 남아시아가 지중해 동부보다 오빌과 먼저 접촉했을지 모름
  − 이 단어들이 남아시아에서 유래했다는 것을 보여주는 증거는 없음

노트 & 답변 연결

주제

읽기 The reading and the lecture both discuss where the Kingdom of Ophir was located. The reading cites three reasons why Ophir may have been located in South Asia based on records from the Eastern Mediterranean, which traded with Ophir.
듣기 However, the lecturer argues that those reasons are not convincing.

지문과 강의에서는 모두 오빌 왕국이 어디에 위치해 있었는지에 대해 논한다. 지문에서는 오빌과 무역을 했던 지중해 동부 지역의 기록을 바탕으로 그 왕국이 남아시아에 위치해 있었을지 모른다는 세 가지 이유를 든다.
그러나 강의자는 그 이유들이 설득력이 없다고 주장한다.

요점 1

읽기 The first reason given in the reading is that most of the imported goods from Ophir seem to have originated in South Asia.
듣기 While the lecturer admits that those goods are from South Asia, she says that Ophir could have been just a trade center, not a country of origin. Therefore, the goods from many different countries may have been traded in Ophir.

지문에서 주어진 첫 번째 이유는 오빌에서 수입된 상품들 중 대다수의 원산지가 남아시아였던 것으로 보인다는 점이다.
강의자는 이런 상품들이 남아시아산이라는 것은 인정하지만, 오빌은 원산지가 아니라 단지 교역의 중심지였을 수도 있다고 말한다. 따라서 여러 다양한 국가로부터 온 상품들이 오빌에서 거래되었던 것일 수도 있다.

읽기 The author mentions the long distance from Ophir to the Eastern Mediterranean as the second reason. This is because it usually took three years for ships to return from Ophir.

듣기 However, the lecturer contradicts this idea by mentioning the possibility that the voyage took so long due to poor navigation technologies and maps at that time.

필자는 오빌에서 지중해 동부 지역까지의 먼 거리를 두 번째 이유로 언급한다. 이는 선박이 오빌에서 돌아오기까지 보통 3년이 걸렸기 때문이다.

그러나 강의자는 그 당시의 부족한 항해 기술과 지도 때문에 여행이 너무 오래 걸렸을 가능성을 언급하면서 이 견해를 반박한다.

읽기 Finally, the reading suggests that the terms used for the goods from Ophir are quite similar to the words used in South Asia. It is suspected that the Eastern Mediterranean borrowed the names from Ophir.

듣기 However, the lecturer suggests that there might have been earlier contact between South Asia and Ophir, so they possibly shared those terms long before the Eastern Mediterranean did.

마지막으로, 지문에서는 오빌에서 들어온 상품에 사용되었던 용어들이 남아시아에서 사용되었던 단어들과 상당히 유사하다고 말한다. 지중해 동부 지역이 이 명칭들을 오빌로부터 차용했다고 추측된다.

그러나 강의자는 남아시아와 오빌이 이보다 앞서 접촉했을지도 모르며, 따라서 그들이 지중해 동부 지역보다 훨씬 이전에 그 용어들을 공유했을 가능성이 있다고 말한다.

어휘 country of origin 원산지

Q10 Reading

The Glen Canyon Dam was constructed on the Colorado River in northern Arizona to regulate water flow. By building it, a manmade reservoir called Lake Powell was created. Although the dam has performed its task quite well, many people have demanded that it be removed, which would drain Lake Powell. However, there are many important reasons to continue using the dam.

First, Lake Powell is a major vacation spot that attracts an average of 2 million people per year. These people come to enjoy the lake and its rugged surroundings, which are made more beautiful by the plants that grow along its shores. This lake makes tourism the main industry of the region, generating the majority of the area's revenue. Therefore, the entire local economy would be crippled if the dam were removed.

Second, it would be extremely difficult to satisfy the demand for water if the dam were removed. This is because regulating the flow of water from the upper to the lower Colorado River Basin was the original purpose of constructing the dam. The dam provides a reliable source of water to the surrounding area and the communities downriver, which would be parched desert without it. This is the most efficient way to provide water to the people and agriculture that depend upon the Colorado River.

Third, draining the lake and removing the dam would have a negative effect on the surrounding ecosystem. The Colorado River descends from the Rocky Mountains full of sediment, and the dam prevents some of that sediment from continuing downstream. This makes the water cleaner and keeps the

글렌캐니언 댐은 물의 흐름을 조절하기 위해 애리조나주 북부의 콜로라도강에 건설되었다. 그 댐을 건설하면서 파월호라는 인공 저수지가 조성되었다. 그 댐이 본연의 과업을 상당히 잘 수행했음에도 불구하고 많은 사람들은 여러 가지 이유로 그 댐을 없앨 것을 요구했는데, 그러면 파월호의 물이 모두 마를 것이다. 그러나 그 댐을 계속 사용해야 하는 많은 중요한 이유가 있다.

첫째로, 파월호는 연간 평균 2백만 명의 사람들이 몰리는 주요 휴양지이다. 이 사람들은 호숫가를 따라 자라는 식물들로 인해 아름다움이 배가되는 호수와 그곳의 바위투성이 경치를 즐기기 위해 온다. 이 호수는 관광업을 그 지역의 주요 산업으로 만들어서, 그 지역 수입의 대부분을 창출한다. 그러므로 그 댐이 없어진다면 지역 경제 전체가 마비될 것이다.

둘째로, 그 댐을 없앤다면 물에 대한 수요를 충족시키기가 매우 어려울 것이다. 콜로라도강 유역의 상류에서부터 하류까지 물의 흐름을 조절하는 것이 댐을 건설한 본래 목적이었기 때문이다. 그 댐은 만약에 댐이 없었다면 바싹 마른 사막이었을 주변 지역과 강 하류에 있는 지역 공동체들에게 믿을 만한 물 공급원을 제공한다. 이것은 콜로라도강에 의존하고 있는 사람들과 농업에 물을 공급하는 가장 효율적인 방법이다.

세 번째로, 호수의 물을 빼고 댐을 없애는 것은 주변 생태계에 부정적인 영향을 미칠 것이다. 콜로라도강은 로키산맥에서부터 퇴적물을 가득 품고 흘러 내려오는데, 댐은 그 퇴적물의 일부가 하류로 계속 내려가는 것을 막아준다. 이

river channel deeper. Therefore, the dam creates a pleasant environment for wildlife downstream by removing that sediment, which is beneficial for the ecosystem.

는 물을 더 깨끗하게 만들어주며 수로를 더 깊게 유지시켜 준다. 그러므로 이 댐은 그 퇴적물을 제거함으로써 강 하류의 야생 동물들에게 쾌적한 환경을 조성하는데, 이는 생태계에 유익한 일이다.

어휘 regulate **v** 조절하다, 통제하다 | manmade **adj** 인공의 | reservoir **n** 저수지, 비축 | drain **v** 물을 빼내다 | vacation spot 휴양지 | rugged **adj** 울퉁불퉁한, 바위투성이의 | revenue **n** 수익, 수입 | cripple **v** 제 기능을 못 하게 만들다 | downriver **adv** 강 하류에 | parched **adj** 바싹 말라 버린 | sediment **n** 퇴적물 | downstream **adv** (강의) 하류로 | channel **n** 수로

Listening

As you all know, dam removal is a difficult and costly process, but leaving it in place is often far worse. In your reading, the author presented three arguments against removing the Glen Canyon Dam, which contains Lake Powell. However, upon closer examination, these reasons seem less compelling and more misguided. In fact, they indicate reasons to remove it sooner rather than later.

The first point the author made was that Lake Powell is a major tourist attraction and vacation spot. This is true, but the area held far more natural beauty before the lake existed. The lake filled in not only Glen Canyon, but it also extended into many smaller canyons along streams that feed into it. These held lush plant life, abundant animals, beautiful rock formations, and many archaeological sites. Their beauty was unknown to most of the public at the time, but surely they would attract more tourists than water sports and camping at the lake do today.

Next, the author explained that the dam is the most efficient way to provide water to the people that depend on the Colorado River. This seems like a valid point, until you realize that the water outflow is limited during droughts so that the hydroelectric turbines have enough to function. On top of that, the lake loses around 6 percent of the water that flows into it each year to evaporation. That hardly sounds efficient.

Finally, the author gives his most misguided argument. He states that removing the dam would have a negative effect on the ecosystem by releasing sediment back into the river. This is wrong for a very clear reason. The wildlife downriver depends upon that sediment for its survival. It is rich in nutrients and minerals that the plants and animals need to live, so removing the sediment and making the water clearer is hurting rather than helping them.

다들 알다시피 댐 제거는 어렵고 큰 비용이 드는 과정이지만 그대로 남겨두는 것이 훨씬 더 좋지 않은 경우가 많죠. 여러분이 읽은 자료에서 필자는 파월호를 비롯한 글렌캐니언 댐 제거에 반대하는 세 가지 주장을 제시했습니다. 그러나 엄밀히 조사해보면 이런 이유들은 설득력이 적고 더욱 터무니없는 것처럼 보입니다. 사실 그 이유들은 일찌감치 그 댐을 제거해야 하는 이유를 보여주고 있어요.

필자가 주장했던 첫 번째 요점은 파월호가 주요 관광 명소이자 휴양지라는 것이었죠. 이것은 사실입니다만 그 지역은 호수가 존재하기 전에 훨씬 더한 자연미를 지니고 있었어요. 그 호수는 글렌캐니언을 차지하고 있었을 뿐 아니라 그곳으로 흘러 들어가는 지류를 따라 위치한 많은 작은 협곡들에까지 이어져 있었습니다. 그 소협곡 지역에는 우거진 식물, 많은 동물, 아름다운 암석층 및 고고학적 유적지가 있었죠. 그 지역의 아름다움은 당시에 대다수의 사람들에게 알려지지 않았었지만, 그곳들은 분명히 오늘날 호수의 수상 스포츠와 캠핑보다 더 많은 관광객들을 유치했을 것입니다.

다음으로, 필자는 그 댐이 콜로라도강에 의존해 사는 사람들에게 물을 공급하는 가장 효율적인 방법이라고 설명했습니다. 이는 타당한 주장인 것처럼 보이지만 수력 발전 터빈이 작동 가능한 만큼의 충분한 물을 확보할 수 있도록 가뭄 기간에는 물의 유출이 제한된다는 것을 금세 깨닫게 되죠. 그뿐 아니라 매년 그 호수로 흘러들어오는 물의 약 6퍼센트가 증발됩니다. 그것은 효율적이라고 하긴 힘들어요.

마지막으로, 필자는 가장 그릇된 주장을 펴고 있어요. 그는 댐을 제거하는 것이 퇴적물을 강으로 다시 방출함으로써 생태계에 부정적인 영향을 줄 것이라고 말합니다. 이것은 매우 명백한 이유로 사실이 아닙니다. 하류의 야생 동물들은 생존을 위해 그 퇴적물에 의존하고 있어요. 퇴적물에는 동식물이 생존하기 위해 필요한 영양소와 미네랄이 풍부하므로 퇴적물을 제거하여 물을 더 깨끗하게 만드는 일은 그들을 돕는 것이 아니라 해치는 것입니다.

어휘 compelling **adj** 설득력 있는, 강제적인 | misguided **adj** 엉뚱한, 잘못 판단한 | sooner rather than later 일찌감치, 늦기 전에 | tourist attraction 관광 명소 | extend **v** 이르다, 달하다, 연장하다 | lush **adj** 무성한, 우거진 | abundant **adj** 많은, 풍부한 | rock formation 암반층, 암석 형성 | archaeological **adj** 고고학적인 | valid **adj** 타당한 | outflow **n** 유출 | drought **n** 가뭄 | hydroelectric **adj** 수력 발전의 | on top of that 게다가, 그뿐 아니라 | evaporation **n** 증발

주제 Glen Canyon Dam – created manmade reservoir Lake Powell, but ppl want the dam to be removed(Lake Powell will disappear). The dam is important!

1. Lake Powell = vacation spot
   - attracts 2 mil. ppl/year
   - tourism = main industry of region → economy will be crippled
2. X satisfy demand for water
   - the dam provides water to nearby area & communities → w/o it, they will suffer
3. neg. effect on ecosystem
   - the dam keep sediment from Rocky M. → cleaner water → create good envi. for wildlife

글렌캐니언 댐 – 파월호라는 인공 저수지를 만들었지만, 사람들은 이 댐이 제거되길 원함(파월호는 사라지게 됨). 댐은 중요하다!

1. 파월호 = 휴양지
   – 1년에 2백만 명이 찾아옴
   – 관광 = 이 지역의 주된 산업 → 경제가 마비될 것
2. 물 수요를 충족할 수 없음
   – 댐이 근처의 지역 & 지역 사회에 물을 공급함 → 댐이 없으면 사람들이 고통받을 것
3. 생태계에 부정적 영향
   – 댐이 로키산맥의 퇴적물을 막아줌 → 더 깨끗한 물 → 야생 동물을 위해 좋은 환경 만듦

주제 Glen Canyon Dam – created manmade reservoir Lake Powell, but ppl want the dam to be removed(Lake Powell will disappear). The dam needs to be removed!

1. Lake Powell = vacation spot
   - true, but the area was more beautiful before the lake existed
   - ppl just didn't know this place at the time
2. X satisfy demand for water? Limited anyway
   - dam can't provide water to ppl during droughts
   - lose 6% of water b/c evaporation = X efficient
3. neg. effect on ecosystem
   - wildlife actually need that sediment to survive
   - sediment = nutrients & minerals for animals & plants

글렌캐니언 댐 – 파월호라는 인공 저수지를 만들었지만, 사람들은 이 댐이 제거되길 원함(파월호는 사라지게 됨). 댐은 없어져야 한다!

1. 파월호 = 휴양지
   – 맞다, 하지만 이 지역은 호수가 존재하기 전이 더 아름다웠음
   – 당시 사람들은 그저 이곳을 몰랐을 뿐이다
2. 물 수요를 충족할 수 없음? 어차피 제한됨
   – 가뭄 동안 댐이 사람들에게 물을 공급할 수 없음
   – 증발 때문에 물의 6%를 잃음 = 효율적이지 않음
3. 생태계에 부정적 영향
   – 야생 동물들은 생존하기 위해 사실 그 퇴적물을 필요로 함
   – 퇴적물 = 동물과 식물을 위한 영양분 & 미네랄

주제

읽기 Lake Powell is an artificial reservoir created by the Glen Canyon Dam on the Colorado River. The reading passage gives three reasons why this dam and lake should not be removed.

듣기 On the other hand, the lecturer casts doubt on the opinions maintained by the reading passage.

파월호는 콜로라도강의 글렌캐니언 댐에 의해 조성된 인공 저수지이다. 읽기 지문은 이 댐과 호수가 없어지지 말아야 하는 세 가지 이유를 들고 있다.
반면에, 강의자는 읽기 지문에서 주장하는 의견들에 의구심을 제기한다.

요점 1

읽기 Firstly, the author states that Lake Powell is a very famous tourist attraction. This is a highly lucrative business, so the local economy will be damaged if the lake disappears.

듣기 However, the lecturer suggests that the natural scenery of that area was more beautiful before the lake was created. Many people would have visited there without the lake and its outdoor activities.

첫째로, 필자는 파월호가 매우 유명한 관광 명소라고 말한다. 이는 매우 수익성이 높은 사업이므로 만약에 호수가 사라지면 지역 경제가 타격을 입을 것이다.
그러나 강의자는 호수가 조성되기 전에 그 지역의 자연경관이 더 아름다웠다는 것을 시사한다. 많은 사람들은 호수와 야외 활동이 없어도 그곳을 방문했을 것이다.

Integrated Task

Part 2

읽기 Secondly, according to the reading, the dam should be maintained to provide a source of water to the people who rely on the Colorado River.

듣기 Yet again, the lecturer points out that this is not efficient because a certain amount of water should be reserved for generating hydroelectric power during the dry season. In addition, almost 6 percent of the water in the lake evaporates into the air every year.

둘째로, 읽기 지문에 따르면 그 댐은 콜로라도강에 의존하고 있는 사람들에게 수원을 공급하기 위해 유지되어야 한다.

또다시 강의자는 이것이 효율적이지 않다고 지적하는데, 건기에는 수력 발전을 위해 일정한 양의 물이 비축되어야 하기 때문이다. 게다가 매년 호수의 거의 6퍼센트에 달하는 물이 공기 중으로 증발한다.

읽기 Lastly, the reading passage claims that the dam's removal would have a bad influence on the surrounding ecosystem. He says that the water would get dirty by releasing sediment into the river.

듣기 However, the lecturer contradicts this by explaining that deposition is necessary for the organisms downstream. This is because the sediment mentioned in the reading contains abundant nourishment and minerals for their survival.

마지막으로, 읽기 지문에서는 댐의 제거가 주변 생태계에 악영향을 미칠 것이라고 주장한다. 그는 퇴적물을 강으로 흘려보냄으로써 물이 더러워질 것이라고 말한다.

그러나 강의자는 퇴적물이 강 하류에 사는 생물체들에게 필요한 것이라고 설명하면서 이를 반박한다. 이는 지문에서 언급된 퇴적물에 그들의 생존을 위한 풍부한 영양분과 미네랄이 함유되어 있기 때문이다.

어휘 artificial **adj** 인공의 ㅣ lucrative **adj** 수익성이 좋은 ㅣ reserve **v** 비축하다 ㅣ dry season 건기 ㅣ evaporate **v** 증발하다 ㅣ contradict **v** 반박하다 ㅣ deposition **n** 퇴적, 퇴적물 ㅣ nourishment **n** 영양분

Test　　　　　　　　　　　　　　　　　　　　　　　　　　　　　본서 / P. 108

Q1

Reading

It is a well established fact that many plants either fold up their leaves or close up their flowers after night falls. This behavior is called nyctinasty, and while scientists fully understand the physical process responsible for this ability, the reasons behind this behavior remain a mystery. Many hypotheses have been proposed to explain this behavior, and these are three of the most popular ones.

The first is that the plants are trying to protect themselves from the cold. Even in tropical climates, temperatures are typically lower at night than they are during the day. When the leaves are unfolded, their surface area is increased, which is ideal for gathering sunlight to perform photosynthesis. However, at night, increased surface area means that more heat will be lost into the cool air. The internal parts of flowers are also delicate, so closing can protect them from the effects of the cold.

The second is that the leaves and flowers close so that they will collect less dew. When they are open, they will collect more moisture, which can be used by fungi and other parasites to grow on them. For flowers, moisture is even more

많은 식물들이 해가 저문 후에 잎을 접거나 꽃잎을 닫는 것은 기정사실이다. 이런 습성을 '주야 운동'이라고 하는데, 과학자들이 이런 능력을 발현시키는 물리적 과정을 충분히 이해하고 있는 반면에 이 습성에 대한 이유는 수수께끼로 남아 있다. 이런 습성을 설명하기 위해 많은 가설들이 제기되었으며, 다음은 가장 많은 사람들이 공유하는 세 가지 가설이다.

첫 번째 가설은 식물들이 추위로부터 스스로를 보호하려 한다는 것이다. 열대성 기후에서도 밤 기온은 일반적으로 낮 기온보다 더 낮다. 잎이 펼쳐져 있으면 그 표면적은 증가하는데, 이것은 광합성 작용을 하기 위한 햇빛을 모으는 데 이상적이다. 그러나 밤에는 증가한 표면적이 더 많은 열을 차가운 공기 중으로 잃게 될 것임을 의미한다. 또한 꽃의 내부는 연약해서 꽃잎을 닫는 것은 꽃을 추위의 영향으로부터 보호해줄 수 있다.

두 번째 가설은 나뭇잎과 꽃들이 이슬을 덜 모으기 위해 잎을 닫는다는 것이다. 그 잎과 꽃잎이 열려 있으면 더 많은 수분을 모으게 될 것이며, 이는 곰팡이와

of a problem. If they are filled with water, insects will not visit them, and moisture will affect how their pollen works. They need their pollen to stick to insects temporarily so they will transport it, but water will cement it to the insects, keeping them from depositing it on another flower.

The third is that plants can limit their exposure to light by closing at night. Like animals, plants have daily and yearly cycles that determine their activity levels called circadian rhythms. This cycle is particularly important for reproduction, so they have to use the length of the day to track the seasons. So, by closing their leaves at night, they can avoid unusually bright nighttime conditions that could throw off their circadian rhythms.

다른 기생충들이 그곳에서 자라는 데 이용될 수 있다. 꽃의 경우에 수분은 훨씬 더 심각한 문제다. 꽃이 수분으로 가득 차 있으면 곤충은 꽃을 찾아가지 않을 것이며 수분은 꽃가루가 작용하는 방식에 영향을 줄 것이다. 꽃은 꽃가루를 곤충에 일시적으로 붙여 운반시켜야 하지만, 물은 꽃가루를 곤충에 단단히 붙여 그것이 다른 꽃에 내려앉지 못하도록 할 것이다.

세 번째 가설은 식물들이 밤에 닫힘으로써 빛에 노출되는 것을 제한할 수 있다는 것이다. 동물들과 마찬가지로 식물은 그들의 활동 수준을 결정하는 '24시간 주기 리듬'이라는 일일 및 연간 주기를 가지고 있다. 이 주기는 특히 번식에 중요하므로 식물들은 계절의 흐름을 추적하기 위해 낮의 길이를 이용해야 한다. 그리하여 밤에는 잎을 닫음으로써 식물들은 그들의 24시간 주기 리듬에 혼선을 주는 유난히 밝은 밤 환경을 피할 수 있다.

어휘　well established **adj** 확립된, 확고부동한 ｜ fold up 접다 ｜ nyctinasty **n** 주야 운동 ｜ hypothesis **n** 가설 ｜ unfolded **adj** 펼쳐진 ｜ photosynthesis **n** 광합성 ｜ delicate **adj** 연약한, 섬세한 ｜ dew **n** 이슬 ｜ moisture **n** 수분, 습기 ｜ fungi **n** fungus(곰팡이)의 복수형 ｜ parasite **n** 기생충 ｜ insect **n** 곤충 ｜ pollen **n** 꽃가루, 화분 ｜ stick **v** (달라) 붙다 ｜ temporarily **adv** 일시적으로 ｜ transport **v** 나르다, 옮기다 ｜ cement **v** 단단히 붙이다, 결합시키다 ｜ deposit **v** 두다, 놓다 ｜ circadian rhythm 24시간 주기 리듬 ｜ reproduction **n** 번식 ｜ track **v** 추적하다 ｜ unusually **adv** 유별나게, 평소와 달리 ｜ throw off 내던지다, 떨쳐버리다

Listening

The reading discusses the possible causes for nyctinasty, which is how some plants fold their leaves or close their flowers at night. The author focuses upon hypotheses that have been proposed to explain this phenomenon. Unfortunately, the three ideas that the author has chosen are flawed for fairly obvious reasons.

The first idea put forward is that the plants close up to protect themselves from the cold. The majority of plants do not have an internal source of heat, so they are already vulnerable to the cold, and folding up would not help them in this regard. If folding up helped them to stay warm, they would fold up on cold days as well. Since they do not, it seems very unlikely that plants would close at night to conserve warmth.

The second idea suggested is that flowers and leaves close up at night so that they will collect less moisture from the morning dew. This would prevent fungi and other parasites from starting to grow. However, fungi don't need much moisture to live. The amount of moisture that these plants normally have on their surface is enough for the fungi. In addition, the author mentions that moisture prevents their pollen from working. Nevertheless, closing at night won't help because flowers do not fold up when it rains, which makes them far wetter than dew can.

The third idea offered is that they close to limit their exposure

지문에서는 주야 운동의 가능한 원인들에 대해 논하고 있는데, 주야 운동은 식물들이 밤에 잎을 접거나 꽃잎을 닫는 방식에 관한 것입니다. 필자는 이런 현상을 설명하기 위해 제기되었던 가설들에 초점을 맞추고 있어요. 안타깝게도 필자가 선택한 세 가지 아이디어는 꽤 명백한 이유들로 오류가 있다고 볼 수 있습니다.

제기된 첫 번째 견해는 식물들이 추위로부터 스스로를 보호하기 위해 닫힌다는 겁니다. 대부분의 식물들은 내부의 열원을 가지고 있지 않으므로 이미 추위에 취약하며, 이런 점에서 잎을 접는 것은 식물에 도움이 되지 않을 것입니다. 잎을 접는 것이 따뜻함을 유지하는 것에 도움이 된다면 식물은 추운 날에도 잎을 접겠지요. 그렇게 하지 않는 것을 보면 식물들이 온기를 지키기 위해 밤에 닫힐 가능성은 매우 적어 보입니다.

제시된 두 번째 견해는 꽃과 나뭇잎들이 아침 이슬에서 나오는 수분을 덜 모으기 위해 밤에 닫힌다는 것입니다. 이는 그들이 곰팡이와 다른 기생충들이 자라기 시작하는 것을 막아 주겠지요. 그러나 곰팡이는 생존하는 데 많은 수분을 필요로 하지 않아요. 평소에 이 식물들 표면에 있는 수분만으로도 곰팡이가 살기엔 충분하죠. 게다가 필자는 수분이 꽃의 꽃가루 활동을 방해한다고 언급합니다. 그럼에도 불구하고 밤에 닫히는 것은 도움이 되지 않을 것인데, 이는 꽃들이 비가 올 때는 닫히지 않으며 비는 이슬보다도 훨씬 더

to moonlight, which could confuse their growing cycle. This sounds very plausible, but there is an obvious problem with this. Many of the plants that fold up their leaves at night live in very shady conditions where light is already scarce even during the day. This means that at night they would be in complete darkness. So, they clearly don't have to fold up at night because moonlight would not even reach them.

식물을 축축하게 만들기 때문이에요.

제안된 세 번째 견해는 식물이 그들의 성장 주기에 혼란을 줄 수 있는 달빛에의 노출을 제한하기 위해 닫힌다는 것입니다. 이는 매우 그럴듯하게 들리지만, 여기에는 명백한 문제점이 있죠. 밤에 잎을 접는 많은 식물들은 낮 동안에도 이미 빛이 부족한 매우 그늘진 환경에서 살고 있습니다. 이는 그 식물들이 밤에는 칠흑 같은 어둠 속에 놓이게 된다는 것을 의미하죠. 따라서 달빛이 그들에게 도달하지도 못할 것이므로 분명히 밤에는 접을 필요가 없습니다.

어휘   phenomenon **n** 현상 I flawed **adj** 결함이 있는 I put forward 제안하다, 내세우다 I internal **adj** 내부의 I vulnerable **adj** 취약한 I in this regard 이런 점에서 I conserve **v** 보존하다, 보호하다 I exposure **n** 노출 I confuse **v** 혼란시키다 I plausible **adj** 그럴듯한 I shady **adj** 그늘이 드리워진 I scarce **adj** 부족한, 드문

예시 답변

Both the reading and the lecture discuss nyctinasty, which is how plants fold up their leaves or close up their flowers at night. The reading passage mentions three hypotheses to explain why many plants do this. On the other hand, the lecturer casts doubt on the causes suggested by the author.

Firstly, the author maintains that the leaves and flowers close up to keep themselves from losing heat by reducing their surface area. In addition, they don't need to open for photosynthesis at night. However, the lecturer claims that just folding up doesn't help to conserve warmth. This is supported by the fact that the plants cannot generate heat by themselves, and they don't fold up on cold days.

Secondly, according to the reading, one of the causes for nyctinasty is that the plants need to avoid collecting moisture. This is because it can grow fungi and other parasites as well as disturb the pollination of flowers. The lecturer, however, refutes the argument by saying that fungi can start growing with a small amount of water. Also, closing at night is not due to moisture because the flowers do not close up on rainy days.

Lastly, the reading states that the plants are trying to avoid excessive moonlight that could confuse their stable circadian rhythms, which are crucial for reproduction. However, the lecturer points out that many of those plants grow in the shade. Their habitat must be very dark at night, so the moonlight would not influence their cycles.

읽기와 듣기 지문 둘 다 식물이 밤에 잎을 접거나 꽃 잎을 닫는 주야 운동에 관해 논의한다. 읽기 지문은 왜 많은 식물들이 이러한지 설명하기 위한 세 가지 가설을 언급한다. 반면 강의자는 필자가 제시한 원인들에 의구심을 제기한다.

첫째로, 필자는 잎과 꽃이 표면적을 줄임으로써 열 손실이 없도록 하기 위해 닫힌다고 주장한다. 게다가 밤에는 광합성을 위해 열릴 필요도 없다. 그러나 강의자는 단순히 잎을 접는 것만으로는 온기를 지키는 데 도움이 안 된다고 주장한다. 이는 식물들이 스스로 열을 발생시키지 못하며, 추운 날에는 잎을 접지 않는다는 사실에 의해 뒷받침된다.

두 번째로, 읽기 지문에 따르면 주야 운동의 원인 중 하나는 식물들이 수분을 모으는 것을 피해야 한다는 것이다. 이는 수분이 곰팡이와 다른 기생충들을 자라게 할 뿐 아니라 꽃의 수분 작용을 방해하기 때문이다. 그러나 강의자는 곰팡이가 적은 양의 물로도 자라날 수 있다고 말하며 이 주장에 반박한다. 또한 꽃은 비 오는 날에는 닫히지 않으므로 밤에 닫히는 것은 수분 때문이 아니다.

마지막으로, 지문에서는 식물이 번식에 결정적인 안정적인 24시간 주기 리듬을 혼란시킬 수 있는 과도한 달빛을 피하려 한다고 말한다. 그러나 강의자는 그런 식물들 중 다수가 그늘에서 자란다고 지적한다. 그들의 서식지는 밤에 매우 어두울 것이므로 달빛은 그들의 주기에 영향을 미치지 않을 것이다.

어휘   pollination **n** 수분 (작용) I excessive **adj** 과도한 I crucial **adj** 중대한, 결정적인 I habitat **n** 서식지

Q2

Reading

There are approximately 5,880 species of mammals currently living on our planet. Nearly all of these animals are contained within two categories: marsupial and placental mammals. Marsupial mammals give birth after only a few weeks, and their young finish developing in an outer pouch of skin. In contrast, placental mammals are pregnant for much longer, and their offspring are much better adapted for survival when born. This means that marsupial mammals are inherently inferior to placental mammals.

Firstly, when a marsupial is born, it is at a very early stage of development compared to placental mammals. It must climb inside its mother's pouch unaided, or it will die. Once inside the pouch, a marsupial has access to its mother's nipples, but if she cannot find enough food, she will not be able to produce milk for the baby. So, even in the pouch, the infant is still vulnerable to environmental influences. Conversely, many placental mammals are much more developed when born and can move around independently just a few hours after birth.

Secondly, the internal body temperature of marsupials varies widely, which shows that they are more primitive than placental mammals. An infant marsupial cannot control its body temperature, so it must stay in its mother's pouch. However, even as an adult, a marsupial's body temperature is heavily influenced by its environment, which makes them more like cold-blooded animals. Such variation makes them vulnerable to extreme temperatures, unlike placental mammals that maintain a high internal temperature regardless of environmental conditions.

Thirdly, some evidence shows that marsupials are unable to compete with placental mammals. Most marsupials flourish in Australia, whereas placental mammals live everywhere. However, since marsupials exist in the fossil record on all continents, this means that marsupials used to live in places other than Australia, but most of them died out due to placental mammals. This is further proven by the fact that placental mammals have recently been introduced to Australia, and now marsupials are being outcompeted even there.

현재 지구상에는 대략 5,880종의 포유류가 살고 있다. 이중 거의 모든 동물들은 육아낭이 있는 유대목 포유류와 태반이 있는 포유류의 두 가지 범주에 속한다. 유대목 포유류는 단 몇 주 후에 새끼를 낳으며, 그들의 새끼는 가죽 바깥쪽에 있는 주머니에서 마저 발달한다. 그에 반해서 태반이 있는 포유류는 훨씬 더 오랜 임신 기간을 거치며, 그들의 새끼는 태어났을 때 생존 적응력이 훨씬 더 강하다. 이는 유대목 포유류가 태반이 있는 포유류보다 선천적으로 열등하다는 것을 의미한다.

첫째로, 유대 동물은 태어났을 때 태반이 있는 포유류에 비해 발육의 매우 초기 단계에 있다. 새끼는 아무런 도움을 받지 않고 어미의 주머니 안으로 들어가야 하는데, 그러지 못하면 죽게 될 것이다. 일단 주머니 안에 들어가면 유대 동물은 어미의 젖꼭지에 접근할 수 있지만, 만약 어미가 충분한 식량을 찾지 못하면 새끼에게 줄 모유를 생산하지 못할 것이다. 따라서 주머니 안에서조차 새끼는 여전히 환경적 영향에 취약하다. 정반대로, 다수의 태반 포유동물들은 태어났을 때 발육이 훨씬 더 잘된 상태이며, 태어난 지 단 몇 시간 만에 독립적으로 돌아다닐 수 있다.

두 번째로, 유대 동물들의 체내 온도는 변화 폭이 크며, 이것은 그들이 태반이 있는 포유류보다 원시적이라는 것을 보여준다. 새끼 유대 동물은 체온을 조절할 수 없으므로 계속 어미의 주머니 안에 있어야 한다. 그러나 성체 동물의 경우에도 유대 포유류의 체온은 환경의 영향을 크게 받는데, 이 때문에 그들은 변온 동물에 더 가깝다. 환경 조건과 상관없이 높은 체내 온도를 유지하는 태반 동물들과는 다르게 그런 변화는 그들을 극한 환경에 취약하게 만든다.

세 번째로, 몇몇 증거에서는 유대 동물들이 태반 포유동물들과 경쟁하지 못한다는 것을 보여준다. 대부분의 유대 동물은 호주에서 번성하는 반면에 태반 포유동물들은 도처에 서식한다. 그러나 유대목 동물들은 모든 대륙의 화석 기록에 존재하므로 이는 유대 동물들이 호주 외의 다른 지역에서 살았으나 대다수가 태반 포유류로 인해 멸종되었다는 것을 의미한다. 태반 포유동물들이 최근에 호주로 유입되었으며 현재는 유대 동물들이 그곳에서조차 경쟁에서 밀린다는 사실은 이를 강하게 뒷받침한다.

어휘 placental adj 태반이 있는 I marsupial adj 육아낭이 있는, 유대류의 I give birth (새끼를) 낳다, 출산하다 I pregnant adj 임신한 I inherently adv 선천적으로, 본질적으로 I inferior adj 열등한, 질 낮은 I unaided adj 도움을 받지 않는 I nipple n 젖꼭지, 유두 I vulnerable adj 취약한 I conversely adv 정반대로, 역으로 I internal adj 내부의 I primitive adj 원시적인 I cold-blooded animal 변온 동물, 냉혈 동물 I variation n 변화 I outcompete v 더 우세하다

In the reading, the author tries to prove that marsupial mammals are inferior to placental mammals. While he does introduce many facts about both types of mammals, these have clearly been misunderstood. Marsupial mammals are not less evolved than placental mammals; they have just followed a different evolutionary path. This has given them a different set of strengths and weaknesses, some of which give them an edge over placental mammals.

First, the author talks about their level of development at birth. He contends that since marsupials are born so early, they are extremely vulnerable even in their mother's pouch, whereas many placental mammals are much more developed and can move around soon after birth. However, this doesn't mean that all placental mammals could survive on their own right after birth. In fact, predatory ones like humans are physically weak long after that, requiring much time to finish developing. In contrast, marsupials have an advantage because they are fully capable of living independently when they leave the pouch.

Next, the reading focuses on internal body temperature variation. The author says that marsupials are less evolved since many of them have internal temperatures that vary widely and are easily influenced by outside temperatures. However, this is controlled variation that is done with a specific purpose. These marsupials live in extremely arid environments where there is a large difference between day and night temperatures. These animals can raise or lower their internal temperatures so that they expend less energy and lose less water.

Finally, according to the author, the distribution of both types of mammals shows that marsupials are unable to compete with placental mammals. The recent introduction of placental mammals to Australia also appears to threaten marsupials. However, those animals were actually introduced by humans, which allowed them to become invasive. In fact, marsupials have been competing with other placental mammals in Australia for a long time. For example, rats and other rodents showed up around 5 million years ago, but marsupials have survived competition with those mammals.

지문에서 필자는 유대목 포유류가 태반 포유류보다 열등하다는 것을 입증하려 합니다. 그가 두 종류의 포유류에 대한 여러 사실을 소개하고 있긴 하지만 이런 사실들은 명백히 잘못 알려져 있죠. 유대목 포유류는 태반 포유류보다 덜 진화한 것이 아니라 그저 다른 진화 경로를 따랐을 뿐이에요. 이것은 그들에게 다른 강점과 약점을 부여했으며, 이중 일부는 그들이 태반 포유류보다 우위를 점하도록 해 줍니다.

첫째로, 필자는 그들이 태어날 때의 발달 수준에 대해 이야기합니다. 그는 유대 동물들은 너무 일찍 태어나기 때문에 어미의 주머니 속에서조차 극히 취약한 반면에 많은 태반 포유류는 발육이 훨씬 더 잘된 상태이며 출생 직후에 돌아다닐 수 있다고 주장합니다. 그러나 이것이 모든 태반 포유류가 태어난 직후부터 혼자서 살아남을 수 있다는 것을 의미하지는 않아요. 사실, 인간과 같은 포식성의 포유류는 태어난 후 오랫동안 신체적으로 약하며, 발달을 끝마치기까지 오랜 시간이 걸립니다. 그에 반해서 유대 동물들은 주머니를 떠날 때 충분히 독립적으로 살아갈 수 있다는 점에서 유리하죠.

다음으로, 지문은 체내 온도 변화에 초점을 맞춥니다. 필자는 많은 유대 동물들의 체내 온도가 변화 폭이 매우 크며 외부 온도로부터 쉽게 영향을 받기 때문에 덜 진화되었다고 말하죠. 그러나 이것은 특정 목적으로 이루어지는 통제된 변화입니다. 이런 유대 동물들은 밤낮의 기온 차이가 큰 매우 건조한 환경에서 서식합니다. 이런 동물들은 에너지를 덜 쓰고 수분을 덜 빼앗기기 위해 자신의 체내 온도를 높이거나 낮출 수 있어요.

마지막으로, 필자에 따르면 이 두 포유류의 분포는 유대 동물들이 태반 포유류와 경쟁할 수 없다는 것을 보여줍니다. 태반 포유류가 최근 호주로 유입된 것 또한 유대 동물들을 위협하는 것으로 보입니다. 그러나 그 동물들은 실제로 사람들에 의해 유입되었으며, 이로 인해 급속히 퍼질 수 있었던 것입니다. 사실 유대 동물들은 오랫동안 호주에서 다른 태반 포유류와 경쟁해 왔어요. 예를 들어, 쥐와 그 외 설치류들은 약 5백만 년 전에 나타났지만, 유대 동물들은 그런 포유류들과의 경쟁에서 살아남았습니다.

어휘 edge **n** 우위, 유리함 I on one's own 혼자서 I predatory **adj** 포식성의 I arid **adj** 건조한, 메마른 I expend **v** (돈, 시간, 에너지를) 쏟다, 들이다 I distribution **n** 분포, 분배 I invasive **adj** 급속히 퍼지는 I rodent **n** 설치류

예시 답변

The reading and the lecture both compare marsupial mammals to placental mammals. The writer contends that marsupials are inferior to placental mammals because they are less

지문과 강의 모두 유대목 포유류와 태반 포유류를 비교하고 있다. 글쓴이는 유대 동물들이 태어났을 때 덜 발달된 상태이기에 태반 포유류보다 열등하다고 주장

developed when born. However, the lecturer argues back that both types of mammals have just evolved in different ways.

Firstly, the reading says that young marsupials need to stay in their mother's pouches to survive, where they are still influenced by external factors, whereas many placental mammals are more developed when born. However, the lecturer points out that it takes time for placental mammals to survive on their own, even if they can move shortly after birth. In contrast, marsupials have better chances of survival because they are fully developed when they leave the pouch.

Secondly, the writer states that marsupials are less evolved because their internal temperatures vary widely and are easily affected by the environment, while placental mammals have stable body temperatures. However, the lecturer claims that many marsupials live in very dry areas, so the ability to vary their temperature is helpful to prevent them from losing too much energy and water where the daily temperature range is huge.

Thirdly, the reading suggests that marsupials were outcompeted by placental mammals in places other than Australia, as their bones have been found worldwide, and that they are losing in Australia as well. However, the lecturer explains that placental mammals came to Australia because they were introduced by humans. In addition, some placental mammals such as rodents have been competing with marsupial mammals in Australia for a long time.

한다. 그러나 강의자는 이 두 포유류들이 그저 서로 다른 방식으로 진화한 것이라고 주장하며 이에 반박한다.

먼저, 지문은 어린 유대 동물들이 생존을 위해 어미의 주머니 안에 있어야 하고 그 안에 있을 때도 외부 요인들로부터 여전히 영향을 받지만, 많은 태반 포유류들은 태어났을 때 발육이 더 잘된 상태라고 이야기한다. 그러나 강의자는 태반 포유류들이 태어난 직후에 움직일 수 있다고 해도 스스로 생존하기까지는 시간이 걸린다고 지적한다. 그에 반해 유대 동물들은 어미의 주머니를 떠날 때 완전히 성장한 상태이기 때문에 생존할 기회가 더 많다.

두 번째로, 글쓴이는 유대 동물들이 덜 진화한 것이라고 말하는데, 유대 동물들은 내부 온도 변화가 심하고 환경에 쉽게 영향을 받지만 태반 포유류들은 안정적인 체온을 가지고 있기 때문이다. 그러나 강의자는 많은 유대 동물들이 매우 건조한 지역에 서식하므로 체온을 변화시키는 그들의 능력이 일교차가 큰 그 지역에서 너무 많은 에너지와 수분을 잃는 것을 방지하는 데 도움이 된다고 주장한다.

세 번째로, 지문에서는 유대 동물들의 뼈가 전 세계에서 발견되었기 때문에 그 동물들이 호주를 제외한 다른 지역에서 태반 포유류들에게 밀려났으며, 지금은 호주에서조차 밀리고 있다고 말한다. 그러나 강의자는 태반 포유류들이 사람들에 의해 호주로 유입되었다고 설명한다. 게다가 설치류와 같은 몇몇 태반 포유류들은 호주에서 오랫동안 유대목 포유류와 경쟁해왔다.

어휘   external **adj** 외부의 I chance **n** 가능성 I stable **adj** 안정된, 안정적인 I range **n** 범위, 폭

II. Academic Discussion Task   Part 1. 기초 다지기

유형 1. 찬성/반대

본서 I P. 118

Q1

Professor: When it comes to spending money, some argue that it is better to invest in something long-lasting, like an expensive piece of jewelry, rather than indulging in short-term pleasures, such as a vacation. What are your thoughts on this matter?

교수: 돈을 쓸 때, 어떤 사람들은 비싼 보석 같은 오래가는 것에 투자하는 것이 휴가처럼 단기적인 즐거움에 빠져들기보다 나은 것이라고 주장합니다. 이에 대한 여러분의 생각은 무엇인가요?

어휘   when it comes to ~에 관한 한 I invest in ~ 에 투자하다 I indulge **v** 빠져들다 I short-term pleasure 단기의 기쁨

Jeorge: jewelry / **April:** vacation

조지: 보석 / **에이프릴:** 휴가

A. From my perspective, both made excellent statements, but I'm on the same page as April.

A. 제 관점에서, 두 사람 모두 훌륭한 주장을 했지만 저는 에이프릴과 같은 생각입니다.

Q2

Professor: Many cities nowadays are devising plans to improve themselves, yet they are unsure of an optimal solution. When it comes to a city's benefit, some argue that the best way to achieve it is by focusing on constructing new buildings rather than preserving nature. What are your thoughts on this matter?

교수: 요즘 많은 도시가 스스로를 개선하기 위한 계획을 세우고 있지만, 최선의 해결책을 모르고 있습니다. 도시의 이익에 관해서는 새로운 건물을 건설하는 데 중점을 두는 것이 자연을 보존하는 것보다 더 나은 방법이라고 주장하는 사람들도 있습니다. 여러분은 이에 대해 어떻게 생각하시나요?

어휘 devise **v** 고안하다 | argue **v** 언쟁하다 | unsure of ~ 에 확신이 없는 | preserve **v** 보존하다

Jeorge: constructing new buildings / **April:** preserving nature

A. From my perspective, both made excellent statements, but I'm on the same page as April.

조지: 새로운 건물을 건설하는 것 / **에이프릴:** 자연을 보존하는 것

A. 제 관점에서, 두 사람 모두 훌륭한 주장을 했지만 저는 에이프릴과 같은 생각입니다.

Q3

Professor: Some argue that it is more important for parents to spend quality time playing and bonding with their children, rather than focusing solely on academic achievements. What are your thoughts on this statement?

교수: 어떤 사람들은 부모가 자녀의 학업 성취에만 집중하기 보다 자녀와 깊고 의미 있는 시간을 보내고 유대감을 형성하는 것이 더 중요하다고 주장합니다. 여러분은 이 주장에 대해 어떻게 생각하시나요?

어휘 quality time 깊고 의미 있는 시간 | bond **n** 유대 | solely **adv** 오로지 | achievement **n** 성취

Jeorge: agree / **April:** disagree

A. From my perspective, both made excellent statements, but I'm on the same page as Jeorge.

조지: 찬성 / **에이프릴:** 반대

A. 제 관점에서, 두 사람 모두 훌륭한 주장을 했지만 저는 조지와 같은 생각입니다.

Q4

Professor: We often hear the saying "Families should have meals together on a regular basis." What are your thoughts on this statement?

교수: "가족은 정기적으로 함께 식사를 해야 한다."는 말을 종종 듣습니다. 이 주장에 대한 여러분의 생각은 무엇인가요?

어휘 meal **n** 식사 | regular **adj** 규칙적인 | on a regular basis 정기적으로

Jeorge: agree / **April:** disagree

A. From my perspective, both made excellent statements, but I'm on the same page as Jeorge.

조지: 찬성 / **에이프릴:** 반대

A. 내 관점에서, 두 사람 모두 훌륭한 주장을 했지만 저는 조지와 같은 생각입니다.

유형 2. 아이디어 말하기

본서 | P. 120

Q1

Professor: People can benefit from traveling all around the world. Tell me one benefit you can gain from world travel.

교수: 사람들은 전 세계 여행에서 혜택을 얻을 수 있습니다. 전 세계 여행에서 얻을 수 있는 혜택 중 하나를 말해 보세요.

어휘　benefit 🅥 ~에서 득을 보다 l enable 🅥 가능케 하다 l broaden 🅥 확장하다 l perspective 🅝 관점, 식견

Jeorge: relieving stress / **April:** meeting different people

A. From my perspective, both made excellent statements, but I would like to add that traveling all over the world enables people to broaden their perspectives.

조지: 스트레스를 완화하는 것 / 에이프릴: 다양한 사람들을 만나는 것

A. 제 관점에서, 두 사람 모두 훌륭한 발언을 했지만, 전 세계를 여행하는 것이 그들의 관점을 넓힐 수 있다는 것을 덧붙이고 싶습니다.

Q2

Professor: Please describe a new experience you have had recently that significantly impacted your life. Explain how this experience has influenced your perspective and personal growth.

교수: 최근에 겪은 새로운 경험 중에 당신의 삶에 큰 영향을 미친 것에 대해 설명해 주세요. 이 경험이 여러분의 시각과 개인적인 성장에 어떤 영향을 미쳤는지 설명하세요.

어휘　significantly 🔤 상당히 크게 l impact 🅝 영향 l growth 🅝 성장 l laboratory 🅝 실험실

Jeorge: volunteer program / **April:** internship at a laboratory

A. From my perspective, both made excellent statements, but I would like to add that an internship at a small company had a significant impact on my life.

조지: 자원봉사 프로그램 / 에이프릴: 실험실에서의 인턴십

A. 제 관점에서, 두 사람 모두 훌륭한 발언을 했지만, 작은 회사에서의 인턴십이 제 삶에 큰 영향을 미쳤다는 것을 덧붙이고 싶습니다.

Q3

Professor: Which significant scientific breakthrough or technological innovation from the past two centuries would you select as a crucial advancement?

교수: 지난 200년 동안 중요한 과학적 발견이나 기술적 혁신 중에서 어떤 것을 중요한 발전으로 선택하겠습니까?

어휘　breakthrough 🅝 획기적 발전 l crucial 🔤 중대한, 결정적인 l antibiotic 🅝 항생제, 항생 물질 l by far 단연코

Jeorge: antibiotics / **April:** computer

A. From my perspective, both made excellent statements, but I would like to add that the Internet is the most important technological invention by far.

조지: 항생제 / 에이프릴: 컴퓨터

A. 제 관점에서, 두 사람 모두 훌륭한 발언을 했지만, 제가 추가하고 싶은 것은 인터넷이 현대에 가장 중요한 기술 발명이라는 것입니다.

Q4

Professor: Technology has made the world a better place to live, so please tell me one aspect that impacts your life.

교수: 기술은 세상을 더 좋은 곳으로 만들었다는 점에서, 여러분의 삶에 영향을 미치는 한 가지 측면을 말씀해 주세요.

어휘　aspect 🅝 측면 l gain 🅥 얻다 l contribute 🅥 기여하다 l management 🅝 관리

Jeorge: communication / **April:** gaining information

A. From my perspective, both made excellent statements, but I would like to add that technology can contribute to effective time management.

조지: 소통 / 에이프릴: 정보를 얻는 것

A. 제 관점에서, 두 사람 모두 훌륭한 발언을 했지만, 제가 덧붙이고 싶은 것은 기술이 효과적인 시간 관리에 기여할 수 있다는 것입니다.

Lesson 01 스트레스 관련 표현

01. Participating in club activities can contribute to alleviating stress.

02. Nowadays, students often get stressed out from their heavy workloads and the competition with those around them.

03. They need a pleasant diversion to relax mentally.

04. By spending quality time with enjoyable club activities, they will eventually be able to relax and get back to their work.

05. He used to suffer from a huge workload and pressure.

06. He sometimes stayed up all night getting his work done.

07. Because of this, he was basically exhausted physically and mentally.

08. Playing inline hockey allowed him to escape from the stress of his work.

09. Thanks to this, he was able to get back to his work feeling refreshed.

10. He now has a relaxed and confident mental state.

Lesson 02 분위기 관련 표현

01. Students experience a positive ambiance while engaging in energetic activities during PE class.

02. Most students can be influenced by the atmosphere in their surroundings.

03. The impact of the atmosphere is a lot more important than they might realize.

04. Students should feel a good atmosphere while they are at school.

05. The school used to be very competitive and strict.

06. However, things changed little by little after the school principal tried to change the atmosphere.

07. A lot of time and effort were put into making the school curriculum better with more enjoyable PE classes.

08. The current students at my school genuinely appreciate the cheerful and energetic atmosphere.

09. The school has also gained a good reputation that students want to be accepted into.

10. I honestly think that the current state of the school is much more desirable compared to the past.

Lesson 03 사람들과의 관계 관련 표현

01. Parents can truly interact with their children while playing together.

02. It creates an optimal condition for improving their relationship.

03. When they play together, they have more opportunities to share various experiences and emotions.

04. These shared experiences can possibly lead to sincere conversations later on.

05. He used to drift apart from his son due to his job.

06. He had a hard time interacting with his son.

07. Then, one day, he decided to go hiking with his son at least once a week, not just to maintain his health but also to improve their relationship.

08. Becoming familiar with his son seemed awkward at first.

09. It was challenging for them to get close to each other.

10. His son slowly opened up to him, and a strong bond was built between them.

Lesson 04 관점의 확장 관련 표현

| Practice | 본서 P. 136 |

01. Traveling all over the world enables people to gain inspiration.

02. Traveling all over the world enables people to broaden their perspectives.

03. While traveling to different places, people gain exposure to many different matters they haven't experienced before.

04. This provides them with valuable insights.

05. These insights are needed as they navigate unpredictable situations in the future.

06. He often moved, and had numerous experiences.

07. However, it was exciting to learn how to embrace diversity.

08. In fact, while traveling all over the world with him, I kept my distance from different people.

09. Whereas he was open-minded toward people from various backgrounds.

10. Furthermore, there were no uncomfortable or awkward moments between him and others.

Lesson 05 조언 관련 표현

| Practice | 본서 P. 140 |

01. People can gain a lot of advice from their work experience.

02. These experiences have a significant impact on their lives.

03. These experiences also provide them with practical and valuable advice as they navigate unpredictable situations.

04. Through these moments, people have the opportunity to evaluate themselves objectively, leading to a better life in the future.

05. I used to be naive and less sociable due to my introverted personality.

06. Due to his personality, it was challenging for him to integrate with new people.

07. Initially, it was uncomfortable and challenging for me to integrate with new people and learn from real-world experience.

08. However, as I became accustomed to it, I started to contemplate matters I hadn't considered before.

09. This valuable experience provided me with practical advice.

10. This also contributed to my mental growth.

Lesson 06 편리함 관련 표현

본서 | P. 144

Practice

01. The Internet provides people with convenience in terms of communicating with others.

02. This has replaced traditional offline settings.

03. Thanks to the Internet, people can skip unnecessary processes.

04. With the help of the Internet, people don't have to go through any tedious processes.

05. When his friend moved to another city, he signed up for an online video chat platform.

06. That offered a variety of functions.

07. When he visited the website, he found it had useful features.

08. That enabled him to communicate with his friend on a daily basis.

09. As a result, he didn't need to travel a long distance in person.

10. This illustrates how the Internet frees people from the inconvenient offline processes when communicating with others.

Lesson 07 시간 활용 관련 표현

본서 | P. 148

Practice

01. Making specific plans in advance can significantly contribute to effective time management.

02. It's a proven fact that a considerable amount of time is wasted when people make instant plans and simply go with the flow.

03. Having a specific plan helps individuals utilize their time more efficiently.

04. It enables workers to handle various tasks at a faster pace.

05. It also allows them to focus better and show more outstanding performance.

06. When he worked as a teaching assistant, he had to assist his professor with research.

07. Everything went smoothly except for one thing.

08. One day, he decided to change his lifestyle by making specific plans for his time in advance.

09. He ended up saving a substantial amount of time.

10. He completed his TA work on schedule.

II. Academic Discussion Task　　Part 2. 실전 굳히기

본서 | P. 154

Lesson 01 스트레스 관련 주제 문단 구성

Your professor is teaching a class. Write a post responding to | 당신의 교수님께서 강의 중입니다. 교수님의 질문에

the professor's question.

In your response, you should:
- express and support your opinion
- make a contribution to the discussion

An effective response will contain at least 100 words. You will have 10 minutes to write it.

Dr. Springer: When it comes to spending money, some argue that it is better to invest in something long-lasting, like an expensive piece of jewelry, rather than indulging in short-term pleasures, such as a vacation. What are your thoughts on this matter?

Jeorge: Personally, I believe that investing in something that lasts, like an expensive piece of jewelry, is a wise decision. Not only does it provide a lasting value, but it can also be seen as an investment that retains or even appreciates in worth over time. Furthermore, owning a valuable piece of jewelry can be a symbol of prestige and accomplishment.

April: While I acknowledge the appeal of long-lasting investments, I believe that spending money on pleasurable experiences, such as a vacation, can be equally valuable. Pleasurable experiences have the potential to create lifelong memories and broaden one's horizons. Additionally, they can contribute to personal growth, cultural understanding, and stress relief, which are all essential aspects of a well-rounded life.

답하는 글을 쓰세요.

- 당신의 의견을 표현하고 뒷받침하세요
- 토론에 기여하세요

효과적인 답변은 최소한 100단어를 포함할 것입니다. 당신은 10분 동안 글을 작성할 수 있습니다.

스프린져 교수: 돈을 쓸 때, 어떤 사람들은 비싼 보석과 같이 오래가는 물건에 투자하는 것이 휴가와 같은 단기적인 즐거움에 빠지는 것보다 나은 것이라고 주장합니다. 이 문제에 대한 당신의 생각은 무엇인가요?

조지: 개인적으로 저는 오랫동안 가치가 유지되는 비싼 보석과 같은 것에 투자하는 것이 현명한 결정이라고 생각합니다. 이것은 지속적인 가치를 제공할 뿐만 아니라 시간이 지남에 따라 가치를 유지하거나 더 높아질 수 있는 투자로도 볼 수 있습니다. 더구나 소중한 보석을 소유하는 것은 명예와 성취의 상징이 될 수 있습니다.

에이프릴: 오래 지속되는 투자의 매력을 인정하면서도 저는 휴가와 같은 즐거운 경험에 돈을 쓰는 것이 동등하게 가치 있을 수 있다고 믿습니다. 즐거운 경험은 평생 기억을 만들고 시야를 넓힐 수 있는 잠재력이 있습니다. 더불어 이러한 경험은 개인적인 성장, 문화적 이해, 스트레스 해소에 기여할 수 있으며, 이는 모두 균형 잡힌 삶의 필수적인 측면입니다.

어휘 long-lasting **adj** 오래 지속되는 | indulge **v** 빠져들다 | prestige **n** 명성 | acknowledge **v** 인정하다 | lifelong **adj** 일생의 | horizon **n** 시야, 지평선 | well-rounded life 균형 잡힌 삶

아웃라인

일반적 진술

short-term pleasure: alleviate stress → stressed from work + competition → quality time enjoying short-term pleasure → relax + get back to work

구체화 사례

example → stressed out from work → "family trip" → relaxed mental state

단기적인 즐거움: 스트레스 완화 → 일과 경쟁으로부터의 스트레스 → 단기적인 즐거움을 즐기는 값진 시간 → 편안해지고 + 다시 일로 돌아갈 수 있음

예시 → 일 때문에 스트레스를 받음 → 가족 여행 → 편안해진 정신 상태

예시 답변

일반적 진술

From my perspective, both made excellent statements, but I'm on the same page as April. Simply put, experiencing short-term pleasures can contribute to alleviating stress. Nowadays, people often get stressed out from their heavy workloads and the competitions with those around them, so they need a

제 관점에서는 두 사람 모두 훌륭한 주장을 했지만, 저는 에이프릴과 동일한 견해를 가지고 있습니다. 간단히 말해 단기적인 즐거움을 경험하는 것은 스트레스 해소에 기여할 수 있습니다. 요즘 사람들은 무거운 업무 부담과 주변 사람들과의 경쟁에서 스트레스를

pleasant diversion to relax mentally. By spending quality time on short-term pleasures such as vacations, they will eventually be able to relax and get back to their work.

구체화 사례

A perfect example of this is a close friend of mine. He used to suffer from a heavy workload and its pressure. He sometimes stayed up all night getting his work done, so he was basically exhausted physically and mentally. Then one day, he got to have a chance to take a family trip, and it truly allowed him to escape from all the stressful matters while enjoying the trip. Thanks to this, he now has a relaxed and confident mental state.

받는 경우가 많아서, 정신적으로 편안해질 수 있는 즐거운 기분 전환이 필요합니다. 휴가와 같은 단기적인 즐거움에 깊고 의미 있는 시간을 보내면 결국에는 휴식을 취하고 업무로 돌아갈 수 있을 것입니다.

이에 대한 완벽한 예시는 제 친한 친구 중 한 명입니다. 그는 무거운 업무 부담과 압박으로 고통받았습니다. 그는 때때로 일을 끝내기 위해 밤을 새워야 했기 때문에 신체적으로나 정신적으로 완전히 지쳤습니다. 그러던 어느 날, 그는 가족 여행을 떠날 기회를 얻었고, 이 여행을 즐기면서 모든 스트레스에서 벗어날 수 있었습니다. 이로 인해 그는 이제 편안하고 자신감 있는 정신 상태를 가지고 있습니다.

Practice

본서 P. 156

Q

Your professor is teaching a class. Write a post responding to the professor's question.

In your response, you should:
- express and support your opinion
- make a contribution to the discussion

An effective response will contain at least 100 words.
You will have 10 minutes to write it.

Dr. Springer: It's interesting to see the differing viewpoints regarding the balance between work-related hobbies and unrelated leisure activities, and the potential benefits they offer for personal well-being and professional growth. Do you agree or disagree with the given statement? Because people spend so much of their time working, it is vital that they use their free time to engage in hobbies that are different from their work.

Jeorge: I agree with the statement. Engaging in hobbies that are different from one's work is crucial for overall well-being and personal growth. Hobbies provide an avenue for individuals to explore their passions, interests, and talents outside the constraints of their professional responsibilities. It allows them to unwind, relax, and recharge, which ultimately improves their productivity and creativity when they return to work.

April: I believe it is equally important to find a balance between work and leisure. In some cases, individuals may find fulfillment in pursuing hobbies related to their work, as it allows them to further develop their expertise and explore new dimensions within their field. Additionally, dedicating time to enhance professional skills during free time can be advantageous for career advancement.

당신의 교수님께서 강의 중입니다. 교수님의 질문에 답하는 글을 쓰세요.

- 당신의 의견을 표현하고 뒷받침하세요
- 토론에 기여하세요

효과적인 답변은 최소한 100단어를 포함할 것입니다. 당신은 10분 동안 글을 작성할 수 있습니다.

스프린져 교수: 직업과 관련된 취미와 관련 없는 여가 활동 간의 균형 및 그것들이 개인의 웰빙과 직업적 성장에 제공하는 잠재적 이점에 대한 다양한 시각을 보는 것은 흥미로운 일입니다. 주어진 주장에 동의하십니까, 반대하십니까? 사람들은 많은 시간을 일에 쓰기 때문에 그들이 여가를 적절하게 활용하여 일과 다른 취미에 참여하는 것이 매우 중요합니다.

조지: 해당 주장에 동의합니다. 자신의 일과 다른 취미에 참여하는 것은 전반적인 웰빙과 개인적인 성장에 중요합니다. 취미는 개인이 전문적인 책임의 제약을 벗어나 자신의 열정, 흥미 및 재능을 탐험할 수 있는 수단을 제공합니다. 이는 그들이 긴장을 풀고 휴식을 취하며 에너지를 충전할 수 있도록 해 주어 궁극적으로 업무로 돌아갈 때 생산성과 창의성을 향상시킵니다.

에이프릴: 저는 일과 여가 사이에서 균형을 찾는 것이 똑같이 중요하다고 믿습니다. 어떤 경우에는 개인이 자신의 일과 관련된 취미를 추구함으로써 그들의 전문성을 더욱 발전시키고 그 분야에서 새로운 차원을 탐험할 수 있게 되어 만족을 느낄 수 있습니다. 게다가 여가에 전문 기술을 향상시키기 위해 시간을 할애하는 것은 경력 향상에 유리할 수 있습니다.

어휘 viewpoint **n** 관점, 시각 ｜ work-related **adj** 업무에 관련된 ｜ vital **adj** 중요한 ｜ engage in 참여하다 ｜ avenue **n** 수단, 방법 ｜ unwind **v** 풀리다, 휴식을 취하다 ｜ expertise **n** 전문 지식, 전문성

예시 답변

From my perspective, both made excellent statements, but I'm on the same page as Jeorge. Simply put, engaging in hobbies that are different from one's work can contribute to alleviating stress. Nowadays, people often get stressed out from their heavy workloads and the competitions with those around them, so they need a pleasant diversion to relax mentally. By spending quality time on hobbies that are different from work, they will eventually be able to relax and get back to their work. A perfect example of this is a close friend of mine. He used to suffer from a heavy workload and its pressure. He sometimes stayed up all night getting his work done, so he was basically exhausted physically and mentally. Then one day, he got to have a chance to join an inline hockey club, which had nothing to do with his profession, and it truly allowed him to escape from all the stressful matters while engaging in this activity. Thanks to this, he now has a relaxed and confident mental state.

제 관점에서는 두 사람 모두 훌륭한 주장을 했지만, 저는 조지와 동일한 견해를 가지고 있습니다. 간단히 말해 직업과는 다른 취미에 참여하는 것은 스트레스 해소에 기여할 수 있습니다. 요즘 사람들은 무거운 업무 부담과 주변 사람들과의 경쟁에서 스트레스를 받는 경우가 많아서, 정신적으로 편안해질 수 있는 즐거운 기분 전환이 필요합니다. 직업과는 상관없는 취미에 깊고 의미 있는 시간을 보내면 결국에는 휴식을 취하고 업무로 돌아갈 수 있을 것입니다. 이에 대한 완벽한 예시는 제 친한 친구 중 한 명입니다. 그는 무거운 업무 부담과 압박으로 고통받았습니다. 그는 때때로 일을 끝내기 위해 밤을 새워야 했기 때문에 신체적으로나 정신적으로 완전히 지쳤었습니다. 그러던 어느 날, 그는 직업과는 관련이 없는 인라인 하키 동아리에 가입할 기회를 얻었고, 이 활동에 참여하면서 모든 스트레스에서 벗어날 수 있었습니다. 이로 인해 그는 이제 편안하고 자신감 있는 정신 상태를 가지고 있습니다.

Lesson 02 분위기 관련 주제 문단 구성

Your professor is teaching a class. Write a post responding to the professor's question.

In your response, you should:
- express and support your opinion
- make a contribution to the discussion

An effective response will contain at least 100 words.
You will have 10 minutes to write it.

Dr. Lucas: When it comes to designing a school's curriculum, there are numerous classes to choose from, each offering its own unique benefits. However, if you had to select just one class to be mandatory for the school's curriculum, which class would you prioritize?

Bobby: Personally, I believe that a class focusing on personal finance and financial literacy should be mandatory for all students. In today's society, financial knowledge is crucial for individuals to navigate the complexities of managing their finances effectively. Such a class would equip students with essential skills like budgeting, saving, and understanding investments, ensuring they have a solid foundation to make informed financial decisions throughout their lives and achieve accomplishments.

당신의 교수님께서 강의 중입니다. 교수님의 질문에 답하는 글을 쓰세요.

- 당신의 의견을 표현하고 뒷받침하세요
- 토론에 기여하세요

효과적인 답변은 최소한 100단어를 포함할 것입니다. 당신은 10분 동안 글을 작성할 수 있습니다.

루커스 교수: 학교 교육 과정을 설계할 때는 각각이 특유한 이점을 제공하는 다양한 수업이 있습니다. 그러나 학교 교육 과정의 필수 과목으로 딱 한 과목을 선택해야 한다면 어떤 과목을 우선시하겠습니까?

바비: 개인적으로 저는 모든 학생들에게 개인 금융과 금융 이해력에 중점을 둔 수업이 필수적이라고 생각합니다. 현대 사회에서 재무 지식은 각 개인이 자신의 재무를 효과적으로 관리하기 위한 복잡성을 다루는 데 중요합니다. 이러한 수업은 학생들에게 예산 편성, 저축, 투자 이해와 같은 필수 기술을 제공하여 평생 정보에 입각한 재무 결정을 내릴 수 있는 견고한 기반을 갖도록 보장합니다.

Kelly: While I recognize the importance of financial literacy, I would argue that a class on critical thinking and problem-solving should be the mandatory choice. These skills are universally applicable and essential for success in any field. By developing critical thinking abilities, students can learn to analyze and evaluate information, think creatively, and make sound judgments.

켈리: 금융 이해력의 중요성을 인정하지만 저는 비판적 사고와 문제 해결력에 중점을 둔 수업이 필수 선택이 되어야 한다고 주장하겠습니다. 이러한 기술은 보편적으로 적용 가능하며 모든 분야에서 성공하는 데 필수적입니다. 학생들이 비판적 사고 능력을 개발함으로써 정보를 분석하고 평가하며 창의적으로 생각하고 적절한 판단을 내릴 수 있게 됩니다.

어휘 numerous **adj** 다수의 I mandatory **adj** 의무적인 I navigate **v** 다루다, 항해하다 I complexity **n** 복잡성 I equip **v** 익히게 하다, 갖추다 I ensure **v** 보장하다, 확보하다 I accomplishment **n** 성취

아웃라인

일반적 진술

a positive atmosphere in PE class → influence of the atmosphere: important → Students should feel a good atmosphere. → PE: make students feel more cheerful and energetic

체육 수업의 긍정적 분위기 → 분위기의 영향 : 중요함 → 학생들은 좋은 분위기를 느껴야만 한다. → 체육 수업: 학생들을 활기차게 만들어 줄 수 있다는 점 강조

구체화 사례

example → competitive and strict atmosphere in the school → the principal's plan to change the atmosphere → a lot of time and effort to provide enjoyable PE class → positive atmosphere in the school

예시 → 치열하고 엄격한 학교의 분위기 → 분위기를 쇄신하려는 학교장의 계획 → 즐길 수 있는 체육 수업을 제공하기 위한 많은 시간과 노력 투자의 과정 → 긍정적으로 변화된 학교의 분위기

예시 답변

일반적 진술

From my perspective, both made excellent statements, but I would like to add that PE class should be a mandatory part of the school curriculum. Essentially, students experience a positive ambiance while engaging in energetic activities during PE class. This is primarily because most students can be influenced by the atmosphere in their surroundings. The impact of the atmosphere is a lot more important than they might realize. Therefore, students should feel a positive atmosphere while they are at school. PE class simply makes students feel so cheerful and energetic that they have a more enjoyable school life.

제 관점에서는 두 사람 모두 훌륭한 주장을 했지만, 저는 체육 수업이 학교 교육 과정의 필수 과목이어야 한다고 생각합니다. 기본적으로 학생들은 체육 수업에서 활기찬 활동에 참여하면서 긍정적인 분위기를 경험합니다. 이는 대부분의 학생들이 주변 환경의 분위기에 영향을 받을 수 있기 때문입니다. 분위기의 영향은 그들이 생각하는 것보다 훨씬 더 중요합니다. 따라서 학생들은 학교에서 긍정적인 분위기를 느껴야 합니다. 체육 수업은 학생들이 정말로 기분 좋고 활기찬 느낌을 갖게 만들어 더 즐거운 학교생활을 할 수 있게 합니다.

구체화 사례

A perfect example of this is the high school I attended. The school used to be very competitive and strict. However, things changed little by little after the school principal tried to change the atmosphere. A lot of time and effort were put into making the school curriculum better with more enjoyable PE classes. Now, the current students at my school genuinely appreciate the cheerful and energetic atmosphere. The school has also gained a good reputation that students want to be accepted into.

이에 대한 완벽한 예시는 제가 다녔던 고등학교입니다. 학교는 이전에 매우 치열하고 엄격했습니다. 그러나 교장이 분위기를 변화시키기 위해 노력한 후에 조금씩 변화가 일어났습니다. 더 즐거운 체육 수업으로 교육 과정을 개선하기 위해 많은 시간과 노력이 들어갔습니다. 이제 우리 학교의 재학생들은 즐겁고 활기찬 분위기에 진심으로 감사하고 있습니다. 학교는 또한 학생들이 입학하고 싶어 하는 좋은 평판을 얻었습니다.

Q

Your professor is teaching a class. Write a post responding to the professor's question.

In your response, you should:
- express and support your opinion
- make a contribution to the discussion

An effective response will contain at least 100 words. You will have 10 minutes to write it.

Dr. Lucas: Many cities nowadays are devising plans to improve themselves, yet they are unsure of the exact answer. When it comes to the city's benefit, some argue that the best way to achieve it is by focusing on constructing new buildings rather than preserving our nature. What are your thoughts on this matter?

Bobby: Personally, I agree with the notion that constructing new buildings can bring financial benefits to the government. The development of infrastructure and new constructions can attract investments, boost the economy, and create job opportunities. These economic gains can then be utilized for various public welfare programs, ultimately benefiting the citizens.

Kelly: While I understand the potential benefits of constructing new buildings, I strongly believe that preserving our natural environment should be a top priority. Our natural resources are invaluable, providing us with clean air, water, and biodiversity. Neglecting environmental preservation can have severe consequences for our planet and future generations.

당신의 교수님께서 강의 중입니다. 교수님의 질문에 답하는 글을 쓰세요.

- 당신의 의견을 표현하고 뒷받침하세요
- 토론에 기여하세요

효과적인 답변은 최소한 100단어를 포함할 것입니다. 당신은 10분 동안 글을 작성할 수 있습니다.

루커스 교수: 요즘 많은 도시가 스스로를 개선하기 위한 계획을 세우고 있지만 정확한 대답을 모르는 상황입니다. 도시의 이익에 관해서는 자연을 보존하는 대신 새로운 건물 건설에 중점을 두는 것이 가장 좋은 방법이라고 주장하는 사람들이 있습니다. 이에 대한 여러분의 의견은 어떠한가요?

바비: 개인적으로 저는 새로운 건물을 건설하는 것이 정부에 재정적 이익을 가져올 수 있다는 의견에 동의합니다. 기반 시설 및 새로운 건축물의 개발은 투자를 유치하고 경제를 촉진하며 일자리 창출에 도움이 될 수 있습니다. 이러한 경제적 이익은 다양한 공공복지 프로그램에 활용될 수 있으며 궁극적으로 시민들에게 혜택이 될 것입니다.

켈리: 새로운 건물을 건설하는 것의 잠재적 이점을 이해하지만, 저는 우리의 자연환경을 보존하는 것이 최우선 과제여야 한다고 강력하게 믿습니다. 우리의 자연 자원은 귀중하며, 우리에게 깨끗한 공기, 물 및 생물 다양성을 제공합니다. 환경 보존을 무시하면 지구와 향후 세대에 심각한 결과를 초래할 수 있습니다.

어휘 devise ⓥ 고안하다 | be unsure of 확신이 없다 | notion ⓝ 의견, 생각 | infrastructure ⓝ 기반 시설 | economic gain 경제적 이익 | public welfare 공공복지 | biodiversity ⓝ 생물 다양성

예시 답변

From my perspective, both made excellent statements, but I'm on the same page as Kelly. Essentially, people experience a positive ambiance while living in a city with well-preserved nature. This is primarily because most people can be influenced by the atmosphere in their surroundings. The impact of the atmosphere is a lot more important than they might realize. Therefore, people should feel a positive atmosphere while in their cities. Well-preserved nature simply makes the city so calm and peaceful that they have a more enjoyable urban life. A perfect example of this is the city I'm living in. The city used to be very distracting and noisy with frequent constructions. However, things changed little by little

제 관점에서는 두 사람 모두 훌륭한 주장을 했지만, 저는 켈리와 의견이 일치합니다. 기본적으로 자연이 잘 보존된 도시에서 생활하면 사람들은 긍정적인 분위기를 경험합니다. 이는 대부분의 사람들이 주변 환경의 분위기에 영향을 받을 수 있기 때문입니다. 분위기의 영향은 그들이 인식하는 것보다 훨씬 더 중요합니다. 따라서 사람들은 도시에서 긍정적인 분위기를 느껴야 합니다. 자연을 잘 보존하면 도시가 평온하고 평화로워져 더 즐거운 도시 생활을 할 수 있게 합니다. 이에 대한 완벽한 예시는 제가 살고 있는 도시입니다. 이 도시는 이전에는 잦은 건설로 소란하고 시끄러웠습니다. 그러나 시장이 분위기를 변화시키기 위해 노력

Academic Discussion Task

Part 2

after the mayor tried to change the atmosphere. A lot of time and effort were put into making the city better by preserving nature. Now, the people in my city genuinely appreciate the calm and peaceful atmosphere. The city has also gained a good reputation, becoming the most desirable place to live in.

한 후에 조금씩 변화가 일어났습니다. 도시를 더 나아지게 하기 위해 자연을 보존하는 데 많은 시간과 노력이 들어갔습니다. 지금은 저희 도시의 사람들이 평온하고 평화로운 분위기를 진심으로 감사하고 있습니다. 이 도시는 가장 이상적인 거주지로 손꼽히게 되어 좋은 평판도 얻었습니다.

Lesson 03 사람들과의 관계 관련 주제 문단 구성

Your professor is teaching a class. Write a post responding to the professor's question.

In your response, you should:
- express and support your opinion
- make a contribution to the discussion

An effective response will contain at least 100 words.
You will have 10 minutes to write it.

Dr. Emilie: Many busy parents struggle to balance their work and family life, and may not have much time to devote to helping their children with schoolwork. Some argue that it is more important for parents to spend quality time playing and bonding with their children, rather than focusing solely on academic achievements. What are your thoughts on this statement?

Oliver: I completely agree with the statement. Spending quality time with your children is essential for building strong relationships and developing their emotional intelligence. Parents who prioritize play-time over academics are sending an important message to their children: that their love and attention are not contingent on academic performance.

Lucy: While I agree that spending quality time with your children is important, I think that academic achievement should not be overlooked. It's important for parents to be involved in their children's education and to provide them with the support they need to succeed in school. This doesn't mean sacrificing play-time, but finding a balance between academic and non-academic activities.

당신의 교수님께서 강의 중입니다. 교수님의 질문에 답하는 글을 쓰세요.

- 당신의 의견을 표현하고 뒷받침하세요
- 토론에 기여하세요

효과적인 답변은 최소한 100단어를 포함할 것입니다. 당신은 10분 동안 글을 작성할 수 있습니다.

에밀리 교수: 많은 바쁜 부모들은 직장과 가정생활을 균형 있게 유지하는 데 어려움을 겪으며, 아이들의 공부를 돕는 데 많은 시간을 할애하기 어려울 수 있습니다. 어떤 사람들은 부모가 아이들과 놀고 유대감을 형성하며 깊고 의미 있는 시간을 보내는 것이 학업 성취에만 중점을 두는 것보다 더 중요하다고 주장합니다. 이에 대한 여러분의 의견은 무엇인가요?

올리버: 그 주장에 완전히 동의합니다. 아이들과 깊고 의미 있는 시간을 보내는 것은 강한 관계를 형성하고 그들의 정서 지능을 발전시키기 위해 중요합니다. 학업보다 놀이를 우선시하는 부모들은 중요한 메시지를 자녀들에게 전달하고 있습니다. 즉, 그들의 사랑과 관심은 학업 성취에 달려있지 않다는 것입니다.

루시: 아이들과 깊고 의미 있는 시간을 보내는 것이 중요하다는 데 동의하지만, 학업 성취를 간과해서는 안 된다고 생각합니다. 부모는 자녀 교육에 참여하고 학교에서 성공하기 위한 지원을 제공하는 것이 중요합니다. 이는 놀이 시간을 희생하는 것이 아니라 학문과 비학문 활동 간의 균형을 찾는 것을 의미합니다.

어휘 balance **v** 균형을 유지하다 | devote **v** 헌신하다 | quality time 깊고 의미 있는 시간 | emotional intelligence 정서 지능 | prioritize **v** ~에 우선순위를 매기다 | contingent **adj** (~을) 조건으로 하는 | overlook **v** 간과하다

아웃라인

일반적 진술

interaction between parents and children → play together → share experiences and emotions → lead to sincere conversations later

부모와 자식 사이에서의 소통 → 같이 놀면서 어울림 → 경험들을 함께하고 감정들을 공유함 → 진지한 대화들을 나눌 수 있는 기회

구체화 사례

example → drift apart from his son due to his job → decided to play with his son → awkward and challenging at first → gradually better → a strong bond between father and son

예시 → 일 때문에 아들과의 관계가 소원함 → 아들과 같이 노는데 더 많은 시간을 보내기로 결정 → 처음에는 어색하고 힘들었음 → 점차 나아짐 → 아빠와 아들 사이에서의 끈끈한 유대가 생기게 됨

예시 답변

일반적 진술

From my perspective, both made excellent statements, but I'm on the same page as Oliver. Essentially, parents can truly interact with their children while playing together, creating an optimal condition for improving their relationship. This is mainly because, when they play together, they have more opportunities to share various experiences and emotions. These shared experiences can possibly lead to sincere conversations later on.

제 관점에서는 두 사람 모두 훌륭한 주장을 했지만, 저는 올리버와 의견이 일치합니다. 기본적으로 부모는 함께 놀면서 자녀와 진정한 상호 작용을 할 수 있으며, 이는 관계 향상을 위한 최적의 상태를 만들어 낼 수 있습니다. 이는 주로 함께 놀 때 다양한 경험과 감정을 공유할 수 있는 더 많은 기회가 있기 때문입니다. 이러한 공유된 경험은 나중에 진정한 대화로 이어질 수 있습니다.

구체화 사례

A perfect example of this is my uncle. He used to drift apart from his son due to his job, making it challenging for them to interact. Then, one day, he decided to go hiking with his son at least once a week, not just to maintain his health but also to improve their relationship. At first, it seemed awkward and challenging for them to get close to each other, but it gradually improved. His son slowly opened up to him, and a strong bond was built and developed between them.

이에 대한 완벽한 예시는 제 삼촌입니다. 그는 직업 때문에 아들과 멀어져 상호 작용하기 어려웠습니다. 그러던 어느 날, 그는 건강을 유지하기 위해서 뿐만 아니라 관계를 개선하기 위해 매주 적어도 한 번 아들과 등산하기로 결정했습니다. 처음에는 서로 가까워지기가 어색하고 어려웠지만, 점차 나아졌습니다. 그의 아들은 천천히 그에게 마음을 열고, 그들 사이에 강한 유대가 형성되고 발전했습니다.

Practice

본서 P. 164

Q

Your professor is teaching a class. Write a post responding to the professor's question.

In your response, you should:
- express and support your opinion
- make a contribution to the discussion

An effective response will contain at least 100 words.
You will have 10 minutes to write it.

Dr. Emilie: As we discuss the importance of family dynamics, let's delve into the topic of regular family meals. We often hear the saying "Families should have meals together on a regular basis." What are your thoughts on this statement? Does having regular family meals provide significant benefits?

Oliver: Thank you, Professor. I believe that families should indeed prioritize having regular meals together. These shared moments offer more than just nourishment; they provide an opportunity for family members to connect, share their

당신의 교수님께서 강의 중입니다. 교수님의 질문에 답하는 글을 쓰세요.

- 당신의 의견을 표현하고 뒷받침하세요
- 토론에 기여하세요

효과적인 답변은 최소한 100단어를 포함할 것입니다. 당신은 10분 동안 글을 작성할 수 있습니다.

에밀리 교수: 우리가 가족 역동의 중요성을 논의하는 가운데 정기적인 가족 식사에 대한 주제를 좀 더 자세히 이야기해 보겠습니다. 우리는 종종 "가족은 정기적으로 함께 식사를 해야 한다."는 말을 듣습니다. 이 진술에 대한 여러분의 의견은 어떠한가요? 정기적인 가족 식사가 중요한 이점을 제공합니까?

올리버: 감사합니다. 교수님. 저는 가족들이 정기적으로 함께 식사하는 것이 정말로 우선되어야 한다고 믿습니다. 이러한 공유된 순간은 영양뿐만 아니라 가족 구성원들이 연결되고 그들의 경험을 나누며 결속을

experiences, and strengthen their bonds. It's during these meals that we often engage in meaningful conversations, providing a sense of togetherness and support.

Lucy: I understand the importance of family meals, but I'd like to emphasize the challenges many families face in today's hectic lifestyles. While it's a wonderful idea, the reality is that demanding work schedules, extracurricular activities, and other commitments can make it difficult for everyone to sit down together regularly. Nonetheless, the value of family meals should not be understated, and finding ways to make it work can bring numerous benefits.

강화하는 기회를 제공합니다. 이런 식사 중에 우리는 종종 의미 있는 대화를 나누며 유대감과 지지를 느낄 수 있습니다.

루시: 가족 식사의 중요성을 이해하지만, 오늘날의 바쁜 생활에서 많은 가족이 직면하는 어려움을 강조하고 싶습니다. 멋진 아이디어일 수 있지만 현실적으로는 바쁜 업무 일정, 여러 활동 및 다른 약속으로 모두가 정기적으로 함께 앉아 식사하는 것이 어려울 수 있습니다. 그럼에도 불구하고 가족 식사의 가치는 과소평가되어서는 안 되며, 이를 실현할 방법을 찾는다면 다양한 이점을 가져올 수 있습니다.

어휘 family dynamic 가족 역동 | indeed **adv** 정말로 | nourishment **n** 영양 | strengthen **v** 강화하다 | bond **n** 유대 | hectic **adj** 바쁜 | extracurricular activity 교외 활동

From my perspective, both made excellent statements, but I'm on the same page as Oliver. Essentially, family members can truly interact with one another while having a meal together regularly, creating an optimal condition for improving their relationships. This is mainly because when they have meals together, they have more opportunities to share various experiences and emotions. This can possibly lead to sincere conversations later on. A perfect example of this is my uncle. He was drifting apart from his family due to his job, making it challenging for them to interact. Then, one day, he decided to have meals with his family on a daily basis, not just to maintain his health but also to improve their relationship. At first, it seemed awkward and challenging for his family to get close to one another, but it gradually improved. His family slowly opened up to him, and a strong bond was built and developed among them.

저의 시각에서 두 분 모두 매우 훌륭한 주장을 하셨다고 판단합니다만, 저는 올리버와 동일한 견해를 가지고 있습니다. 본질적으로 가족 구성원이 정기적으로 함께 식사를 하는 것은 서로에게 진정한 소통의 기회를 제공하는 최적의 환경을 조성할 수 있다고 믿습니다. 함께 식사할 때 다양한 경험과 감정을 공유할 수 있기 때문입니다. 이는 나중에는 보다 진솔한 대화로 이어질 수 있습니다. 이에 대한 완벽한 사례로 제가 들 수 있는 것은 제 삼촌의 경험입니다. 그는 직업 때문에 가족에게서 떨어져 지냈고 그들과 소통이 어려웠습니다. 그러나 어느 날, 건강 유지뿐만 아니라 가족과의 관계 개선을 위해 매일 가족과 함께 식사하기로 결심했습니다. 처음에는 가족끼리 가까워지는 것이 어색하고 어려웠지만, 점차 상황은 개선되었습니다. 그의 가족은 천천히 그에게 마음을 열고, 끈끈한 유대 관계를 형성하고 발전시켰습니다.

Lesson 04 관점의 확장 관련 주제 문단 구성

Your professor is teaching a class. Write a post responding to the professor's question.

In your response, you should:
- express and support your opinion
- make a contribution to the discussion

An effective response will contain at least 100 words. You will have 10 minutes to write it.

Dr. Logan: As we explore the enriching aspects of travel, let's delve into the topic of how people can benefit from traveling from all around the world. We often hear the saying, "People

당신의 교수님께서 강의 중입니다. 교수님의 질문에 답하는 글을 쓰세요.

- 당신의 의견을 표현하고 뒷받침하세요
- 토론에 기여하세요

효과적인 답변은 최소한 100단어를 포함할 것입니다. 당신은 10분 동안 글을 작성할 수 있습니다.

로건 교수: 여행의 풍부한 측면을 탐험하는 동안, 세계 각지에서 여행하는 것이 어떻게 사람들에게 이로움을 줄 수 있는지에 대한 주제를 살펴보겠습니다. "사람들은 세계 각지에서 여행함으로써 이로움을 얻

can benefit from traveling from all around the world." What are your thoughts on this statement? Do you believe that travel can provide significant advantages?

Noah: I strongly agree with the statement. Traveling offers a unique opportunity for individuals to broaden their horizons, immerse themselves in different cultures, and gain a deeper understanding of the world. It allows us to break free from our comfort zones, challenge our perspectives, and foster personal growth.

Helen: While I agree that travel can be beneficial, I believe that academic studies should still remain a top priority. Education provides a strong foundation and equips individuals with essential knowledge and skills. However, incorporating travel experiences into one's educational journey can enhance their understanding of diverse cultures and global issues, providing a more holistic and well-rounded education.

을 수 있다."는 말을 종종 듣습니다. 이 주장에 대한 여러분의 생각은 무엇인가요? 여행이 상당한 이점을 제공할 수 있다고 생각하시나요?

노아: 저는 그 주장에 강력히 동의합니다. 여행은 개인들이 시야를 넓히고 다양한 문화에 몰두하며 세계를 더 깊이 이해할 수 있는 독특한 기회를 제공합니다. 여행은 편안한 지역에서 벗어나 우리의 관점을 의심하고 개인적인 성장을 촉진하는 기회를 제공합니다.

헬렌: 여행이 유익할 수 있다는 데는 동의하지만, 학문적인 연구가 여전히 최우선 사항이어야 한다고 생각합니다. 교육은 강력한 기초를 제공하며, 필수적인 지식과 기술을 개인에게 제공합니다. 그러나 여행 경험을 자신의 교육 여정에 통합하면 다양한 문화와 세계적인 문제에 대한 이해를 향상시킬 수 있어 더 전체적이고 균형 있는 교육을 제공할 수 있습니다.

어휘 significant adj 중요한 ㅣ immerse v 몰두하다 ㅣ comfort zone 편안함을 주는 상황 ㅣ foundation n 기초, 기반 ㅣ incorporate v 통합하다 ㅣ diverse adj 다양한 ㅣ holistic adj 종합적인

아웃라인

일반적 진술

traveling the world : broaden perspectives → exposure to different matters they haven't experienced before → get valuable insights for the future

구체화 사례

example → a friend who often moved + had numerous experiences → not challenging but exciting to learn how to embrace diversity → traveling all over the world with that friend → me: keeping distance from differences → him: open-minded to everything

전세계를 여행하는 것: 관점/시야의 확장 → 이전에 경험해 보지 않았던 다른 것들에 대한 노출 → 미래를 위해 필요한 가치 있는 통찰을 얻게 됨

예시 → 자주 이사를 다니고 수많은 경험을 겪었던 한 친구 → 많은 곳을 돌아다니면서 다양성을 포용하는 법을 배우게 되어 매우 즐거웠음. → 그 친구와의 세계 여행 → 나: 다름에 대해 거리를 둠 → 그 친구: 모든 것들에 대한 열려 있는 태도

예시 답변

일반적 진술

From my perspective, both made excellent statements, but I'm on the same page as Noah. Simply put, traveling all over the world enables people to gain inspiration and broaden their perspectives. While traveling to different places, people gain exposure to many different matters they haven't experienced before. This provides them with valuable insights that are needed as they navigate unpredictable situations in the future.

구체화 사례

A perfect example of this is a close friend of mine, whose father was a diplomat traveling the world. Due to his father's job, he often moved and had numerous experiences. He said that even though it was challenging to lead such a lifestyle, it

제 시각에서 두 분 모두 훌륭한 주장을 하셨다고 생각하지만, 저는 노아와 동일한 견해를 가지고 있습니다. 간단히 말씀드리면, 전 세계를 여행하는 것은 사람들이 영감을 얻고 시야를 넓히는 것을 가능케 만든다고 생각합니다. 다양한 장소를 여행하면서 사람들은 이전에 경험하지 못한 많은 다양한 문제에 노출되게 됩니다. 이는 미래에 예측할 수 없는 상황에서 필요한 귀중한 통찰력을 제공한다고 생각합니다.

이에 대한 완벽한 사례로 언급할 수 있는 것은 제 친한 친구인데, 그의 아버지는 세계를 여행하는 외교관이셨습니다. 그의 아버지의 직업 때문에 자주 이사를 다니면서 다양한 경험을 쌓았습니다. 그는 이러한 생

was exciting to learn how to embrace diversity. In fact, while traveling all over the world with him, I kept my distance from unfamiliar people, whereas he was open-minded toward people from various backgrounds because he had experienced similar situations before. Furthermore, there were no uncomfortable or awkward moments between him and others.

활 방식이 도전적이었지만, 다양성을 포용하는 법을 배우는 것은 흥미로웠다고 말했습니다. 실제로 그와 함께 전 세계를 여행하면서 저는 친숙하지 않은 사람들과 거리를 두었지만, 그는 이전에 비슷한 상황을 경험했기 때문에 다양한 배경을 가진 사람들에게 열린 마음을 가졌습니다. 더 나아가 그와 다른 사람들 사이에 불편하거나 어색한 순간은 전혀 없었습니다.

Practice

본서 | P. 168

Q

Your professor is teaching a class. Write a post responding to the professor's question.

In your response, you should:
- express and support your opinion
- make a contribution to the discussion

An effective response will contain at least 100 words. You will have 10 minutes to write it.

Dr. Logan: While academic studies are important for a child's education, there is an ongoing debate about whether studying abroad at an early age is beneficial for children. Considering the advantages and potential drawbacks, what factors should parents and educators consider when deciding whether to recommend studying abroad at an early age for children?

Noah: Personally, I believe that studying abroad at an early age can be highly recommended for children. It offers them a unique opportunity to immerse themselves in a different culture, learn a new language, and gain a global perspective. This experience not only enhances their academic knowledge but also helps them develop invaluable life skills, such as adaptability and independence.

Helen: While I understand the potential benefits of studying abroad, I think it's essential to prioritize a child's academic studies. A strong foundation in traditional education provides the necessary skills and knowledge for future success. Although studying abroad can offer cultural exposure, it should not overshadow the importance of a comprehensive academic curriculum.

당신의 교수님께서 강의 중입니다. 교수님의 질문에 답하는 글을 쓰세요.

- 당신의 의견을 표현하고 뒷받침하세요
- 토론에 기여하세요

효과적인 답변은 최소한 100단어를 포함할 것입니다. 당신은 10분 동안 글을 작성할 수 있습니다.

로건 교수: 어린이 교육에 있어서 학과 공부는 중요하지만, 조기 유학이 유익한지에 대한 논쟁이 계속되고 있습니다. 장점과 잠재적인 단점을 고려할 때, 어린이에게 조기 유학을 권할지 결정할 때 부모와 교육자가 고려해야 할 요소는 무엇인가요?

노아: 제 개인적인 의견으로는 어린이에게 조기 유학을 권하는 것이 매우 유익할 수 있다고 생각합니다. 이것은 그들에게 다른 문화에 몰두하고, 새로운 언어를 배우며, 세계적인 시각을 얻을 수 있는 독특한 기회를 제공합니다. 이 경험은 그들의 학문적 지식뿐만 아니라 적응력과 독립성과 같은 귀중한 삶의 기술을 개발하는 데 도움이 됩니다.

헬렌: 해외 유학의 잠재적 이점을 이해하지만, 어린이의 학업에 우선순위를 두는 것이 중요하다고 생각합니다. 전통적인 교육의 견고한 기초는 미래의 성공을 위한 필수적인 기술과 지식을 제공합니다. 해외 유학이 문화적 경험을 제공할 수 있지만, 이것은 종합적인 학문 과정의 중요성을 무색하게 할 수 없습니다.

어휘 ongoing **adj** 진행 중인 | debate **n** 논쟁 | potential **adj** 잠재적인 | drawback **n** 단점 | invaluable **adj** 귀중한 | adaptability **n** 적응력 | overshadow **v** ~을 무색하게 하다

예시 답변

From my perspective, both made excellent statements, but I'm on the same page as Noah. Simply put, studying abroad at

제 시각에서 두 분 다 훌륭한 주장을 하셨다고 생각하지만, 저는 노아와 동일한 견해를 가지고 있습니다.

an early age enables children to gain inspiration and broaden their perspectives. While studying in different countries, children gain exposure to many different matters they haven't experienced before. This provides them with valuable insights that are needed as they navigate unpredictable situations in the future. A perfect example of this is a close friend of mine, whose father was a diplomat traveling the world. Due to his father's job, he often moved and had numerous experiences. He said that even though it was challenging to lead such a lifestyle, it was exciting to learn how to embrace diversity. In fact, while studying in the United States with him, I kept my distance from people of different cultures, whereas he was open-minded toward everything from various backgrounds because he had experienced similar situations before. Furthermore, there were no uncomfortable or awkward moments between him and others.

간단히 말씀드리면, 어린 나이에 해외에서 공부를 하는 것은 어린이들이 영감을 얻고 시야를 확장하는 것을 가능케 만든다고 생각합니다. 다양한 나라에서 공부하는 동안 어린이들은 이전에 경험하지 못한 다양한 문제에 노출됩니다. 이는 미래에 예측할 수 없는 상황에서 필요한 소중한 통찰력을 제공합니다. 이에 대한 완벽한 사례로는 제 친한 친구인데, 그의 아버지는 세계를 여행하는 외교관이셨습니다. 아버지의 직업으로 인해 자주 이사를 가야 했으며 많은 경험을 쌓았습니다. 그는 이러한 생활 방식이 도전적이었지만, 다양성을 받아들이는 법을 배우는 것이 흥미로웠다고 말했습니다. 실제로 그와 함께 미국에서 공부하면서 저는 다른 문화의 사람들과 거리를 두었지만, 그는 이전에 비슷한 상황을 경험했기 때문에 다양한 배경에서 오는 모든 것에 대해 개방적이었습니다. 게다가 그와 다른 사람들 간에 불편하거나 어색한 순간은 전혀 없었습니다.

Lesson 05 조언 관련 주제 문단 구성

Your professor is teaching a class. Write a post responding to the professor's question.

In your response, you should:
- express and support your opinion
- make a contribution to the discussion

An effective response will contain at least 100 words.
You will have 10 minutes to write it.

Dr. Bliss: I'd like to share your recent experiences that have had a significant impact on your lives. It's remarkable how diverse experiences can shape our perspectives and contribute to personal growth. So, please describe a new experience you have had recently that significantly impacted your life. Explain how this experience has influenced your perspective and personal growth.

James: Recently, I had the opportunity to participate in a volunteer program in a rural community. This experience has had a profound impact on my life. It exposed me to the realities and challenges faced by underprivileged communities, deepening my empathy and understanding of social issues. Interacting with the locals and working together to improve their living conditions sparked a sense of purpose and a desire to contribute positively to society.

Emma: In contrast, my recent experience was completing a research internship at a prestigious laboratory. This opportunity allowed me to work closely with leading scientists

당신의 교수님께서 강의 중입니다. 교수님의 질문에 답하는 글을 쓰세요.

- 당신의 의견을 표현하고 뒷받침하세요
- 토론에 기여하세요

효과적인 답변은 최소한 100단어를 포함할 것입니다. 당신은 10분 동안 글을 작성할 수 있습니다.

블리스 교수: 여러분의 삶에 큰 영향을 미친 최근 경험을 나누고 싶습니다. 다양한 경험이 어떻게 우리의 관점을 형성하고 개인적인 성장에 기여할 수 있는지 놀랍습니다. 그러니 최근에 겪은 여러분의 삶에 큰 영향을 미친 새로운 경험을 설명해 주세요. 이 경험이 어떻게 여러분의 관점과 개인적인 성장에 영향을 미쳤는지 설명해 주세요.

제임스: 최근에 저는 시골 지역에서 자원봉사 프로그램에 참여할 기회가 있었습니다. 이 경험이 제 삶에 깊은 영향을 미쳤습니다. 이것은 빈곤한 지역이 직면하는 현실과 어려움을 접하게 되었고 사회 문제에 대한 제 공감과 이해가 깊어졌습니다. 현지 주민들과 소통하며 그들의 생활 조건을 개선하기 위해 협력하는 경험은 저에게 목적감과 사회에 긍정적으로 기여하고자 하는 열망을 일깨웠습니다.

에마: 대조적으로, 제 최근 경험은 명성 있는 연구실에서 연구 인턴십을 완료한 것이었습니다. 이 기회를 통해 저는 제가 관심을 가지고 있는 분야에서 선도적인 과학자들과 밀접하게 협력할 수 있었습니다. 이 경

in my field of interest. Through this experience, I gained valuable insights into cutting-edge research and acquired practical laboratory skills. It reinforced my passion for scientific inquiry and provided clarity regarding my career path.

힘을 통해 저는 최첨단 연구에 대한 소중한 통찰력을 얻었으며 실질적인 실험실 기술을 습득했습니다. 이는 저의 과학적 탐구에 대한 열정을 강화하고 제 진로에 대한 명확성을 부여했습니다.

어휘 significant **adj** 중요한 I shape **v** ~을 형성하다 I volunteer **n** 자원봉사자 I profound **adj** 깊은, 심오한 I rural **adj** 시골의 I underprivileged **adj** 불우한 I prestigious **adj** 명성 있는

아웃라인

일반적 진술

advice from experiences → valuable and practical advice for future → through the experiences, evaluate oneself objectively → better life in the future

경험들로부터 얻는 조언 → 미래를 위한 가치 있고 실용적인 조언 → 그러한 경험들을 통해서, 자신들을 객관적으로 평가하게 됨 → 미래에 더 나은 삶을 가지게 됨

구체화 사례

example → me: less sociable → live in my own world → internship as a graduation requirement → challenging to learn from the internship opportunity → get used to the situation → got to contemplate a lot of matters → gained advice + mental growth

예시 → 나: 사회성이 결여되어 있었음 → 나만의 세계에서 살고 있었음 → 졸업 요구조건으로서 인턴십을 해야만 함 → 인턴십 기회로부터 배우는 것은 처음에 굉장히 힘들었음 → 상황에 익숙해지게 됨 → 많은 것들에 대해 깊이 생각하게 되는 기회를 가지게 됨 → 조언과 정신적 성장을 얻게 됨.

예시 답변

일반적 진술

From my perspective, both made excellent statements, but I would like to add that an internship at a small company had a significant impact on my life. In essence, people can gain a lot of advice from their work experience. It's obvious that these experiences provide them with practical and valuable advice as they navigate unpredictable situations. Through these moments, people have the opportunity to evaluate themselves objectively, leading to a better life in the future.

제 시각에서 두 분 모두 훌륭한 발언을 하셨다고 생각하지만, 저는 작은 회사에서의 인턴 경험이 제 삶에 상당한 영향을 끼쳤다는 점을 덧붙이고 싶습니다. 본질적으로 사람들은 직무 경험을 통해 많은 조언을 얻을 수 있습니다. 이러한 경험은 예측할 수 없는 상황에서 실질적이고 가치 있는 조언을 제공합니다. 이러한 순간을 통해, 사람들은 객관적으로 자기 자신을 평가할 수 있는 기회를 얻게 되어 미래에 더 나은 삶을 살아갈 수 있게 됩니다.

구체화 사례

A perfect example of this is my own experience. I used to be naive and less sociable due to my introverted personality. This led me to isolate myself from others and live in my own world. Then, one day, I had an internship experience as a graduation requirement. Initially, it was uncomfortable and challenging for me to integrate with new people and learn from real-world experience. However, as I became accustomed to it, I started to contemplate matters I hadn't considered before. This valuable experience not only provided me with practical advice but also contributed to my mental growth.

완벽한 예시로는 제 자신의 경험이 있습니다. 예전에는 내성적인 성격으로 인해 순진하고 사회성이 부족한 편이었습니다. 이로 인해 저는 다른 사람들로부터 저를 고립시키고 저만의 세계에 머무르곤 했습니다. 그런데 어느 날, 졸업 요건으로 인턴 경험을 하게 되었습니다. 처음에는 새로운 사람들과 어울리고 현실 경험을 통해 배우는 것이 불편하고 어려웠습니다. 그러나 익숙해지면서 저는 이전에 생각하지 못한 문제를 고찰하게 되었습니다. 이 소중한 경험은 실질적인 조언뿐만 아니라 저의 정신적인 성장에도 기여하였습니다.

Practice

Q

Your professor is teaching a class. Write a post responding to the professor's question.

당신의 교수님께서 강의 중입니다. 교수님의 질문에 답하는 글을 쓰세요.

92 II Academic Discussion Task

In your response, you should:
- express and support your opinion
- make a contribution to the discussion

An effective response will contain at least 100 words.
You will have 10 minutes to write it.

Dr. Bliss: Over time, we've seen numerous cases where people and societies have improved by acknowledging and fixing their errors. Today, we'll discuss a topic that's relevant to people from different cultures and eras: "Do people learn from their mistakes? What's your take on this?"

James: I wholeheartedly agree with this statement. Mistakes are invaluable learning experiences. They teach us important lessons that often can't be gained through success alone. Take, for instance, a student who makes an error in a math problem. That mistake can lead to a deeper understanding of the concept when corrected. Similarly, in life, personal mistakes often lead to self-reflection and personal growth.

Emma: Learning from mistakes is not guaranteed. Some people may repeat the same mistakes without improvement. In certain situations, mistakes can have serious consequences that can't be easily rectified. It's also worth noting that not all lessons need to come from mistakes: guidance, education, and knowledge sharing are proactive ways to learn.

- 당신의 의견을 표현하고 뒷받침하세요
- 토론에 기여하세요

효과적인 답변은 최소한 100단어를 포함할 것입니다. 당신은 10분 동안 글을 작성할 수 있습니다.

블리스 교수: 시간이 지남에 따라 우리는 사람들과 사회가 자신들의 실수를 인정하고 수정함으로써 개선된 수많은 사례를 모았습니다. 오늘은 서로 다른 문화와 시대의 사람들에게 관련 있는 주제에 대해 논의할 것입니다: "사람들은 자신의 실수에서 배우는 걸까요? 이에 대한 여러분의 견해는 무엇인가요?"

제임스: 이 주장에 전적으로 동의합니다. 실수는 값진 학습 경험입니다. 실수를 통해 얻을 수 있는 중요한 교훈은 종종 성공만으로는 얻을 수 없습니다. 예를 들어, 수학 문제에서 실수를 범한 학생을 생각해 보세요. 그 실수는 수정될 때 그 개념에 대한 더 깊은 이해로 이어질 수 있습니다. 마찬가지로 삶에서 개인적인 실수는 자기 성찰과 개인적인 성장으로 이어질 수 있습니다.

에마: 실수로부터 배우는 것은 보장되지는 않습니다. 어떤 사람들은 개선 없이 동일한 실수를 반복할 수 있습니다. 특정 상황에서는 실수가 쉽게 바로잡을 수 없는 심각한 결과를 초래할 수 있습니다. 또한 모든 교훈이 실수에서 나올 필요는 없으며, 지도, 교육 및 지식 공유는 적극적인 학습 방법입니다.

어휘 acknowledge **v** 인정하다 | relevant **adj** 관련된 | wholeheartedly **adv** 진심으로 | self-reflection **n** 자기 성찰 | personal growth 개인적인 성장 | consequence **n** 결과 | proactive **adj** 적극적인

예시 답변

From my perspective, both made excellent statements, but I'm on the same page as James. Essentially, people can gain a lot of advice from their mistakes. It's obvious that these errors provide them with practical and valuable insights as they navigate unpredictable situations. Through these moments, people have the opportunity to evaluate themselves objectively, leading to a better future. A perfect example of this is my own experience. I used to be naive and less sociable due to my introverted personality, which led me to isolate myself from others and live in my own world. Then, one day, I had an internship experience as part of my graduation requirements. Initially, it was uncomfortable and challenging for me to integrate with new people and learn from real-world experiences. I made many mistakes along the way. However, as I became more accustomed to it, I started to contemplate matters I hadn't considered before. This valuable experience not only provided me with practical advice but also contributed to my personal growth.

제 시각에서는 두 분 모두 훌륭한 주장을 하셨다고 생각하지만, 저는 제임스와 동일한 의견을 가지고 있습니다. 본질적으로 사람들은 자신의 실수에서 많은 조언을 얻을 수 있다고 생각합니다. 이 실수들은 예측할 수 없는 상황을 헤쳐나갈 때 실질적이고 가치 있는 통찰력을 제공합니다. 이러한 순간을 통해 사람들은 객관적으로 자기 자신을 평가할 수 있는 기회를 얻게 되어 더 나은 미래로 나아갈 수 있습니다. 이에 대한 완벽한 예시로는 제 자신의 경험입니다. 예전에는 내성적인 성격으로 인해 순진하고 사회성이 부족한 편이었습니다. 이로 인해 다른 사람들로부터 저를 고립시키고 저만의 세계에만 머무르곤 했습니다. 그런데 어느 날, 졸업 요건으로 인턴 경험을 하게 되었습니다. 처음에는 새로운 사람들과 어울리고 현실 경험을 통해 배우는 것이 불편하고 어려웠습니다. 그 길에는 많은 실수가 있었습니다. 그러나 익숙해지면서 저는 이전에 생각하지 못한 문제를 고찰하게 되었습니다. 이 소중한 경험은 실질적인 조언뿐만 아니라 제 개인적인 성장에도 기여하였습니다.

Your professor is teaching a class. Write a post responding to the professor's question.

In your response, you should:
- express and support your opinion
- make a contribution to the discussion

An effective response will contain at least 100 words. You will have 10 minutes to write it.

Dr. Ethan: Good day, class. Scientific discoveries and technological innovations have been instrumental in shaping the world as we know it. Today, we'll delve into a captivating question: "Which significant scientific breakthrough or technological innovation from the past two centuries would you select as a crucial advancement?" Let's explore the remarkable achievements that have transformed our lives.

Daniel: Thank you, Professor. When considering significant advancements from the past two centuries, I would definitely pick the discovery of antibiotics. When Alexander Fleming stumbled upon penicillin in 1928, it revolutionized medicine and saved countless lives. The ability to treat bacterial infections transformed healthcare, making surgery safer and preventing deaths from once-fatal diseases.

Judy: I understand the importance of antibiotics, but I'd select the development of the computer. Starting from the 1960s, the computer has changed the way we communicate, work, and access information. It has connected people globally, accelerated research and innovation, and transformed industries. Today, it's an integral part of modern life, driving progress in countless fields.

당신의 교수님께서 강의 중입니다. 교수님의 질문에 답하는 글을 쓰세요.

- 당신의 의견을 표현하고 뒷받침하세요
- 토론에 기여하세요

효과적인 답변은 최소한 100단어를 포함할 것입니다. 당신은 10분 동안 글을 작성할 수 있습니다.

에단 교수: 안녕하세요, 여러분. 과학적 발견과 기술 혁신은 우리가 아는 세계를 형성하는 데 중요한 역할을 해왔습니다. 오늘은 매혹적인 질문에 대해 논의해 보겠습니다: "지난 200년 동안의 중요한 과학적 발견 또는 기술 혁신 중 어떤 것을 중요한 발전으로 선택하겠습니까?" 우리 삶을 변화시킨 놀라운 성취를 살펴보죠.

다니엘: 감사합니다, 교수님. 지난 200년 동안의 중요한 발전을 고려할 때, 저는 확실히 항생물질의 발견을 선택하겠습니다. 1928년 알렉산더 플레밍이 페니실린을 우연히 발견한 것은 의학을 혁신하고 무수한 생명을 구했습니다. 세균 감염을 치료할 수 있는 능력은 수술을 더 안전하게 만들고 예전에는 치명적이었던 질병으로 인한 사망을 예방했습니다.

주디: 항생물질의 중요성을 이해하지만, 저는 컴퓨터의 발전을 선택할 것입니다. 1960년대부터 컴퓨터는 우리의 의사소통, 업무, 정보 접근 방식을 바꿨습니다. 이는 전 세계적으로 사람들을 연결하고, 연구와 혁신을 가속하며, 산업을 변형시켰습니다. 오늘날 이는 현대 생활에서 불가결한 부분으로, 무수한 분야에서 진보를 이끌고 있습니다.

어휘 breakthrough n 돌파구 | innovation n 혁신 | advancement n 발전, 진보 | stumble upon ~을 우연히 발견하다 | once-fatal disease 한때 치명적이었던 질병 | access n 접근 | integral adj 불가결한 | countless adj 무수한

아웃라인

일반적 진술
the Internet: provide convenience → communicate with people anytime → replace traditional offline settings → × go through tedious process

구체화 사례
example → cousin's friend moved → signed up for online video chat → useful features to communicate → × travel a long distance in person

인터넷: 편리함을 제공 → 언제라도 사람들과의 소통할 수 있음 → 기존의 오프라인 환경들을 대체 → 번거로운 과정을 겪지 않아도 됨

예시 → 사촌의 친구가 이사를 갔음 → 온라인 화상 채팅에 가입 함 → 화상 채팅은 소통하기 위한 유용한 기능들을 가지고 있음 → 친구를 보기 위해 직접 장거리를 이동하지 않아도 되었음

일반적 진술

From my perspective, both made excellent statements, but I would like to add that the Internet is the most important technological invention by far. The Internet provides people with convenience in terms of communicating with others. It's a proven fact that people can always communicate with others whenever they have Internet access. This has replaced traditional offline settings. Thanks to this, people don't have to go through any tedious processes.

구체화 사례

A perfect example of this is my cousin. When his friend moved to another city, he signed up for an online video chat platform that offered a variety of functions. When he visited the website, he found it had useful features that enabled him to communicate with his friend on a daily basis. As a result, he didn't need to travel a long distance in person. This illustrates how the Internet frees people from the inconvenience of offline processes when communicating with others.

제 시각에서는 두 분 모두 훌륭한 주장을 하셨다고 생각하지만, 저는 인터넷이 현존하는 기술 발명 중에서 가장 중요한 발명일 것이라고 추가하고 싶습니다. 인터넷은 사람들에게 다른 사람들과 소통하는 측면에서 편리함을 제공합니다. 인터넷 접속이 가능한 경우 언제든지 사람들은 다른 사람들과 소통할 수 있다는 것은 입증된 사실입니다. 이것은 전통적인 오프라인 환경을 대체하였습니다. 덕분에 사람들은 귀찮은 과정을 거치지 않아도 됩니다.

이에 대한 완벽한 예시로는 제 사촌입니다. 그의 친구가 다른 도시로 이사를 가자, 그는 다양한 기능을 제공하는 온라인 비디오 채팅 플랫폼에 가입했습니다. 그가 웹사이트를 방문하자, 그는 친구와 매일 소통할 수 있도록 도와주는 유용한 기능이 있다는 것을 발견했습니다. 결과적으로, 그는 직접 멀리 여행할 필요가 없었습니다. 이는 인터넷이 다른 사람들과 소통할 때 오프라인 과정의 불편함에서 사람들을 어떻게 해방해 주는지를 보여 주는 사례입니다.

Practice

본서 P. 176

Q

Your professor is teaching a class. Write a post responding to the professor's question.

In your response, you should:
- express and support your opinion
- make a contribution to the discussion

An effective response will contain at least 100 words.
You will have 10 minutes to write it.

Dr. Ethan: It is crucial to have access to reliable and comprehensive information in today's society. People have various methods for obtaining the information or data they need. Some individuals acquire information from those around them, while others prefer to visit libraries to gather data. What do you believe is the most effective way to gain information?

Daniel: In my opinion, the Internet is the most effective way to gain information. With its vast resources and convenience, the Internet allows us to access a wide range of information quickly. We can conduct online research, access academic databases, and find reliable sources for our inquiries. Moreover, the Internet provides various multimedia formats, such as videos and interactive tutorials, that enhance our learning experience.

당신의 교수님께서 강의 중입니다. 교수님의 질문에 답하는 글을 쓰세요.

- 당신의 의견을 표현하고 뒷받침하세요
- 토론에 기여하세요

효과적인 답변은 최소한 100단어를 포함할 것입니다. 당신은 10분 동안 글을 작성할 수 있습니다.

에단 교수: 오늘날의 사회에서 신뢰할 수 있고 포괄적인 정보에 접근하는 것은 중요합니다. 사람들은 필요한 정보나 데이터를 얻기 위해 다양한 방법을 사용합니다. 어떤 사람들은 주변 사람들로부터 정보를 얻는 반면, 다른 사람들은 도서관을 방문하여 자료를 수집하는 것을 선호합니다. 당신은 어떤 방법이 정보를 얻는 가장 효과적인 방법이라 생각하십니까?

다니엘: 제 의견으로는 인터넷이 정보를 얻는 데 가장 효과적인 방법입니다. 인터넷은 방대한 자원과 편의성으로 인해 우리에게 다양한 정보에 빠르게 접근할 수 있는 기회를 제공합니다. 우리는 온라인에서 연구를 할 수 있고 학술 데이터베이스에 접근하며 문의 사항에 대한 신뢰할 수 있는 출처를 찾을 수 있습니다. 게다가 인터넷은 비디오나 대화형 자습서와 같은 다양한 멀티미디어 형식을 제공하여 학습 경험을 향상시킵니다.

Judy: While I agree that the Internet is a valuable source of information, I believe that a combination of methods is essential for comprehensive knowledge. Libraries, for example, provide access to in-depth books, scholarly journals, and historical archives that may not be readily available online. They offer a quieter and focused environment for studying and conducting research.

주디: 인터넷이 정보 획득에 중요한 자원이라는 점에 동의하지만 포괄적인 지식을 얻기 위해서는 여러 방법의 조합이 중요하다고 생각합니다. 예를 들어 도서관은 깊이 있는 책, 학술 저널, 역사적 자료에 접근할 수 있는 기회를 제공하며 이러한 자료는 쉽게 온라인에서 찾을 수 없을 수도 있습니다. 도서관은 공부하고 연구를 진행할 수 있는 조용하고 몰입할 수 있는 환경을 제공합니다.

어휘 reliable **adj** 신뢰할 만한 l comprehensive **adj** 포괄적인 l acquire **v** 획득하다 l gather **v** 모으다 l range **n** 범위 l in-depth **adj** 심층적인 l archive **n** 기록 보관소

예시 답변

From my perspective, both made excellent statements, but I would like to add that the Internet is the most effective way to gain information. (but I'm on the same page as Daniel) Simply put, the Internet provides people with convenience in terms of collecting data. It's a proven fact that people can always gain a lot of information whenever they have Internet access. This has replaced traditional offline settings. Thanks to this, people don't have to go through any tedious processes. A perfect example of this is my cousin. When he was preparing for his exam, he signed up for an online class that offered a lot of information. When he visited the website, he found it had useful information and features that enabled him to learn by himself on a daily basis. As a result, he didn't need to be taught by someone in person. This illustrates how the Internet frees people from the inconvenience of offline processes when gaining information.

제 시각에서는 두 분 모두 훌륭한 주장을 하셨다고 생각하지만, 인터넷이 정보를 얻는 가장 효과적인 방법이라고 덧붙이고 싶습니다. (저는 대니엘과 동일한 의견을 가지고 있습니다.) 간단히 말해서, 인터넷은 데이터 수집 측면에서 사람들에게 편리함을 제공합니다. 인터넷에 접속할 때마다 사람들이 항상 많은 정보를 얻을 수 있다는 것은 입증된 사실입니다. 이것은 전통적인 오프라인 환경을 대체하였습니다. 덕분에 사람들은 귀찮은 과정을 거치지 않아도 됩니다. 나의 사촌이 이에 대한 좋은 예시입니다. 그가 시험 준비를 할 때, 그는 많은 정보를 제공하는 온라인 강의에 등록했습니다. 웹사이트를 방문하자, 그가 매일 학습을 할 수 있게 하는 유용한 정보와 기능이 있다는 것을 발견했습니다. 결과적으로, 그는 누군가에게 직접 배울 필요가 없었습니다. 이는 어떻게 인터넷이 정보를 얻을 때 오프라인 과정의 불편함에서 사람들을 해방해주는지를 보여 주는 사례입니다.

Lesson 07 시간의 활용 관련 주제 문단 구성

Your professor is teaching a class. Write a post responding to the professor's question.

In your response, you should:
- express and support your opinion
- make a contribution to the discussion

An effective response will contain at least 100 words.
You will have 10 minutes to write it.

Dr. Joanna: It's interesting to see the contrasting viewpoints regarding the benefits of structured plans versus the advantages of being flexible and open to new experiences. Each approach has its merits, and it ultimately depends on individual preferences and circumstances. Some people make a specific plan for their time in advance, while others make

당신의 교수님께서 강의 중입니다. 교수님의 질문에 답하는 글을 쓰세요.

- 당신의 의견을 표현하고 뒷받침하세요
- 토론에 기여하세요

효과적인 답변은 최소한 100단어를 포함할 것입니다. 당신은 10분 동안 글을 작성할 수 있습니다.

조애너 교수: 구조화된 계획과 유연하며 새로운 경험에 열린 태도의 이점에 대한 대조적인 견해를 보는 것은 흥미로운 일입니다. 각 접근법은 각각의 장점이 있으며, 결국 개인의 선호와 상황에 따라 달라집니다. 어떤 사람들은 미리 시간에 대한 구체적인 계획을 세우는 반면, 다른 사람들은 즉흥적인 계획을 세우고 흐름에 맡기는 것을 선호합니다. 여러분은 어떤 생활 방

instant plans and just go with the flow. Which lifestyle do you prefer?

Justin: Personally, I prefer making specific plans in advance. Having a well-thought-out schedule allows me to prioritize my tasks, manage my time effectively, and stay organized. By planning ahead, I can set clear goals, allocate sufficient time for each activity, and ensure that I make progress towards my objectives. This approach also helps me maintain a sense of discipline and focus, as I have a road map to guide my actions.

Anna: I personally prefer going with the flow. I find that being spontaneous allows me to embrace new opportunities, adapt to unexpected situations, and remain flexible. Sometimes, rigid plans can limit creativity and prevent me from exploring different avenues. By going with the flow, I can seize the present moment, follow my instincts, and embrace serendipity. It allows me to be more open-minded, responsive to changes, and comfortable with uncertainty.

식을 선호하시나요?

저스틴: 개인적으로 저는 사전에 구체적인 계획을 세우는 것을 선호합니다. 신중하게 계획된 일정을 가지면 작업의 우선순위를 정하고 시간을 효과적으로 관리하며 조직적으로 일할 수 있습니다. 사전에 계획을 세우면 명확한 목표를 설정하고 각 활동에 충분한 시간을 할당하며 목표에 대한 진전을 확실히 할 수 있습니다. 또한 이 접근법은 행동을 안내할 로드맵이 있기 때문에 훈련과 집중감을 유지하는 데 도움이 됩니다.

애나: 저는 개인적으로 흐름에 맡기는 것을 선호합니다. 저는 즉흥적으로 행동하는 것이 새로운 기회를 포용하고 예상치 못한 상황에 적응하며 유연할 수 있게 해 준다고 생각합니다. 때로는 엄격한 계획이 창의성을 제한하고 다양한 가능성을 탐험하는 것을 방해할 수 있습니다. 흐름에 따라가면서 현재의 순간을 즐길 수 있으며 직관에 따라 행동할 수 있고 우연을 받아들일 수 있습니다. 이는 저를 더 개방적이고 변화에 민감하며 불확실성에 편안하게 만듭니다.

어휘 structured plan 체계적인 계획 I flexible **adj** 유연한 I preference **n** 선호도 I circumstance **n** 상황 I well-thought-out 신중히 계획된 I ensure **v** 보장하다 I spontaneous **adj** 즉흥적인 I seize **v** 잡다

아웃라인

일반적 진술

making specific plan: effective time management → instant plan: time is wasted → specific plan: utilize time efficiently → handle tasks at a faster pace + focus better + outstanding performance

구체화 사례

example → cousin who used to make instant plans + go with the flow → assist professor as TA → x enough time for TA work → change lifestyle by making specific plans → save time + complete TA work on schedule

구체적인 계획을 세우는 것: 효과적인 시간 관리 → 즉석에서 만든 계획: 시간이 낭비 됨 → 구체적 계획: 효과적으로 시간 활용 → 일들을 좀 더 빠른 속도로 다루게 됨 + 집중을 더 잘하게 됨 + 눈에 띄는 성과를 거두게 됨

예시 → 즉석에서 계획을 세우고 흐름에 맡기는 사촌 → 교수를 조교로서 도움 → 조교 업무를 하기엔 충분치 못한 시간 → 구체적인 계획들을 세우는 것으로 라이프 스타일 변화를 시도함 → 시간 절약 + 일정대로 조교 업무를 완료

예시 답변

일반적 진술

From my perspective, both made excellent statements, but I'm on the same page as Justin. Simply put, making specific plans in advance can significantly contribute to effective time management. It's a proven fact that a considerable amount of time is wasted when people make instant plans and simply go with the flow. Having a specific plan helps individuals utilize their time more efficiently. In detail, it enables workers to handle various tasks at a faster pace, allowing them to focus better and show more outstanding performance.

제 시각에서는 두 분 모두 훌륭한 주장을 하셨다고 생각하지만, 저는 저스틴과 동일한 의견을 가지고 있습니다. 간단히 말해서, 미리 구체적인 계획을 세우는 것은 효과적인 시간 관리에 큰 기여를 할 수 있다고 생각합니다. 즉석에서 계획을 세우고 흐름에 맡기는 경우에는 상당한 시간이 낭비된다는 것이 입증된 사실입니다. 구체적인 계획을 가지는 것은 개인이 시간을 더 효율적으로 활용할 수 있게 도와줍니다. 자세히 말하면, 이는 근로자들이 다양한 업무를 더 빠른 속도로 처리하도록 하여 더 집중하고 뛰어난 성과를 내도록 돕습니다.

구체화 사례

A perfect example of this is my cousin, who used to make instant plans and go with the flow in everything he did. When he worked as a teaching assistant, he had to assist his professor with research. Everything went smoothly except for one thing: he didn't have enough time to complete the TA work, which involved collecting a substantial amount of research data, due to his part-time job after school. One day, he decided to change his lifestyle by making specific plans for his time in advance. Thanks to this change, he ended up saving a substantial amount of time and completed his TA work on schedule.

이에 대한 완벽한 예시로는 저의 사촌이 있는데, 그는 이전에 모든 것을 즉석에서 계획하고 흐름에 맡기던 사람이었습니다. 그가 교수 조교로 일할 때, 교수님의 연구를 도와야 했습니다. 모든 것은 원활하게 진행되었지만 한 가지 문제가 있었습니다. 방과 후 아르바이트 때문에 많은 연구 데이터를 수집해야 했던 조교 업무를 마무리하는 데 충분한 시간이 없었습니다. 어느 날, 그는 미리 시간에 대한 구체적인 계획을 세우기로 결정했습니다. 이 변화 덕분에 그는 상당한 시간을 절약하고 조교 업무를 예정대로 완료할 수 있었습니다.

Practice

Q

Your professor is teaching a class. Write a post responding to the professor's question.

In your response, you should:
- express and support your opinion
- make a contribution to the discussion

An effective response will contain at least 100 words.
You will have 10 minutes to write it.

Dr. Joanna: It's evident that technology has brought about significant benefits, but it's important to consider the potential challenges and societal implications as well. I would like to share your insights on the impact of technology on our world. Technology has made the world a better place to live. Do you agree or disagree?

Justin: I agree with the statement. Technology has revolutionized various aspects of our lives, leading to significant improvements in many areas. For instance, advancements in healthcare technology have enhanced medical treatments, increased life expectancy, and improved the overall well-being of individuals.

Anna: While I acknowledge the benefits of technology, I also believe that it has its drawbacks. One of the major concerns is the impact of technology on social interactions. With the rise of smartphones and social media, people are becoming more isolated and less engaged in face-to-face interactions. There is a risk of losing genuine human connections and fostering a sense of loneliness.

당신의 교수님께서 강의 중입니다. 교수님의 질문에 답하는 글을 쓰세요.

- 당신의 의견을 표현하고 뒷받침하세요
- 토론에 기여하세요

효과적인 답변은 최소한 100단어를 포함할 것입니다. 당신은 10분 동안 글을 작성할 수 있습니다.

조애너 교수: 기술은 상당한 이점을 가져 온 것은 분명하지만 잠재적인 도전과 사회적 영향도 고려하는 것이 중요합니다. 기술이 우리 세계에 미치는 영향에 대한 여러분의 의견을 나누고 싶습니다. 기술은 세계를 살기 좋은 곳으로 만들었습니다. 동의하십니까 아니면 동의하지 않으십니까?

저스틴: 그 주장에 동의합니다. 기술은 우리 삶의 여러 측면을 혁신하여 다양한 분야에서 큰 향상을 이뤄냈습니다. 예를 들어, 의료 기술의 발전으로 의료 치료가 향상되었고, 수명이 연장했으며, 개인의 전반적인 안녕이 증진됐습니다.

애나: 기술의 이점을 인정하는 한편, 그것은 단점도 가지고 있다고 생각합니다. 주요 우려 중 하나는 기술이 사회적 교류에 미치는 영향입니다. 스마트폰과 소셜 미디어의 등장으로 인해 사람들은 더욱 고립되고 대면 상호 작용에 덜 참여하게 되고 있습니다. 진정한 인간관계를 상실하고 고독감을 조장할 위험이 있습니다.

어휘 **evident** adj 명백한 | **implication** n 영향 | **life expectancy** 기대 수명 | **drawback** n 단점 | **interaction** n 상호 작용 | **genuine** adj 진정한 | **foster** v 조장하다, 육성하다 | **loneliness** n 외로움

From my perspective, both made excellent statements, but I'm on the same page as Justin. Simply put, advanced technology can significantly contribute to effective time management. It's a proven fact that a considerable amount of time is wasted when people do their work without the help of technology. Advanced technology helps individuals utilize their time more efficiently. In detail, it enables workers to handle various tasks at a faster pace, allowing them to focus better and show more outstanding performance. A perfect example of this is my cousin. When he worked as a teaching assistant, he had to assist his professor with research. Everything went smoothly except for one thing: he didn't have enough time to communicate with his professor because of his part-time job after school. One day, he decided to use online messenger to communicate with his professor. Thanks to this technology, he ended up saving a substantial amount of time and completed his TA work on schedule.

제 시각에서는 두 분 모두 훌륭한 주장을 하셨다고 생각하지만, 저는 저스틴과 동일한 의견을 가지고 있습니다. 간단히 말해서, 선진 기술은 효과적인 시간 관리에 상당한 기여를 할 수 있다고 생각합니다. 기술의 도움 없이 일을 처리할 때 상당한 시간이 낭비된다는 것은 입증된 사실입니다. 선진 기술은 개인이 시간을 더 효율적으로 활용할 수 있게 도와줍니다. 자세히 말하면, 이는 근로자들이 다양한 업무를 더 빠른 속도로 처리하도록 하여 더 집중하고 뛰어난 성과를 내도록 돕습니다. 이에 대한 완벽한 예시로는 저의 사촌이 있습니다. 그는 교수 조교로 일할 때, 교수님의 연구를 도와야 했습니다. 모든 것이 원활하게 진행되었지만 한 가지 문제가 있었습니다. 방과 후 아르바이트로 인해 교수님과 소통할 충분한 시간이 없었습니다. 어느 날 그는 교수님과 소통하기 위해 온라인 메신저를 사용하기로 결정했습니다. 이 기술 덕분에 그는 상당한 시간을 절약하고 조교 업무를 계획대로 완료할 수 있었습니다.

Test

본서 ▶ P. 182

Q1

Your professor is teaching a class. Write a post responding to the professor's question.

In your response, you should:
- express and support your opinion
- make a contribution to the discussion

An effective response will contain at least 100 words.
You will have 10 minutes to write it.

Dr. Liam: Today, we will explore a topic that revolves around the different modes of communication. Our focus will be on the statement that face-to-face communication is superior to other forms, such as letters, emails, or telephone calls. We will examine the reasons and details behind this assertion. Do you agree or disagree that face-to-face communication is superior to other types of communication? Support your answer with specific reasons and details.

Jacob: I strongly agree with the statement. Face-to-face communication allows for nonverbal cues, such as facial expressions and body language, which enhance understanding and build stronger connections between individuals. It also enables immediate feedback and promotes active listening, leading to more effective and meaningful interactions.

당신의 교수님께서 강의 중입니다. 교수님의 질문에 답하는 글을 쓰세요.

- 당신의 의견을 표현하고 뒷받침하세요
- 토론에 기여하세요

효과적인 답변은 최소한 100단어를 포함할 것입니다. 당신은 10분 동안 글을 작성할 수 있습니다.

리암 교수: 오늘은 서로 다른 의사소통 방식을 중심으로 한 주제를 다루어 보겠습니다. 우리의 초점은 대면 소통이 편지, 이메일, 또는 전화 등 다른 형태의 소통보다 우월하다는 주장에 있습니다. 이 주장의 이유와 세부 내용을 살펴보겠습니다. 대면 소통이 다른 형태의 소통보다 우월하다고 생각하십니까 아니면 그렇지 않다고 생각하십니까? 구체적인 이유와 세부 내용을 통해 답해 주세요.

제이콥: 해당 주장에 강력하게 동의합니다. 대면 소통은 표정과 몸짓과 같은 비언어적인 단서를 허용하여 이해를 증진하고 개인 간의 더 강한 연결을 형성할 수 있게 합니다. 또한 즉각적인 피드백을 가능하게 하며 적극적인 청취를 촉진하여 더 효과적이고 의미 있는 상호 작용으로 이어집니다.

Test

Academic Discussion Task

Bella: While I acknowledge the benefits of face-to-face communication, I believe that other forms of communication can be equally valuable. In today's fast-paced world, digital communication offers convenience, allowing people to connect regardless of physical distance. Additionally, written communication provides a permanent record and allows for careful articulation of thoughts, which can be especially important in professional settings.

벨라: 대면 소통의 이점을 인정하면서도, 다른 형태의 소통도 동등하게 가치 있을 수 있다고 생각합니다. 현대의 급변하는 세계에서 디지털 소통은 물리적 거리에 관계없이 사람들이 연결될 수 있도록 편의를 제공합니다. 게다가 서면 소통은 영구적인 기록을 제공하며 생각을 신중하게 표현할 수 있는 기회를 제공하여 전문적인 환경에서 특히 중요할 수 있습니다.

어휘 revolve [v] ~에 관한 것을 다루다 l assertion [n] 주장 l nonverbal cue 비언어적 신호 l immediate [adj] 즉각적인 l fast-paced [adj] 빠른 속도의 l regardless of ~에 관계없이 l articulation [n] 명료한 표현

예시 답변

From my perspective, both made excellent statements, but I'm on the same page as Bella. Simply put, online communication methods provide people with convenience when communicating with others. It is a proven fact that people can always communicate with others whenever they have Internet access. This has replaced traditional offline settings. Thanks to this, people don't have to go through any tedious process. A perfect example of this is my cousin. When his friend moved to another city, he signed up for an online video chat platform that offered a variety of functions. When he saw the website, he thought it had useful features that enabled him to communicate with his friend on a daily basis. Hence, he didn't need to travel a long distance in person. This illustrates how the Internet frees people from the inconvenience of offline processes when communicating with others.

제 시각에서는 두 분 모두 훌륭한 주장을 하셨다고 생각하지만, 저는 벨라와 동일한 의견을 가지고 있습니다. 간단히 말해서, 온라인 소통 방법은 사람들이 다른 사람들과 소통할 때 편의를 제공합니다. 인터넷에 접속이 가능한 경우 언제든지 사람들은 다른 사람들과 소통할 수 있다는 것은 입증된 사실입니다. 이는 전통적인 오프라인 환경을 대체하였습니다. 이 덕분에 사람들은 귀찮은 과정을 거치지 않아도 됩니다. 이에 관한 완벽한 예시로는 저의 사촌이 있습니다. 그의 친구가 다른 도시로 이사를 가자 그는 다양한 기능을 제공하는 온라인 비디오 채팅 플랫폼에 가입했습니다. 그가 웹사이트를 방문하자, 그는 친구와 매일 소통할 수 있도록 도와주는 유용한 기능이 있다는 것을 발견했습니다. 결과적으로, 그는 직접 멀리 여행할 필요가 없었습니다. 이는 인터넷이 다른 사람들과 소통할 때 오프라인 과정의 불편함에서 사람들을 어떻게 해방해주는지를 보여 주는 사례입니다.

Q2

Your professor is teaching a class. Write a post responding to the professor's question.

In your response, you should:
- express and support your opinion
- make a contribution to the discussion

An effective response will contain at least 100 words.
You will have 10 minutes to write it.

Dr. Catherine: Today, our discussion will revolve around the importance of maintaining friendships. Specifically, we will explore the statement that the ability to maintain friendships with a small number of people over a long period of time is more crucial for happiness than the ability to easily make many new friends. Do you agree or disagree that the ability to maintain long-term friendships is more crucial for happiness

당신의 교수님께서 강의 중입니다. 교수님의 질문에 답하는 글을 쓰세요.

- 당신의 의견을 표현하고 뒷받침하세요
- 토론에 기여하세요

효과적인 답변은 최소한 100단어를 포함할 것입니다.
당신은 10분 동안 글을 작성할 수 있습니다.

캐서린 교수: 오늘은 우리의 토론은 오랫동안 친구 관계를 유지하는 것의 중요성에 중점을 둘 것입니다. 구체적으로는 많은 새로운 친구를 쉽게 사귀는 능력보다는 소수의 사람들과 오랜 기간에 걸쳐 친구 관계를 유지하는 능력이 행복에 더 중요하다는 진술에 대해 다루어 볼 것입니다. 새로운 친구를 쉽게 사귀는 능력보다는 오랫동안 친구 관계를 유지하는 능력이 행복에 더 중요하다라는 진술에 동의하십니까 그렇지 않

than the ability to make many new friends easily? Provide specific reasons and examples to support your viewpoint.

Isaac: I completely agree with the statement. Long-term friendships provide a sense of deep connection, trust, and support that is essential for lasting happiness. These friendships often involve shared experiences, memories, and a deep understanding of one another, which cannot be easily replicated in new friendships.

Dorothy: While I agree that long-term friendships have their value, I believe that the ability to make new friends easily is equally important. As life evolves, circumstances change, and new opportunities arise, having the flexibility to connect with new individuals can expand our perspectives, introduce us to diverse experiences, and provide fresh sources of happiness.

으십니까? 당신의 견해를 뒷받침하기 위해 구체적인 이유와 예시를 제시해 주세요.

아이삭: 해당 주장에 완전히 동의합니다. 오랫동안 유지되는 친구 관계는 지속적인 행복을 위해 필수적인 깊은 연결, 신뢰, 그리고 지지를 줍니다. 이러한 친구 관계는 종종 공유된 경험, 추억, 서로에 대한 심층적인 이해를 포함하며, 이러한 것들은 새로운 친구 관계에서 쉽게 똑같이 만들어질 수 없습니다.

도로시: 오랫동안의 친구 관계가 가치 있다는 점에 동의하지만, 저는 새로운 친구를 쉽게 만드는 능력이 똑같이 중요하다고 믿습니다. 삶이 변화하고 상황이 바뀌며 새로운 기회가 나타날 때, 새로운 개인들과 연결할 수 있는 유연성을 가지는 것은 우리의 시야를 확장하고 다양한 경험을 소개하며 새로운 행복의 원천을 제공할 수 있습니다.

어휘 crucial **adj** 중대한 I long-term friendship 오래 지속되는 우정 I trust **n** 신뢰 I shared experience 함께한 경험 I replicate **v** 복제하다 I arise **v** 생기다, 일어나다 I expand **v** 확장하다

예시 답변

From my perspective, both made excellent statements, but I'm on the same page as Dorothy. Simply put, making numerous new friends enables people to gain a lot of inspiration and broaden their perspectives. While interacting with numerous new friends, people gain exposure to many different matters they haven't experienced before. This provides them with valuable insights they need as they navigate unpredictable situations in the future. A perfect example of this is a close friend of mine whose father was a diplomat traveling the world. Due to his father's job, he often moved and had a chance to interact with people from diverse backgrounds. He said that even though it was challenging to lead such a lifestyle, it was exciting and happy to learn how to embrace diversity. In fact, when participating in social events with him, I kept my distance from different people, whereas he was open-minded to people from various backgrounds because he had experienced similar situations before. Furthermore, there were no uncomfortable or awkward moments between him and others.

제 시각에서는 두 분 모두 훌륭한 주장을 하셨다고 생각하지만, 저는 도로시와 동일한 의견을 가지고 있습니다. 간단히 말해서, 많은 새로운 친구를 사귀는 것은 사람들에게 많은 영감을 주고 시야를 확장할 수 있게 만듭니다. 다양한 새로운 친구와 소통하면서 사람들은 이전에 경험하지 못한 다양한 상황에 노출됩니다. 이는 미래의 예측할 수 없는 상황에서 필요한 소중한 통찰력을 제공합니다. 이에 관한 완벽한 예로 언급할 만한 것은 아버지가 세계를 여행하는 외교관이었던 저의 친한 친구 중 한 명입니다. 아버지의 직업 때문에 그는 자주 이사를 다녔고 다양한 배경을 가진 사람들과 소통할 기회가 있었습니다. 그는 이러한 생활 방식이 힘들었지만, 다양성을 포용하는 법을 배우는 것이 흥미롭고 행복했다고 말했습니다. 실제로 그와 함께 사회적인 행사에 참여할 때, 저는 다른 사람들과 거리를 두었지만, 그는 이전에 비슷한 상황을 경험했기 때문에 다양한 배경의 사람들에게 열린 마음을 가졌습니다. 게다가, 그와 다른 사람들 간에 불편하거나 어색한 순간은 전혀 없었습니다.

Actual Test 1

본서 ┃ P. 188

Question 1

`Reading`

In the late 14th century, an unknown poet from the Midlands composed four poems titled *Pearl*, *Sir Gawain and the Green Knight*, *Patience*, and *Cleanness*. This collection of poems is referred to as *Cotton Nero A.x* and the author is often referred to as the Pearl Poet. Up to this day, there have been many theories regarding the identity of this poet, and these are three of the most popular ones.

The first theory is that the author's name was Hugh, and it is based on the *Chronicle of Andrew of Wyntoun*. In the chronicle, an author called Hucheon (little Hugh) is credited with writing three poems, one of which is about the adventures of Gawain. Not only that, but all three poems are written in alliterative verse, as are all four of the poems in *Cotton Nero A.x*. Since they are written in the same style and one poem from each set concerns Gawain, some people contend that all of the *Cotton Nero A.x* poems were written by Hugh.

The second theory is that John Massey was the poet, and it is supported by another poem called *St. Erkenwald* and penmanship. Although the actual authorship of *St. Erkenwald* is unknown, John Massey was a poet who lived in the correct area and time for scholars to attribute it to him. This manuscript was written in very similar handwriting to that of the Pearl Poet, which indicates that one person is likely the author of all five of the poems.

The third theory is that the poems were actually written by different authors from the same region of England. This comes from the fact that there is little linking the poems to each other. Two are concerned with the Arthur legends, but the only link connecting the other two is that they describe the same area of the countryside. They also seem to be written in the same dialect. Taken together, these facts indicate that they were written in the same region, but they probably were not written by the same person.

14세기 말, 잉글랜드 중부 지방 출신의 한 무명 시인은 〈진주〉, 〈거웨인 경과 녹색 기사〉, 〈인내〉, 〈순수〉라는 제목의 시 네 편을 썼다. 이 시집은 〈코튼 네로 A.x〉라고 불리며 저자는 흔히 펄 시인이라고 불린다. 오늘날까지 이 시인의 정체에 관한 많은 이론들이 있었고, 다음이 가장 널리 퍼진 세 가지 이론이다.

첫 번째 이론은 저자의 이름이 '휴'라는 것으로, 〈윈턴의 앤드류의 연대기〉에 근거를 둔다. 이 연대기에서는 휴천(작은 휴)이라는 저자가 세 편의 시를 썼다고 하는데, 그중 하나가 거웨인의 모험에 관한 것이다. 그뿐 아니라 세 편의 시는 모두 〈코튼 네로 A.x〉에 있는 네 편의 시와 마찬가지로 두운체로 쓰였다. 그 시들이 같은 문체로 쓰였으며 각 세트에 거웨인을 다루는 시가 한 편씩 있으므로 일부 사람들은 〈코튼 네로 A.x〉에 실려 있는 시를 모두 휴가 썼을 거라고 주장한다.

두 번째 이론은 존 매시가 시인이라는 것이며, 이는 〈성 어컨월드〉라는 또 다른 시와 필체가 뒷받침한다. 〈성 어컨월드〉의 실제 원저자는 알려져있지 않지만 존 매시가 해당 지역과 시기에 살았던 시인이었기에 학자들은 그가 저자일 것이라고 추정한다. 이 원고는 펄 시인의 원고와 매우 비슷한 필적으로 쓰였으며, 이는 한 사람이 시 다섯 편을 모두 쓴 저자일 가능성이 높다는 것을 나타낸다.

세 번째 이론은 그 시들이 잉글랜드의 같은 지역에 살던 각기 다른 저자들의 작품이라는 이론이다. 이는 시들 사이에 연관성이 거의 없다는 사실에서 기인한다. 두 편의 시는 아서 왕의 전설과 관련이 있긴 하지만 다른 두 편의 시를 잇는 연결 고리는 그 시골의 같은 지역을 묘사하고 있다는 것뿐이다. 또한 그 시들은 같은 방언으로 쓰인 것으로 보인다. 종합해보면 이런 사실들은 그 시들이 같은 지역에서 쓰였지만 같은 사람에 의해 쓰인 것은 아닐지도 모른다는 것을 나타낸다.

어휘   poet ⓝ 시인 ┃ the Midlands 잉글랜드 중부 지방 ┃ compose ⓥ 쓰다, 구성하다 ┃ up to this day 오늘날까지 ┃ identity ⓝ 정체, 신원, 정체성 ┃ chronicle ⓝ 연대기 ┃ be credited with ~이 있다고 간주되다 ┃ alliterative ⓐⓓⓙ 두운체의 ┃ verse ⓝ 운문, 시, (시의) 연, (노래의) 절 ┃ penmanship ⓝ 필체, 서법 ┃ authorship ⓝ (원)저자 ┃ attribute ⓥ ~것이라고 보다 ┃ manuscript ⓝ 원고, 필사본 ┃ handwriting ⓝ 친필, 필적 ┃ be concerned with ~와 관련이 있다 ┃ dialect ⓝ 방언, 사투리

`Listening`

Due to the fact that the author failed to sign his manuscript,

저자가 자신의 원고에 서명하지 못했다는 사실 때문

the true identity of the Pearl Poet may never be known. The text that you read for your homework detailed three theories that people have suggested regarding his identity, but they are all flawed in serious ways.

The first theory that the author was a man named Hugh seems plausible at first, but upon further examination that idea falls apart. The *Chronicle of Andrew of Wyntoun* speaks of a poet named Hucheon, who was writing around the appropriate time about related topics and in the same style as the poems in *Cotton Nero A.x.* However, this theory overlooks one significant factor, the dialect in which the poems were written. Hucheon's poems were written in a Yorkshire dialect, whereas the Pearl Poet wrote in a Midlands dialect closer to those of Staffordshire or Cheshire. Therefore, it is highly unlikely that Hucheon was the Pearl Poet.

The second theory that the Pearl Poet was John Massey is also difficult to support. Firstly, there is no concrete proof that Massey wrote *St. Erkenwald*, let alone the Pearl Poet's poems. The theory also points out that the Pearl Poet and John Massey had similar handwriting, but this too is problematic. The poems were all reproduced before the printing press had spread throughout Europe, so they were copied by hand. Therefore, it is possible that they were reproduced by the same scribe, but this in no way clarifies who composed them originally.

The third theory that the poems were actually written by four entirely different authors who lived in the same region is also questionable. It allows for the similar landscapes they depict and for them being written in the same dialect. However, their linguistic similarities go beyond dialect. The author actually uses many terms that he invented, and the poems share these terms. It is difficult to believe that four separate poets could have created the same words and used them, so it is clear that there was only one author.

에 펄 시인의 정체는 밝혀지지 않을지도 모릅니다. 여러분이 과제를 하기 위해 읽었던 지문에는 그의 신원에 관해 사람들이 제시한 세 가지 이론이 열거되어 있지만 모두 심각한 결함이 있습니다.

저자가 '휴'라는 사람이었다는 첫 번째 이론은 처음에는 그럴듯해 보이지만, 더 깊이 조사해보면 그 발상은 힘을 잃고 맙니다. 〈윈턴의 앤드류의 연대기〉에서는 휴천이라는 시인에 대해 언급하는데, 그 시인은 적절한 시기에 관련 주제에 대한 저술 활동을 하고 있었으며 〈코튼 네로 A.x〉에 실린 시들과 같은 문체로 썼어요. 그러나 이 이론은 한 가지 중요한 요인, 즉 시에서 쓰인 방언을 간과하고 있습니다. 휴천의 시는 요크셔 방언으로 쓰인 반면, 펄 시인은 스태퍼드셔나 체셔 지방의 것과 가까운 잉글랜드 중부 방언을 사용했어요. 그러므로 휴천이 펄 시인이었을 가능성은 매우 낮습니다.

펄 시인이 존 매시였다는 두 번째 이론 또한 옹호하기 어렵습니다. 먼저, 존 매시가 펄 시인의 시들은 고사하고 〈성 어컨월드〉의 저자라는 구체적인 증거가 없어요. 이 이론은 또한 펄 시인과 존 매시가 비슷한 필적을 가지고 있었다고 언급하는데, 여기에도 문제가 있습니다. 그 시들은 모두 인쇄기가 유럽 전역에 보급되기 전에 복제되었으므로 손으로 베껴 적었을 것입니다. 그러므로 같은 필경사가 베껴 썼을 가능성은 있습니다만 누가 그 시들을 쓴 원저자인지는 결코 명확하게 말해 주지 않아요.

그 시들이 사실 같은 지역에 살았던 네 명의 완전히 다른 저자에 의해 쓰였다는 세 번째 이론 또한 의심의 여지가 있습니다. 이는 그 시들이 비슷한 풍경을 묘사하고 있으며 같은 방언으로 쓰였다는 점을 고려한 것이지요. 그러나 그들의 언어학적 유사성은 방언의 수준을 넘어서고 있습니다. 저자는 실제로 자신이 지어낸 용어들을 다수 사용하고 있으며, 그 시들은 이런 용어들을 함께 사용하고 있습니다. 네 명의 서로 다른 시인들이 같은 단어를 지어내 사용했을 거라고 생각하기 어려우므로 저자는 단 한 명이었음이 분명합니다.

어휘 flawed **adj** 결함이 있는 | plausible **adj** 그럴듯한, 이치에 맞는 | fall apart 무너지다 | overlook **v** 간과하다 | concrete **adj** 구체적인, 사실에 의거한 | let alone ~은 고사하고 | problematic **adj** 문제가 있는 | printing press 인쇄기 | scribe **n** 필경사 | in no way 결코 ~ 않다 | allow for ~을 감안하다 | depict **v** 묘사하다 | linguistic **adj** 언어(학)의 | go beyond ~을 넘어서다

강의에서 제시한 요점을 요약하시오. 읽기 지문의 요점에 대해 강의에서 어떻게 반박하는지 설명하시오.

예시 답변

The reading gives three possible theories regarding the identity of the Pearl Poet, who wrote the four poems in a collection titled *Cotton Nero A.x.* However, the lecturer indicates that the reading's theories have flaws and errors in their arguments.

지문은 〈코튼 네로 A.x〉 시집에 있는 네 편의 시를 집필한 펄 시인의 정체에 관해 세 가지 가능한 이론을 제시한다. 그러나 강의자는 지문의 이론에서 주장하는 바에는 결함과 오류가 있다고 말한다.

Firstly, the reading proposes that the Pearl Poet was an author named Hugh. This is because his poems were written in the same style as *Cotton Nero A.x* and some of the poems concern Gawain. However, the lecturer points out that the Pearl Poet and Hugh's dialects are not the same. It is highly likely that they are the two different people who lived in different regions.

Secondly, the reading suggests that another poet named John Massey may be the author of *Cotton Nero A.x*. This is supported by the fact that the handwriting of *Cotton Nero A.x* and *St. Erkenwald*, a poem thought to have been written by John Massey, look quite similar. However, the lecturer contradicts this by arguing that the same scribe could have reproduced all the poems.

Lastly, the reading states that the poems in *Cotton Nero A.x* could have all been written by different authors. This is because there is no clear link among the four poems except for similar landscapes and the same dialect. However, the lecturer undermines this idea by saying that the author used his own invented words in all of his poems. It is hardly likely that four different people created the same words.

첫 번째로, 지문에서는 펄 시인이 휴라는 이름의 저자였다고 제시한다. 이는 그의 시들이 〈코튼 네로 A.x〉와 같은 문체로 쓰였으며 일부 시에서 거웨인을 주제로 하고 있기 때문이다. 그러나 강의자는 펄 시인과 휴가 사용한 방언이 같지 않다는 점을 지적한다. 그들은 다른 지역에 살았던 각기 다른 두 명의 인물일 가능성이 높다.

두 번째로, 지문에서는 존 매시라는 또 다른 시인이 〈코튼 네로 A.x〉의 저자일지도 모른다고 제시한다. 이것은 〈코튼 네로 A.x〉와 존 매시가 쓴 시라고 여겨지는 〈성 어컨월드〉의 필적이 매우 유사해 보인다는 사실에 의해 뒷받침된다. 그러나 강의자는 같은 필경사가 모든 시들을 베껴 썼을 수 있다고 주장하며 이를 반박한다.

마지막으로, 지문은 〈코튼 네로 A.x〉의 시들이 모두 각기 다른 저자에 의해 쓰였을 수 있다고 언급한다. 이는 비슷한 풍경과 동일한 방언을 제외하면 네 편의 시 사이에 분명한 연결 고리가 없기 때문이다. 그러나 강의자는 저자가 모든 시에서 자신이 직접 만들어 낸 단어를 사용했다고 말하면서 이 견해를 일축한다. 네 명의 각기 다른 인물이 같은 단어를 만들어 냈을 것이라고 보기는 어렵다.

어휘 contradict ⓥ 반박하다 | except for ~을 제외하고는 | undermine ⓥ 훼손시키다

Question 2

Your professor is teaching a class. Write a post responding to the professor's question.

In your response, you should:
- express and support your opinion
- make a contribution to the discussion

An effective response will contain at least 100 words.
You will have 10 minutes to write it.

Dr. Michael: Good day, class. As we navigate through the intricacies of resource allocation in universities, a pressing question emerges: "Should universities give the same amount of money to their students' sports activities as they give to their university libraries?" This topic invites us to consider the equilibrium between physical and intellectual development. In the pursuit of a comprehensive discussion, let's explore the dynamics of funding priorities.

Ian: Thank you, Professor. I find merit in the idea that universities should allocate equal funding to sports activities and libraries. While libraries are crucial for academic pursuits, sports play a pivotal role in students' holistic development. Investing in sports fosters physical well-being, teamwork, and

당신의 교수님께서 강의 중입니다. 교수님의 질문에 답하는 글을 쓰세요.

- 당신의 의견을 표현하고 뒷받침하세요
- 토론에 기여하세요

효과적인 답변은 최소한 100단어를 포함할 것입니다. 당신은 10분 동안 글을 작성할 수 있습니다.

마이클 교수: 안녕하세요, 여러분. 대학에서 자원 할당의 복잡한 사항을 다루다 보면 떠오르는 중요한 질문이 있습니다: "대학은 학생들의 스포츠 활동에 대학 도서관에 주는 것과 같은 금액을 주어야 할까요?" 이 주제는 우리에게 육체적 및 지적 발전 사이의 균형을 고려하도록 합니다. 좀 더 포괄적인 토론을 위해 자원 할당 우선순위의 역학을 다뤄 보겠습니다.

이안: 감사합니다, 교수님. 저는 대학이 도서관과 스포츠 활동에 동일한 자금을 할당해야 한다는 생각에서 장점을 찾았습니다. 도서관은 학문적 추구에 중요하며, 스포츠는 학생들의 종합적인 발전에 중요한 역할을 합니다. 스포츠에 투자하는 것은 신체적 웰빙, 팀워크, 그리고 공동체 의식을 육성합니다. 이러한 측면은 학생의 전반적인 교육 경험에 크게 기여합니다.

a sense of community. These aspects contribute significantly to a student's overall educational experience.

Linda: I appreciate Ian's perspective, but I lean towards a different stance. I believe that universities should prioritize allocating funds based on academic needs rather than equal distribution. Libraries are the heart of academic resources, supporting research, study, and intellectual growth. While sports are valuable for physical well-being, the primary mission of a university is academic excellence. Therefore, a greater allocation to libraries aligns more closely with the core educational mission of universities.

린다: 이안의 관점을 높이 평가하지만, 저는 다른 입장을 가지고 있습니다. 저는 대학이 균등한 분배보다는 학문적 필요에 따라 자금을 할당하는 것이 더 나은 것이라 생각합니다. 도서관은 연구, 공부, 지적 성장을 지원하는 학문적 자원의 중심입니다. 스포츠는 신체적 웰빙에 중요하지만, 대학의 주요 임무는 학문적 우수성입니다. 따라서 도서관에 대한 더 큰 할당이 대학의 핵심 교육 임무와 더 잘 부합한다고 생각합니다.

어휘 intricacy **n** 복잡한 사항 ǀ emerge **v** 출현하다, 드러나다 ǀ equilibrium **n** 균형 ǀ merit **n** 장점 ǀ pivotal **adj** 중요한 ǀ allocate **v** 할당하다 ǀ align **v** 일치시키다, 맞추다

예시 답변

From my perspective, both made excellent statements, but I'm on the same page as Ian. Simply put, if the university spends its budget on providing various sports activities, students can interact with many people while participating in these activities, creating an optimal condition for broadening their relationships. This is mainly because when they engage in various sports activities at school, they have more opportunities to share diverse experiences and emotions with one another. These shared experiences can potentially create opportunities for various conversations later on. A perfect example of this is a close friend of mine. He used to drift apart from his friends due to his introverted personality, having a serious problem with them. Then, one day, his school decided to allocate more budget to providing students with various sports activities. He decided to participate in these activities not only to maintain his health but also to expand his relationships with friends. At first, it seemed awkward and challenging for him to get close to new people through the activities, but it gradually got better. The people playing sports together slowly opened up to him, and a strong bond was developed between him and his friends.

제 관점에서는 두 사람 모두 훌륭한 주장을 했지만, 저는 이안과 동일한 의견입니다. 간단히 말해서, 대학이 예산을 다양한 스포츠 활동 제공에 사용한다면 학생들은 이러한 활동에 참여하면서 많은 사람들과 상호작용할 수 있어 관계를 확장하기에 최적의 상태를 만들 수 있습니다. 학교에서 다양한 스포츠 활동에 참여할 때 다양한 경험과 감정을 공유할 수 있는 기회가 더 많아집니다. 이러한 공유된 경험은 나중에 다양한 대화의 기회를 만들 수 있습니다. 저의 친한 친구 중 한 명이 이를 완벽하게 보여 줍니다. 그는 내성적인 성격 때문에 친구들과 멀어져 그들과 심각한 문제가 있었습니다. 그런데 어느 날 학교에서는 학생들에게 다양한 스포츠 활동을 제공하기 위해 예산을 더 할당하기로 결정했습니다. 그는 이러한 활동에 참여함으로써 건강을 유지하는 것뿐만 아니라 친구들과의 관계를 확장하기로 결정했습니다. 처음에 그는 새로운 사람들과 가까워지는 것이 서투르고 어려웠지만, 그것은 점차 좋아졌습니다. 함께 스포츠를 하는 사람들이 그에게 마음을 열며 그와 친구들 간에 강한 유대감이 형성되었습니다.

Actual Test 2

본서 ǀ P. 192

Question 1

Reading

Researchers have found that wind turbines kill hundreds of thousands of bats every year. This mostly happens because many migrating bat species fly through areas where wind farms are built, but even non-migrating species are being killed. For this reason, it is important to develop ways to

연구자들은 풍력 발전용 터빈으로 인해 매년 수많은 박쥐가 죽는다는 사실을 발견했다. 이는 대개 이주하는 대다수 박쥐들이 풍력 발전 단지가 세워진 지역들을 통과하여 날아가기 때문에 일어나는 현상인데, 이주하지 않는 박쥐조차 죽임을 당한다. 이러한 이유로

protect bats from wind turbines. Here are three strategies that could help to protect bats.

First, the most basic solution is to avoid building wind turbines in areas where bats are common. Since migrating bats follow the same paths every year, it is easy to figure out where they usually fly and not build in those areas. Bat species that do not migrate usually sleep in caves, and these are also easy to locate and avoid. By carefully researching where bats live and fly, we can build wind farms in areas where they will have little effect on bats.

Second, power companies can protect bats by changing their operating schedules. They can shut down their turbines at night, when bats are most active. If the turbines are not moving, the bats can safely fly around them. This would have little effect on the power companies since the demand for electricity is much lower at night. In fact, one wind power company in the U.S. tested out this method, and they reported far fewer bat deaths with only a tiny loss in annual power generation.

Third, the power companies can use radar to discourage the bats from coming near the turbines. Bats dislike radar waves, which is why they usually avoid areas where radar is used, like airports. So if radar emitters are installed in wind farms and on wind turbines, that will make the bats avoid the area. This method would be ideal, since it keeps the bats safe and allows the wind turbines to operate at any time.

풍력 발전용 터빈으로부터 박쥐를 보호하는 방법을 강구해 내는 것이 중요하다. 박쥐를 보호하는 데 도움을 줄 수 있는 세 가지 전략들이 있다.

첫째, 가장 기본적인 해결책은 박쥐들이 흔한 지역에 풍력 발전용 터빈을 설치하는 것을 피하는 것이다. 이주하는 박쥐들은 매년 같은 경로를 따라가기 때문에, 그들이 통상 날아가는 곳을 파악해서 그 지역에 설치하지 않는 것은 쉬운 일이다. 이주하지 않는 박쥐들은 보통 동굴에서 잠을 자며, 이 동굴을 찾아내 피하기는 쉽다. 박쥐들이 사는 곳과 날아다니는 곳을 신중히 조사함으로써, 박쥐에게 영향을 거의 주지 않는 지역에 풍력 발전 단지를 조성할 수 있다.

둘째, 전력 회사들은 가동 일정을 변경함으로써 박쥐를 보호할 수 있다. 박쥐가 가장 활동적인 밤 시간대에 터빈을 꺼 두면 된다. 터빈이 가동되지 않으면 박쥐들은 그 주변을 안전하게 날아다닐 수 있다. 전기 수요가 밤에는 현저히 낮기 때문에 전력 회사에 별 지장이 없을 것이다. 실제로 미국의 한 풍력 발전소가 이 방법을 시험했는데, 연간 발전량을 극미량만 감소시키면서 박쥐 살상을 상당히 줄였다고 보고했다.

셋째, 전력 회사들은 레이더(전파 탐지기)를 사용하여 박쥐들이 터빈 근처로 오는 것을 막을 수 있다. 박쥐들은 레이더파를 싫어하는데, 이것이 박쥐들이 공항처럼 레이더가 사용되는 지역을 피하는 이유이다. 그래서 레이더 방출기가 풍력 발전 단지와 풍력 발전용 터빈에 설치된다면, 박쥐가 그 지역을 피하게 될 것이다. 이 방법은 박쥐를 안전하게 보호하면서도 풍력 발전용 터빈을 언제든 가동할 수 있다는 점에서 이상적이라고 할 수 있다.

어휘 migrate ◪ 이동하다, 이주하다 | wind farm 풍력 발전 단지 | strategy ◐ 전략, 계획 | locate ◪ ~의 정확한 위치를 찾아내다 | operate ◪ 작동하다, 가동하다 | shut down 정지시키다 | demand ◐ 수요 | annual **adj** 매년의, 연례의 | power generation 발전(發電) | discourage ◪ 막다, 말리다 | install ◪ 설치하다 | ideal **adj** 이상적인

Listening

Bats live long lives, but they reproduce slowly. This combination makes them very vulnerable because they cannot respond quickly when a large number of them are killed. This is why it is so important to protect them from wind turbines, which kill hundreds of thousands of them. However, the strategies suggested in the reading would be ineffective.

First, the reading explains that it is easy to determine where bats often fly. That is true, but it does not mean that we can simply avoid building wind turbines in those areas. Wind turbines must be built on high ground where the wind is strongest, but these areas are where bats like to fly. Bats do not usually like lowland areas because the air does not move as much, and there are fewer insects to catch. Thus,

박쥐는 수명이 길지만, 번식을 느리게 하지요. 이 두 가지 사실 때문에 박쥐들은 매우 취약한데, 많은 수의 박쥐들이 죽으면 빨리 대응을 할 수 없기 때문입니다. 이것이 수많은 박쥐를 살상하는 풍력 발전용 터빈에서 박쥐를 보호하는 것이 아주 중요한 이유입니다. 하지만, 지문에서 제시된 전략들은 효과가 없을 것입니다.

첫째로, 지문은 박쥐들이 자주 날아다니는 곳을 알아내기가 쉽다고 설명하고 있습니다. 그것이 사실이긴 하지만, 그렇다고 해서 우리가 그 지역에 풍력 발전용 터빈을 짓는 것을 단순히 피할 수 있다는 건 아닙니다. 풍력 발전용 터빈은 바람이 가장 강한, 고도가 높은 지역에 설치해야만 하는데, 이런 지역은 박쥐들이 즐겨 날아다니는 곳입니다. 박쥐들은 보통 저지대를

separating wind turbines and bats is nearly impossible.

Second, shutting wind turbines down at night would prevent the turbine blades from killing flying bats. But keeping the turbines still at night creates a new problem. During the daytime, bats often sleep in trees or any other tall structure, including wind turbines. Many bats would land on turbines in the early morning to rest. When the turbines started to operate, they would kill the bats that are sleeping in the machinery. Therefore, only operating in the daytime would not protect bats.

Third, it is true that bats dislike radar, and they would definitely avoid wind turbines with radar emitters. However, bats have a very good reason to dislike radar: it hurts them. Even brief exposure to radar waves can damage their reproductive organs, which prevents them from having babies. Radar emitters would keep the turbines from killing bats directly, but the emitters would cause the bat population to decline. So using radar would have the opposite effect from the one it is intended to have.

좋아하지 않는데, 그 이유는 공기가 그만큼 많이 이동하지 않고, 잡아먹을 곤충이 적기 때문입니다. 그래서 풍력 발전용 터빈과 박쥐를 떼어놓기란 거의 불가능해요.

둘째로, 풍력 발전용 터빈을 밤에 중단시키는 것은 날아다니는 박쥐들이 터빈의 날에 맞아 죽는 것을 예방할 수 있을지도 모릅니다. 하지만 밤에 터빈을 중지시키는 것은 인해 새로운 문제를 일으킵니다. 낮에는 박쥐들이 주로 나무나 풍력 발전용 터빈 같은 높은 구조물에서 잠을 잡니다. 많은 박쥐들이 이른 아침에 휴식을 취하기 위해 터빈에 내려앉습니다. 터빈이 작동하기 시작하면 그 장치에서 자고 있던 박쥐들이 죽게 됩니다. 그래서 낮에 가동하는 것만으로는 박쥐를 보호할 수 없습니다.

셋째로, 박쥐들이 레이더를 싫어하는 것은 사실이고, 그래서 레이더 방출기가 달린 풍력 발전용 터빈을 피할 거라는 점은 분명하죠. 하지만 이렇게 박쥐들이 레이더를 싫어하는 데는 그만한 이유가 있습니다. 자신들을 해치기 때문입니다. 레이더파에 잠깐만 노출되어도 생식 기관이 손상될 수 있는데, 이는 임신을 막습니다. 레이더 방출기로 터빈이 박쥐를 직접적으로 죽이는 것을 막을 수 있을지는 모르지만, 방출기가 박쥐의 개체 수 감소를 야기할 수도 있습니다. 그래서 레이더 사용은 의도하는 바와 정반대 효과를 가져올 수도 있습니다.

어휘   reproduce ⓥ 번식하다 Ι vulnerable adj 취약한, 연약한 Ι ineffective adj 효과 없는 Ι lowland adj 저지대의 Ι separate ⓥ 분리하다, 떼어놓다 Ι blade ⓝ (칼이나 도구 등의) 날 Ι exposure ⓝ 노출 Ι reproductive organ 생식 기관 Ι population ⓝ 개체 수 Ι decline ⓥ 감소하다, 줄어들다 Ι opposite adj 정반대의 Ι intend to~ 하려고 하다, ~할 작정이다

강의에서 제시한 요점을 요약하시오. 읽기 지문의 요점에 대해 강의에서 어떻게 반박하는지 설명하시오.

예시 답변

The reading and the lecture both talk about the dangers posed to bats by wind turbines. The reading says that it is not difficult to solve this problem by using several strategies. However, the lecturer argues that the strategies suggested in the reading would not be effective.

Firstly, the reading says that it is easy to locate where bats usually fly because they follow the same paths every year when they migrate. We should not build wind turbines in those areas. However, the lecturer says it is almost impossible to separate bats and turbines in that way because the places liked by bats and the ones suitable for building turbines are the same.

Secondly, the reading suggests the strategy of shutting down wind turbines at night when bats are active. Since the demand for electricity is quite low at night, it would not cause much

지문과 강의 모두 풍력 발전용 터빈이 박쥐에게 끼치는 위험에 관해 이야기하고 있다. 지문에서는 몇 가지 전략을 사용하여 이 문제를 해결하는 것이 어렵지 않다고 말한다. 하지만 강의자는 지문에서 제시한 전략들이 효과가 없을 거라고 주장한다.

첫째로, 지문에서는 박쥐들이 매년 이주할 때마다 같은 경로를 따르기 때문에 그들이 통상적으로 날아다니는 곳을 파악하기가 쉽다고 말한다. 그 지역에 터빈을 설치하지 않으면 되는 것이다. 하지만 강의자는 박쥐들이 좋아하는 장소와 풍력 발전용 터빈을 설치하기에 적합한 장소가 일치하기 때문에 이런 식으로 그 둘을 떼어놓기가 거의 불가능하다고 말한다.

둘째로, 지문은 전력 회사들이 박쥐가 주로 활동하는 밤에 터빈을 잠시 꺼 두는 방법을 제시한다. 밤에는 전기 수요가 적기 때문에 전력 회사에 큰 손실을 끼치

harm to power companies. However, according to the lecturer, if they stopped the turbines at night, bats that land on turbines to sleep would be killed by them once the turbines start to work again.

Thirdly, the reading suggests that they can discourage bats from coming near the turbines with devices that send out radar signals, which bats dislike. This is an ideal solution because power companies could operate turbines at any time. However, the lecturer contends that bats dislike radar because it harms them. Radar waves are known to damage their reproductive organs. If the power companies used this strategy, it would lead to a decline in bat populations in the long run.

지 않을 것이다. 그러나 강의자에 따르면, 만일 밤에 터빈을 중지시키면 잠을 자기 위해 터빈에 내려앉은 박쥐들이 터빈 가동이 재개됨과 동시에 터빈에 살상될 것이다.

셋째로, 지문은 박쥐들이 싫어하는 레이더 신호를 방출하는 장치를 이용해서 박쥐들이 터빈 근처로 오는 것을 막을 수 있다고 말한다. 전력 회사들이 풍력 발전용 터빈을 언제든 가동할 수 있다는 점에서 이것은 이상적 해결책이다. 하지만 강의자는 레이더가 자신들에게 해를 입히기 때문에 박쥐들이 레이더를 싫어한다고 주장한다. 레이더파는 박쥐들의 생식 기관을 손상시키는 것으로 알려져 있다. 전력 회사들이 이 전략을 사용한다면 장기적으로 박쥐 개체 수가 감소하게 될 것이다.

어휘 suitable **adj** 적합한 I cause harm to ~에게 해를 끼치다 I decline **n** 감소

Question 2

Your professor is teaching a class. Write a post responding to the professor's question.

In your response, you should:
- express and support your opinion
- make a contribution to the discussion

An effective response will contain at least 100 words.
You will have 10 minutes to write it.

Dr. Irene: Greetings, class. Today, our focus is on the belief that early exposure to studying abroad is essential for broadening horizons and personal development. The question before us is simple yet profound: Do you agree or disagree with this perspective? Studying overseas at an early age is crucial for evolving as individuals. As we embark on this exploration, let's delve into the dynamics of studying abroad and its potential effects on personal development.

Henry: Thank you, Professor. I wholeheartedly agree with the idea that studying abroad at an early age is crucial for personal development. Experiencing different cultures, meeting diverse people, and navigating unfamiliar environments offer unparalleled opportunities for self-discovery. The challenges and joys of studying abroad shape individuals in ways that traditional education might not.

Lottie: While I acknowledge the benefits Henry highlights, I find myself leaning towards disagreement. Not everyone has the privilege or inclination to study abroad early in life. Moreover, local education can also foster personal development through exposure to diverse perspectives and cultures. The emphasis should be on creating a globally aware

당신의 교수님께서 강의 중입니다. 교수님의 질문에 답하는 글을 쓰세요.

- 당신의 의견을 표현하고 뒷받침하세요
- 토론에 기여하세요

효과적인 답변은 최소한 100단어를 포함할 것입니다. 당신은 10분 동안 글을 작성할 수 있습니다.

아이린 교수: 안녕하세요, 여러분. 오늘은 해외 유학에 대한 초기 노출이 시야를 확장하고 개인적인 발전에 중요하다는 믿음에 중점을 두겠습니다. 우리 앞에 있는 질문은 간단하면서도 깊은 의미가 담긴 것입니다: 이 관점에 동의하십니까, 동의하지 않으십니까? 어린 나이에 유학을 하는 것은 개인적인 성장에 중요합니다. 이 탐구를 시작할 때, 유학의 역학과 개인적 발전에 미치는 잠재적 영향을 자세히 살펴보겠습니다.

헨리: 감사합니다. 교수님. 저는 해외에서 조기 교육을 받는 것이 개인적 발전에 중요하다는 생각에 전적으로 동의합니다. 다양한 문화를 경험하고 다양한 사람들을 만나고 익숙하지 않은 환경에서 적응하는 것은 자아 발견에 탁월한 기회를 제공합니다. 해외에서의 공부의 도전과 기쁨은 전통적인 교육이 제공하지 못하는 방식으로 개인을 형성합니다.

로티: 헨리가 강조한 이점을 인정하면서도 저는 반대로 기울고 있다고 느낍니다. 모든 사람이 삶 초반에 해외에서 공부할 권리나 경향을 가지고 있지 않습니다. 게다가 현지 교육도 다양한 관점과 문화에 노출함으로써 개인적 성장을 촉진할 수 있습니다. 중점은 지역에서도 모든 학생이 개인적으로 발전할 수 있도록

curriculum locally, ensuring that all students, regardless of their ability to study abroad, can develop as individuals.

전 세계적인 인식을 가진 교육 과정을 만드는 데 있어야 합니다.

어휘 evolve **v** 진화하다 | delve **v** 탐구하다 | personal development 개인 발전 | unparalleled **adj** 비길 데 없는 | disagreement **n** 불일치 | inclination **n** 성향 | emphasis **n** 강조

예시 답변

From my perspective, both made excellent statements, but I'm on the same page as Henry. Simply put, children can gain a lot of advice while studying abroad at an early age. It is obvious that this gives them such valuable and practical advice as they go through unpredictable situations. Through these moments, children can have a chance to evaluate themselves in a more objective way, leading to a better life in the future. A perfect example of this is my own experience. I used to be naive and less sociable due to my introverted personality. This made me segregate myself from people and live in my own world. Then, one day, I got a chance to go to elementary school in the United States. At first, it was uncomfortable and challenging for me to blend in with new friends and learn from a new environment. However, as I was getting used to it, I started to engage in many new experiences I hadn't had before. This not only gave me valuable advice but also made me more grown up mentally.

제 입장에서는 두 사람 모두 훌륭한 주장을 펼쳤지만, 저는 헨리와 의견이 일치합니다. 간단히 말하면, 어린 나이에 해외에서 공부하는 동안 어린이들은 많은 조언을 얻을 수 있습니다. 예측할 수 없는 상황을 겪을 때마다 그들에게 귀중하고 현실적인 조언을 제공한다는 것은 분명합니다. 이러한 순간을 통해 어린이들은 미래에 더 나은 삶으로 이어질 수 있도록 더 객관적으로 자신을 평가할 기회를 갖게 될 것입니다. 이에 대한 완벽한 예는 저의 경험입니다. 저는 예전에 순진하고 내성적인 성격 때문에 사교적이지 못했습니다. 이로 인해 남들과 격리되어 저만의 세계에서 살았습니다. 그러던 어느 날 미국의 초등학교에 다니게 되었습니다. 처음에는 새로운 친구들과 새로운 환경에서 적응하기가 불편하고 어려웠습니다. 그러나 익숙해지면서 저는 이전에 경험하지 못한 많은 새로운 경험에 참여하기 시작했습니다. 이것은 저에게 귀중한 조언뿐만 아니라 정신적으로 더 성숙해지게 만들었습니다.

PAGODA TOEFL 80+ Writing

PAGODA TOEFL 80+ Writing

PAGODA TOEFL 80+ Writing

PAGODA
TOEFL
80+ Writing │해설서